D1083283

TO LEAD THE FREE WORLD

American Nationalism and the Cultural Roots of the Cold War

JOHN FOUSEK

The University of North Carolina Press   Chapel Hill and London

© 2000

The University of North Carolina Press

All rights reserved

Manufactured in the United States of America

This book was set in Minion and Meta types

by Tseng Information Systems, Inc.

The paper in this book meets the guidelines for

permanence and durability of the Committee on

Production Guidelines for Book Longevity of the

Council on Library Resources.

Library of Congress

Cataloging-in-Publication Data

Fousek, John, 1959–

To lead the free world : American nationalism and the

cultural roots of the Cold War / by John Fousek.

    p. cm.

Includes bibliographical references (p.   )

and index.

ISBN 0-8078-2525-5 (cloth: alk. paper). —

ISBN 0-8078-4836-0 (pbk.: alk. paper)

1. United States — Foreign relations — 1945–1953 — Public

opinion. 2. United States — Foreign relations — 1945–

1953 — Philosophy. 3. Nationalism — United States —

History — 20th century. 4. Popular culture — Political

aspects — United States — History — 20th century.

5. Discourse analysis — United States. 6. Public

opinion — United States — History — 20th century.

I. Title.

E813.F68   2000

327.73′009′045 — dc21   99-34166

CIP

04   03   02   01   00   5   4   3   2   1

To the memory and spirit of my father,

PETER JIRI FOUSEK (1923–1987)

CONTENTS

PREFACE

This book is a study of public culture, concerned more with popular perceptions of United States foreign policy than with the policy itself. Like practitioners of the "new cultural history," I approach popular perceptions primarily through the prism of public discourse.[1] Language shapes thought in significant ways, and language in the public sphere sets the terms readily available to ordinary citizens for thinking about public issues. As I use it, the term "public culture" is defined as the sphere in which the various segments of a society contend over its development. Public culture is the arena in which social and political conflict is played out and in which consensus is forged, manufactured, and maintained, or not. It is the place where all the segments of the society either speak to each other or fail to speak to each other — where they must contend if they wish to advance their own interests and values or to influence the direction of the larger society. It is a "place" that exists in print, on the airwaves, and in the meeting hall. To the extent that nations are "imagined communities," as the political scientist Benedict Anderson has argued, they are imagined in and through the public culture.[2] I use the term "discourse" primarily in its ordinary-language sense, rather than in the more rarefied sense associated with poststructuralist literary criticism and philosophy. Nonetheless, I believe that any given discourse develops its own patterns, involving key words, phrases, metaphors, and images that set the contours of legitimate discussion within its field. In examining public discourse about America's world role from 1945 to 1950, I have attempted to discern the development of such patterns. Following Daniel Rodgers's shrewd analysis of "keywords in American politics," I treat public discourse as contested terrain.[3]

The potential sources for any study of U.S. public life in the mid-twentieth century are overwhelming. Consequently, this study is based primarily on a set of sources chosen to represent key segments of the nation's public culture: the Truman administration, the mass print media, the African American community, and organized labor.[4] The decision to focus on these four areas reflects, on the one hand, an interest in the relative roles of the government and the media in fostering the Cold War consensus and, on the other hand, an interest in the relationships between race, class, and American nationalism. In examining the public discourse of the Truman administration, I analyze the president's major, nationally broadcast, foreign-policy speeches in relation to letters that citizens wrote back in response. The citizens' letters merit close examination not because they were influential (they were not), but because they provide a rare window on how ordinary Americans responded, in their own words, to more prominent voices and to the major international events of their time. They also reveal a great deal about how individual citizens viewed their relationship to the nation and the head of state. Such letters to the president constitute a rich yet little-studied source for the study of twentieth-century U.S. history. Some scholars, most notably Alan Brinkley, have made extensive and highly suggestive use of the mass of citizens' mail to President Franklin Roosevelt during the Great Depression. But no similar works examine or present citizens' letters to Truman or other postwar presidents.[5] For the mass media, I make extensive use of mass-circulation magazines, including *Life*, *Saturday Evening Post*, *Collier's*, and *Ladies' Home Journal*, as well as the period's one true mass-circulation newspaper, the *New York Daily News*, and editorial cartoons from around the country. Television was in its infancy in the late 1940s, and magazines and tabloids remained major sources of visual images in U.S. commercial culture as well as common sources of information and ideas about world affairs.[6] Glossy picture magazines like *Life* addressed a vast, predominantly middle-class readership. Under Henry Luce's leadership, *Life* had always been ardently "internationalist." By the end of the war its competitors were as well. The *Daily News*, by contrast, spoke mainly to a working-class readership and subscribed to a viewpoint generally deemed "isolationist" both by contemporaries and by historians. In reality, that viewpoint emphasized that the United States should maintain the freedom to act unilaterally in international affairs, not that it should be isolated from the rest of the world. In many ways, particularly concerning military policy, the *News*'s perspective increasingly converged with the "internationalist" positions of the Truman administration.

I have sampled the African American and labor sources of the period selectively to focus on points of contention with the prevailing discourse of the official and mass cultures, as expressed by the government and the media. Many complexities within each of these sectors have necessarily been excluded. In examining African American discourse, I focus on two major civil rights organizations, the National Urban League and especially the National Association for the Advancement of Colored People (NAACP), and on periodicals with national circulation, specifically the *Pittsburgh Courier* and *Ebony* (a new picture magazine launched in 1945 and modeled after *Life*), as well as the venerable NAACP publication, *The Crisis*. With local editions tailored to cities around the country and by far the largest circulation of any African American newspaper, the *Courier* was both the *New York Times* and the *Daily News* of the African American press. It was, in many respects, the paper of record within the black community. Whereas papers like the *Amsterdam News* in New York City covered mainly local news of the black community, the *Courier* covered international news extensively and featured nearly four pages of opinion pieces by leading African American columnists who held varying views but were all deeply concerned with world affairs. For the viewpoint of organized labor, I have focused mainly on two unions, the United Automobile Workers (UAW) and the United Electrical Workers (UE), two of the largest and most important labor organizations of the period. Foreign policy issues were important in the internal politics of both the UAW and the UE, particularly because discussions pertaining to U.S.-Soviet relations also related to discussions about communism and national loyalty within the labor movement. The politics of anticommunism was central to the histories of both of these unions, and the politics of Cold War foreign policy was as well.[7] My analysis of foreign-policy discourse within the unions is based primarily on a close reading of the pertinent discussions at their annual national conventions. The floor debates recorded in the convention proceedings provide important evidence of how national labor leaders, such as Congress of Industrial Organizations (CIO) president Philip Murray or the UAW's Walter Reuther, spoke to their membership. More important still, from the perspective of this study, they provide a fascinating glimpse of less exalted union members discussing their nation's foreign policy in often heated exchanges. Both the UE and the UAW were among the most democratic, large-membership organizations in the country. Convention delegates spoke their minds freely and did so as representatives of the rank and file. Their words may give some approximation of how ordinary union members thought and felt about their nation's foreign policy.

ACKNOWLEDGMENTS

This book has been a long time coming, and so I am long overdue in the acknowledgment of many debts. The work began as a doctoral dissertation at Cornell University, and I am forever grateful to Cornell's history department for affording me a remarkable educational opportunity. Much of what I know of the art of history I learned from Cornell's fine historians, including Walter LaFeber, Larry Moore, and Nick Salvatore. As numerous members of the historical profession know, Michael Kammen is in a class by himself. His enthusiasm for this project and faith in its author have helped to sustain the project. Comments from and conversations with all four of these scholars helped to improve the manuscript in its earlier manifestations. Michael in particular has now read numerous drafts, and each one has benefited from his incisive reading. At the University of North Carolina Press, Lewis Bateman has provided unflagging support for the book from the first; Kathy Malin has been a superb copy editor.

In addition to Cornell's history department, support for my research and writing came from the Cornell University Peace Studies Program, the John D. and Catherine T. MacArthur Foundation, the John Anson Kittredge Fund, the Mellon Foundation, and the Daughters of the American Revolution. To all these institutions, I am deeply grateful. Of course, research support would be of little use to historians without research libraries and archives — and librarians and archivists. I am forever indebted to the staffs of the Cornell University Libraries, the New York Public Library, the Library of Congress (especially the Manuscript Division), the National Archives, and the Harry S. Truman Library. I often tell my students that a good reference librarian is a historian's best friend; certainly this historian could never have completed this piece of work without the intelligence and collegiality of the dedicated librarians and archivists at these institutions. At Franklin and Marshall College, Joshua Hagelgans provided invaluable research assistance, particularly with some of the visual material.

The ideas developed in this book were previously aired in a variety of venues, including the University of Wisconsin's 1991 conference "Re-thinking the Cold War," a Cornell Peace Studies seminar, and Marilyn Young's graduate seminar on the Cold War at New York University (NYU). Feedback I received on those occasions proved invaluable in assuring me I was onto something, encouraging me to go further, and forcing me to clarify my arguments. I am especially grateful for encouragement I received from Paul Boyer at the University of Wisconsin at Madison, Judith Reppy at Cornell's Peace Studies Program, and Marilyn Young at NYU. Thoughtful readings by Ann Foster, Michael Kammen, Allan Winkler, and Michael Sherry have strengthened the final manuscript immeasurably. My colleague Richard Langhorne, director of the Center for Global Change and Governance at Rutgers University, provided incisive comments on the introduction, for which I am grateful.

A small number of close friends outside the historical profession have helped to sustain me in my intellectual endeavors over the years. You know who you are, but I'll tell everyone else: Adrienne Asch, Jon Frankel, Derek van der Tak, and especially Craig Anton McDonald, whose wide-ranging knowledge and curiosity and unique sensitivity and charm will be deeply missed. Above all, my closest friend, my wife Alberta Crum Fousek, has helped to sustain me in this and all other worthwhile pursuits. Our pursuits together now focus on our son, Peter Sinclair Onacona Fousek. Without Alberta's wisdom, spirit, and strength, this book and its author would be far poorer. The book is dedicated to my father, whose insights would have enriched it. It is really for both of my parents, from whom I learned to love ideas, to know that they matter, and to care passionately about American public life. It is also for you, Birdie: "In my dreams we fly." And for Peter, in a world beyond the Cold War.

TO LEAD THE FREE WORLD

INTRODUCTION

When Japan surrendered in August 1945, finally ending the global cataclysm of World War II, most Americans yearned for nothing more than lasting peace. Many called on their government to "bring the boys back home" from Europe and Asia as quickly as possible. The United States and the Soviet Union remained formal allies, though they were no longer bound together by common foes. Many U.S. policymakers and opinion leaders worried that the public would be reluctant to support the kind of active U.S. involvement in overseas affairs that they saw as necessary. By the summer of 1950, however, the United States was engaged in a limited war in Korea and a total, global, cold war with the Soviet Union. Most significantly, a broad public consensus supported these engagements. At the end of World War II, few observers would have predicted the rise of this Cold War consensus. Fewer still would have foreseen it in the years before Pearl Harbor. How and why did this rapid transformation come to pass?

One easy answer holds that events unfolding on the world stage convinced an overwhelming majority of U.S. citizens that the Soviet Union was an expansionist force bent on world conquest, much as Nazi Germany had been. In this view, the Truman administration adopted an anti-Soviet foreign policy to keep up with an increasingly anticommunist public mood — and to gain Harry Truman's election to a full term as president in 1948. In a prize-winning 1972 study, for example, the historian John Lewis Gaddis argued that the Truman administration initially adopted a "get tough with Russia" policy in early 1946 "largely in response to public opinion." Other historians, including Walter LaFeber and Thomas Paterson, have argued the opposite: that Truman exerted enormous influence in shaping public opinion on foreign affairs in the immediate postwar years. Most recently, Frank Kofsky argued that Truman and his advisers deliberately fomented a war scare in 1948, using the consolidation of Communist control in Czechoslovakia and the Soviet blockade of Berlin as pretexts for rapid hikes in military spending. While I find these arguments more compelling than those claiming that Truman's foreign policy decisions were significantly constrained by popular views, such explanations seem excessively reductionist.[1]

Throughout his presidency, Harry Truman sought to build public support for a globally activist foreign policy. His administration no doubt played a dominant role in shaping the new consensus, using its control of foreign policy information along with tactics of co-optation, intimidation, and repression.[2] But in this general goal, the administration had potent allies in the media, churches, and other public institutions. Executive manipulation was an important causal factor in creating the Cold War consensus, but explanations that make it the sole factor are less than satisfactory. Such explanations, moreover, deny historical agency to the public at large and to most of the people in it, reducing their views of world affairs to blank slates to be sketched in as their leaders (or rulers) deem appropriate. Even if the government, the media, and other influential institutions were united in seeking to create public support for a globally activist, anti-Soviet foreign policy, the question remains why the public was responsive to their efforts. The answer to that question may be found through the study of public discourse about U.S. foreign policy. President Truman's public discourse continuously linked U.S. global responsibility to anticommunism and enveloped both within a framework of American national greatness. In his famous whistle-stop campaign tour in 1948, for example, he repeatedly referred to the U.S. as "the greatest nation the sun ever shone upon" while asserting that this greatness brought with it the obligation to check communist expansionism around the world. This discursive (and ideological) triad of national greatness, global responsibility, and anticommunism pervaded American public life in the later 1940s. The appeal to nationalist sentiment resonated widely with ordinary middle-class and working-class Americans. Public consent, in this sense, was shaped from a ready supply of suitable materials. It was not manufactured from whole cloth.

My central thesis is that American nationalist ideology provided the principal underpinning for the broad public consensus that supported Cold War foreign policy. Seen through the prism of that ideology, the U.S. had emerged from World War II as a fully matured great power, dedicated to realizing freedom throughout the world and prepared to usher in a new golden age in its own image. Henry Luce, the hugely influential publisher of *Time, Life,* and *Fortune* magazines, had christened this new age "the American Century" even before Pearl Harbor. After the war, the Soviet Union became an implacable foe because it threatened this idea of the American Century. From the late 1940s through the late 1980s, the United States waged cold war against the Union of Soviet Socialist Republics not primarily in the name of capitalism or Western civilization (neither of which would have united the American people behind the cause), but in the name of America—in the name, that is, of the nation. The potency of the Cold War ideology that emerged between 1945 and 1950—an ideology that dominated U.S. public life at least until the collapse of the Soviet Union in 1991—derived largely from its nationalist appeal. Yet despite the vast scholarly literature on the Cold War, American nationalism remains a little-studied element of postwar U.S. history. Indeed, as Stephen Vaughn noted nearly twenty years ago in his study of democracy and nationalism in the propaganda work of the Committee on Public Information during World War I, twentieth-century American nationalism remains a subject badly in need of further study.[3]

But what exactly is "American nationalism"? The question "What is a nation?" has dogged students of politics since the nineteenth century. As we prepare to enter the twenty-first, it dogs us still. Since the implosion first of the Soviet empire and then of the Soviet Union itself, nationalism has again asserted itself as a force on the world scene, one not likely to fade away soon. The scholarly literature on nationalism is voluminous and seems to expand exponentially, particularly in the years since the earth-shaking events of 1989–91. This literature, moreover, is increasingly complex and multidisciplinary. Recent anthologies, such as the Oxford reader *Nationalism,* edited by John Hutchinson and Anthony D. Smith, display the richness of this discourse and the difficulties of formulating one all-encompassing conception of the phenomena it concerns. We are no closer than ever to scholarly consensus on central questions: What is a nation? And what, then, is nationalism? These questions are particularly problematic for students of the United States, which has not figured prominently in the current renaissance of scholarly interest in such matters. Since much recent work focuses on nationalist movements in the creation of new nation-states, the operation of nationalism within established, more or less stable politics, such as the United States in the postwar years, has not received adequate attention.[4]

If, as John Dunn writes in framing an important collection of essays on the "contemporary crisis of the nation state," the nation is defined as "a community of birth," consisting "of those who belong together by birth (genetically, lineally, through familially inherited language and culture)," then how can such a polyglot polity as the United States of America be a nation? Indeed, Dunn admits that few contemporary nation states conform to this idea of the nation. A more fluid, more contextually sensitive definition is needed. Anthony D. Smith, one of the most prolific students of nationalism, offers a more flexible "working definition" of the nation as "a named human population which shares myths and memories, a mass public culture, a designated homeland, economic unity and equal rights and duties for all members." Smith's definition contains useful elements, particularly in its attention to shared myth and memory, public culture, and territoriality. But the notion that "economic unity and equal rights and duties" are essential characteristics of the nation is problematic. "Nations" exist in diaspora settings or across state borders in ways that make "economic unity" impossible, and few nations, if any, have existed on a basis of absolute equality of rights and duties among all members. Indeed, the extent to which a sense of national solidarity can exist despite exploitation and inequality within the national group testifies to the power of nationalism as a subjective phenomenon. In the context of mid-twentieth-century America, for example, most African Americans felt themselves to be Americans — members of the nation — despite their general exclusion from the national economy and the systematic denial of their rights as citizens. For these reasons, among others, I follow Benedict Anderson's conception of the nation as "an imagined political community." Anderson's definition is sufficiently open that it can help to comprehend nations and nationalisms in a wide variety of contexts. His apt phrase, moreover, is especially germane to the study of American nationalism. If ever a nation was an imagined community, surely it is the United States of America.[5]

This brings us to the question of defining nationalism, a matter on which Anderson is less explicit though still suggestive. If the nation is an imagined community, nationalism would seem to be the ideas or processes through which it is imagined. But Anderson makes a compelling argument that nationalism cannot be properly understood as *an* ideology. It should be treated, he writes, "as if it belonged with 'kinship' and 'religion,' rather than with 'liberalism' or 'fascism.' " This view suggests that nationalism is rooted at a deeper ontological level than modern political ideologies, which helps to explain its ubiquity, its emotional power, and, as Anderson emphasizes, the willingness of millions of people to die for the sake of their nations. Nationalism is a cultural form readily adaptable to a wide range of contexts and open to a variety of ideological contents. Smith, however, treats nationalism as "a universally applicable ideology" serving to legitimate modern nations. According to Smith, this ideology consists of the following precepts: "that the world is divided into nations, each of which has its own character and destiny; that an individual's first loyalty is to his or her nation; that the nation is the source of all political power; that to be free and fulfilled, the individual must belong to a nation; that each nation must express its authentic nature by being autonomous; and that a world of peace and justice can only be built on autonomous nations." Smith's analysis here is flawed. To begin with, the last item in this list seems gratuitous. The Nazi variant of German nationalism, for instance, held no such vision of peace and justice based on a world of autonomous nations. More seriously, Smith's concept of "a universally applicable ideology" is ahistorical. History, as E. P. Thompson put it, "is above all the discipline of context." From a historical perspective, any actually existing ideology is necessarily contingent on the context in which it operates; it must be understood in relation to the conditions of a particular time and place. Yet Smith's precepts may also be construed as elements of nationalism as a more general cultural form, comparable, as Anderson says, to kinship or religion. These are the rules by which the nation is imagined as a specific form of community different from other imagined communities.[6]

Liah Greenfield offers a definition that falls somewhere between those of Smith and Anderson, combining elements of each. The distinguishing characteristic of nationalism, she argues, is that it "locates the source of individual identity within a 'people,' which is seen as the bearer of sovereignty, the central object of loyalty, and the basis of collective solidarity." Within the nationalist frame, according to Greenfield, the "people" is always fundamentally unitary or "homogeneous," and "only superficially divided by the lines of status, class, locality, and in some cases even ethnicity." Greenfield classifies nationalism not as an ideology but as "a style of thought." I would add that it is a style of thought about identity, loyalty, and solidarity that values the nation above all other sources or objects of identity, loyalty, and solidarity.[7]

For purposes of this study, nationalism as a general phenomenon may be defined as a way of thinking or "style of thought" through which individuals identify themselves as members of a nation. Any particular nationalism includes a specific set of widely shared ideas, beliefs, values, attitudes, and images. To borrow language from both Greenfield and Anderson, I view the nation, in turn, as an "imagined community" that those individuals view as "the bearer of sovereignty, the central object of loyalty, and the basis of collective solidarity." I would add to this one characteristic taken from a standard dictionary definition: that nationalism as a style of thought exalts the particular nation concerned over all other nations. American nationalism, in the sense that I understand it and the contexts in which I have examined it, certainly does that.

Like many midcentury observers, Hans Kohn, perhaps the foremost scholar of comparative nationalism of the time, argued that "nationalism in the United States differs in many ways" from its usual pattern. In his 1957 study, *American Nationalism,* Kohn wrote that the United States of America "was not founded on the common attributes of nationhood—language, cultural tradition, historical territory or common descent—but on an idea which singled out the new nation among the nations of the earth." That idea, embodied in the U.S. Constitution, was "the English tradition of liberty" transformed through the American Revolution and the Enlightenment into "a universal message" proclaiming the rights of humankind.[8] This notion that the United States has a unique and universal message of benefit to all the world is indeed a core theme of American nationalism. In narrative form, this theme has most commonly found expression in the long-standing tradition of thought about American chosenness, mission, and destiny—a tradition that extends back at least to the early Puritan settlers in seventeenth-century New England, long before the American nation was ever imagined. These are the elements of American nationalism that played such a potent role in the origins of the Cold War.

From Albert K. Weinberg's classic 1935 study through Anders Stephanson's recent synthesis, both entitled *Manifest Destiny,* the best analyses of this tradition have always treated it as a central element of American nationalism. Weinberg explained Manifest Destiny as the ideological justification of nineteenth-century landed expansionism. In his view, the end of territorial aggrandizement and Woodrow Wilson's renunciation of explicitly nationalistic objectives in favor of universal values marked the closing of the story. Taking issue with Weinberg on this point, Ernest Tuveson's *Redeemer Nation* firmly links Wilson to the traditional nationalist belief in the providential mission of America and suggests also that this tradition played a role in post-1945 thinking. But as a rule the persistence of these ideas into the mid-twentieth century and beyond has been alternately neglected, dismissed, taken for granted, or discussed in generalities.[9] Stephanson's synthetic essay brilliantly links the themes of chosenness, destiny, and mission together within a common frame of "destinarian discourse" and elegantly demonstrates how this discourse framed the expansionist episodes of the 1840s and 1890s. He provides valuable historical perspective on how these themes operated in the Cold War era but offers no detailed analysis or empirical investigation beyond 1914. Through close readings of diverse materials, from presidential speeches to popular magazines to labor union debates and the African American press, I have attempted to show how this discursive tradition influenced postwar public culture and shaped U.S. foreign policy discourse during this crucial period.

As Clifford Geertz suggested years ago, in relation to his own examinations of Indonesian nationalism, periods of turmoil and change, in which established patterns break down, tend to bring ideological thinking to the fore. Ideology provides clear and familiar explanations for developments that are disturbingly unclear and unfamiliar.[10] In terms of foreign relations, the 1940s constituted just such a period for the United States. World War II was a crisis of unprecedented magnitude, with enormous implications for the nation's sense of itself and its place in the world. U.S. involvement in the fighting began at Pearl Harbor with a piercing blow to the national myth of invulnerability and ended with the lingering images of mushroom clouds over Hiroshima and Nagasaki, symbols of an unsettling new threat. The conclusion of hostilities hardly brought global tranquility. Wartime propaganda suggested that American power combined with the new United Nations organization would assure a lasting peace, but the postwar world proved far more complex and intractable than any propaganda image could allow. The collapse of European colonialism, the near collapse of European capitalism, and the emergence of the Soviet Union as a world power able and willing to challenge U.S. objectives all combined to confute the wartime notion of "One World" that would thrive under American leadership after the war. With Geertz's work in mind, it is not surprising that many Americans, from foreign-policy makers to the proverbial men and women on the street, fell into patterns of ideological thinking in struggling to make sense of often frightening developments. Between 1945 and 1950, an increasingly cohesive ideology, which I call "American nationalist globalism," provided the most compelling explanation for international events that most Americans found deeply disturbing. This ideology combined traditional nationalist ideologies of American chosenness, mission, and destiny with the emerging notion that the entire world was now the proper sphere of concern for U.S. foreign policy. In a global age, America was called upon to exercise its now extraordinary power globally in the name of traditional American values— values that had always been deemed universal. The nationalist elements of this ideology were essential to its success. Ultimately, in an atmosphere of apparently unceasing international crises, Americans tended to rally around the flag.

U.S. foreign policy since the era of World War II is generally characterized as "internationalist" or "globalist" in its orientation. Coined, unsurprisingly, in 1943, the term "globalism" itself is self-explanatory. Webster's *Tenth New Collegiate Dictionary* provides a satisfactory definition: "a national policy of treating the whole world as a proper sphere for political influence." In American historical writing, descriptions of a "rise to globalism" or "the triumph of internationalism" reveal a teleological or "whiggish" interpretation of U.S. foreign policy that posits the new global orientation of the 1940s as a mark of progress beyond "isolationist" views.[11] Several historians have noted the nationalist elements in American globalism or internationalism, but they have not analyzed its significance sufficiently.[12] I argue, by contrast, that the American globalism of the 1940s was nationalistic at its core. From this perspective, the dominant ideology of U.S. foreign policy in the postwar era is best understood as an ideology of "American nationalist globalism."[13] American nationalism has always been rooted in universal values—freedom, equality, and justice under law—that the United States claimed to stand for.[14] This universalism had long been a component of U.S. foreign-policy ideology. But in the 1940s, the U.S. pursued a foreign policy ostensibly aimed at realizing these values throughout the world. The belief that the universal nature of American national values justified and even necessitated the global expansion of U.S. power embodies the essence of American nationalist globalism in the postwar era. Variations on traditional ideas of American mission and destiny pervaded U.S. public culture in this period. But the American mission was now global in a concrete sense as well as universal in the abstract, since American power was now global in reach. Ironically, this ideology of American nationalist globalism justified major departures from national tradition— such as entangling overseas alliances, a peacetime draft, large standing armies, and protracted land wars in Asia—in the name of traditional nationalist ideas of chosenness, mission, and destiny.

Within the framework of American nationalist globalism, national self-interest and global altruism were identical. To paraphrase the famous line about General Motors, what was good for America was good for the world. U.S. power was global in scope. The interests of the U.S. and the rest of humanity were convergent. And the U.S. was the natural, destined leader of the world—possessing values, institutions, and a "way of life" to which all other peoples aspired. Dean Acheson, perhaps the most influential architect of postwar U.S. foreign policy, gave this perspective paradigmatic expression when he said: "We are willing to help people who believe the way we do, to continue to live the way they want to live."[15] To the extent that they can be disentangled at all, postwar American nationalism and postwar American globalism were two sides of the same coin (or two halves of the same walnut, to borrow a phrase from Harry Truman). By the end of World War II, the developing ideology of nationalist globalism was based on increasingly intertwined notions of national greatness and global responsibility. In the Truman Doctrine speech of March 12, 1947, President Truman effectively redefined U.S. global responsibility in terms of global anticommunism and the containment of Soviet power. Interestingly, he did so without mentioning the Soviet Union by name but rather by framing the new anti-Soviet policy in terms of American national greatness and global responsibilities:

> The free peoples of the world look to us for support in maintaining their freedoms. If we falter in our leadership, we may endanger the peace of the world—and we shall surely endanger the welfare of our own Nation. Great responsibilities have been placed upon us by the swift movement of events.[16]

As the containment policy was publicly adopted from March 1947 on, global anticommunism was fully incorporated as a third key idea within the ideology of American nationalist globalism, but it remained a corollary to the preceding conceptions: National greatness brought global responsibility, which required the containment of communism.

From a historical perspective, neither the conflation of American nationalism with the new American globalism nor the development of a broad public consensus behind Cold War foreign policy was a foregone conclusion. The aftermath of the first world war had witnessed a widespread public rejection of Woodrow Wilson's efforts "to make the world safe for democracy." In the interwar period, many Americans felt burned by their experience of Wilson's failed crusade. The public mood of the 1920s and 1930s is generally characterized as "isolationist" even though the United States remained very much involved in world affairs.[17] As deepening global crises in the late 1930s led to a second world war, a protracted debate between interventionists and noninterventionists—or "internationalists" and "isolationists," as they were called—virtually dominated U.S. public life. The tensions of those years reveal deep-seated popular resistance to becoming involved in another "European war."[18]

From 1937 until the attack on Pearl Harbor in December 1941, Franklin Delano Roosevelt engaged in a long, intricate dance with public opinion, which he viewed as predominantly isolationist. The president sought to lead his reluctant partner toward a full embrace of U.S. intervention against the totalitarian tide in Europe and Asia. Total war could be waged only with total public support, and Roosevelt feared entering the fray in a manner that might provoke a popular backlash. Pearl Harbor united the nation behind Roosevelt's foreign policy, pulling the rug out from under the anti-interventionist position more swiftly and completely than anyone imagined possible. The very name Pearl Harbor burned into the nation's consciousness. Along with Munich and Hiroshima, Pearl Harbor would enter U.S. public discourse as one of the code words for the almost universally accepted "lessons" of World War II — never appease aggressors and always remain militarily prepared.[19] These lessons effectively undermined the isolationist position in American public life. Pearl Harbor and Hiroshima destroyed the popular belief that the Atlantic and Pacific oceans shielded the United States from foreign attack. Many old isolationists would persist on their anointed path in the postwar era. But their position became thoroughly marginal, suspect, and virtually incomprehensible to those who accepted the official lessons taught by what Winston Churchill called "the unnecessary war."[20]

The years from 1937–38 to 1941 also witnessed a widespread democratic revival in the United States, which continued through the war years and beyond.[21] During the interwar period, the eclipse of progressivism and disillusionment over the First World War led to considerable cynicism concerning American democracy. That jaundiced attitude, most pronounced in the 1920s, contrasts sharply with the generally celebratory view of U.S. political values that prevailed after World War II.[22] But in the late 1930s, against the backdrop of rising totalitarianism abroad, renewed interest in and commitment to American democracy largely overcame the more cynical view prevalent earlier. This trend continued through the war, setting the stage for a postwar era in which Americans proudly called their country "the leader of the free world."

This democratic revival must also be seen as an outgrowth of the rising American nationalism of the 1930s, which among other things brought the terms "American Way of Life" and "American Dream" into common usage.[23] In the late 1930s, the rising threat of fascism and Nazism, along with a certain disillusionment with the New Deal, cast these terms in bold relief. By the 1940s, as a result, these and related notions, such as the American Creed and the American Idea, were conceived more explicitly in terms of democratic values. When Henry

Luce coined the notion of the American Century some nine months before Pearl Harbor, he did so within this context of resurgent democratic nationalism. In proclaiming the arrival of the American Century, Luce argued that the moment had come to construct a world order based on American democratic values. He sought to provide a vision of this American Century that would rally the nation to assume its "manifest duty" as the world's most powerful nation: "America as the dynamic center of ever-widening spheres of enterprise, America as the training center of the skillful servants of mankind, America as the Good Samaritan, really believing again that it is more blessed to give than to receive, and America as the powerhouse of the ideals of Freedom and Justice—out of these elements surely can be fashioned a vision of the 20th Century to which we can and will devote ourselves in joy and gladness and vigor and enthusiasm."[24] Especially after the U.S. and its allies won the war, many Americans came to believe that in some fashion the American Way of Life, the American Dream, or the American Creed held the solutions to problems that plagued a war-ravaged world.

The ideology of American nationalist globalism originated in the thinking of native-born, white Protestants of upper- or middle-class backgrounds—a group heavily represented in the nation's foreign-policy elite, in the government generally, in international business, and in the media. In the mid-twentieth century, the white Anglo-Saxon Protestant elite constituted the dominant *ethnie* or ethnic grouping within a polyglot nation that did not yet recognize itself as "multicultural." From this culturally privileged position within the imagined community of the American nation, the middle-aged, white, Anglo-Saxon, Protestant men of the foreign-policy elite functioned as a hegemonic bloc in the formation of this ideology.[25] By that I mean simply that they were able to project their own values and beliefs into a dominant position in the nation's public life and largely to set the terms of public discussion concerning "America's world role." They were able to do so in part because of the historically privileged position of mainline Protestantism within American culture, but also because the U.S. political economy was being transformed by the intertwined processes of militarization and globalization. The era of World War II brought new preoccupations with "national security" as well as a vastly expanded "military-industrial complex" which sought to perpetuate itself after the war. The concept of national security fit nicely with the ideology of nationalist globalism, which in turn provided further justification for a permanent military economy.[26] During the New Deal, as Thomas Ferguson argues effectively, a new historical power bloc composed of "capital-intensive industries, investment banks, and internationally oriented commercial banks" secured positions of primacy within U.S. business and the Democratic Party.[27] By the end of World War II, these multinational interests were even more secure in these positions. They also exerted tremendous influence in the media and other opinion-shaping institutions.

Many leading figures of this "multinational bloc" became leading architects of U.S. foreign policy during the Roosevelt and Truman administrations, including Dean Acheson, James Forrestal, and W. Averell Harriman, to name just a few. But whether we think of them as agents of multinational capital or as the "wise men" of foreign affairs and hard-headed "realists" who understood the rules of power in international politics, members of the postwar foreign-policy elite were deeply influenced by the traditional nationalist myths.[28] Most were born in the late nineteenth century, when both the U.S. and the world looked very different than they did in the mid-twentieth. Wartime Secretary of Defense Henry Stimson, for example, was born two years after the Civil War and was directly touched by the nationalist, missionary spirit of the Spanish-American War, which occurred when he was in his early thirties.[29] Not surprisingly, given their personal roots in the simpler, Protestant America of the nineteenth century, their "international-ist" thinking was shaped by ideas of Manifest Destiny and providential mission.

Two quotations neatly illustrate the significance of this traditional discourse in the central foreign policy debates of the later 1940s. In his quasi-official elaboration of the new policy of containment, published anonymously in July 1947, George Kennan concluded by draping the anti-Soviet policy in the mantle of these deep-seated American ideas: "the thoughtful observer of Russian-American relations will find no cause for complaint in the Kremlin's challenge to American society. He will rather experience a certain gratitude to a Providence which, by providing the American people with this implacable challenge, has made their entire security as a nation dependent on their pulling themselves together and accepting the responsibilities of moral and political leadership that history plainly intended them to bear."[30] From a very different political position, Henry A. Wallace, who emerged as the leading critic of containment policy after resigning as Secretary of Commerce in September 1946, made a more millennialist claim about America's historic role. "By reason of history, geography and sheer economic strength," Wallace wrote in January 1947, "America has it in her grasp to furnish that great and last [sic] peace which the prophets and sages have preached for thousands of years."[31] This sort of rhetoric, drawing on traditional themes of providential destiny and millennial mission, extended far beyond the thinking of elite figures like Kennan and Wallace.

At the end of World War II, significant out-groups—most notably within organized labor and the African American community—espoused their own distinctive and often contentious visions of America's world role. Like the rest of U.S. society, these groups were strongly affected by the democratic and nationalist revivals of the 1930s and 1940s. From their viewpoints, equality was a particularly important component of America's democratic ideals. During World War II, patriotism ran high among blacks and workers despite continuing racial conflict and labor strife. Especially after the publication of Gunnar Myrdal's *An American Dilemma* in 1944, most prominent African American leaders and their allies framed the public discussion of U.S. race relations in terms of the gap Myrdal highlighted between the American Creed and the persistence of racial oppression. That Myrdalian framework was very much part of the democratic and nationalist revivals of the period, and it became central to the strategy of the emerging postwar civil rights movement.[32] The predominant African American demand from the 1940s through the early 1960s was that America live up to its creed. That demand had been central to the work of the National Association for the Advancement of Colored People (NAACP) since its founding in 1909, but it gained added impetus during and after World War II. In a somewhat analogous development, the idea and politics of "Americanism" assumed a heightened importance in the labor movement during the years of the democratic revival.[33]

The wartime rhetoric that proclaimed the nation's dedication to the worldwide struggle for human freedom resonated deeply with many union members and African Americans committed both to the American idea and the struggles of their fellows in other lands. Indeed, they frequently made this rhetoric their own and used it to advance working-class and African American visions of the American mission. But as the world scene changed, particularly from 1947 on, the domestic political climate shifted rightward amid a rising anticommunist uproar. The contours of public debate were consequently redrawn. To maintain their own places in the national conversation, central elements of these groups increasingly employed the dominant foreign-policy language of anticommunist nationalist globalism. Like other Americans, many blacks and workers held strong anticommunist views which they now learned to situate in an international context. During this period, major organizations such as the NAACP and the UAW came to support the broadly stated objectives of the Truman administration's foreign policy, even while continuing to dissent on specific issues. Leaders of these groups, and no doubt many of their followers, believed passionately in the American ideals they espoused in support of the Cold War. Out of their belief in the nation's ultimate commitment to individual freedom, equality, and justice under law, they willingly dampened their criticism of the nation's foreign policy in the name of national loyalty during a period of deepening international conflict. Yet by engaging in the dominant discourse, supporting the administration, and demonstrating their own national loyalty, they also sought to advance their own agendas and to protect their movements from the mounting waves of anticommunist attacks. These rhetorical and political strategies helped to shape the subsequent histories of the labor and civil rights movements as well as the history of U.S. foreign-policy discourse and public culture more generally.

The range of acceptable public discourse narrowed considerably between 1945 and 1950, as its basic terms concerning the U.S. world role increasingly limited any room for dissent. By 1950, national loyalty became equated with global anti-communism and a correspondingly global, interventionist foreign policy. In that context, anything but tactical criticism of U.S. foreign policy was defined as inherently disloyal and hence illegitimate. Tactical debate on specific foreign policy issues continued and even proliferated. But on fundamental questions of national purpose, of the nation's role in world affairs and of grand strategy to guide U.S. foreign policy, the range of permissible discourse and legitimate debate became increasingly constricted. "Isolationism," whether of the left or the right, was delegitimized by the experience of World War II. By 1947 and 1948, once the idea took hold that the U.S. needed to combat Soviet-led communism around the world, remaining oppositional perspectives were similarly cast outside the sphere of acceptable discourse. Both "isolationist" and "pro-Soviet" perspectives were so easily dismissed in the postwar era because they were deemed to signify fundamental disloyalty to the nation. By 1950, the only major question left was how best to wage the global struggle. In this context, the notion that "politics stops at the water's edge" in the interest of national unity curtailed more than just excessive partisanship. It curtailed significant public debate about the nation's proper role in world affairs — and about its domestic priorities as well.

By 1950, then, American nationalist globalism provided the ideological framework for a broad public consensus behind the Truman administration's Cold War stance. Some Americans held opinions outside of that consensual framework, of course, but such opinions were now thoroughly marginal, culturally demonized, and politically irrelevant. Criticism of Truman's foreign policy persisted, but it was mainly directed at questions of the administration's tactics and basic competence, particularly concerning the so-called "loss" of China and the inability to gain a quick, decisive victory in Korea. Much of that criticism came from the Republican right. Rather than contributing to a retrenchment of U.S. overseas efforts, these conservative attacks prodded successive administrations into a more expansive, more militarized brand of globalism that went largely unchecked until the rise of the anti–Vietnam War movement in the mid-1960s.

The foreign-policy elite and its allies viewed public opinion as an integral instrument of Cold War foreign policy. As James Reston of the *New York Times* pointed out in 1949, as part of a study sponsored by the influential Council on Foreign Relations, the president of the United States is always "the Number One Voice" in the national conversation about foreign affairs.[34] The president generally has the first word in announcing and explaining major international developments to the American public. Harry Truman took advantage of this fact to significantly shape the terms of public discussion. The Truman administration also exaggerated international crises and the Soviet military threat to scare Congress and the public and to intimidate potential critics. It used anticommunist smear tactics to delegitimize some critics (most notably Henry Wallace), while using loyalty oaths and anticommunist legislation to silence others.[35] It built relationships with the CIO and the NAACP that helped to soften foreign-policy criticism from those organizations. Yet the Truman administration did not single-handedly create the period's growing anticommunist impulse, which effectively undermined left-wing critics of Cold War foreign policy. Nor did the anticommunist right later associated with Senator Joseph McCarthy. The CIO expelled communist-led unions. The NAACP dismissed W. E. B. Du Bois, who supported Henry Wallace and vociferously condemned Truman's foreign policy. African American opinion leaders closed ranks against Paul Robeson after he declared in 1949 that blacks would not fight in a war against the Soviet Union. These and related actions were not taken by the Truman administration, nor by the Republican right. They were taken by leaders of subordinate groups with an eye to demonstrating national loyalty and maintaining friendly relations with the federal government.

The politics of national loyalty ultimately constrained foreign-policy debate and cemented the Cold War consensus. It was not just a one-way street flowing from the elite to the masses. As the sense of long-term international crisis deepened, African Americans and union members, along with most other Americans, became more nationalistic, more anticommunist, and more persuaded by the hegemonic ideology of nationalist globalism. That ideology, in any event, increasingly filtered the international news most Americans read or heard. And the Truman administration generally emphasized the long-term, global nature of the Cold War. But the key point is that, for most Americans, the ideology of American nationalist globalism provided the clearest, most powerful explanation for events as they unfolded between 1945 and 1950 and the most convincing basis for U.S. policy. That was true, in part, because competing views were increasingly unavailable, but it was true nonetheless. Indeed, by the end of the 1940s, the predominance of nationalist globalism was such that one had to speak its terms to be heard at all. Red-baiting, along with the lessons of Munich, Pearl Harbor, and Hiroshima, had silenced, marginalized, or delegitimized the most critical voices. Others voiced criticism only in terms that guaranteed their own anticommunist, internationalist credentials. Still others saw the light after some new act of perceived Soviet aggression.

Ideas concerning a beneficent national mission and a destined national greatness served to justify the expansion of U.S. power during and after World War II, just as they had throughout much of earlier U.S. history. Yet such beliefs were genuinely shared by policymakers and large segments of the public, even if policymakers and other elites took a leading role in articulating these ideas and thereby shaping public discourse. The Truman administration was able to pursue a foreign policy rooted in the ideology of American nationalist globalism at least in part because much of the American public shared the same ideology.

This book is a study in public culture, rather than a study of foreign policy making per se. Previous studies have examined the ideological thinking of policymakers in this period, though more work is badly needed in that area.[36] My focus, however, is on the cultural context in which policymakers operated and in which the Cold War consensus developed, and on questions of continuity and change in popular attitudes, beliefs, perceptions, and values as they related to foreign affairs. Some important work in this direction has been done, notably by Paul Boyer and Michael Sherry.[37] But the role of American nationalism, and especially the nationalist symbolism of American world power, remains a neglected factor in our understanding of the Cold War's origins. As the Cold War itself recedes into history and the view that the Russians started it and the Americans won it becomes increasingly commonplace, it is more important than ever to examine the ways in which the United States contributed to the Cold War's origins, particularly through the universalist pretensions of its political culture. The triumphalism embedded in Francis Fukuyama's view that the end of the Cold War marked "the end of history" constitutes a new, historically contingent variation on the ideology that framed that conflict from the beginning.[38] In a world growing less rather than more pliable to the dictates of U.S. policy, such ideological thinking is potentially quite dangerous.

1 THE MOMENT OF VICTORY

For many Americans, the end of World War II came more swiftly than expected, appearing suddenly with the enormous, mushroomlike clouds over Hiroshima and Nagasaki. Japan's defeat had been within grasp for weeks. But on August 6, 1945, victory became palpable, as the United States unleashed a new weapon so awesome that Japanese surrender seemed the necessary consequence of its use. According to public opinion polls in August 1945, a large majority of Americans approved the use of atomic bombs against Japan. They did so because they believed the bomb had hastened the war's end and their nation's victory. In other words, they believed what President Harry S. Truman and his administration told them.[1]

Despite fears and anxieties concerning the atomic bomb itself, the end of the war brought most Americans a sense of relief and national pride.[2] The American way of life had survived the challenge of total war against totalitarian foes. At this moment of victory, nationalist sentiments suffused all corners of U.S. public life, including the widespread talk of international cooperation. An essentially nationalistic construction of the moment of victory set the parameters for public understanding of the main purposes of U.S. foreign policy in the postwar era.

By announcing the war's end and the events that led up to it, and by subsequently proclaiming national days of celebration and prayer, President Truman helped to shape that moment. In Truman's public pronouncements, the victory signified the greatness of the United States, the righteousness of its cause, and the guidance that God granted the nation. The victory of the United States and its allies over the forces of Hitler, Mussolini, and the Japanese militarists, the president emphasized, demonstrated "the basic proposition of the worth and dignity of man" — of the individual as master rather than servant of the state. The mass media echoed these themes. The Truman administration and the media alike construed the victory as belonging primarily to the United States rather than to all the Allies equally.[3] In the official discourse and in the mass culture, the nation's righteousness stood beyond question. Yet some voices in the national discussion did question both the completeness of the victory and the righteousness of the nation. Those voices included members of a peace movement shriveled by the wartime consensus, small numbers of independent leftists and conservative nationalists, and others who had opposed U.S. entry into the war to begin with. But the strongest chorus of voices to question the triumphalist view of America's victory issued from the African American press.[4]

THE ATOMIC MOMENT

The first public disclosure of the atomic bomb came in a terse written statement issued by President Truman August 6, 1945, the day the bomb was unleashed on the people of Hiroshima. The president described a weapon possessing "more than two thousand times the blast power of the British 'Grand Slam,'" previously the largest bomb ever used. Yet comparison to other merely human efforts was insufficient, both in scale and in drama. Truman stressed that the atomic bomb was "a harnessing of the basic power of the universe." The United States, he told his listeners, had mastered "the force from which the sun draws its power" and unleashed it "against those who brought war to the Far East."[5] How, then, could Japan or any foe resist America's will?

While acknowledging British cooperation, the president emphasized that this remarkable achievement was made possible by the unique know-how, material abundance, and physical security of the United States. The technical feat itself, Truman suggested, was a national triumph of historic magnitude: "We have spent two billion dollars on the greatest scientific gamble in history — and won."[6] Such world-historical superlatives recurred throughout the president's brief statement. "What has been done," he assured his constituents, "is the greatest achievement of organized science in history."[7] If Japan's leaders still failed to accept "unconditional surrender," he warned, "they may expect a rain of ruin from the air, the like of which has never been seen on this earth."[8] The unequaled rain of ruin Japan had already experienced, in the form of the "conventional" U.S. aerial assault, went unmentioned.

Before Hiroshima, the U.S. press had conveyed some sense of the enormity of the ongoing air war against Japan, but it treated the atomic bomb as a new departure in destructiveness.[9] The *New York Daily News,* the nation's best-selling newspaper and a staunch booster for U.S. air power, amplified Truman's view of the new weapon's vast significance. On August 7, the top half of the tabloid's front page spelled it out in big, bold print: "Atomic Bomb Spells Japs' Ruin: Truman."[10] As one Washington correspondent described the mood in the nation's capital, "For forty-eight hours now, the new bomb has been virtually the only topic of conversation and discussion. . . . For two days it has been an unusual thing to see a smile among the throngs that crowd the streets. The entire city is pervaded by a kind of sense of oppression."[11]

But to many Americans the bomb brought a sense of relief as well, because it signaled the imminence of the war's end. The week of the surrender, for example,

Life magazine published a powerful photo-essay featuring the surreal, billowing clouds over Hiroshima and Nagasaki, under a title that implicitly equated the bomb with the peace: "The War Ends: Burst of Atomic Bomb Brings Swift Surrender of Japanese." [12] Even in the days immediately following its debut, public discussion of the atomic bomb focused less on its use against Japan than on its meaning for the nascent postwar world and America's place in it. Japan's defeat and America's victory were taken as givens, as though both eventualities were embedded in the official news releases concerning Hiroshima. The bomb itself "spells Japs' ruin," as the *News*'s headline put it. The media presented this atomic triumph as more than simply a triumph against Japan. One news story, for example, reported that "Congressional sources" believed the bomb "puts [the] USSR virtually in the position now of an also ran." [13] The bomb gave the United States incontestable power over all actual and potential adversaries.

In its August 8 editorial, "The Split Atom," the *Daily News* argued that the bomb would be essential to American security for the foreseeable future. Noting that Canada held the greatest known deposits of the necessary uranium, the editorial concluded that this northern neighbor and World War II ally "should make itself our out-and-out and exclusive ally" in terms of its uranium trade. In such matters, the *News* asserted, "it is a question of kill or be killed in wartime, and of lining up the best possible weapons in peacetime lest others line them up against us and in due time deal us a Pearl Harbor." Ignoring Truman's vague appeal about controlling the spread and use of the new weapon, the *News* called for controlling the necessary resource to ensure a perpetual preponderance of U.S. atomic power, even if the existing atomic monopoly could not be maintained. Canada should realize that U.S. interests were its interests as well. If not, the *News* suggested, "enough patriotic Americans can probably be found to see to it that Canada does the right thing by us and by itself with its uranium," possibly by threatening it with atomic bombs. Though the Pacific War was not yet over, this editorial, like most post-Hiroshima discourse, concerned itself primarily with the postwar security of the United States. The victory over Japan was more or less in hand, and the commonplace "lesson" of Pearl Harbor—that eternal vigilance is the price of peace, as the saying goes—was taken as the most reliable guide to the postwar future.

On the same page, an editorial cartoon entitled "The Family" amplified one aspect of the editorial's basic theme. The drawing depicted an affluent white couple, probably in their forties, leisurely reading their morning paper in the shade of a glorious old elm or oak. She holds the paper, bearing the banner headline "First Atom Bomb Falls on Hiroshima," and says to him "This atom bomb seems to be the most terrific instrument of destruction ever invented." "Yes," he replies, "and let's use it on our enemies first instead of our enemies using it on us." By this means, the proverbial American Way of Life, which this couple seems to represent, is to be preserved against any and all adversaries. The self-assurance of this obviously successful man no doubt served to discourage doubt in those who might think otherwise.[14]

Other editorial cartoons revealed less sanguine views of the bomb. Two revealing cartoons from the *Newark Evening News* appeared in the first weeks of the atomic age. One depicted a powerful forearm labeled "Control of Atomic Power" struggling to wrest the globe from the grip of a huge, ape-man monster labeled "Future Threat of War." The other depicted a roundtable of United Nations diplomats in the guise of an enormous scale weighed down to one side by a tiny ball representing "atomic power"; a giant globe hung in the balance. Another cartoon that appeared within days of the atomic bombings showed a geeky-looking scientist (glasses, white lab jacket, a slip of paper in his pocket marked "The Atom") standing over an arc of the globe revealing the Americas and a crawling infant identified as "Humanity." The man held out a tiny ball in his extended hand, and the caption posed a question: "Baby play with nice ball?" Unlike the *Daily News,* these cartoonists saw the bomb less as a sign of American power than as a symbol of world vulnerability. But they instantly grasped its global implications, as well as the speed with which it spelled the end of the war and the beginning of a dangerous new era.[15]

Palpable though it was, the final, total victory remained to be realized. Public anticipation of the war's denouement continued to grow until August 14, when Truman announced that Japan's surrender met U.S. demands. In the intervening days, this rising anticipation produced waves of nervous energy throughout the nation. For several consecutive days before the surrender was accepted, for example, crowds gathered in New York's Times Square and other public spaces, awaiting triumphant celebrations that people evidently felt were in the air.[16]

THE PRESIDENT REPORTS

In the nine-day span from the bombing of Hiroshima to the announcement of Japan's surrender, President Truman repeatedly fed the anticipation of victory while shaping the meaning that victory would assume in the nation's public life. On August 9, most notably, Truman delivered a "radio report to the American people" that proved pivotal in influencing public discussion of the war's end and of America's role in the emerging, postwar international order. The bulk of the speech discussed the situation in Europe and the results of the Potsdam Conference in Berlin, from which Truman had just returned. But Truman also discussed the state of the war against Japan, the significance of the atomic bomb, and the new position of the United States in a changed world.

Truman starkly portrayed the ravages he had seen in Europe. He described

Berlin, "the city from which the Germans intended to rule the world," as "a ghost city." He described haunting scenes in the ruins of other devastated German cities, where "women and children and old men were wandering over the highways, returning to bombed-out homes or leaving bombed-out cities, searching for food and shelter." Truman spoke also of the "terrific destruction" he had seen in Western Europe and England. The images of war-torn Europe — of a land "in ruins," of people wandering in despair amid their bombed-out communities — were all familiar enough to the American public by August 1945. They had become stock phrases in any discussion of the war, employed recurrently in the press, on the radio and elsewhere. But by using these phrases to express his own first-hand observations, the president invested them with the full symbolic weight of his office.[17]

After sketching this picture of Europe in ruins, the president gave thanks to God for the well-being of the United States, and expressed a sense of urgency concerning the need to protect the nation against any future war:

> How glad I am to be home again! And how grateful to Almighty God that this land of ours has been spared!
>
> We must do all we can to spare her from the ravages of any future breach of the peace. That is why, though the United States wants no territory or profit or selfish advantage out of this war, we are going to maintain the military bases necessary for the complete protection of our interests and of world peace.

This passage reflects important elements of American "internationalist" thought in the 1940s, but it also conveys strong nationalist sentiments. By proclaiming his pleasure at returning home, especially against the bleak European backdrop he had sketched, Truman voiced the love of country so essential to war talk in any nation-state. By bringing God into the equation, he delivered a classic formulation of what Conor Cruise O'Brien has called "holy nationalism," implying that God had chosen to spare America from war's devastation.[18] Most tellingly, the nationalism Truman espoused here was self-consciously benevolent and "disinterested," characteristics typical of, though hardly unique to, American nationalism. The self-conscious denial of self-aggrandizement runs far back in the tradition of American nationalist thought and was accentuated in the twentieth century with the renunciation of landed expansionism, particularly in the rhetoric of Woodrow Wilson and Franklin Roosevelt.[19]

Still, no matter how selfless the United States proclaimed itself, Americans had to take action to ensure that God's will would be realized. The act of acquiring military bases, for instance, involved no selfish desire because it was entirely defensive, benevolent, and necessary to realize God's will. In the same August 9 speech, Truman presented U.S. interests and world peace as concentric circles, if not identical spheres. Speaking in the national voice of the United States, the president declared that the United States would acquire whatever bases "our military experts" think necessary "for our protection." Yet these acquisitions would be "consistent with the United Nations Charter," Truman promised, voicing a central precept of the internationalist mantle he had inherited from Roosevelt.

Truman proceeded to assert the increasingly commonplace notion that any future war would wreak devastation of unimaginable magnitude, dwarfing the horrors of the present conflict. The possibility of unforeseeable destruction from which the United States might not be spared served as the core of Truman's evocation of the spirit and purpose of the United Nations. National self-interest, or the concept of national security, clearly underlay the language of international cooperation.

After these introductory remarks, Truman explained the results of the Potsdam Conference, including military arrangements related to the Soviet declaration of war against Japan and the political and economic principles by which the Allies would govern occupied Germany. These principles, Truman said, "seek to rebuild democracy by control of German education, by reorganizing local government and the judiciary, by encouraging free speech, free press, freedom of religion, and the right of labor to organize." The president summarized the broadest aims of the occupation in even bolder terms: "We are going to do what we can to make Germany over into a decent nation, so that it may eventually work its way from the economic chaos it has brought upon itself, back into a place in the civilized world." [20] Within the dual contexts of the entire speech and the broader tradition of discourse about America's world role of which the speech is a part, the voice in this passage appears ambiguous. On the one hand, Truman's use of "we" clearly seems intended to speak for the occupying powers collectively, since it immediately follows the president's explication of the jointly declared Potsdam principles. On the other hand, when Truman used the pronoun "we" earlier in his radio speech, he used it to speak in the unified voice of all Americans, and many U.S. listeners may have heard it that way in this paragraph as well. Once this "we" is construed as the voice of America, the sentence appears in many ways to fit into the deep tradition of talk about America as a redeemer nation, whose higher purpose is to bring the rest of the world (particularly the Old World) out of its sinful state of self-created chaos and back to the light of civilization, American-style.[21]

Truman returned to this theme, on a more expansive scale, in concluding his discussion of Europe. He did so in words that invested America's victory there with a very specific, very significant set of meanings. "Europe today is hungry," he said. In the newly liberated countries of Western Europe, many people lacked clothing, shelter, and the basic means of rebuilding their devastated societies:

As the winter comes on, the distress will increase. Unless we do what we can to help, we may lose next winter what we won at such terrible cost last spring. Desperate men are liable to destroy the structure of their society to find in the wreckage some substitute for hope. If we let Europe go cold and hungry, we may lose some of the foundations of order on which the hope for worldwide peace must rest.

We must help to the limits of our strength. And we will.[22]

Truman was suggesting, of course, that "the foundations of order on which the hope for worldwide peace must rest" were vital to U.S. self-interest and national security. To "let Europe go cold and hungry" would be self-injurious as well as ungenerous. Truman's use of what I have earlier called the national voice is revealing. The president avowed international responsibilities and moral commitments not merely as head of state but in the name of "we" the people.

Truman next turned "to the day of victory in Japan." While use of the atomic bomb was not undertaken lightly, the president said, the United States would use it repeatedly until Japan surrendered.[23] He then raised the question of the new weapon's implications for the postwar world, accentuating the sense that the war's end was at hand. "The atomic bomb," Truman explained, "is too dangerous to be loose in a lawless world." Consequently, the United States and its atomic partners, Great Britain and Canada, would not reveal "the secret of its production . . . until means have been found to control the bomb so as to protect ourselves and the rest of the world from the danger of total destruction." The danger itself was presented as inherently global. The president vowed to seek congressional cooperation toward the goal of controlling the bomb's production and use and making its power "an overwhelming influence towards world peace."[24] Yet Truman's speech failed to suggest how this ambitious, globalist goal might be accomplished. That it could be done at all was left as a matter of faith, either in God's mysterious wisdom, the United States's demonstrable ingenuity, or both working in tandem.

Significantly, the president presented the United States as the prime actor behind the bomb, mentioning Great Britain and Canada only casually. In discussing efforts to promote the control and peaceful application of the bomb, he mentioned only Secretary of War Stimson, Secretary of State Byrnes, and the Congress. In the name of the American people, the president told the American people,

We must constitute ourselves trustees of this new force — to prevent its misuse, and to turn it into the channels of service to mankind.

It is an awful responsibility which has come to us.

We thank God that it has come to us, instead of to our enemies; and we pray that He may guide us to use it in His ways and for His purposes.[25]

This pivotal passage presented a profession of universal benevolence on behalf of the United States. Americans were to serve as trustees of the bomb in the interest of all humanity—an "awful responsibility" but one that accompanied victory itself, like the responsibility for restoring order in Europe. Truman suggested that God had given these international responsibilities to the United States, revealing his tendency to interpret American history, at least recent American history, in Providential terms.[26] Indeed, Truman implied that the ability of the United States to wipe out entire cities with one blow was a sign of divine favor. By asserting that the United States alone could "prevent its misuse," Truman reified the notion that use of the bomb against Hiroshima was proper and justified. (The bombing of Nagasaki occurred the day Truman delivered this speech but remained unknown to the public until the next day.) As in his initial public statement on the bomb, Truman portrayed Hiroshima as a military base, ignoring its role as home to over a quarter-million civilians. The president was engaging in war talk, full of sharp contrasts between good and evil, devoid of subtle moral shadings: the United States was purely a force for good in the world; only its enemies, and forces beyond its control, were to be feared. Subtleties like dead children had no place.

After thanking God for the bomb and praying for His guidance in its use, Truman closed his speech by expounding on the meaning of victory in its loftiest terms. The victory already achieved in Europe was "more than a victory of arms," the president proclaimed:

> It was a victory of one way of life over another. It was a victory of an ideal founded on the rights of the common man, on the dignity of the human being, on the conception of the State as the servant—and not the master—of its people. . . .
>
> We tell ourselves that we have emerged from this war the most powerful nation in the world—the most powerful nation, perhaps, in all history. That is true, but not in the sense some of us believe it to be true.

The central lesson of America's victory, Truman concluded, was that

> a society of self-governing men is more powerful, more enduring, more creative than any other kind of society, however disciplined, however centralized.
>
> We know now that the basic proposition of the worth and dignity of man is not a sentimental aspiration or a vain hope or a piece of rhetoric. It is the strongest, most creative force now present in this world.
>
> Now let us use that force and all our resources and all our skills in the great cause of a just and lasting peace![27]

Despite the president's reference to the victory already achieved in Europe, his words encompassed the anticipated victory in the Pacific. In fact, he spoke of "the war" exclusively in the past tense.

Precisely as the public sensed the imminence of final victory, the president had publicly explicated that victory as a worldwide triumph of the American "way of life" over another, un-American way of life. Significantly, Truman posited "the rights of the common man" and "the dignity of the human being" as central to the meaning of victory and thus to the very purpose of the war. In the same vein, the war marked the triumph of free Americans over amoral, professional soldiers. The presumption that the United States had emerged from the war as the most powerful nation ever is treated as a commonplace belief shared by all Americans. But the important point Truman sought to make here was that the nation's preponderant power rested primarily not on its material abundance or military might but on the moral force of its ideals, and that the power of those ideals had been freshly demonstrated, as never before, in the course of total, global war.

The outpouring of mail President Truman received in response to this speech showed that his message struck deep chords with its intended audience, the American people. The responses ranged widely and richly, from bellicosity to religiosity, from the pragmatic to the utopian. Even the most critical agreed that Truman's speech marked a major statement at a pivotal moment in the intertwined histories of the United States and the world. Few letter writers protested the president's decision to use the atomic bomb. Many more supported his willingness to use as many as needed. A telegram from Kansas urged the use of two bombs the next day then doubling the number until Japan surrendered. Religious sentiments were more widespread, appearing most strikingly in letters that echoed Truman's invocation of divine providence concerning the atomic bomb. An elderly man from rural Florida thought the president's speech was divinely inspired and concurred that since God had denied the atomic bomb to America's enemies, "we will use it in his name and for his purposes," making possible a world in which "we will have war no more." A Lutheran pastor from Portland, Oregon, expressed similar views with a less utopian slant: "Christian America is today thankful for your desire to make and keep America great by assuming a godly guardianship over the future of the possibilities inherent in the atomic bomb. Your assurance in this direction will prove increasingly cheering to all mankind." This last sentence tacitly acknowledged that humanity might initially find the bomb less than "cheering," while asserting that the world would eventually come to trust in Christian America's guardianship over its future.[28] Many other writers praised Truman simply for asking God's guidance and let him know that they also prayed for God to guide their president in leading "our Great Nation" in the cause of world peace. A Wisconsin farmer expressed deep gratitude for Truman's "godly mission of declaring 'Peace' terms to the world." A telegram from New York City asked God to make possible the "unconditional application . . . all over the world of the principles and ideas of the President of the United States and the American people." These letters convey a widespread awareness of the global reach of American power, as well as a faith in the nation's moral righteousness.[29]

Other presidential correspondents wrote both out of a visceral enthusiasm for the president's message and out of a desire to argue for their own political positions. Harris Wofford Jr., a nineteen-year-old Army Air Force corporal and future U.S. senator from Pennsylvania, wrote in admiration of Truman and in support of world federalism. He applauded Truman for proclaiming "America's purpose as the survival and world-wide extension of the free principles" before arguing that the logical conclusion of Truman's policy would be "World Federal Democracy." The bomb, Wofford wrote, cast the challenge in bold relief: "either the Earth is governed or it will be blown up, either the free peoples boldly lead in building a World United States or a new Caesar will take over the world." This young liberal assured his commander-in-chief that his generation would take up the task when their time came. In contrast to Wofford's youthful idealism, the New York financier E. F. Hutton wrote President Truman an equally enthusiastic letter about the same August 9th radio address arguing for a very different political tack. Seizing on Truman's assertions about the power of self-governing men, Hutton said the world was in a head-on collision between collectivist tyranny (witnessed by the Labor victory in Britain) and "return to God" and constitutional democracy, as embodied in the United States. The world looked to the United States for guidance, wrote Hutton, which it could provide only if its economy prospered. The best way to insure increased prosperity, in Hutton's view, was to remove all checks that had been imposed on industry and capital. Only then could the United States provide a "beneficent force" to its dependents. Wofford and Hutton expressed wildly divergent agendas from a basis of shared enthusiasm for the president's radio speech. The ideological abstractions of Truman's rhetoric left ample room for argument.[30]

MEDIA MESSAGES

The news media covered the president's August 9th radio speech extensively, amplifying its core messages in ripples that continued to spread out for many days after Truman's broadcast. Though the bombing of Nagasaki provided the day's other big story, and Japan finally surrendered just days later, the president's speech was widely discussed throughout the following week and beyond. Not surprisingly, different publications construed Truman's words in different ways.

To the editors of *Life* magazine, the speech's import lay in Truman's discussion of the bomb and of American power in "The Atomic Age," to use the title of its August 20 editorial.[31] *Life* praised Truman for his "cool and unimaginative tone" as an antidote to public anxieties about the bomb, and for his apparent refusal "to use . . . the atomic bomb as a diplomatic weapon against Russia." The very vastness of American power, the editorial suggested, gave new cause to use it with restraint. Quoting Truman's broadcast, the editorial argued: "America . . . is now 'the most powerful nation in the world — the most powerful nation perhaps in all history.' All the more reason, therefore, to stick to the Russian policy we had made before: to welcome Russia's entrance into the Japanese war and confirm our intention to keep world peace on a genuinely Allied basis. There were Americans who felt a Jovian impulse to redress the wrongs of Eastern Europe by threatening to hurl atomic thunderbolts from British bases. Instead we stood by Potsdam and our word." The emphasis on keeping the peace "on a genuinely Allied basis" reflects a central theme of American internationalism in the 1940s. This passage juxtaposes its own knowingly enlightened internationalism against the bellicose, crudely nationalistic urge "to hurl atomic thunderbolts." Yet *Life* restated Truman's assertion of America's unprecedented power without linking it directly to the president's emphasis on the moral, as opposed to military or economic, sources of that power. The important thing, it seems, was for readers to appreciate that theirs was "the most powerful nation perhaps in all history."[32]

Life then returned to dwell on the Jovian analogy it had raised, rooting it this time in a verse from English poetry:

> *Ay, do thy worst. Thou art omnipotent.*
> *O'er all things but thyself I gave thee power . . .*

Thus, in Shelley's vision, did Prometheus defy his enemy Jove. But when America's omnipotence passes like Jove's it will not go down with a Promethean curse. So far, at least, we have shown some power over ourselves; Prometheus, the subtle artificer and friend of man, is still an American citizen. Not naked force but "the basic proposition of the worth and dignity of man . . ." as Truman put it, "is the strongest, most creative force now present in the world."

In this passage, *Life* cites and then interprets Truman's most potent statement concerning moral power, but it separated this notion of moral force from American power itself, which is implied at the editorial's outset to be of a more traditional sort. Still, the principal message here is that the United States had not yet succumbed to the temptations to Jovian arrogance that understandably beset the nation. Moreover, this passage construes "America's omnipotence" as the product of a specific historical moment, which will, like all others, recede into the past. Most significantly, though, the editorial emphasized that the United States had managed to demonstrate its self-control precisely because it valued "the basic proposition of the worth and dignity of man" more than naked force. As in Truman's speech and throughout a wide range of public discourse at the end of the war, this proposition was seen to be the single feature that irrefutably distinguished the United States from other great powers in history.

Despite its efforts to distance itself from the Jovian impulse, *Life* hardly shied away from the belief in America's greatness. In the closing lines of this editorial, for example, the magazine called on the nation to embark upon an immense, even utopian mission in the postwar atomic age: "No limits are set to our Promethean ingenuity, provided we remember that we are not Jove. We are not ants either; we can abolish warfare, and mitigate man's inhumanity to man. But all this will take some doing. And we are in a strange new land." Talk of abolishing war was widespread in 1945, and this passage suggests that the United States could unilaterally abolish both warfare and human injustice. The possibilities of what the United States could achieve were indeed limitless. Such grandiose claims might seem hollow or naïve, but they represent a classic statement of American nationalism in the heady days of August 1945, when triumphalism washed away most doubts about the limits of American power. The most powerful nation in history was poised to make the world over again in its own benevolent image.

By contrast with *Life,* the *New York Daily News* emphasized Truman's pronouncements concerning military bases. On August 10, the paper featured a huge front-page headline reading "U.S. Will Keep War Bases, Truman Says." The corresponding article noted that "Truman made it clear that while this country wants no territory out of the global war it is determined to have our flag fly over all key points considered vital to our defense." Any consciousness of the contradiction involved in this move was thoroughly repressed. This story also reported that many people had listened attentively to the president's broadcast in the hope that he would announce Japan's surrender.[33] On August 11, the *News*'s editorial heralded "Truman's Wise Speech," saying it "was loaded with factual, rock-bottom information, was delivered in an earnestly matter-of-fact Midwestern voice, and did not contain one wisecrack or purple passage," all in implied contrast to Franklin Roosevelt, whose death the *News*'s editors had hardly mourned. The editorial asserted that his point concerning military bases was "the most important part of the whole statement." The *News* suggested that the president would not have made this statement without prior agreement from the Australians and British "that we are to have such of those bases as our military experts want." After all, the argument proceeded, "It would be only common sense for the British and Australians to let us have them. Otherwise, in event of future trouble in the Pacific, there would be a pronounced feeling in the United States of: 'Oh, well, let the

Australians, etc., take care of themselves this time — if they can.'" This passage assumes that popular feelings of international responsibility, concerning the Pacific at least, depended upon a sense of national possession. Only if the islands belong to "us" will the region's problems be experienced as "our" problems too, and consequently as problems that "we" will be responsible for solving. This formulation is essentially nationalistic (which is hardly surprising coming from the *Daily News*) in that the "imagined community" of the nation is by definition tied to an identification with the nation's land.[34] The interesting thing about this expression of American nationalism is the extent to which other listeners might have appropriated Truman's remarks in a similar vein. As I suggested earlier, the president's statement contained strong nationalistic ingredients. But this passage from the *News* editorial goes further in suggesting a view of the emerging, postwar relationship between the United States and its allies, if not the rest of the world, in which the true self-interest of all other nations is seen to be simultaneously identical with and subordinate to the perceived self-interest of the nearly omnipotent United States. Over the next five years, this kind of view would become increasingly potent, even as the sense of American omnipotence was shaken.

The *News* found Truman's brief remarks concerning control of atomic weaponry to represent "a noble concept that could not be guaranteed." While acknowledging that "knowledge of these things gets around," the *News* put little faith in international cooperation on such matters. Instead, it argued that the United States should seek to maintain an overwhelming edge in atomic power: "Our only safe policy with regard to this weapon will be to have more atom bombs and bomb plants than the rest of the world until a counter-weapon is discovered; and to hire ample spies of our own to keep our Government advised of what goes on in other nations, militarily and scientifically."[35] Under the caption "Japs About To Quit?" the editorial's closing section suggested "that the Japanese would like to surrender if they could keep their Emperor intact in his person, privileges, perquisites and prestige." While such terms would be less than "unconditional surrender," the *News* emphasized that the Emperor was "only a symbol" and that keeping him on the throne might save many American lives.[36] Besides, the editorial concluded, a quick Japanese surrender would minimize Russian leverage in Asia and the Pacific once the war was over. This editorial most likely left many readers with a reinforced sense that final victory was close at hand, and that U.S. supremacy in the postwar world was an accepted fact.

In those first few days of the atomic age, the *Daily News* printed several letters to the editor concerning the bomb and its consequences. Almost all of them either supported the bomb's use against Japan, as well as its potential diplomatic use against the Soviet Union, or made light of it in some fashion that combined irony with avoidance. But one letter, from Elizabeth Dwyer of Manhattan, ran directly against this belligerent grain. Dwyer's letter suggested that the United States's use of the atomic bomb had tarnished its claims to moral enlightenment: "Speaking of atrocities, is not our atomic bombing as vicious as anything perpetrated by the Japs or the Nazis with their death camps, so much deplored? Are we not morally guilty in having held out for unconditional surrender, which gave the excuse for this ghastly gesture?" Dwyer concluded that if America continued these tactics, it would become "the most feared and despised nation on earth."[37] But such efforts to complicate the war's Manichaean distinctions between the international forces of good and evil did not generally get very far. In this case, Dwyer's letter stands as an isolated expression of such sentiments within the *News*'s "Voice of the People" feature, as the paper called its published letters to the editor. It did, however, prompt one printed letter in response, which granted that the bomb was an atrocity but argued that "to fight evil you must fight it with itself." The writer, one Alyce M. Anderson, also of Manhattan, then quickly moved to reassert the moral purity of the United States, saying that "we should trust our Government enough, and our military leaders, to know that they wouldn't have used the atom bomb except in a case of sheer need."[38] In 1945, clearly, the official story about Hiroshima and Nagasaki carried considerable authority, as it would for more than half a century to follow. Yet, by 1990s standards, such unquestioning faith in the legitimacy of government authorities would seem startlingly naïve.

"DOUBLE V"?: AFRICAN AMERICANS AND THE QUESTION OF VICTORY

While *Life,* the *Daily News,* and other voices in the commercial mass culture amplified elements of President Truman's rhetoric even while appropriating them toward their own ends, African American voices generally expressed a radically different perspective on the bomb and the war's end. Consequently, the writings on these subjects in the African American press held an almost elliptical and at times subversive relationship to that employed by the president and the white-controlled mass media.

African Americans held concerns that the dominant white discourse simply did not speak to. Specifically, diverse African American voices contended that the nation's victory would be without real meaning unless it brought with it an end to both European colonialism and American racial injustice. (Indeed, the two were often treated as components of a single, underlying problem rooted in the long history of European exploitation of darker peoples. In this perspective, the United States was viewed as an outgrowth of Europe, and Jim Crow as simply a variant on white methods of oppressing nonwhites throughout the world.) Consequently, when African American commentators touched on themes contained in Presi-

dent Truman's public discourse, they often did so in a way that was sharply contentious, even when they did not specifically take Truman to task for his remarks
or policies. Where American ideals were professed in the name of the nation's foreign policy objectives, African American commentators tended to emphasize the
disparity between the professed ideals and the day-to-day realities of American
life, between the dominant public image of America as a force of moral leadership in the world and the practices of racial injustice embedded in the nation's
history and social structure. This kind of argument served as a double-edged
sword. On the one side, it cut to the need to resolve such disparities by mitigating
racial injustice at home. On the other side, it cut to the question of hypocrisy in
the nation's stated foreign-policy goals, suggesting, either implicitly or explicitly,
that U.S. foreign policy was driven less by morality than by avarice.

So, where Truman proclaimed that the United States would take the lead in
reforming Germany and bringing it back into the fold of Christian civilization,
African American commentators questioned America's fitness for such a role.
Pittsburgh Courier columnist Marjorie McKenzie, for example, questioned the
very ability of the United States to carry out the Potsdam principles aimed at
overcoming the legacy of Nazism. With heavy irony, McKenzie argued that the
proposed experiment in abolishing discrimination and establishing democratic
ideas and justice under law was "so novel to the 'American way' " that the United
States was particularly ill-suited to the task. By contrast, she suggested, the Russians at least "have some experience in administering such principles." [39]

Another *Courier* columnist, the self-trained and often controversial historian
and anthropologist J. A. Rogers, took a slightly different tack on the same problem, arguing that "the United States, even with its self-crowned halo of democracy, is due for a housecleaning" as much as the Axis powers or Great Britain
[where the Tories had just been turned out of office]. As Rogers construed the
situation, the Potsdam Conference had abolished racism in the former Third
Reich, "which means that Germany, Nazi-land, will be ahead of the United States
in actual democracy." Since the United States was going to try Nazi leaders for
racial bigotry among other crimes, Rogers asked, "who is going to try Bilbo, East-
land, Rankin [the most notorious white supremacists in the U.S. Congress], and
others for their racial bigotry here?" [40] The United States could not hold itself
above its own professed ideals of international justice. But whereas the African
American press treated the United States as simply a part of the rest of the world,
with comparable moral status and comparable social and political problems, the
white-controlled mass media tended to present images of a dichotomous, hierarchical relationship between the United States and the rest of the world, morally
and otherwise.

African American commentators took a similarly critical stance regarding both the use of the atomic bomb and general public support for it. George S. Schuyler, the noted satirist and increasingly conservative iconoclast, effectively dismissed Truman's claims to righteousness in the bombing of Hiroshima, simply by ignoring them and describing the event as he saw it:

> Not satisfied with being able to kill people by the thousand, we have now achieved the supreme triumph of being able to slaughter whole cities at a time. . . . It seems that just yesterday we were bemoaning German barbarism in bombing Warsaw, Rotterdam, London and other industrial centers, and citing as evidence of Japanese savagery the slaughter of a few thousand innocents in Shanghai. There was also much Christian head-wagging over the mistreatment and beheading of some American soldiers by Nipponese gorillas, but now there is little except praise for the exploit of our airmen in wiping out 200,000 human beings at one blow.[41]

In a way that both the president and the mass media seemed to disallow, Schuyler drew the link between national triumph and national acquiescence to mass slaughter.[42] Despite the president's repeated protestations that Hiroshima had been targeted precisely as a military installation, Schuyler remarked that such pretense had been abandoned. Finally, the last sentence in the passage above presented an interesting commentary on U.S. public attitudes toward the Japanese. In the first clause, Schuyler noted the "Christian head-wagging" over atrocities committed by "Nipponese gorillas," playing on the widespread wartime metaphor of the Japanese as a form of subhuman simian, as well as on white American racism more generally.[43] Schuyler then proceeded, however, to note the widespread praise for the achievement of "wiping out 200,000 human beings at one blow," rhetorically restoring the enemy to a shared species identity. The effect is at once to reassert the humanity of the Japanese (something that was unheard of in the commercial mass culture or in official discourse in mid-1945) and to dryly castigate (white) American Christians not just for their self-righteous "head-wagging" but for dismissing the Japanese as subhuman.

Schuyler proceeded to argue that the bomb "puts the Anglo-Saxons definitely on top," reducing Russia "to a secondary power." His use of "Anglo-Saxons" here served to overlay racial categories onto the description of American power Truman had offered. Schuyler showed little faith in utopian claims regarding atomic control. Instead, he reasoned, "the Anglo-Saxons, led by the U.S.A., will have their way in the world until other people discover and perfect a weapon more devastating than the uranium bomb. That way, it must be admitted, is the way of white imperialism which fire-arms enabled them to establish two centuries ago." In this view, "naked force" and Anglo-Saxon imperialism clearly undermined U.S. claims concerning "the basic proposition of the worth and dignity of man." It should be noted, too, that Schuyler was an anti–New Deal conservative, an African American isolationist of sorts, whose foreign-policy views often seemed closer to those expressed in the *New York Daily News* than those of other, generally more progressive, African American commentators.

Concerning the atomic bomb, however, Schuyler shared common ground with colleagues considerably to his left. *Courier* columnist Marjorie McKenzie, for example, expressed alarm at the American people's lack "of moral and instinctual reserves for dealing with the problems before them" in the postwar era. To McKenzie, "the most profoundly shocking aspect" of the war's "fantastic" final week was "the callousness with which the American public accepted [the] wiping out of several hundred thousand Japanese, many of them civilians, women and children, when two bombs neatly erased Hiroshima and Nagasaki."[44] Whereas white-controlled publications like *Life* and the *Daily News* cited Truman's rhetoric and effectively made parts of it their own, McKenzie, Schuyler, and other black commentators implicitly undermined certain of the president's rhetorical claims (which were or were becoming, in effect, the claims of the broader official culture and of the white-owned mass media as well) without explicitly naming the views they were contending against. McKenzie, for example, undermined Truman's proposition that the overwhelming power of the United States flowed from the moral force of its ideals and its people, not by citing this proposition and arguing against it, but simply by noting, with pain, an "absence of moral and instinctual reserves" on the part of the American people.

Indeed, African Americans generally seem to have interpreted the nation's final victory in World War II with an ambivalence seldom expressed by their white compatriots, let alone by the mass media or spokesmen of officialdom. During the war, this ambivalence was most widely expressed through the symbol and slogan of the "Double V"—victory over fascism abroad and victory over racial injustice at home.[45] The spirit expressed in this slogan remained vital long after fascism's defeat abroad. Moreover, it contributed significantly both to the birth of the modern civil rights movement (because the other half of the "Double V" remained unfulfilled) and to the specific path along which the ideology of the Cold War consensus developed in the United States in the late 1940s (because African American leaders and commentators constantly used the persistence of racial injustice in the United States to critique the nation's widespread claims to world moral leadership, often quite scathingly and with brilliant rhetorical effect).

The end of the war actually widened the gap between the nation's achievements abroad and the frustration of its Negro citizens at home. The full irony of the situation was perhaps most acutely expressed in discussion of the postwar fate of the Fair Employment Practice Committee (FEPC), which was scheduled to end along with the war effort.[46] Only a permanent FEPC, civil rights advocates argued, would give America's minority peoples a sense that real victory had been achieved. In the September editorial of its journal, *The Crisis,* the National Association for the Advancement of Colored People called on supporters to urge their congressional representatives to back the permanent-FEPC bill then mired in the House Rules Committee. Without passage of such a bill, the editorial noted dryly, "The ending of the war with Japan meant also the ending of the life of the Fair Employment Practice Committee."[47] Mrs. Anna Hedgeman, executive secretary of the National Council for a Permanent FEPC, highlighted the ironic fate of the "Double V" dream in concrete terms: "The world rejoiced when the news came from Potsdam that Truman, Stalin and Atlee had issued a decree abolishing all discriminatory Nazi laws. . . . Yet here in the United States, unless Congress acts quickly, FEPC is automatically abolished by the winning of the same war that made the Potsdam declaration possible."[48] From this perspective, victory was neither fully achieved nor purely benevolent.

The African American press presented ambivalent images of the war's end in other ways as well. On the one hand, a news story reported that black GIs had started to celebrate the war's end upon learning over the radio of Japan's surrender offer. Their celebration was spurred on as "Lionel Hampton's 'Flying Home' poured out of the radio," even though the announcer quickly explained the war was still on.[49] On the other hand, *Pittsburgh Courier* gossip columnist Toki Schalk wrote that "with peace hovering in the air . . . we stop to wonder when we will win the real peace. That which deals with minority groups and economics." More significantly, Schalk suggested that such concerns dampened the general African American response to the anticipated peace: "There was a noticeable lack of mad enthusiasm over this long-awaited peace. Perhaps you noticed it in your community . . . there was no gay abandon here in Pittsburgh . . . rather there was a restrained happiness tinged with doubt." Indeed, Schalk predicted that "with this end of the legal war, there will be an upping of the [social and racial] strife which illegally disrupts our country."[50]

VICTORY CELEBRATIONS, PROFANE AND SACRED

The war officially ended on August 14, when President Truman announced that Japan had accepted Allied terms of "unconditional surrender." This was the news the public had been waiting for, and the radio networks broadcast Truman's words almost immediately. The president proclaimed a two-day holiday to celebrate the earlier victory in Europe as well as the victory over Japan.[51] His official announcement simply excused federal employees from work on Wednesday and Thursday, August 15 and 16, as a token of thanks, "on behalf of the nation," for their contribution to the war effort. Yet the public quickly transformed this announcement into a de facto national holiday providing two days for public celebration.[52] The celebrations began immediately. Twenty minutes after Truman's press conference a crowd of thousands cheered the president from Pennsylvania Avenue as he and Mrs. Truman strolled on the White House lawn. Truman responded with an impromptu speech proclaiming the end of fascism and declaring exultantly that "This is the day for [the] democracies."[53]

Not surprisingly, published photographs of the wild festivities in New York's Times Square and the centers of other large cities show crowds that were overwhelmingly if not exclusively white. In part, this may simply reflect de facto segregation. But neither the white press nor the black press showed any pictures of comparable crowds of jubilant blacks. (Indeed, the closest thing I have seen to a photograph of blacks celebrating the war's end shows a handful of uniformed men and women, all identified as members of the armed forces, looking somewhat posed, smiling politely at the newspapers in a Parisian cafe. Though it appeared in the Pittsburgh Courier, this photo was produced by an Army public relations bureau.[54])

African American communities celebrated the victory, but at least one observer, Courier gossip columnist Toki Schalk, observed "a noticeable lack of [the] gaiety that characterized the downtown crowds." In contrast to the general abandon of the white crowds, Schalk noted that on Wylie Avenue, in the heart of Pittsburgh's black community, "only the very young made noise. The older folk were thankful in a quieter way."[55] Within the downtown celebrations, Schalk noted that "in sharp contrast to the white people, there were the little knots of colored people, just standing, watching. Not shouting, nor crying, nor waving their hands . . . just standing quietly by, expressionless." To Schalk, the explanation was simple. "It wasn't that all of us don't have something to be thankful for," she wrote, "But for Negroes, another war has already started . . . the war for economic freedom."[56]

Having declared two days of national celebrations, Truman subsequently proclaimed the first postwar Sunday a national day of prayer. The president called upon all Americans "to unite in offering their thanks to God for the victory we have won, and in praying that He will support and guide us into the paths of peace."[57] Then, on September 1, President Truman delivered a radio speech broadcast nationwide along with the official surrender ceremonies from across the Pacific.[58] The president declared the following day, September 2, 1945, to be V-J Day, marking the official ending of the war. His principal message on the day of Japan's formal surrender was that global victory had been achieved primarily by the fruit of American abundance and that it marked the triumph of American ideals and the American "way of life" in a colossal struggle against the forces of evil. It was "a victory of liberty over tyranny," fueled by the seemingly unlimited productive capacity of America's war plants, shipyards, farms, mines, and factories.[59] On the one hand, Truman presented the war's final end as the triumph of liberty, which he construed as the defining ideal of American government and the American way of life. On the other hand, he repeatedly emphasized not simply the military power produced by American abundance but also the global reach of that power, which in effect "bridged all the oceans of the world" and supplied fighting forces "in all the corners of the earth." In the end, however, he returned to the theme of liberty—of American values as the source of the nation's greatness and hence the wellspring of its global victory.[60] America's ideals, in short, contained the essence of its greatness.

Consequently, the president defined V-J Day as a day of renewed pride in the American way of life, "of renewed consecration to the principles which have made us the strongest nation on earth and which, in this war, we have striven so mightily to preserve." V-J Day was not simply a national holiday but a nationalistic holy day, as the president called for "renewed consecration" to the nation's defining principles. Consecration is not an act generally applied toward secular entities like political culture, but in the United States, as elsewhere, the spirit of holy nationalism can transport national political values into the realm of the sacred. In the United States, moreover, political values are perhaps more central to the nationalist creed than they are in most other nation-states.[61] For Truman, American values were not quite a panacea, but they provided human beings with their best hope for a decent life: "Liberty . . . has provided more solid progress and happiness and decency for more people than any other philosophy of government in history. And this day has shown again that it provides the greatest strength and the greatest power which man has ever reached."[62] This passage further reveals the triumphalist attitude that Truman shared with other American nationalists at the end of World War II. The American philosophy of government, in this view, had been the most successful in history, on both humanitarian and utilitarian grounds. And V-J Day demonstrated that liberty, as embodied in the United States, had made possible the pinnacle of human achievement, which Truman expressed in terms of "strength" and "power."

But if victory signified the greatness of the United States, its political values, and its way of life, this victory, this greatness itself brought with it large responsibilities. Yet the very national qualities that had guaranteed victory also guaranteed that these responsibilities would be met:

> A free people with free Allies, who can develop an atomic bomb, can use the same skill and energy and determination to overcome all the difficulties ahead.

Victory always has its burdens and its responsibilities as well as its rejoicing. But we face the future and all its dangers with great confidence and great hope. America can build for itself a future of employment and security. Together with the United Nations, it can build a world of peace founded on justice, fair dealing, and tolerance.[63]

For all Truman's emphasis on international cooperation, this passage places a large weight on American leadership, if not American supremacy. The United States is not merely one nation among the free peoples of the world who together can overcome the anticipated challenges; rather, it is "a free people" which can accomplish anything it desires by virtue of its own inner strength and power, and which is fortunate in having "free Allies" also. Similarly, the United States is not one among equal partners in a United Nations organization capable of achieving a just and lasting peace; rather, it is a great nation which "can build a world of peace," based upon American principles, with the assistance of the United Nations.

So by the end of August the long-awaited moment of final victory had come and gone. But the webs of significance that gave meaning to that victory were still being spun — by the president, by the mass media, by the black press, and by others able to articulate their own gloss on the event and project it into the public sphere. Many strands of these webs reached back to long before the war was won, or even begun. But in the weeks surrounding Japan's surrender, the dominant themes in the mass media reinforced Truman's pronouncements. The nation's victory in World War II was construed as a watershed in human history, at least in part because it signaled, beyond doubt, the long-heralded arrival of the United States as the recognized — indeed, the necessary — leader of the world. The notion that "America is the number-one nation," which has been so central to public discourse about both U.S. foreign policy and American national identity throughout the postwar era, in effect achieved its hegemony at this moment.

Life magazine put the matter plainly in its first editorial written and published after the triumph: "The Meaning of Victory: What We Have Won Is Clearer Goals and a New Chance To Work For Them."[64] Even the subtitle suggested that the victory had clarified the nation's mission of world leadership. The text of the editorial developed this theme. It substituted a tough, modern-sounding phrase — "national purpose" — for the mystical, old-fashioned word "mission," but the meaning was substantially the same.

Under the subheading "At the World's Summit," *Life*'s editors argued that the United States had had greatness thrust upon it, to paraphrase the Shakespearean adage, by virtue of its participation in a war it had been forced into against its will:

When we so gradually fell — or were pushed — into this war, our national purpose seemed to be no more than to resist aggression and perhaps to establish the notion in the world that aggression does not pay. Later this aim was embellished . . . with more ambitious doctrines like the Four Freedoms and still later with the hope of ending all world wars and knitting the nations into a kind of political unity, the hope of the San Francisco Charter.

During the war many Americans also learned for the first time about power politics and America's place as a nation in the world power equation. That place has grown so far and fast during the war that, as Mr. Churchill said last week, "the U.S. at this minute stands at the summit of the world."

Historically, of course, the United States had seldom been shy about its ambitions in the world at large, so the claim that the United States had had world power thrust upon it against its will (a posture various U.S. opinion makers had taken since the 1890s) seems disingenuous. Still, *Life*'s editors thought it important to tell their readers that "many Americans" (presumably including their own audience) were just coming to grips with the nation's arrival "at the world's summit." This fit well with the magazine's general aim, under Henry Luce, of propagandizing for the cause of American internationalism and for Luce's own vision of a worldwide "American Century." [65]

In a corresponding editorial entitled "A Time for Patience," the *Saturday Evening Post* cast the war as a challenge to the nation's sense of self-worth, declaring that "American arms and ideals have triumphed in the most severe test this country has ever faced" and that the nation had emerged from the humiliation of Pearl Harbor "with two great victories to add to the proud book of American history." The miracle of American war production had dazzled the world. But most significantly, the *Post* concluded, "The leading democracy of the world has proved again that it knows how to fight as well as how to live. It is only natural that there should be exultation in our hearts." [66] With this severe test put successfully behind it, the nation had no reason to doubt its achievements or abilities. The only question had been whether the United States knew "how to fight as well as how to live." (The exemplary nature of the American Way of Life had never been in doubt.) That question had been answered affirmatively, of course, and the end of the war simply added "two great victories . . . to the proud book of American history." Clearly, the book imagined in this sentence had several crucial pages torn out, including those on the Civil War, arguably still "the most severe test this country has ever faced" (unless of course one considers the entire legacy of slavery). But this editorial presented national pride and exultation as natural responses to the triumph. Nonetheless, it called for patience, as opposed to complacency, in the coming period of reconversion to peacetime.

Internationally, the *Post* editors delineated two essential aspects of the patience necessitated by America's triumph: patience as responsibility, and patience as compromise. Patience as responsibility served to frame the discussion of overseas relief. The *Post* recognized that some Americans would be reluctant to ship large amounts of food and fuel abroad when they remained in short supply at home: "Yet to cut off this flow of supplies, while we sat at home enjoying abundance, would be a disastrous mistake. . . . It is true that we can't feed and warm the whole world, but we can and must help until the emergency eases." These lines echo the sense of America's international responsibility that Truman had articulated in his radio speech upon returning from Europe. Like the president, the editors of the *Saturday Evening Post* and other mass-circulation magazines did what they could to bring the "misery of war-torn lands" to life in the minds of U.S. citizens. The frank admission in this particular editorial that "we can't feed and warm the whole world" is noteworthy.

The idea of patience as the ability to compromise served to frame the editorial's discussion of U.S.-Soviet relations. Within this context, the editorial said, "We must remember that we are only one of several large nations that have a voice in the peace settlements. We should fight, with all the diplomatic tools we possess, for what we believe to be right, but there is a point at which compromise comes into the picture. . . . We can't right all the wrongs of the world overnight." This recognition of the limits of U.S. power and of the need to compromise with opposing points of view provides a stark contrast to sentiments expressed, for example, in the *Daily News*. Yet this recognition of limited power is subverted by the editorial's central theme of patience itself. "We can't right all the wrongs of the world overnight," the passage concludes, leaving distinctly open the possibility that "we" (meaning the United States) can indeed right them over time, if only we are patient and don't botch the job by rushing it.

In discussing U.S. power directly, in its concluding paragraph, this editorial drew on the president's own remarks to provide the framework for discussion:

> President Truman spoke sober truth when he said recently that the United States is the strongest nation in the world today, perhaps in all history. But it is not a power that we can use in proud arrogance. Rather, it is a responsibility which we must accept with humble determination to rise above selfishness, petty jealousies and petulance. If we approach the gigantic problems which confront us with patience and common sense, we can face the future with high hope, perhaps even with confidence. Depending on how we conduct ourselves, we can turn toward the light — or toward darkness.

The basic ideas here bear striking similarities to those in the *Life* editorial, discussed earlier, which used the analogy of Jove and Prometheus to make much the same point. (It is worth noting that this passage paraphrases Lincoln's Second Inaugural Address in suggesting that "we can face the future with high hope," though Lincoln's own meaning was far from triumphalist.[67]) Most significantly, though, this editorial appeared several weeks afterward, in the *Post*'s September 8 issue, and Truman's August 9 radio address still provided the terms for discussion. Despite its cautionary call for patience, this notably judicious editorial still construed victory primarily in terms of a triumphalist American nationalism.

Though it was nearly ubiquitous in the official culture and the mass media and was expressed in a range of forms, from the drum-beating of the *Daily News* to the reasoned quietude of the *Saturday Evening Post,* the triumphalist, celebratory response to the nation's "final, total victory" was not shared by all Americans. As shown earlier, African Americans frequently displayed a more subdued and ambiguous reaction to the war's end than did their white compatriots. Perhaps the sharpest dissent on the meaning of victory at the moment of its final achievement came from the idiosyncratic African American journalist and author J. A. Rogers. As an independent scholar, Rogers prided himself on his broad knowledge of world history, which he drew upon frequently in his newspaper columns to make sweeping judgments about contemporary developments. As a correspondent covering the Italian invasion of Ethiopia in the 1930s, he had seen the beginnings of the war that was now finally concluded a decade later. In his August 25 column for the *Pittsburgh Courier,* Rogers seemed to thoroughly subvert the triumphalist, nationalist interpretation of the war's end, as he argued that war weakens "victors and vanquished alike." [68] The completeness of its dissidence is exceptional, but Rogers's column merits close examination because the exception can shed light on the rule.

Rogers rejoiced that the slaughter had ended, but he added acidly, "I cannot, however, rejoice in victory of any one part of the human race over any other part of it no matter what its so-called race or color. All are losers. Victory is a delusion. History shows too, that the winners of today are the losers of tomorrow." Noting that Britain and France, despite their places among the victorious, had been reduced to second- and third-rate nations, Rogers even went so far as to question the presumed international stature of the United States, writing that "her position seems the most favorable of all, but is it?" Purportedly the greatest victor, the United States had in fact dissipated huge portions of its nonrenewable natural resources "in almost every corner of the globe" while accumulating a $300 billion federal debt in order to vanquish its adversaries. "What is worse," Rogers continued, "this fancied prosperity is going to make her the envy of even her allies as it was after the last war." In the white-controlled mass media, by contrast, American prosperity was generally represented as something that made the

United States an inspiration to other nations, and the wartime depletion of natural resources as reason for the United States to secure access to those resources in other parts of the world, particularly oil in the Middle East.

Rogers's discussion is noteworthy because it cut deeply through the webs most widely spun around the meaning of the war. Indeed, he denied the war any meaning at all, beyond the profit motive that he located at the root of all wars. "Victory is a delusion." Within the context of U.S. public life in August 1945, this sentence was remarkably dissident. Even if victory alone was all the war had been about, Rogers cast the war's stated purpose as an exercise in self-deception. Delusions, once recognized as such, give no cause for pride or exultation. What is more, if the victory that signified America's true greatness was in fact a delusion, then that greatness itself was delusional.

Such ideas, however pointed, failed to puncture the dominant discourse concerning the war's end, in which victory signified America's greatness, which in turn entailed vast international responsibilities in a war-ravaged world. The White House exerted tremendous power in shaping the contours of that discourse, and the mass media generally operated within the discursive parameters established in the president's own talk. Nonetheless, the meaning of victory remained a field of contention, and while African American voices generally proved the most contentious, they were not alone.

2 THE MEANING OF VICTORY

Even in 1945, the American public shared no clear consensus on U.S. war aims, beyond the aim of winning. Victory itself provided the nation's unifying, undisputed goal—a sort of lowest common denominator. As the historian John Morton Blum put it in his classic survey of American politics and culture during the war, "Victory was what it had all been about."[1] Yet important voices in the public culture sought to invest that narrow aim with larger, deeper meanings.

Within public discourse about the war's end, and about America's place in the world once the killing had stopped, there emerged certain core themes—national greatness, global responsibility, and the triumph of freedom—that almost every writer and speaker touched upon. If the meaning of victory was a field for contention, these themes constituted the boundaries of the field; legitimate discussion was largely constrained by what these terms could be made to do. In a sense, then, the meaning of these terms and their auxiliaries was contested more than the meaning of victory itself. Of course, the construction of that meaning began long before the actual moment of victory occurred, and it continued after the moment had passed. By 1945, victory meant many things. But in the dominant discourse of the day, it meant above all that the United States had come of age as a great nation ready to lead the world. Even before the bombing of Hiroshima, a Gallup poll showed that 63 percent of Americans surveyed believed that the United States would have more influence in world affairs after the war than any other nation. And an overwhelming majority supported U.S. membership in the new world organization designed to maintain the peace.[2] The Bomb and the final victory itself surely augmented those majorities.

NATIONALISM AND INTERNATIONALISM,
FROM ROOSEVELT TO TRUMAN

Perhaps no individual did more to shape public discussion about the nation's war aims than President Franklin D. Roosevelt. From the mounting international crises of the late 1930s until his death in April 1945, Roosevelt employed a considerable amount of his energy, power, and charm toward building public support for an active role for the U.S. government in foreign affairs. The course of world events, including, most dramatically, the bombing of Pearl Harbor, as well as the nation's undisputed emergence "as the world's foremost Power," surely aided these efforts. To the extent that Roosevelt succeeded in fostering an internationalist consensus, however, the rhetoric he employed in speaking to the public proved vital to that success.[3] Roosevelt's conception of national security, based on the view that technological and economic developments had made the world smaller and more dangerous to U.S. interests than ever before, was a component of that rhetoric.[4] But so were more traditional components of American political culture, including ideas of national mission and destiny and especially including the core value of freedom.

From the start of U.S. involvement in the war, the nation's official rhetoric featured talk of freedom. As Roosevelt put it in his Annual Message to Congress on January 6, 1942, just one month after Pearl Harbor, "Victory for us means victory for freedom." He expanded this thought by delineating what he called "the four freedoms" and positing them as the central U.S. war aims: "Our own objectives are clear: the objective of smashing the militarism imposed by war lords upon their enslaved peoples — the objective of liberating the subjugated nations — the objective of establishing and securing *freedom of speech, freedom of religion, freedom from want, and freedom from fear everywhere in the world* [emphasis added]."[5] Such talk accomplished three important ends. First, it anchored the nation's war aims in one of the fundamental precepts of American political culture. Second, it defined those aims as being global in scope. And third, it made vivid the contrast between the United States and its enemies in terms of a powerful, dichotomous metaphor of liberation versus subjugation, freedom versus slavery — a contrast made particularly compelling by the image of Nazi Germany.

As the historian Daniel Rodgers has argued, "freedom" became a war word, a rallying cry. In 1941, Roosevelt spoke of a world "divided between human slavery and human freedom."[6] In 1942, Vice President Henry Wallace described the war as "a fight between a slave world and a free world."[7] This stark opposition, harking back to Lincoln's image of a house divided, unable to stand half slave and half free, became the central metaphor of U.S. public discourse during the war years. As Rodgers argues, it would later provide "the controlling metaphor of the Cold War" as well. In his *Prelude to War,* the classic propaganda film he made for the U.S. Army, the great Hollywood director Frank Capra dramatized this metaphor with a striking, surreal image of two globes: the Free World bathed in glowing light, the Slave World engulfed in dark shadows. Shown to millions of recruits and draftees throughout the course of the war, Capra's film also won the Academy Award for Best Documentary in 1942. Its globalist iconography would redound at the war's end.[8]

Talk of the four freedoms as universal goals ran the risk of sounding as though the United States thought it knew what was best for everyone, everywhere. The four freedoms were often reconflated into the simple abstraction of freedom itself as a global objective, and such talk of freedom could seem to suggest that American political values alone held the key to lasting peace. Either the free world would triumph, with the United States at its head and the American creed in its heart, or a slave world would prevail, with Hitler in command, war and suffering everywhere, and civilization in collapse. Some observers held more nuanced views, of course. The liberal radio commentator Raymond Gram Swing noted that while the war was in a sense a war for freedom, Americans were not "fighting to bring our particular kind of freedom and our particular kind of government to everybody in the world." Freedom, Swing noted, meant different things to different peoples. But such critical self-awareness was largely blocked by a deep-rooted belief that such core values of U.S. political culture expressed universal human yearnings, as well as by the fundamental opposition between fascism and freedom and the general revulsion with Nazism.[9]

Whatever his own political and intellectual relationship to Wilsonian idealism, FDR's rhetoric was carefully gauged to avoid the mistakes that had brought down Woodrow Wilson a generation earlier.[10] Yet Roosevelt often espoused Wilsonian themes, albeit in self-consciously muted form. On at least one occasion Roosevelt explicitly linked the "mission" of "the present generation of Americans" to that of their predecessors in the First World War, saying that "this generation must act not only for itself, but as a trustee for all those who fell in the last war — a part of their mission unfilled." That mission, he suggested, was to build "a world fellowship" and to grant future generations "a heritage of peace" — a rather Wilsonian mission, indeed. Like Wilson, he stigmatized "isolationist" views by labeling his anti-interventionist opponents "ostriches."[11]

Roosevelt repeatedly linked national strength to international obligations, and international obligations, in turn, to national self-interest. The argument that power brought responsibility, which in turn brought the opportunity for world leadership "in the name of peace and humanity" and in the interests of the United States, formed the core around which Roosevelt's administration sought to build an internationalist consensus.[12] This line of thinking would resonate long after Roosevelt's death, as the Truman administration carried it forward into the postwar era. Roosevelt presented the acceptance of worldwide responsibilities as a sign of the nation's coming-of-age, a theme many opinion leaders would invoke after the war's end: "We shall not again be thwarted in our will to live as a mature nation, confronting limitless horizons. We shall bear our full responsibility, exercise our full influence, and bring our full help and encouragement to all who aspire to peace and freedom."[13] In linking responsibility, maturity, and power, Roosevelt was appealing to the American public's self-image. Who wants to be immature, or powerless? The enormous achievements of the war years, including the growing imminence of victory over hated enemies across two oceans, constituted an undeniable sign of America's power. But while military victory alone might signify vast national power, victory in building a lasting peace and a world of freedom would signify national maturity and moral power — power of a higher order which would testify to America's true greatness.

In his fourth and final inaugural address, President Roosevelt spoke of the war as "a test of our courage — of our resolve — of our wisdom — of our essential democracy." The test was not simply to win the war, but to build a just, honorable, and durable peace. To meet that test, he suggested, would be to "perform a service of historic importance" that future generations would "honor throughout all time." While the notion of a test implies that success cannot be taken for granted, Roosevelt expressed supreme confidence in the nation's fortitude, saying, "in the presence of our God," that he knew "that it is America's purpose that we shall not fail." Roosevelt concluded by suggesting that God not only set this test for the nation but also enabled the United States to meet it:

> The Almighty God has blessed our land in many ways. He has given our people stout hearts and strong arms with which to strike mighty blows for our freedom and truth. He has given to our country a faith which has become the hope of all peoples in an anguished world.
>
> So we pray to Him now for the vision to see our way clearly — to see the way that leads to a better life for ourselves and for all our fellow men — to the achievement of His will to peace on earth.[14]

In short, God had singled out the United States as the agent for realizing His will to world peace — had even equipped it for the purpose. The only question was whether the nation could follow His guidance in its "period of supreme test." But Roosevelt implied that the outcome of the test was in the nation's own hands, for clearly the righteous prayers of such a divinely favored nation would be answered, especially when they sought simply the realization of God's will. Such intimations of providential destiny revealed the nationalist hubris within Roosevelt's internationalist talk.

Roosevelt's death on April 12, 1945, marked an important transition in American political culture. The dominant political figure of a generation had passed from the scene, but his presence would continue to be felt. Most of the young men and women in the U.S. armed forces had never known another president. The press memorialized him as both a national leader and a world leader. A cartoon in the *Philadelphia Record* showed a globe draped in mourning cloth with the flags of many nations flying at half mast and a placard proclaiming: "Franklin Roosevelt, Died in Action, 4-12-45." The *Philadelphia Inquirer*, by contrast, portrayed Uncle Sam laying an olive branch on a casket labeled "Roosevelt." As generally presented in the public culture, Harry Truman's job was to carry on the work of this heroic figure. One cartoon displayed the new man ("The President" stamped on his jacket for all those who wouldn't yet recognize a drawing of Truman) at work cementing a giant stone labeled "World Peace Program" atop an equally enormous block labeled "Roosevelt Foundation." "Construction job goes on," declared the caption. Another, captioned "Truman at the Helm," showed a Truman figure pulling on a captain's hat and stepping up to a big ship's wheel marked "USA" as Uncle Sam beckons him to take command, saying "Carry on!" Other cartoons invested tremendous symbolic faith in the new president without direct reference to Roosevelt. One, from the *Detroit Free Press,* showed Truman rolling up his sleeves to reveal bulging forearms, standing beneath a giant hand pointing him forward "On to Victory." Just to be clear, the cartoonist identified the hand as "Humanity's Ideals." [15]

Upon ascending to the presidency, Truman repeatedly professed his dedication to Roosevelt's ideals, both at home and abroad. In the spring and summer of 1945, his speeches reiterated the main themes of Roosevelt's foreign-policy discourse. He even brought longtime Roosevelt speech writer Samuel Rosenman back to the White House for this purpose. Truman's legitimacy as president rested on his position as FDR's constitutional successor, and many liberals questioned his legitimacy in that role in any event; they saw former vice president Henry Wallace as Roosevelt's true heir. [16]

Almost from the beginning, though, subtle differences emerged between Truman's public rhetoric and Roosevelt's. By the end of 1945, Truman still spoke an intertwined language of national greatness, global responsibility, and the triumph of freedom, but he emphasized the notion of national greatness more stridently than Roosevelt generally had. Both Roosevelt and Truman were American nationalists. Each had his own style of nationalism that shaped his discussions of American internationalism. [17] But Truman's nationalism was more pronounced, more transparent, and less subtle, while Roosevelt's was always cloaked in the cosmopolitan garb of the patrician. Significantly, Truman was the first president who belonged to the American Legion, certainly a kind of badge of nationalist honor. In many regards, as leading Truman scholars have suggested, the new president's beliefs, ideals, and outlook were very much those of the typical—and typically provincial—white American male of his generation. The same can hardly be said of Roosevelt, whose privileged background set him apart.

Rhetorically, Truman departed from the Roosevelt model mainly in terms of his relatively greater emphasis on America, American greatness, and American distinctiveness; the new president, even more than his predecessor, was a staunch exponent of American exceptionalism. [18] When Truman addressed a joint session of Congress on April 16, 1945, just four days after FDR's death, he invoked Roosevelt as a symbol both of America's world leadership and of American national unity. Yet in the same speech, Truman called the war a "struggle to preserve . . . our American way of life," a more nationalistic statement of the war's purpose than Roosevelt generally offered.[19] This shift in presidential rhetoric may have been consciously intended for political purposes, first to keep national energies focused on the Pacific War once the Nazis had been defeated, then to promote national unity during the frictions of reconversion after the war's unexpectedly rapid close. But it also reflected the attitudes, assumptions, and language of the two men involved. Roosevelt, the cosmopolitan patrician from New York, could conceive of himself as a citizen of the world; Truman, the former haberdasher from Missouri, was above all a proud citizen of "the greatest nation that the sun ever shone upon," to use one of his own favorite phrases — and his nationalism was notably unconstrained.[20]

Truman's emphasis on national greatness, and on the nation's dominant international position, reflected broader currents in American culture at the end of the war. The widespread belief in America's inherent greatness was a matter of long tradition. But that tradition had received new impetus during World War II, most notably perhaps from Henry Luce's influential prophecy about the dawning of the American Century.[21] No doubt the change in presidential tone reflected the changing circumstances of 1945 as well. As V-E Day and V-J Day each approached and passed, the self-conscious emphasis on American greatness swelled with the pride of triumph, as the fears of the Depression years and the early war years of Axis aggression faded into the past (although many Americans continued to fear a postwar depression). This growing sense of power and triumph was nicely illustrated in an editorial cartoon from the *Kansas City Star*. The legs of a giant in combat boots strode across the globe. The left foot, labeled "VE," was planted firmly, grinding down on whatever lay beneath it, while the right foot, labeled "VJ," stepped forward, a tiny buck-toothed caricature of a Japanese soldier cowering in its shadow. When the United States emerged from the war as the world's dominant power, the long-standing belief in America's inherent greatness was widely expressed in a new language and iconography of global supremacy. This cartoon was an early example.[22]

POWER, PRIDE, AND THE PRESS

The leading popular magazines, for their part, continuously touted the nation's strength while occasionally warning against the dangers of hubris.[23] Displaying greater self-awareness than Truman generally did, *Life* magazine repeatedly cautioned that "pride goeth before a fall." Between V-E Day and V-J Day, Truman emphasized the remaining, difficult tasks of defeating Japan and winning the peace; but he never directly warned against what Senator William Fulbright would later term "the arrogance of power."[24]

With the end of the war in Europe, *Life* depicted the United States as "a vast, productive country unsure what 'victory' meant but joyous, noisy and hopeful." As *Life*'s editorial put it the week after V-E Day, U.S. forces had "played a sizeable, even a preponderant, part" in reducing Germany "to a pile of slag." While noting that Americans had agreed, for the moment, "to call this destruction victory," the editorial suggested that they would in time come to see that the victory had a positive side as well: "We haven't yet had time to ponder the fact that the power to destroy is also the power to build." According to *Life*'s editorialists, Americans were traditionally reluctant to wield power, and the GI who simply wanted to return home symbolized a great nation that had "no desire to kick anybody around." Still, Americans now had the opportunity, "in the full mandate of victory," to use their power "to remake the world in order to insure the future for their own life-sustaining myth" of progress — "of moving toward a world 'where life is better.'"[25]

In its 1945 Fourth of July editorial, *Life* restated this theme with an even clearer warning against the arrogance of power: "Our nation is a great instrument for good, and power is safer in our hands than most. But that will be so only while we remember that our nation and our sovereignty are not ends but instruments. The purpose of American strength is to promote liberty and self-government throughout the human race."[26] Here as elsewhere, *Life* projected the traditional nationalist belief that the United States had a beneficent global mission, which distinguished it from other nations and without which it would become as dangerous as any other great power. For *Life*'s editors, as for other influential figures in the mass media and in the nation's political establishment, this belief in the nation's inherent virtue and special destiny served to justify the expansion of U.S. power during and after World War II, much as it had in earlier phases of American history.[27]

In its editorial of July 30, 1945, *Life* applauded Truman for a recent speech in Kansas City in which the president proclaimed that "this great Republic ought to lead the way" toward world peace.[28] But to *Life*'s editorialists, the nation's capacity for world leadership was rooted in its unparalleled economic power. The editorial's closing paragraph argued that foreign aid (including loans, credits, and cash grants) provided potent tools for "the diplomacy of spreading our own principles of freedom" in the emerging competition with the Soviet Union.[29]

That same month, as the UN Conference proceeded in San Francisco, feature articles in both the *Saturday Evening Post* and *Collier's* encouraged Americans to assert themselves more boldly in world affairs. The *Collier's* piece is especially interesting. Its author, Russell W. Davenport, was a former managing editor of

Luce's *Fortune* magazine and a key figure in Wendell Willkie's 1940 presidential campaign. Earlier in 1945, Davenport had published a book-length poem entitled "My Country." In 1951, he edited *Fortune*'s famous paean to American capitalism, *U.S.A.: The Permanent Revolution.* As these fragments of his career suggest, Davenport wrote from the perspective of an ardent American nationalist. His *Collier's* article betrayed little concern about the nation lapsing into hubris: "The American people do not yet realize the importance of their voice in world affairs. This voice may not always prevail. . . . *But the important thing is that we speak . . .* that we formulate American aims fearlessly in American terms and lay them before the peoples of the earth. And if the peoples' leaders choose to oppose those aims, they will do so at their own risk." [30] The risk of defying the sole master of the atomic bomb was, of course, a grave risk indeed. Davenport aimed to encourage America's continuing involvement in world affairs, but his rhetoric employed a bellicose, even jingoistic nationalism toward this "internationalist" end. The "we"/"they" or inside/outside distinction that he drew was not between America and any specific enemy Other (such as Nazi Germany or the Soviet Union), but between America and all the other nations of the Earth. The American nation is defined in opposition to any who would block the fulfillment of its desires. Only later, from 1947 on, would the Soviet Union emerge as the predominant symbolic agent of the nation's frustrations, the demonic Other against which the benevolent American nation was most clearly defined. [31]

The notion that Americans were an inherently optimistic people appeared as a recurrent theme in the nation's mass-circulation magazines in the second half of 1945, especially in the *Saturday Evening Post,* where the theme of American optimism was almost always present in the cover art of Norman Rockwell and others working in the same style. [32] Collectively, these magazines suggested that the American people, with their upbeat outlook and vast material power, could meet the challenges of creating a new and better world by simply putting their minds to the task. But their extensive cheerleading most likely masked underlying anxieties. In May 1945, the *Saturday Evening Post* published a poem in this vein. It described

> An acre of good American ground . . .
> With its past, its present and future alive
> And its history mostly yet to arrive —
> What does it mean to an earth so torn?
> This: In such acres a world is born. [33]

These lines seemed to update for the postwar era the famous frontier thesis that the historian Frederick Jackson Turner had elaborated at the turn of the century. [34] The notion that a peculiarly American brand of future-oriented optimism would enable the United States to remake the world also provided the theme for several essays the magazine published later that year.

One essay, by a European scholar who taught history at New York University, advanced the thesis that "the fundamental difference between the American and the European mind" lay "in the gulf between American optimism and European pessimism." The *Post* presented this essay as "a penetrating analysis of why we look at the world through rose-colored glasses," but the author clearly took sides. "The history of the New World," he wrote, "represents a bright page of progress . . . tending toward a millennium based on technology and democracy under American inspiration." By contrast, European history constituted "a fascinating and endless story of ups and downs." So where Europeans were mired in the past, Americans looked with hope to the future. Americans believed "that no evil on earth is incurable," and with the end of the war "they hope that at last the decisive hour has struck to redeem the world, under American inspiration, by means of technology, education, democracy and organization." While the war's devastation would only increase Europe's pessimism, the essay concluded, "America will emerge from this greatest of all wars again triumphant. For the first time in history, America will be called by destiny to become the leading power of our planet." "European pessimism" helped explain Europe's failure "in its great attempt to lead the world." But "American optimism will prove to be a great asset on its way to accomplish this gigantic task." [35] Under the authority of scholarly analysis by a presumably detached European scholar, this essay confirmed all the classic myths of America's special mission and destiny.

Articles by American authors on this theme of American optimism often acknowledged the wave of anxiety and pessimism that seemed to sweep over the country in the war's wake. But they aimed to combat such attitudes, largely by attributing them to urban, liberal, Eastern elites, out of touch with the real America. Such naysayers, it was argued, had become obsessed with security instead of with the ideals of "freedom and opportunity" that had made the nation great. According to a *Saturday Evening Post* article by Marine sergeant Jameson G. Campaigne, the only trouble with the U.S.A. was that "we just don't realize our own powers." Americans just needed to realize that they had by far "the greatest Army and Navy and Air Force in the world," "the highest standard of living in the world," and "the most productive industrial plant in the world." An active, positive role in world affairs would follow. Other countries seemed to appreciate America's strength more than Americans themselves: "The other countries of the world look to us for help in pulling themselves out of their confusion, devastation and hunger. . . . because they know how much we can produce. They know that we can help them more and lead the way better than any other nation in the world." [36] The lead feature article in the *Post*'s Christmas-week issue singled out East Coast cities as the source of all postwar anxieties. Once again, the echo of Frederick Jackson Turner's frontier theme is striking: "Stand on a hilltop with America around you, and you can look out over this whole land, feel its slow, steady pulse of faith in itself and in all its tomorrows. And on the skyline there is only the flicker of metropolitan jitters, like heat waves dancing in the sun."[37] Such texts revealed powerful tensions within the society while aiming to suppress those tensions and to rally the bright, optimistic side of the public psyche behind the flag—and behind the globalist foreign policy for which it increasingly came to stand.

In the wake of war, the mass media and the Truman administration both emphasized that the world was a smaller place and that international matters were consequently "closer to home" than ever before. The media and the government alike placed the United States at the center of this shrinking planet: It was one world, and the United States was its leader. This discussion of America's world leadership as a consequence of its global victory was largely framed by two major strands in the tradition of discourse about American national mission and destiny: America as example; and America as redeemer. Both of these ideas (that the United States should serve as an example for all the world to follow, or, alternately, that it should redeem the world through active involvement in international affairs) were put toward diverse ends throughout U.S. public culture in 1945.

The idea of the United States as example appeared in calls for a United States of Europe modeled after the United States of America, and in the frequently drawn analogy between the United States constitution and either the UN charter or a hypothetical world federation.[38] In a wide range of articles, magazines assured their readers that virtually all the peoples of the world—or at least all right-thinking people in the world—looked to the United States as an example of the Good Society and wanted to be like Americans. A cursory listing of the peoples represented in this manner includes the Czechs, the Italians, the Germans, the Malayans, the Marshallese and other Pacific Island natives, the Arabs, and even the Russians.[39]

Magazines told their American readers that Europeans, too, dreamt the American dream. Orphans recently liberated at Buchenwald, representing "a tiny cross section of Europe's millions of orphans," all wanted to do just one thing: "Go to America." While dedicated to "rebuilding their republic" rather than emigrating, U.S. readers learned, "Czechs worship all things American, including our democratic traditions and our technical skills." In Italy, a department store manager proudly proclaimed, in the *Saturday Evening Post,* that he had had "quite an American career," meaning a career of upward mobility, starting out as an errand boy. "We of the middle class," he added, "want to live the way you do in America."[40] As example and as refuge, American readers received the repeated message that, more than ever before, the rest of the world viewed the United States as a promised land.

According to the magazines, liberated Europeans saw the United States as a refuge and example, but liberated Asians saw it as a savior and redeemer. The latter relationship was depicted in more messianic terms because these fit the racialist, hierarchical discourse of U.S.-Asian relations. Throughout the war, Americans tended to view the Japanese as more barbaric, crueler conquerors than the Germans, and their victims as more thoroughly oppressed and degraded.[41] The mass media, moreover, generally portrayed non-European peoples as needing special tutelage, an idea deeply rooted in the tradition of Christian missionary activity on the part of Europeans and Americans.[42] According to an article bylined by the Philippine general and statesman Carlos P. Romulo, Malayans outside the Philippines, having no word for democracy, articulated their desire for autonomy and self-governance by saying "We hope and pray *America* for our country." After arguing that postwar Asia should be organized into large federations modeled after the United States, General Romulo assured his American readers that "the shot fired at Lexington" still resounded in 1945, louder and more imperative than ever.[43] The nation's anticolonialist heritage lived on. In the dominant U.S. discourse, colonialism was an entirely European affair, and U.S.-Philippine relations stood in direct opposition to European-colonial relations, even if the United States intended "to retain air and naval bases on the islands and a certain control over Philippine foreign policy" and trade after granting independence in 1946.[44]

But the African American press clearly contested this benevolent image of U.S.-Philippine relations. As an American Negro Press service story argued, the U.S. Army had brought Jim Crow practices to the Philippines, and Manila was "being fanned back to life by undemocratic breezes of American influence."[45] (The black press similarly contested the benevolent images, prevalent in official pronouncements and the white-controlled media, of America's influence in postwar Germany. African American writers repeatedly argued that "American style" democracy had, ironically, introduced American-style racism to the country that had spawned the Third Reich.)[46]

The mass-circulation magazines represented victorious American forces elsewhere in Asia not merely as liberators but as God-like saviors. One article, entitled "Psalm From the Islands," presented a Marshall Islander's "lyric" report "on how American deliverance from the Japs came to his people." The author, named Jekeais, assured his readers that during the war the islanders "wanted only to be under the American flag." The people suffered terribly under the Japanese "robbers," but they gained hope from "one of those women to whom spirits come at times." This seeress assured them that "the Americans will come to save us from these evildoers who are destroying us." When the Americans arrived, in planes and warships, the islanders recognized their flags and were not afraid. Once the Americans captured the island, its inhabitants apparently took the U.S. flag as their own. "When our flag had been raised," Jekeais wrote, "we cheered wildly over the victory of the Americans against the hated enemy."[47]

PREPAREDNESS AND THE LESSONS OF PEARL HARBOR

In the late 1930s and early 1940s, a new conception of national security assumed a central place in U.S. public culture. Military preparedness played a prominent role in the national security scheme.[48] By 1945, military power served not simply as an instrument of national security but as a potent symbol of U.S. national greatness; the views of "internationalists" and so-called isolationists almost completely converged on this subject. The global reach and global supremacy of U.S. armed might signified the nation's greatness; both were also seen as prerequisites for preserving the nation's "way of life" and even its survival. According to a series of surveys taken by the Gallup organization throughout 1945, approximately 70 percent of the U.S. public supported Universal Military Training (UMT), one of the keystones of the Truman administration's preparedness program.[49] To many Americans, however, the growing emphasis on military power by the government and the media in the months after the war seemed to undermine America's supposed faith in the United Nations, that ultimate symbol of internationalism.

For the *New York Daily News,* the essential meaning of victory lay in the lessons of Pearl Harbor and the need to maintain the world's greatest air force and navy. This view formed a core element of the paper's editorial line and shaped its news coverage as well. Within the *News*'s pages, talk of global supremacy was clearly fused with nationalist sentiments. An August 3 editorial entitled "U.S. — World's Greatest Air Power," for example, was accompanied by an editorial cartoon depicting an eagle labeled "U.S. Air Forces" perched upon a rock above a white dove labeled "Peace." The caption quoted Army Air Force General H. H. Arnold: "This war has demonstrated that the nation which controls the air controls its own fate. And if that nation's prime objective is a peaceful world, an air force is the implementing instrument of first importance." In December 1945, the paper's regular Washington commentator, John O'Donnell, voiced a kindred fusion of nationalism and globalism. Arguing that demobilization had proceeded too fast and that World War III might be looming on the horizon, O'Donnell cautioned that the United States should "make haste slowly on the proposition of dismantling the greatest fighting organization the planet has ever seen."[50]

Arguments for maintaining preponderant military power were almost always couched in terms of national greatness and its ultimate corollary, global supremacy, often with the suggestion that victory had meaning only if the urge to disarm was successfully resisted. "Today the United States is admittedly the most powerful nation in the world," wrote Secretary of War Robert P. Patterson in a November 1945 *Collier's* article. "But our present triumph may hold the seeds of our future destruction," he warned, if the nation repeated "the tragic mistake of the first World War when future security was sacrificed for a fictitious normalcy." Defeat in any future war, Patterson asserted, would mean national "*extinction.*" Extinction was the alternative to greatness, so preparedness was the cost of greatness. Unlike the magnanimous United States, Patterson claimed, "no future aggressor will have either the forbearance or the reserves" to rebuild a vanquished America. Given this threat to national survival, "a sound system of national security," based on military strength, was essential.[51]

A language and iconography of global superlatives pervaded public discussions of U.S. national security, especially concerning national military strength. Magazine and newspaper editorials, radio commentators, government officials, and corporate advertisements constantly reminded Americans that their nation was the greatest power on earth. Such assertions generally bore on two notions: first, that the United States possessed preponderant military capabilities, which had become necessary for its own security and world peace; second, that the United States was therefore sure to be the first and foremost target of any future aggressor.[52]

By the end of the war, air power became a symbol of America's supremacy and the general shrinking of the world. U.S. planes made the planet smaller while ensuring America's global leadership. Air travel made "one world" possible; U.S. air supremacy guaranteed that it would be America's world. This symbolism was bound up with the intertwined notions of national greatness and the need for military preparedness. One American Airlines advertisement, for example, featured the image of a pale orange globe with a white cut-out of the United States, an "American Flagship" plane above the sphere, and a caption exclaiming, "Let's Keep It the Best Place On Earth." The ad urged Americans "to keep the U.S.A. the *first* among nations as an airfaring people. . . . to help insure our nation's prosperity and security."[53]

Other ads invoked similar themes. Goodyear aircraft ads proclaimed that "Airships Can Help Keep America First In The Air!"[54] The text of one Goodyear ad explicitly invoked Pearl Harbor: "We must zealously guard against the peril of unpreparedness in national air power. The Japanese could have chosen the American mainland for their 'hit and run' attack and the Germans could have bombed New

York from carriers. Let us not expose ourselves to such dangers again. Let America maintain its mastery of the air at all costs."[55] Another Goodyear ad wrapped the idea of global air supremacy in the flag, both with its red, white, and blue imagery and with its text: "Lest we forget their daring and their deeds which kept freedom's flag unfurled and raised man's hopes from despotism's dust — let us pledge our knowledge and our skill to keep the eagle ever poised for fighting flight with an American Air Force second to none."[56] Similar admixtures of nationalist and globalist themes, often employing globalist imagery, were widely used by other major aircraft producers as well. These ads were almost invariably full-page or double-page spreads. Their appearance in mass-circulation consumer magazines like *Life, Collier's,* and the *Saturday Evening Post* was obviously intended not to sell any product but rather to sell the idea of preparedness through air power — and with it the idea of U.S. global supremacy as the prerequisite to national security — to the U.S. public. Not coincidentally, the aircraft industry faced tremendous challenges in the postwar period, having expanded phenomenally during the war. It sought to promote postwar demand by promoting civilian air travel, which proved slow to develop, but it always continued to look to the military as its major customer. During and after the war, that required convincing citizens that air supremacy was essential to maintaining the American way of life. The ads rarely addressed the issue of taxation, but clearly they aimed to prepare citizens to accept high levels of taxes to support the ongoing production of military aircraft.[57]

President Truman emphasized the need for continued U.S. military preeminence in two major speeches in late October of 1945. Significantly, Truman's public calls for preparedness in the name of *national security* came safely after Senate ratification of the new mechanism of *collective security,* the United Nations Charter, on July 28. By October, the president proclaimed that only U.S. military power could keep the peace until the new United Nations Organization proved itself viable. To ensure "a just and lasting peace," Truman told a joint session of Congress of October 23, "we must relentlessly preserve our superiority on land and sea and in the air." Four days later, Truman presented the same basic argument in a major foreign policy speech delivered at a Navy Day celebration in New York's Central Park and broadcast by all the nation's radio networks. In his Navy Day speech, Truman stressed the need to maintain "the greatest naval power on earth" and "one of the most powerful air forces in the world," even after demobilization. This language was significantly toned down compared to the speech to Congress, which apparently was not broadcast. In speaking directly to the people, Truman avoided his most strident language, which he reserved in October 1945 for purposes of stirring Congress into action. But to many Americans, even the Navy Day speech signaled a retreat from the publicly enunciated principles of Rooseveltian internationalism, which stressed collective security through the United Nations and continued cooperation among the great powers, especially the United States and the Soviet Union.[58]

LABOR'S WAR FOR THE COMMON MAN

The integral relationship between the three themes of national greatness, freedom, and global responsibility is well illustrated by the foreign-policy discussions of organized labor, particularly in the Congress of Industrial Organizations, where foreign affairs played a central role in union politics in the 1940s. Unionists expressed nationalism and internationalism with a distinctly progressive slant, frequently declaring their desire for both "a better world" and "a better America."[59] During the 1940s, the annual conventions of America's trade unions were staged as patriotic rallies, intended to demonstrate the fundamental loyalty of the labor movement—to show that organized labor was as American as apple pie. At the conventions of the United Automobile Workers (UAW) and the United Electrical workers (UE), each day's sessions began with the ritual singing of "The Star-Spangled Banner," followed by an invocation summoning the spirit of the nation and the guidance of God.[60] In such contexts, discussions of the nation's purposes in war and peace took on added weight, especially when they could be imbued with meanings that strengthened labor's cause both at home and abroad.[61]

For labor activists and their allies, World War II was mainly a war for freedom. Their rhetoric often echoed Franklin Roosevelt's, but with extra emphasis on workers' rights, especially the right to organize free, independent trade unions. Roosevelt himself tipped his hat to labor's concerns in a telegram read aloud to the 1944 UAW convention. In building the American war machine, the president proclaimed, "American working men and women . . . have shown that free labor can outproduce slave labor."[62]

The invocations that opened the daily convention sessions of both the UAW and the UE in 1944 provide useful windows into the key terms employed in discussing the war's purpose. Almost without fail, they suggested that the United States was fighting to insure the global triumph of human freedom. "We seek not revenge," prayed the Reverend Anthony P. Arsulowicz at the start of the UAW's 1944 convention, "but only assurance that freedom may prevail throughout the world." Later in that same convention, another clergyman voiced these same goals with a clearer social-democratic slant, asking God to grant the principles America was fighting for, namely "the bringing of liberty to all groups and classes in the world, black and white, and red, yellow, and brown, the bringing of equality of opportunity to the children of all kinds of nationalities everywhere, the bringing of justice to all peoples in all parts of the earth as well as to all peoples in our own country." "The bringing of friendship and brotherhood to all," this minister continued, "is the ultimate goal of our democracy." This kind of social-democratic globalism, expressed in the name of America, reflected the prevailing character of the UAW's foreign-affairs discourse in the mid- to late 1940s.[63]

Other invocations linked lofty international goals to labor's domestic aims. At the 1944 UE convention, for example, an army chaplain invoked God's support for the UE's progressive social agenda while expressing gratitude to the union on behalf of "men who today serve in every corner of the earth fighting for our country, for the United Nations, and for human freedom." Speaking before the UAW, Rabbi Jerome D. Folkman offered similar prayers: "May our efforts so improve the lot of humankind that our fellow-workers now on the battlefields of freedom may see in us true comrades working at home for the same cause for which they fight abroad. May the day not be distant when all of us shall work together in peace and harmony for a better world."[64] These speakers were clergyman, not labor leaders. Yet they clearly sympathized with the union cause and probably used similar words with their own congregations. Most tellingly, they employed the same key words and phrases that framed union discussions of the war and foreign affairs.

Throughout the war, the national CIO emphatically endorsed Rooseveltian internationalism. This position reflected a confluence of material interests and ideology. Most national labor leaders saw a postwar expansion of foreign trade as a potential boon to U.S. workers, and to consumers worldwide, not just to U.S. corporations. As CIO president Philip Murray told the 1944 UAW convention, "We should use our immense productive capacity in heavy goods to help rebuild war-torn Europe and Russia, and to industrialize China, India and Latin America. There is a large enough market here to help to stabilize big industry in the United States for decades."[65] In linking the interests of big labor with those of big industry, Murray assumed a globalist stance similar to that of U.S. government and corporate leaders. The 1944 UE convention endorsed similar aims. Murray, like many in the UE, seemed to echo Vice President Henry Wallace, who prophesied the dawning of a worldwide "Century of the Common Man" under the aegis of U.S.-led economic expansion. Wallace was the leading exponent of social-democratic globalism, advocating what many viewed as a global New Deal. But after Truman replaced him as vice president in early 1945, this viewpoint lost whatever prominence it had within official discourse. Yet it retained a certain luster within the labor movement. As Murray explained to the UAW in 1944, this approach to foreign economic policy aimed "to raise standards of living both at home and abroad so that our great industries may continue to operate and the welfare of the common people everywhere in the world may be increased." Class conflict would be unnecessary in a humanized, global capitalism of the common man. Ironically, Murray would vehemently oppose Wallace's 1948 third-party presidential campaign — a campaign that provoked considerable strife within the CIO.[66]

In 1944, both the UAW and the UE passed foreign affairs resolutions explicitly supporting the Roosevelt administration's policies. Some urged the president to remain true to the principles he himself espoused as basic war aims. A UAW resolution on "Freedom for India and Other Colonial Nations," for example, began by defining the war's purpose unambiguously: "Our nation is engaged in a great war of liberation which is intended to bring freedom and democracy to the oppressed peoples of the world." These words echoed Roosevelt's but voiced their anticolonial implications more militantly than Roosevelt typically did. The resolution further called upon the president and leaders of the other United Nations "to assure the people of India, Burma, Malaya, Indo-China and the East Indies that the cause for which our men fight and die is freedom for them as well as all mankind and that the weapons we forge shall not be used to hold in subjugation the people of any land."[67] Like other such resolutions that year, this measure generated little substantive debate. Yet it generated enough discussion to suggest that some union delegates took these words quite seriously and that the lack of dissent on these resolutions may have reflected a lack of disagreement, or even a strong anticolonialist consensus within the UAW's ranks. (Africa's absence from this anticolonialist passage, and from the Murray quotation above, reflects that continent's virtual invisibility in U.S. public culture, save in the African American community, during the mid-1940s.) Resolutions like this one effectively recast Roosevelt's rhetoric of freedom into more militant forms aimed at pushing the president toward specific policy goals to which he had not fully committed himself. Such efforts were less than successful. In fact, the Roosevelt administration's anticolonial rhetoric was beginning to recede in 1944, as the growing certainty of victory brought potential postwar conflicts with the Soviet Union into consideration.[68]

In organized labor, as elsewhere in U.S. public culture, the war's purpose was often framed in negative terms, as a war against fascism rather than for freedom. While this rhetorical move might seem to present U.S. war aims in a less expansive manner, it did not always work that way. A war against fascism was not necessarily a war against colonialism or communism, nor a war to end war or the causes of war. But it remained a moral crusade of universal significance. The speeches of UAW president R. J. Thomas provide a case in point. In his opening speech to the union's 1944 convention, Thomas spoke of his experience during a recent tour of Europe, a tour sponsored by the War Department for top labor leaders. He lauded the many UAW members serving in the armed forces and recounted a visit he paid to several wounded worker-soldiers in a British hospital. "They were up in front," he proudly proclaimed, "fighting hard to whip Nazism and Fascism in the world." Here and elsewhere, Thomas repeatedly framed the nation's war aims in negative yet explicitly global terms. He expressed the hope, for example, that Germany and Japan would be "beaten so damned bad that it will be an example to anyone in the world who wants to start another war." So the war against Nazism and fascism was a universal human struggle that could also function as a war to prevent future wars, provided the victory was total.[69]

The "war against fascism" was also linked to labor's concerns with justice and democracy at home. One speaker, for example, told the 1944 UE convention that eliminating restrictive voting requirements, such as the poll tax, in southern states was needed to fulfill the aims of "our democratic war against fascism and tyranny."[70] In a related albeit more general vein, the UE's Washington representative, Russ Nixon, then on military leave, spoke of "the heroic role" that "the common working people" played in "this victory of unity" among classes and nations. Working people, Nixon declared, had "spark-plugged the struggle against fascism" and so earned decent treatment in the postwar period. An ally of the UE's left-wing leadership, Nixon received a standing ovation from the union's delegates.[71]

In his own speech to the 1944 UE convention, CIO president Philip Murray also emphasized labor's contributions to the war effort. To Murray, global war posed a momentous challenge to the United States as a nation, and labor's primary obligation was to help ensure the nation's triumph. To demonstrate the requisite "spirit of self-sacrifice," Murray advocated strict adherence to the no-strike pledge, which he and other national labor leaders had made to Roosevelt shortly after Pearl Harbor. The no-strike pledge, Murray told the assembled delegates, had already contributed to Allied advances in Africa, Italy, France, and the Pacific. "Your willingness to stay on the job," he declared, "is going to make victory possible for the cause of democracy throughout the entire world." The CIO president made the no-strike pledge sound like a memorial to Woodrow Wilson.[72]

The unions' often heated debates over the no-strike pledge can be read on one level as profound discussions of the relative claims of national unity versus working-class solidarity, and thus of the war's meaning for the nation's workers. Rank-and-file opposition to the no-strike pledge increased toward the end of the war, especially after V-E Day, but the national CIO leadership remained wedded to it. Faced with conservative, antilabor pressures in 1944 and 1945, the CIO pursued a policy of national unity and social peace that sought to minimize class division. Wildcat strikes launched by the rank-and-file dramatically undermined that policy. As the labor historian Nelson Lichtenstein argues, those strikes had "explosive social implications within the national polity." Most wildcat strikers supported the war fully and even the no-strike pledge itself. But, as Lichtenstein writes, "when they downed their tools, they struck a blow at the myth of a common national interest and undivided purpose so important to the ideology of existing union leadership and the effective prosecution of total war."[73] To its proponents (an unlikely coalition that ironically included conservative business unionists, Communist Party labor activists, and anticommunist social democrats like Phil Murray), the pledge was a symbol of labor's loyalty to the American nation. By contributing to the war effort, they argued, it served to protect the rights of American workers, including the right to collective bargaining. To many of its opponents, however, the pledge was an "un-American" constraint on labor's freedom — an infringement on workers' rights to collective bargaining — because it gave employers an unfair advantage by taking away the unions' strongest weapon. To some, opposition to the no-strike pledge was a stand for democracy at home — part of a fight for democracy on two fronts, much like the Double V campaign in the black community. To many militant unionists, the pledge had become a false badge of Communist "Americanism" as well as an obstacle to labor militancy. At the 1944 UAW convention, for example, the delegation from the militant, non-Communist Briggs local taunted top union leaders, especially those linked to the Communist Party, by concertedly waving tiny American flags in response to their patriotic appeals for maintaining the pledge.[74]

Phil Murray's lengthy address to the 1944 UAW convention, delivered the day before the convention opened a fierce and protracted debate over the no-strike pledge, helped frame the subsequent deliberations. As one of its architects and staunchest proponents, Murray expressed the case for maintaining the pledge with power and eloquence. When the question came to the convention floor the following day, delegates supporting the pledge had Murray's words at their disposal, in effect, while those opposing it had to argue against the powerful CIO president.

Not surprisingly, Murray posed the issue in terms of victory, nationalism, and freedom, particularly the freedom of labor to organize. The CIO president urged UAW delegates to give "primary consideration" to the well-being of the United States as a whole, arguing that the labor movement's health depended on the nation's. Murray emphasized that labor remained embattled, even threatened, and that the unions could scarcely afford to take actions that would alienate the public sympathy and governmental support they had so recently won. Against this backdrop, Murray explained that labor leaders supported the no-strike pledge "to win the war," and so "to maintain for ourselves these freedoms that we have enjoyed here in the United States of America during the past eleven years, — freedom of worship, yes; and freedom of the press, yes; and freedom from want and fear, yes . . . and your right to join labor unions of your own choosing."

"Had the war been lost," Murray continued, "the United Auto Workers would have been lost. . . . you would have had no unions, you would have had none of the freedoms to which I have referred."[75]

The CIO president argued further that these original reasons for adopting the no-strike commitment in 1941 still held in 1944, since the war was not yet won. Murray rested his case on the need to avoid alienating the U.S. public from labor's cause, which he believed faced serious threats from the Republican right and the business community. But he buttressed his position with an emotional appeal to the delegates' patriotism, asserting that the commitment to the no-strike pledge was a commitment "to every boy and every girl in the armed services" and "to every man, woman and child in your own country." It had to be maintained both for the good of the workers themselves and "for the good of your country." Murray concluded by telling the delegates that he hoped their decisions would serve "to improve your lot and improve the position of your mighty organization and the well-being of your country, this great country of ours today and in the days to come."[76]

While Phil Murray invoked freedom in support of the no-strike pledge, his opponents invoked it in arguing against him. One delegate, a Brother Campbell of UAW Local 600, rooted his own moderate opposition to the pledge in "the Preamble of the Constitution" which in his view held "that our rights are based on the fact that all men are created equal by their Creator, that the first right is the right to life." In Brother Campbell's Constitution, the right to strike was inseparable from the right to life because "when you take the right to strike away and reduce men to slavery you invalidate that right." For Campbell and others, the no-strike pledge was tantamount to "a condition of slavery" in direct conflict with the "condition of freedom" that American workers desired. "We should get back to a free state as soon as possible," he concluded, by rescinding the pledge.[77]

To some workers, the no-strike question represented a quandary. As one UE militant put it: "We must keep the faith with the people that are left to fight in the far-flung battlefronts all over the world. But we have a double obligation, we have the obligation of preserving for them the very basis, the very democratic things that they went out to fight for, and one of the things that they have gone out to fight for was the right to decent militant collective bargaining."[78] For such working-class militants, labor's loyalty was not really at issue; labor's basic rights were at stake, and these rights were bound up with the war's purpose.

From its inception, the CIO's pledge to President Roosevelt had been premised upon an "Equality of Sacrifice" program, under which labor would sacrifice its right to strike and management would sacrifice its right to maximize profits. By 1944, many labor activists believed that the sacrifice had been lopsided, and that management was taking advantage of labor's no-strike pledge to gain "excessive" profits and undermine the unions. In the UAW, the leader of the movement for completely rescinding the pledge, Ben Garrison of Local 400, agreed with pledge proponents that victory in both Asia and Europe was paramount. "There should be no interruption of production," he said, "for the duration of the war." But Garrison argued that the no-strike pledge had failed to advance this aim, as the spread of wildcat strikes made clear, and that it actually undermined labor's stake in the victory. The equality-of-sacrifice program, said Garrison, had been sold to workers on the idea that "the country comes first and our union second." Garrison and his supporters concurred with that proposition. In their view, management duplicity, rather than labor loyalty, was the underlying issue. As Garrison put it, employers had "taken advantage of the war" to roll back the gains labor had made during the New Deal. He supported the war effort as firmly as anyone, he declared, but sought only "to make damn certain that a just share of victory means that a union will be here" when the troops returned home. Another UAW militant put the point more starkly. Noting that its proponents said the pledge was needed to lick fascists abroad, he asked rhetorically whether after winning that fight, American workers were "going to sit idly by and let all the American fascists knock the hell out of us?" For these pledge opponents, the nation came first, but militant unionism was an essential part of the social fabric that made the United States worth fighting for.[79]

Some pledge supporters agreed that management had not kept its side of the equality-of-sacrifice bargain but saw that as no reason to rescind the pledge. "If management lives in a little glass house," said delegate Richard Leonard, "there is no reason why we should imitate management. We should exploit this condition to the hilt and place the blame where it rightfully belongs."[80] Such a righteous stance would enhance labor's standing in the eyes of the public, and particularly in the eyes of returning veterans.

In this struggle for the mantles of patriotism and militancy, UAW vice president Walter Reuther advanced a compromise proposal to retain the no-strike pledge only in war-production plants. Reuther's proposal was subsequently ruled out in favor of a straight vote for or against the pledge, which he then supported and which the rank-and-file eventually upheld. Yet Reuther emerged as the one UAW leader able to combine patriotism with militancy, a combination that enabled him to undermine Communist influence in the UAW and consolidate power within the union in 1946 and 1947. As the conflict over the no-strike pledge played out in the United Electrical Workers, by contrast, the left-wing, Communist-linked national leadership proved best able to combine the images of union militancy and American patriotism.[81] That combination helped them keep control of the UE until the union was purged by the CIO in 1948 and 1949.

In the UAW's 1944 floor debate, Reuther attempted to recast the no-strike pledge issue as "a difference of opinion" over "practical trade-union problems" rather than the highly emotional "question of patriotism" it was often treated as. To Reuther, the UAW's responsibilities to the nation and to union members were perfectly compatible. "Those who think . . . these two responsibilities are in conflict with each other," he said, "fail to understand the basic fundamentals for which this war is being fought."[82] For Reuther, as for many of his followers and other unionists as well, the union's purpose was to build a better America, and America's purpose was to build a better world. In both cases, betterment meant better realization of the four freedoms and the rights of the common man. Reuther would develop these themes as UAW president in the postwar years.

If labor activists, like many African American leaders and commentators, sought to use the language of national greatness, global responsibility, and the triumph of freedom to advance their own political positions, they nonetheless operated within the contours of that essentially nationalistic language. Neither workers nor blacks set the terms of the discussion, and this fact limited the extent to which they could use these terms toward their own ends, especially if those ends conflicted with the aims of more dominant voices.

According to those dominant voices, emanating from the government and the commercial media alike — from the official culture and the mass culture — victory signified national greatness, which in turn entailed responsibility for ensuring peace and freedom throughout the world. But the meaning of freedom, of global responsibility, and even of national greatness, remained contestable. By reference to national greatness, for instance, one gained the right to hold the United States to the standards of greatness as one defined it. Nonetheless, the "final total victory" over the Axis powers was most tellingly and most immediately taken as a sign of America's greatness: The American Century had arrived.

3 THE MEANING OF GLOBAL RESPONSIBILITY

From late 1945 until early March 1947, both the president and the mass media defined U.S. global responsibility primarily in terms of American national greatness. In the first year after the war's end, the United States was indisputably the most powerful nation in the world. In sharp, self-conscious contrast to the aftermath of the First World War, the prevailing discourse held that this dominant position brought with it vast international obligations. Those duties extended not simply to Europe or Asia but, in name at least, to the world at large. International responsibilities were cast as global responsibilities — responsibilities without bounds — even though the actual reach of American power was more limited. The postwar world meant a new, smaller planet, and the United States was both its economic steward and its moral leader. In part, this self-conscious assumption of global responsibility had to do with America's emerging from the war not only unscathed but enriched, particularly compared to the prewar Depression era, while much of Europe and Asia was devastated. In part, too, it had to do with the burdens of the post–World War I period — with the sense that the nation's "retreat to isolation" twenty-five years earlier had helped to cause the latest global conflagration. But the consciousness of power was as important as the actual extent of U.S. global preeminence.[1]

The collective representations of the nation's responsibilities to the postwar world took a variety of forms. As the world's greatest power, the United States held solemn duties: to feed the starving and rebuild the world economy, to provide moral leadership in the name of American democratic values to a world that had clearly lost its bearings, and to ensure that the peace would be lasting. The duties of world peacekeeper, however, could be discussed only in conjunction with U.S. relations with other major powers, particularly Great Britain and the Soviet Union. But mounting tensions with the USSR challenged the widely held American conception of a unified world under U.S. leadership, eventually forcing a redefinition of U.S. global responsibility. That redefinition — in which the image of One World, a product of wartime imagination concerning the postwar future, gave way to the resurrected image of two worlds, free and unfree — is examined in the next chapter. The following discussion focuses on public representations of U.S. global responsibility in its two primary forms, economic stewardship and moral leadership, from mid-1945 through the beginning of 1947.

The gap between burgeoning prosperity in the United States and languishing misery overseas provoked widespread assertions that the United States bore special responsibilities for world food relief, economic reconstruction, and the revival of international trade. In most discussions of these issues, the world outside the United States was effectively conflated with "the war-torn world," in the ubiquitous phrase of the early postwar years. Indeed, "the war-torn world" appeared frequently as a stock character in editorial cartoons: a small, globe-headed figure with a heavily bandaged scalp and often a cane. Tellingly, this figure was always male and almost always of Caucasian appearance, suggesting that "the war-torn world" was often code for war-torn Europe and that international politics remained a male preserve. One cartoon, appearing the week the war ended, had "Our World," open hand extended, looking up to a courtly, smiling gentleman identified as U.S. Secretary of State James F. Byrnes, loaded up not with one but two doctor's satchels — the United States as benevolent healer to a stricken world. The caption put it plainly: "Doc Byrnes and Patient."[2]

Discursively and symbolically, the entire planet was divided not into "free" and "unfree," and certainly not "Free" and "Communist," but into the untouched United States of America and the ruined societies on whose lands the war was actually fought. Latin America and sub-Saharan Africa often seemed nonexistent. The nation's global preeminence and consequent global responsibilities were widely represented in the culture's popular iconographic forms — editorial cartoons and corporate advertisements. As the world's dominant power, with a political culture widely committed to the universalist claims of its own national values, the United States, many Americans seemed to believe, had always been destined for world moral leadership. According to this view, now that the United States had indisputably arrived at the apex of world power, it was obligated to use its influence to build a world order in accord with American values — a world in which the values of liberal democratic capitalism might be realized around the globe — and to set a proper democratic model for the world to follow.

"RESPONSIBILITY" VS. "ISOLATION"

The historian Michael Sherry has stressed that a new conception of national security arose during the World War II era, dating back to the late 1930s. This new view emphasized the need to make America "secure" in an interdependent world, a world made smaller by technological developments, particularly in transportation and weaponry. Sherry argues compellingly that this new conception of national security propelled an alarming process in the militarization of American society, beginning before World War II and continuing after the Cold War, as high-tech military preparedness became a paramount and permanent need of the state.[3] But as other historians, including Daniel Yergin and Melvyn Leffler, have argued, the key departure in U.S. foreign-policy thinking in the 1940s lay in the redefinition of U.S. national security interests in global terms. On these terms, instability anywhere in the international system posed a potential threat to the well-being of the United States.[4]

The newly expansive, global vision of U.S. security interests was hardly the exclusive ideological property of the foreign-policy elite. The globalist outlook was rooted in an idea of national mission which in turn had deeper roots in American nationalism — roots that the foreign-policy elite shared with broad sections of the public and through which it attempted to educate the public about the nation's new global obligations. This sense of mission grew out of American Protestantism, specifically out of the beliefs of New England Puritans, but its influence transcended its specific religious origins.[5] By the end of the war, American liberals generally believed that U.S. foreign policy should pursue the rather missionary aim of realizing human dignity, freedom, and justice throughout the world. By the end of 1945, Francis Spellman, Roman Catholic Archbishop of New York, could write in *Collier's* that "the American people have a genius for splendid and useful action, and into the hands of America, God has placed the destinies of afflicted humanity." And by late summer 1946, millions of Americans could flip through the pages of a *Life* magazine photo-essay called "Trouble Spots Plague the World" to learn that "for the U.S., in its new position as the world's leading power, trouble anywhere was trouble for America." Featured "trouble spots" included the Balkans, the Middle East, China, Austria, and India. The only question was whether, as *Life* asked, America was prepared to accept the responsibilities that accompanied its greatness.[6]

The idea that global responsibility was a necessary consequence of the nation's greatness helped to delegitimize and marginalize the remaining "isolationist" opposition to an active, global role for the United States. Yet elements of the labor, liberal, and civil rights movements contested the meaning of global responsibility as it was construed by the Truman administration and the commercial mass media. The commercial media themselves frequently criticized the government's specific policies but generally shared its basic outlook. By early 1947, even before the Truman Doctrine speech, the administration's vision of U.S. global responsibilities was gaining sway as a potent force in U.S. public life, uniting such seemingly disparate voices as the allegedly "isolationist" *New York Daily News,* Henry Luce's archly internationalist (and Republican) *Life* magazine, and even, in broad ideological terms, the last great dissenter himself, Henry Wallace.[7]

It would become a cliché of the Cold War era that the president of the United States held the world's hardest job. But the president and the media alike asserted that the burdens of world leadership fell to the ordinary citizen as well as the president. "In this day of a shrinking globe," the *Saturday Evening Post* told its readers, "the President has not only the vexing problems of a nation on his desk but the whole world's in his lap." Another *Post* article told readers that in the postwar era, simply "being a citizen of the United States is going to be the toughest job in the world" — largely because of the nation's new role in complex world affairs, and especially because of its new responsibilities concerning the affairs of Europe, Japan, and the British Empire. One syndicated cartoon showed an "ordinary" (albeit sleek, muscular, and blond) man and woman striding toward a vast expanse of rubble identified as "The War-Wrecked World." He was taking off his jacket as she rolled up her sleeves; " — and now to work," read the caption. Despite such representations of average Americans ready to dedicate themselves to salvaging the war's global wreckage, opinion leaders in government and media alike feared a public desire to return to a domestically oriented postwar "normalcy." But the leading magazines and broadcasters were as dedicated as the Truman administration was to ensuring that the nation accepted its new duties.[8]

The opposing extremes of globalism and apathy were even illustrated in magazine cartoons. One cartoon showed a man watering his lawn, set off by picket fences on a suburban block, but on his lawn sat not a house, like the ones on either side, but a house-sized globe, complete with front steps and door; two men stand in front of the house next door, one staring at the guy, the other one telling him, "It's all his." That was one core element of American globalism in its heyday: the world was ours, so we should have the sense of propriety to water the lawn and keep up the property. Another cartoon depicted, and ridiculed, the much-feared retreat to "normalcy" and apathy. It showed two high-society matrons, in black dresses and pearls, having tea and dessert in a pricey cafe, pinkies raised in the air, with one of them saying to the other: "I just try not to think of anything that has to do with the world." The cartoonist's intent, it seems, was to make isolationism look foolish.[9]

President Truman frequently vowed that the United States would never return to a policy of isolation, and mass-circulation magazines reinforced the sense that isolationism, a once potent force in American life, had thankfully fallen into a state of abject decline. The conversion of Arthur Vandenberg, ranking Republican on the Senate Foreign Relations Committee, from isolationism to internationalism symbolized, according to *Life,* "the beginning of America's coming of age as a world power." In the same article, *Life* reported that in the 1946 primaries "the voters rejected the Senate's four most conspicuous isolationists, LaFollette, Wheeler, Shipstead and Nye," and proclaimed that these results demonstrated the public's rejection of isolationism.[10] Robert Taft, however, remained ensconced in the Senate leadership, "still dominated by the conviction that America can get along with limited world commitments," which he saw mainly as a drain on finite financial resources. For Taft, expansive overseas commitments were just another element of a big-government program that he saw as inimical to individual freedom and the American way of life. But throughout 1946 and early 1947, such views grew increasingly marginal, drowned out by the discourse of global responsibility.[11]

WORLD ECONOMIC STEWARDSHIP

Many Americans experienced the process of economic reconversion from wartime to peacetime as a period of economic anxiety, replete with consumer-goods shortages and fears of rampant inflation, resurgent unemployment, and even economic collapse.[12] Yet the Truman administration and the mass media generally provided an upbeat assessment of the state of the nation's economy. Total war had wreaked havoc abroad but proved a boon to the U.S. economy. According to the editors of *Collier's,* the key question of the postwar era was whether the nation would pursue sound economic policies that would "conserve and increase" this war-born prosperity or simply "fritter it away" in another cycle of boom and bust. "The choice," readers were told, "is up to us." This choice was a weighty one since, as *Life* magazine put it, "the material happiness of the rest of the world largely depends on the export of goods and services from the U.S." These economic responsibilities held moral overtones. As *Life* editorialized in January 1947, echoing Lincoln's words but not his tragic tone, "with the American businessman rests the question of . . . whether the world will now enjoy a new birth of economic freedom."[13]

In this context, official and media discussion of the major U.S. labor strikes of 1946 was widely framed in terms of the worldwide repercussions of disrupting the U.S. economy. *Life*'s editors called resolution of the coal strike "an international must" and had earlier discussed the need to resolve the steel strike as a matter of global concern because "beyond our American need, the world is also clamoring for American production." Even the *Daily News* argued that the challenge of "economic civil war," as represented by the coal and rail strikes, gave the U.S. the opportunity to "show the world the flaws and fallacies in Communism, Fascism, Nazism and kindred isms" by inventing some new, unspecified democratic device — "100% in tune with traditional American liberties and customs" — for resolving such conflicts, and thereby raising "our average living standards higher than ever before." Meanwhile, President Truman argued graphically that the railroad strike threatened to cause mass starvation in Europe by disrupting U.S. relief shipments. As Truman put it in a more general statement after the rail strike's resolution, "Because of our position and influence in world trade and finance, inflation and collapse in this country would shake the entire world."[14]

According to *Life,* people everywhere — including Germany, Japan, Britain, France, Russia, Argentina, and Egypt — saw the United States as "an oasis in the world Sahara." America's material blessings carried moral obligations, especially to Europe. The suffering of European children and the sense that their only hope lay in American generosity received special emphasis in magazine photo-essays and in advertising by humanitarian agencies. The task was defined as global and as belonging to the United States. "World Relief Is America's Job," announced the title of a *Saturday Evening Post* editorial in December 1945, which went on to say, "In meeting the challenge of all this global misery, America will find the opportunity to resume leadership in the struggle for peace and recovery" and to save Europe "from an anarchy which must eventually affect America as well." When the United States produced the second largest wheat crop in its history in 1946, Kansas farmers reportedly said, "It looks as if God wanted this one," echoing the traditional beliefs that God intended America to both feed and redeem the world.[15]

President Truman voiced this theme in a nationally broadcast speech to the Federal Council of Churches (FCC), calling upon the nation to use the moral, religious, and spiritual freedom it had preserved in the war "to save a world which is beset by so many threats of new conflicts, new terror and new destruction" and "to save the starving millions in Europe, in Asia, in Africa." Truman's own expression of religious sentiments in relation to his vision of America's new international role, including his frequently avowed commitment to the Golden Rule, prompted letters of praise from a number of similarly religious citizens. Not surprisingly, the president's speech matched the spirit of the FCC conference, which adopted a foreign affairs statement, written by Republican foreign-policy adviser and future secretary of state John Foster Dulles, urging generous American aid to help war-torn countries rebuild their economies.[16]

Proponents of global relief and reconstruction saw these tasks as matters of self-interest as well as altruism. Recognizing that many Americans were already "sick of the whole damned business" of attending to problems overseas, the *Saturday Evening Post* argued that "we shall have to do what we can to reconstitute civilized life and decent political and commercial relations in the world, if we want those conditions to continue here at home." *Life* and other publications conveyed similar views. President Truman repeatedly asserted that the nation's obligations concerning relief and reconstruction involved both humanitarian concerns and national self-interest.[17]

Such "American generosity" was said to be part of "our national traditions" and to reflect "the general decency of the American people." Material assistance to the world's unfortunate was in the nation's self-interest spiritually as well as materially. As General Dwight Eisenhower put it in a speech to the United Jewish

Appeal, which reprinted his words as part of an extensive advertising campaign, "Whenever tragedy or disaster has struck in any corner of the world, the American people has promptly and generously extended its hand of mercy and help.... *One of the privileges of this great democracy has been its opportunities for us to share with those less fortunate. And the bread we have cast upon the waters has been returned in blessings a hundredfold."* [18]

Ordinary Americans were regularly admonished to sacrifice, to share their abundance with the war-torn world, whether by the media, the president, or other leading public figures such as Eisenhower, Secretary of Agriculture Clinton P. Anderson, and former president Herbert Hoover. One *Life* photo-essay vividly contrasted American abundance with European and Asian scarcity by juxtaposing photographs of meals (a 2,000-calorie dinner in New York City, for instance, set against a 600-calorie dinner in Brunswick, Germany). These pictures preceded a two-page spread on "How To Do With Less Bread," illustrating steps by which "the housewife's crumbs can help feed millions." [19]

Dorothy Thompson, one of the more incisive American commentators on world affairs, saw food distribution as the crucial problem of postwar reconstruction even before the Pacific War had ended. In her August 1945 column in *Ladies' Home Journal,* by far the nation's most popular women's magazine, she issued "A Call to American Women," urging them to press for a vastly more efficient food-distribution system at home to maximize the supplies that could be shipped abroad. The system Thompson proposed would include well-organized rationing, home gardening, sending youth to work on farms during summer vacation, and farming vacant lots in urban areas. She also called for women's vigilance against black marketeers who defied food controls, calling them "assassins of civilization." Women, by contrast, were the guardians of civilization. Thompson admonished her female readership to "look upon this world with the eyes of mothers, realizing that mothers and housewives are perhaps the most important national and international society on earth." As her title suggested, American women had an especially important role to play.[20]

Editorial cartoons treated the food issue as well. Some used Uncle Sam, one of the standard icons of American nationalism, to rally loyal Americans to the cause. In February 1946, a *Philadelphia Record* cartoon portrayed Uncle Sam sitting at one end of a long, formal dining table, an entire feast crowded in front of him while the rest of the table lay bare. A Truman figure stood to his side, beseeching him to look "at the other end of our table," in the caption's words, where a cluster of gaunt apparitions stood beneath a dark cloud labeled "The Starving People of Europe and Asia." Less than a month later, a cartoon in the *Minneapolis Star-Journal* showed an Uncle Sam with a startlingly different attitude toward the problem. This "Sam" was on the attack, running down three hooligans identified as "Anarchy," "Starvation," and "Incipient Fascism," hurling canned goods at their heads from a basket slung over one arm. "Food," the caption proclaimed, "will write the peace." A cartoon in the *Montreal Star* showed that food relief was an issue for Canada as well as the United States, but it had no discernible nationalist content. Its symbolism was limited to a loaf of bread, broken in two, labeled "our" and "food." [21]

Reader response to these messages is difficult to gauge, of course. The radio commentator Eric Sevareid noted that Americans were world-renowned for their generosity but worried that in this instance it was threatened by a rival characteristic, "Yankee skepticism," which led some to question the extent of overseas food needs.[22] Many citizens were reluctant to play the role of Santa Claus—or to be played for a sucker. In the economic uncertainty of the often tumultuous transition from war production to a peacetime economy, many doubted they could afford such generosity. Yet public opinion polls suggest that the admonition to help feed Europe registered strongly with most Americans in 1945 and 1946. Huge majorities of those surveyed indicated their willingness to eat less to help feed the hungry across the Atlantic. In March 1946, for example, 92 percent of those questioned by the Gallup organization said they had read or heard about current plans to ship food overseas. In May 1946, 74 percent of the respondents said their families were actively saving food for this purpose, and 65 percent of those responding to another poll said they would be willing to return to food rationing to help provide for people overseas. Beyond polling data, *Collier's* and *Life* published enough positive letters on the subject to suggest that many Americans found the issues morally compelling. Even the *New York Daily News,* whose editorial policy tended to deride the need for U.S. handouts to Europe, gave voice to ordinary New Yorkers who supported food aid and even personal sacrifice to help people starving overseas.[23] Many Americans, of course, felt otherwise. One letter writer from Norfolk, Virginia, responded harshly to a laudatory news story about the United Nations Relief and Reconstruction Administration (UNRRA). The article proclaimed that "the United States has become synonymous with UNRRA in grateful hearts throughout Europe." But the southern reader told *Collier's* bitterly that after the War Between the States people in the defeated Confederacy "lived on parched corn" for five years, and plenty starved—and they didn't have UNRRA handouts.[24]

In February 1946, when President Truman announced emergency food relief measures, he framed the crisis as a continuation of the war. "I am confident," the president concluded, "that every citizen will cooperate wholeheartedly in the complete and immediate mobilization of this country's tremendous resources to win this world-wide war against mass starvation." As the polling data cited above indicates, many citizens supported such mobilization. The president's February 6th statement prompted hundreds if not thousands of Americans to write Truman letters supporting his program. Many expressed their own sense of generosity and duty, often in the name of America and Christianity, to aid the people of Europe and Asia, especially the children. These letter writers almost always mentioned Europe. Tellingly, when they mentioned Asia too, they invariably mentioned Europe first. Yet this all transpired under the rubric of *world* food relief, even though much of the world was left out altogether.[25]

American generosity had its limits, however, and wholehearted cooperation on the part of "every citizen" remained illusory. One letter writer criticized Truman's "latest move to take care of the world at the expense of the citizens of the U.S.," adding that it was not the president's job "to play Santa Claus to the world." Another told Truman to "start feeding the people of America and to hell with Europe." Others merely criticized any aid to the defeated enemy. Lewis Elvin Hamby of Oak Ridge, Tennessee, believed the war's innocent victims should be attended to but refused to eat black bread, as Truman urged, so that wheat could be shipped to Germans. The Germans, Mr. Hamby wrote the president, "should be made to pay."[26]

On the opposite end of the spectrum, some letter writers explicitly supported food relief to all countries, including Germany and Japan, as part of the nation's moral duties. These letters suggest that the idea of America's global responsibilities resonated deeply with large segments of the public. "Hunger, starvation and the diseases of malnutrition," wrote Lois and Arnold Vaught of Manhattan, "are not conducive to developing the democratic way of life we wish to promote among liberated and defeated peoples." The United States, therefore, was obliged to prevent them. Miss Nora O'Brien of Springfield, Massachusetts, felt that "we are under a moral obligation to care for all Europe." And one New Jersey woman, who said her own relatives were starving in Europe, believed that aid should be given "regardless of race, color or country" because "we got to be better than our enemies. Only so can a foundation for lasting peace be laid."[27] These letters often had religious overtones; many were written by clergymen, who no doubt raised these themes in their sermons.[28] One Chicago woman wrote on behalf of her family of six that "we have never eaten black bread but we shall eat it with thankfulness if it means that our brothers throughout the world may share our blessings."[29] An infantry lieutenant who lost a leg in the war admired Truman's position on food relief. "I'm for building healthy people everywhere," wrote Lt. Aldo Marcucci, "and creating our first line of defense within individuals. It's Christian!"[30]

While these and many other individuals responded viscerally to the moral urgency of relieving mass hunger, the popular magazines asserted vociferously that U.S. responsibilities extended beyond emergency food relief to the need for long-term economic reconstruction. "The American people, whether they like it or not," proclaimed one *Life* editorial, "will be principal factors in rebuilding the world for the next ten years."[31] As the *Saturday Evening Post* put it, food relief was an urgent stopgap measure "in the reconstruction of a world which faces misery, death and revolution."[32] The *Post* called for a positive program for "reconstruction, revival, new production," which its editors believed voters would support. These editorials presented a viewpoint that hungered in advance for something like the Marshall Plan—a viewpoint the editors claimed the general public shared. Significantly, however, the nation's moral obligations concerning relief and reconstruction were framed in global rather than merely European terms. "America is great and powerful," wrote the *Saturday Evening Post* editors, "and the destiny of the nations is largely in her keeping. Let it never be said that in the midst of our vast global plans and designs, we forgot the elementary duty of the good neighbor."[33]

Editors and politicians often employed a language of universal values (such as compassion, peace, stability, and justice) in arguing for specific policies toward individual countries. They believed that broad moral claims would help to sway potentially skeptical taxpayers. Many writers and speakers discussed the 1946 British loan, for example, as a necessary measure for ensuring international stability, rather than simply as an economic boost to an ailing British Empire. Yet despite the widespread spirit of sacrifice for the sake of shipping food overseas, the Gallup poll found that even in the fall of 1945 only 27 percent of those surveyed approved of the proposed loan to Britain, while 60 percent disapproved. A subsequent poll concerning a possible loan to Russia generated exactly the same results, a clear indication that many Americans viewed both allies in a similar light. Food for the world's hungry, as a moral imperative, was one thing; cash for specific governments was another.[34]

By all accounts, the United States held special responsibilities toward its defeated enemies, responsibilities that were often framed in paternalistic language. In discussing the U.S. zone of occupied Germany, the American media frequently referred to "our subjects" and "our Germans" while emphasizing U.S. efforts to instill democratic values in a society that had lapsed into barbarism. The growth of this paternalistic view, which held that the United States was responsible for Germany's economic well-being as well as its moral regeneration, accompanied the policy shift from the Morgenthau Plan for "pastoralization" to the unification of the British and U.S. zones aimed at reviving German industry. Yet even in early 1947, at least some U.S. citizens felt uneasy about the new sympathy toward the Germans on the part of the media and the government.[35] The paternalistic tone was even more pronounced in discussions of U.S. responsibility for occupied Japan. The media generally described the Japanese people as submissive, enigmatic, and somehow grateful to their conquerors. In this view, the American soldiers who occupied Japan were really liberators who had freed that nation from its old regime and the obvious absurdities of its traditional beliefs. The Japanese were on their way to "becoming eventually more American than Americans themselves." [36]

GLOBALIST IMAGERY

In the postwar period, the globalist imagery that had proliferated in U.S. magazine advertising at the end of the war continued to convey pervasive messages about U.S. world leadership and the global reach of "the American way of life." These messages were most conspicuously embodied in representations of worldwide air travel as a defining feature of American consumer culture in the new "Air-Age World." The planet had grown smaller, and U.S. citizens possessed unprecedented—and unrivaled—access to the globe. The closing lines of a poem entitled "Air-Line Timetable" spoke for this newly "airfaring" people in declaiming, "We race the dawn around a shrunken world." Even aircraft manufacturers like Douglas Aircraft and Lockheed advertised in the popular magazines, hoping to expand their civilian market simply by promoting the idea of air travel, as military sales fell precipitously with the end of the war. These corporations, which had expanded rapidly with the war economy, often used the globe as a visual cliché to proclaim both their own product and American aviation as the "world leader." These ads reveal the prevalence of globalist themes in postwar consumer culture, though the advertising strategy had limited success. The aviation industry experienced hard times between 1945 and early 1948. Its future, like its past, would prove dependent on military procurement.[37]

Passenger airlines employed globalist themes even more prominently in their own advertising. Pan American World Airways had long used the globe in its logo, but the globe became a ubiquitous symbol of air travel only in the postwar era. "The Airlines of the United States" even joined together in ads announcing that "The United States Leads the World In Air Transport." An American Airlines ad proclaimed that air travel had transformed "the big, old world" into "the small, new world" and that "our concepts of geography and the relationship of people must change" since "all people now live upon the one universal highway of air . . . with no place on earth isolated from the airplane." The ad was illustrated by a "pictorial map" of the northern arc of the globe, showing much of North America and Eurasia, with colorfully costumed figures representing the peoples of many nations. Its headline invited the reader to "Meet Your Neighbors." Northwest Airlines ads, featuring the image of a plane flying over a globe girdled by commercial air routes, hawked "Around-world connections" and excursions for a "Weekend 'Round the World." A prominent TWA campaign featured a full-color globe in the bottom portion of each of its full-page ads, beneath a drawing of some exotic travel scene or aerial vista. One simply showed two planes in the clouds above a headline telling readers " — and the world at your feet." The world lay at the disposal of the American consumer; Wendell Willkie's vision of "One World" had been commercialized.[38]

Magazine advertisements for a wide array of consumer products and services, from candy bars to banking, also employed the globe as both visual and rhetorical cliché. The sociologist Michael Schudson has suggested quite astutely that advertising art often functions as "capitalist realism." But these images might more aptly be called "capitalist surrealism." Goodyear Tires, for example, ran ads featuring drawings of the earth in dark space, encircled by a huge tire, above a slogan proclaiming Goodyear as "the world's leading builder of tires." Another Goodyear ad showed an automobile circling around above the earth, with the slogan, "You don't stay first *unless* you're best" — a not-so-subtle message to citizens of the world's "No. 1 nation" in a period of mounting U.S.-Soviet tensions. In late 1946, Bell Telephone's overseas service announced to U.S. magazine readers that "The World's in Reach Again," in full-page ads featuring a drawing of the globe with a telephone set in the U.S. heartland and lines extending from it outward to the rest of the earth. In the holiday season that year, Canadian Club liquors ran ads depicting the earth as "a new ornament on trees this year." Beneath the picture, the copy began: "It's bright with promise and burnished with hope. In every home, that globe is an eloquent symbol of the new kinship which we have with all the World."[39]

WORLD MORAL LEADERSHIP

In projecting these images of the worldwide appeal, preeminence, and reach of American commercial culture and of America's "new kinship" with the rest of the globe, corporate advertisers reinforced the notion that the United States was obligated to serve as world moral leader. In December 1945, even the reputedly isolationist congressman John Rankin boasted that the United States, with its atomic monopoly, "could lead the world into that golden age of which Tennyson dreamed." To some, this enormous task posed a test for the nation and its democratic values, on which U.S. claims to world leadership were said to stand. Dorothy Thompson, for example, writing in *Ladies' Home Journal,* insisted that effective American leadership depended on coming to terms with the revolutionary forces transforming the world in the aftermath of the war. As of March 1946, she suggested, the Truman administration had yet to articulate a clear framework to guide its foreign policy. Without such a framework, she argued, "the dynamism of events" would "slip out of control." According to most writers in the nation's mass-circulation magazines, however, as to the Truman administration, the United States was clearly equal to the challenge before it.[40]

In a bylined editorial in the *Saturday Evening Post,* Robert Strausz-Hupé, a political scientist at the University of Pennsylvania, argued that to meet the present test, the United States had to define the broad purposes of its foreign policy in a way the general public could both understand and support, as Britain supposedly had in its heyday. These overarching goals, Strausz-Hupé wrote, could be drawn from the nation's diplomatic tradition: the Monroe Doctrine; freedom of the seas and airways; "a united, independent China"; and "the principle that no single power shall dominate the European continent." These traditions formed the basis for U.S. world leadership: "It is precisely the mission of American foreign policy to see to it that the historic doctrines, fashioned from the nation's blood and treasure, are built into the global model." But the model's success depended on the government's ability to communicate these principles to "the average citizen" and "to confront the public with the cold glare of facts." [41]

Under the headline "Uncle Sam As World Leader," a March 1946 *Collier's* editorial suggested that the United States should play the part of "a combination of world umpire and world leader," mediating between British and Russian interests and providing "a positive, constructive leadership in world affairs ... which it would be to British, Russian and most other interests to accept and follow." (This appeared the same month as Churchill's famous "Iron Curtain" speech calling on the United States to join Great Britain in an anti-Soviet "fraternal association.") With "the excitement and confusion" of the war's end now clearing, the *Collier's* editors opined, "it looks to us as if this combined role of world umpire and world leader is the one for the United States to take and hold," at least until the new United Nations Organization proved it had the strength and durability to keep the peace. In the meantime, the editorial concluded, U.S. world leadership was primarily a question of national will: "We have the power and the world prestige to act that role if we make up our minds to do it." The accompanying editorial cartoon showed Uncle Sam standing behind an arc of the globe, holding reins in each fist, one labeled "conciliation," the other labeled "leadership." With these tools, Uncle Sam could rein in an intractable world.[42]

No voice in U.S. public culture espoused American world leadership more ardently than the *Time-Life* empire of Henry Luce. In the summer of 1946, *Life* launched a new international division, conceived quite consciously as part of the global reach of, and worldwide demand for, American culture. In a letter applauding the magazine's overseas venture, one *Life* reader expressed confidence that America's capacity for world leadership flowed from its national traditions:

"I am convinced that the American people today realize that our deep-seated desire for permanent peace and economic stability requires that we accept the responsibility for world leadership on the international front. They are ready to accept this responsibility and discharge it with all the courage and steadfastness that springs from our pioneering heritage." [43] In *Life*'s pages, U.S. world leadership meant *moral* leadership rooted in the perceived universality of American political values. In a Fourth of July week editorial, for example, *Life* quoted Republican foreign-policy spokesman John Foster Dulles to argue that "the United States ought to take a lead" in reestablishing principle and morality in the postwar world: "It devolves upon us to give leadership in restoring principles as a guide to conduct. If we do not do that, the world will not be worth living in." [44]

In the magazines, then, America's democratic values, particularly individual freedom and justice under law, made U.S. world leadership possible, desirable, and necessary, because these values reflected universal human aspirations. But some citizens remained skeptical about such claims. John Allen of Red Bank, New Jersey, for one, wrote to President Truman in January 1946, supporting Truman's foreign policy aims but insisting that the country's leadership and responsibility should be exercised through the United Nations rather than unilateral measures. Allen denounced "those who hold it our right to tell the rest of the world what they should do, but they in turn should never question our acts. We as a Country or people are not nearly so perfect." In September of that year, a New York *Daily News* reader complained that "our foreign policy is making us the busybodies of Europe, and hated accordingly." [45]

DEMOCRACY, THE COLOR LINE, AND THE COMMON MAN

Though the second World War, unlike the first, had not explicitly been fought as a "war to make the world safe for democracy," the meaning of democracy in world affairs comprised an important subject for U.S. foreign policy discourse in the postwar years. It formed a particular concern for the African American community and the civil rights movement and for the labor movement as well. As an official of the Milwaukee Urban League put it, one crucial lesson of World War II was that "unless there is a workable democracy for *all* people, eventually, there will be democracy for *no* people." No less than Henry Luce or Harry Truman, civil rights and labor leaders held to an expansionist version of democratic ideology.

African American leaders were deeply committed to a globalist perspective, as well as to American democratic values, but they held to a globalism of their own design — and to an Americanism of their own design as well, in which equality, especially racial equality, was the most essential of democratic values. At the

NAACP's 1946 annual conference, for example, Archibald J. Cary Jr., minister of Chicago's Woodlawn AME Church, delivered a keynote address replete with references to Willkie's One World and Wallace's Century of the Common Man, stressing the earth-shattering significance of the atomic bomb and proclaiming that "we must all be citizens of the world." American Negroes had a special role to play as world citizens, he argued, in articulating "the hopes and aspirations of other little people as well as of themselves." Cary urged his audience to make common cause with the Jews, the Indians, the Filipinos, and others of the world's downtrodden, in part as a way of building alliances but also for "the larger reason" that "all of us, Americans, Europeans, Asiatics and Africans are citizens of the world — one world, inextricably interknit and indivisible." [46]

In 1946 the NAACP advocated "an enlightened anti-imperialist foreign policy," in keeping with "the needs of every American, only accentuated by race." For the NAACP — as for the Truman administration, the Luce publications, and American liberalism generally — the globe itself was the necessary sphere of action, the most effective unit of analysis. According to a January 1947 editorial in *The Crisis,* the official NAACP magazine, American Negroes had "a world-wide, blood-spattered, rubble-strewn stage upon which to carry forward their action." In urging the black community to press for greater representation in the U.S. diplomatic corps, political columnist and sociologist Horace Cayton raised the same concern. "It's becoming increasingly important," wrote Cayton, "for the Negro to move out on the world scene." The American Negro, like the American nation, had a leadership role to play in the postwar world. [47]

The labor movement, too, was avowedly internationalist. Both the American Federation of Labor (AFL) and the Congress of Industrial Organizations (CIO) claimed a special role to play in building a better world. In September 1946, at the plumbers' union convention in Atlantic City, New Jersey, AFL leaders William Green and George Meany reiterated their organization's support for the Atlantic Charter and the Four Freedoms. Meany emphasized the AFL's historic opposition to isolationism and its support for most of Roosevelt's foreign policies from 1933 to 1945. In the name of the AFL, he applauded James F. Byrnes's efforts at the Paris conference, where, in Meany's view, the secretary of state was "battling for the Atlantic Charter, battling for a peace based on decency and justice" against Russian truculence. While Meany was hardly the representative man on the street, faith in the Atlantic Charter as a trumpet of worldwide democracy still carried resonance for many Americans, a symbol of the "better world" for which their country had fought. [48]

In the CIO, the left-wing United Electrical workers union treated FDR himself as a symbol of U.S. world leadership. The UE commended Roosevelt as "a leader of the common people of this world" who "led the fight for the Four Freedoms . . . not only for this nation but for the world." UE president Albert Fitzgerald suggested that the CIO had a similar global role, proclaiming that "the common people all over the world" were indebted to CIO president Philip Murray for establishing the World Federation of Trade Unions (WFTU) and the CIO's Political Action Committee (CIO-PAC), "two things that will do more than anything else to assure lasting peace in this world." By 1949, as the Cold War intensified, Murray would expel the UE from the CIO and take the CIO out of the WFTU.[49]

In 1946, though, Murray told the UAW convention that "American wage earners" were committed to working through the WFTU and the UN to put an end to military aggression of any form. "Labor must see to it not only here in America but everywhere throughout the world," said Murray, "that politicians . . . will recognize the sacredness of life, body, and soul" and so "prevent a repetition of this unholy catastrophe" that had so recently ravaged the world. Murray also presented the WFTU as an instrument through which American labor could work to elevate living standards and "fight for the institutions of democracies in all of the countries."[50]

The UAW had an institutional sense of global responsibility that was uniquely its own. By taking the lead in postwar strikes that had defied its critics and raised U.S. living standards, one union leader told the assembled delegates that the UAW had demonstrated "to the entire world" that it could blaze "new trails towards the goal of a better world for all of us." In floor debates, union delegates expressed grave concern over the possible postwar resurgence of isolationist sentiments. One man urged his fellow workers never to forget what had caused the war, as Americans had tended to do in the past. Instead, he implored, "we should condemn all such activities not only in convention but in our daily activities."[51]

The UE convention that year featured Florida's Senator Claude Pepper as its keynote speaker. UE president Fitzgerald introduced Pepper to the convention as "a champion of the rights of the common people of the world," like Roosevelt and Murray, who sought "to restore the original unity that existed among the three great powers of the world." That line prompted applause from the assembled delegates, who evidently saw continued U.S.-Soviet cooperation as the key to postwar peace. Known as "Red" Pepper for his left-leaning politics as well as his hair color, the senator's speech epitomized the left-liberal variant of American globalism most widely associated with former vice president and secretary of commerce Henry Wallace. Pepper equated "Henry Wallace's dream and the human race's dream," adding that humanity stood poised to enter, if it chose, "The Century of the Common Man," as though it were poised at the gates of paradise. Pepper's was a decidedly anti-imperialist form of globalism. "We are not the guarantors of Western European imperialism in any part of the world," he said, in words reminiscent of Mark Twain's barbs against America's playing 'the European game': "We will not let this country . . . sink to the level of a western European power." The following year, Pepper would emerge as a leading critic of the Truman Doctrine, which seemed to do just that.[52]

While emphasizing his own commitment to the nation's international responsibilities and protecting himself from the taint of isolationism, Pepper argued that the historic detachment of the United States from the "old world" and its quarrels was a source of its strength and prestige. Pepper criticized what he perceived as the current drift toward war. He concluded by suggesting that the United States should stand above the fray and mediate in the conflicts between the Soviet Union and the British Empire, which lay at the heart of the present international tensions. The UE delegates responded with a long standing ovation, then unanimously approved a spontaneous motion to print and distribute copies of Pepper's remarks.[53]

The convention's subsequent foreign-policy discussions frequently echoed Pepper's populist, anti-imperialist vision of American globalism. The delegates approved a foreign-policy resolution that claimed roots in "the program of Franklin D. Roosevelt," which placed the United States "on the side of the right of all peoples to form their own governments, for the strengthening of democracy at home and abroad and for the raising of the people's standard of living at home and throughout the world." The resolution argued that in reelecting Roosevelt in 1944, "the people gave their mandate for a foreign policy founded on the democratic traditions and ideals of our country." The overarching aim of such a foreign policy was clear: "To build a peace that is stable and secure because it rests upon the common interests of common people in every nation." Proclaiming that the Truman administration had departed from this mandate, the UE called upon the president to seek another Big Three summit meeting aimed at halting "the development of power politics" and "the division of the world into conflicting spheres of influence." In the predominant view espoused within the UE, the idea of One World, based on the security and well-being of common people everywhere, provided the only proper purpose of U.S. world leadership. But the administration seemed to be moving in the opposite direction, regardless of its rhetorical claims. As UE delegate Emil Asher of Local 447 declared from the convention floor, "With the foreign policy of Secretary of State Byrnes, America is involved in a policy of not freedom but actually of reaction," which was "placing reactionary governments throughout the world."[54]

As in other periods, America's claims to world moral leadership were most sharply tested by the issues of colonialism and imperialism. FDR had been a committed champion of the anticolonialist cause, but with his death and the end of the war, much had changed, both in terms of U.S. policy and in terms of public discussion of the problems of colonialism. Neither President Truman nor the mass media expressed much concern with these problems between 1945 and 1947. The African American community, however, maintained a strongly anticolonialist stance throughout this period.[55]

Both the Truman administration and the commercial mass media treated the granting of Philippine independence, celebrated on July 4, 1946, as an event of historic significance—a model of relations between the West and the nonwhite world. But earlier that year, such disparate journalistic voices as the conservative *New York Daily News* and Edgar Snow, the liberal foreign correspondent of the *Saturday Evening Post,* suggested that the Philippines would do better by applying for U.S. statehood than by accepting formal independence. The Philippine republic would remain economically and militarily dependent on the United States, and Snow argued that this relationship had already become a financial drain. "It may look nice in the history books to have a century all your own," he wrote, in an ironic jab at Henry Luce's vision of the American Century, "but the cost of this American one is running ever higher."[56]

By July, however, such critical voices were drowned out by the dual Independence Day fireworks. *Life* called Philippine independence "an event without real precedent in the history of nations," and featured a full-page photograph of "Fourth of July fireworks, very much like those in the U.S." on the palace grounds in Manila. In a Fourth of July feature article in *Collier's,* Paul C. McNutt, U.S. High Commissioner to the Philippines, wrote that the first Philippine Independence Day "will be a day of history not only for the Philippines, but for the United States" and "for the entire world," because the "former sovereign" would give birth, of its own free will, to "an entirely new nation."

This historic act symbolized America's international responsibilities and moral leadership. "It is the obligation of the United States," McNutt asserted, to help Philippine leaders surmount the obstacles they faced and "to set them on the road to true twentieth-century democracy." By succeeding in this task, he said, "we will have enabled a democracy-loving people to preserve and extend their freedom and to perpetuate the existence in the Orient of a miniature version of our own way of life." Consequently, he predicted "the world will see an off-shoot of the American system, a branch bank of Western democracy, sprung full-grown from 47 years of association with the United States." The Philippines, in short, would be as a city upon a hill, representing "a major tenet" of U.S. foreign policy "as the shining example of enlightened treatment of a dependent people." With the entire "Orient" looking on, McNutt argued, the United States could not afford to let the experiment fail, so it was obligated not just to grant independence "but to insure the new nation's economic survival." That new nation, in turn, would demonstrate and support what McNutt called "the first principle" of U.S. foreign policy: "that American power is to be used for the preservation of peace and the support of democracy wherever possible in the world."[57]

Not all Americans viewed U.S. policies toward dependent peoples in such a glowing light. Writing in *Collier's*, for example, former Secretary of the Interior Harold L. Ickes lambasted the U.S. Navy's administration of various Pacific Islands as fundamentally undemocratic and subversive of the professed ideals of the nation's foreign policies. In his opening paragraph, Ickes pointed out that despite U.S. protestations that it had sought no territory in World War II, it had in fact acquired, in the Micronesian islands (including the Marshall, Marianas, and Caroline archipelagoes) "a land and water area about as large as the United States." These islands were not just "points of geography" or "strategic bases," Ickes emphasized, but "areas inhabited by human beings." From the way these islands were governed, Ickes suggested ironically, "the other nations of the world can read just what the United States and its protestations of democracy really mean." As in the Philippines, the eyes of the world would scrutinize U.S. behavior, and in the Pacific Islands, the naval administration was sending precisely the wrong message overseas.[58]

Less prominent citizens protested postwar foreign policies on similar grounds. In a letter to President Truman, for example, Mrs. Gertrude Avers of Los Angeles, for one, invoked "the principles of Franklin D. Roosevelt" and demanded the withdrawal of U.S. troops from China. "Their presence there," Mrs. Avers wrote, "is a mockery of all our stated war aims." She further urged "no support for Britain in her attacks on the Indonesians." Like UE delegate Emil Asher, an anonymous reader of the *Pittsburgh Courier*, the nation's leading African American newspaper, found the United States appearing all too often on the wrong side in the world struggle for democracy and freedom: "Our record reveals that we supported those forces preventing Iran, Greece and Indonesia from obtaining their freedom and democracy." Moreover, by pursuing such a course, he argued, "we are paving the way to World War III." Instead, he urged fellow *Courier* readers to insist that the nation's representatives "follow a policy that brings freedom for all peoples, white or colored."[59]

The white-controlled press, however, generally suggested that the United States stood apart from, and above, the traditions of European imperialism and colonialism. Examining the postwar colonial troubles of France, Holland, and

Britain, for example, a *New York Daily News* editorial entitled "The Burdens of Empire" concluded: "We're just as glad the United States never went into the empire business, and therefore isn't being harried and shoved and shouted out of that business now." In the *Saturday Evening Post*, the often critical Edgar Snow reviewed British and French efforts to exploit independent Thailand and concluded that "only American intervention . . . saved Siam from being reduced to the status of a British economic colony." Even in the African American press, European colonialism received scorn and vilification that U.S. foreign policy was largely spared. The moderate, photojournalistic monthly *Ebony*, for example, ran a July 1946 editorial entitled "A Spectre Haunts the Empire Builders," which presented a fierce indictment of European colonialism but only implicit criticisms of U.S. policy. That same month, of course, *Ebony*'s white counterparts, such as *Life* and *Collier's*, were busy celebrating the U.S. achievements in granting Philippine independence, an event on which the *Ebony* editorial maintained a provocative silence.[60]

Within U.S. public culture, the question of colonialism was a question of whether the nation's claims of promoting universal values and universal human aspirations held any validity. Did the United States really mean what it said about freedom and democracy for *all* peoples? In the *Saturday Evening Post*, Edgar Snow once again presented a skeptical view that was quite rare within the mainstream press. Under the title "No Four Freedoms for Indo-China," datelined Saigon, Snow argued that the question of "Indo-China's readiness for independence" would not be answered by means of morality and justice, nor, "in this new era of 'American world leadership,' " would it be settled in accord with the U.S. commitment to self-determination. More likely, Snow suggested, it would be settled by force, "as issues of slavery versus freedom have always been settled in the past." The tragedy of the situation, he wrote, was that the people of Indo-China had "built their hopes on the United States." The Vietnamese "could not understand that we did not really mean the Four Freedoms to apply" to them, that Truman's "twelve commandments of foreign policy" did not apply to the French colonies, or that "free democratic elections" were appropriate in former Nazi allies like Romania and Bulgaria but not in Indo-China. "This is one of the reasons," Snow concluded, "why some observers out here keep saying that America ended the war with greater prestige than any nation in history — and is losing it more rapidly than any nation in history."[61]

While Snow's anticolonial skepticism was virtually unique in the white-controlled, print mass media, similar sentiments appeared frequently in the African American press. In *The Crisis*, George Padmore lambasted the idea of international "trusteeships," much heralded as a halfway house between colonialism and freedom, calling it instead "the new imperialism." In the *Pittsburgh Courier*,

George Schuyler cited Egypt, India, Palestine, Vietnam, and Indonesia as places where, in March 1946, "colonial and semi-colonial people languishing under the heels of the 'democracies' continue to show they want their freedom." Schuyler's phraseology clearly subverts the emerging conception of the "free world" in the dominant public discourse, a discourse that associated boot heels with dictatorships and in which democracies did not wear heels. In Schuyler's sardonic view, the rhetoric of U.S. foreign policy was not to be taken at its word. "British, French and Japanese troops helped suppress the Annamite revolt against a return of white imperialism to Indo-China," he wrote that October. "Apparently the natives, in their naive way, took the Atlantic Charter seriously. Meanwhile, thousands of Dutch soldiers, trained at American expense and equipped with Lend-Lease stuff, are going to teach the Javanese what democracy means." The African American press generally kept a close eye on U.S. involvement in the Indonesian conflict in late 1945 and 1946; while the dominant, white-controlled media also reported on Indonesian nationalism, they failed to focus comparable attention on the U.S. role in aiding and abetting the Dutch and the British.[62]

LEADING BY EXAMPLE

As a central tenet of American nationalist ideology, the idea of American mission has traditionally had two main components: America as redeemer and America as exemplar. As redeemer, the United States actively brings its values to the world. As exemplar, it sets a model for the world to follow. Within U.S. foreign-policy discourse in the immediate postwar years, it was widely acknowledged that the former role would depend on the latter. World moral leadership could be provided only by a nation capable of setting a moral example for the world, of practicing at home what it preached abroad. This theme appeared in the mass media, the labor movement, and statements of the Truman administration, but nowhere did it receive sharper, more focused treatment than in the African American press, the civil rights movement, and other voices from the African American community.

To many African Americans and their political allies, U.S. claims to world moral leadership afforded new leverage in the struggle for racial equality at home, which they saw as part of a worldwide struggle against the color line. At best, Jim Crow was colonialism's cousin. From this perspective, racial equality was a matter of world peace as well as domestic tranquility. Though the United States was clearly the "strongest power on earth," its international prestige depended on the fabric of its domestic life. As K. O'Hara Lanier, an Urban League leader and the newly appointed U.S. minister to Liberia, put it in a nationally broadcast radio address in March 1946, "Until equality of opportunity for all becomes a reality in our nation . . . we cannot properly assume our rightful place as leaders in a better world to come." Speakers at the Urban League's annual conference in September 1946 argued quite directly that global responsibility began at home. "America's primary responsibility," said George L. P. Weaver, director of the National CIO Committee to Abolish Discrimination, "is to close the gap between our professed moral creed and our day-to-day practices here at home." Without such domestic reform, the nation could never meet its other obligations.[63]

The Truman administration's concern with free, democratic elections in Poland and other Eastern European countries became the target of scathing criticism in the African American press, focusing especially on the South Carolina background of Secretary of State James F. Byrnes. No one made this point more forcefully than Walter White, executive secretary of the NAACP. In his speech to the association's 1946 annual conference, for example, White ridiculed "the kind of world 'leadership' represented by James F. Byrnes of South Carolina who, as Secretary of State, loftily demands democratic elections in Bulgaria while in his own state of South Carolina there is brazen denial of democratic elections." In a *Chicago Defender* column, White recommended that Byrnes and Texas senator Tom Connally be replaced in the U.S. delegation to the Paris conference by "Americans who are known to have practiced as well as rendered lip service to the ideals of democracy," such as former first lady Eleanor Roosevelt or former undersecretary of state Sumner Welles. "What we need most desperately," White concluded, is "the creation of faith that we mean what we say we mean," a point he would return to throughout the immediate postwar years, in his writing, his public speaking, and in guiding the NAACP.[64]

Like many other African American leaders and writers, White saw the domestic struggle for racial justice as part of "the awakening of the dark world" during and after World War II. In White's view, the NAACP held a position of leadership in the worldwide struggle, in part because he was "more optimistic about the solution of our home problems than . . . about the solution of related world problems" stemming from "international imperialism."[65] Thurgood Marshall, White's NAACP colleague who would go on to become perhaps the most influential American jurist of the twentieth century, expressed a less than sanguine view concerning the postwar gap between professed ideals and hard realities both at home and abroad. "The war against Fascism has so far accomplished absolutely nothing toward the breaking down of imperialism against the darker races of the world," Marshall told the association's annual conference in June 1946, "even though these darker races form the majority rather than the minority of the peoples in the world. The war against fascism likewise has done nothing to break down the vicious system of second-class citizenship in our own country and in many ways has allowed home-grown Fascists to grow in stature."[66] In his own speech to the same conference, White expressed a similarly bleak view of the postwar domestic scene. "America faces possible doom," he said, "because in her mad scramble for wealth and power, she has desecrated her birthright of freedom" and "ignored the rise of racial and economic evils which lead [to] fascism." In the absence of the kind of visionary national leadership formerly provided by Franklin Roosevelt and Wendell Willkie, White declared, "We as a nation play a shoddy game of protection and even perpetuation of imperialism throughout the world."[67]

To White, these postwar developments marked a betrayal of the American creed, a matter he took quite seriously both as a U.S. citizen and as head of the nation's largest and oldest civil rights organization. As the historian James O. Horton has observed, African Americans have always served as the "guardians of the American rhetorical tradition." In the 1940s, more than ever before, the nation's highest ideals served as the most powerful political fulcrum available to civil rights leaders, especially after the 1944 publication of Gunnar Myrdal's hugely influential book, *An American Dilemma,* and the defeat of Germany and Japan the following year. No one was more aware of this fulcrum's potential leverage than Walter White. In effect, White presented the NAACP as the guardian of the nation's soul. "The task ahead of us is enormous," he told the association's membership at its 1946 annual conference, because "what we do will play a considerable part in keeping America faithful to the ideal of freedom on which our country was founded," and because of the new worldwide significance of this goal. White was emphatic on this point, which would guide the NAACP's strategy throughout the early postwar years: "We must pound and pound and pound the conscience of America not only because of what happens to Negroes physically because of discrimination but also because of what is done morally and spiritually to America as a whole."[68]

Lester Granger, executive secretary of the National Urban League, found encouragement "in the new anxiety felt by millions of white American citizens regarding the actual state of democracy in America," particularly concerning the nation's racial practices. As "real Americans," these people were "determined that the Atlantic Charter and its Four Freedoms shall not be regarded as idle talk" and that "the principles and the full meaning of the Charter shall be exemplified in the everyday living experience of citizens throughout our land." In Granger's view, "the fulfillment of American democracy," not Russian expansionism or European colonialism or any other international burden, presented "the sternest challenge and the greatest opportunity of our times." The fulfillment of American democracy, of course, meant the achievement of racial equality. This postwar argument, advanced so eloquently by White, Granger, and other middle-class African American leaders, marked a kind of dialectical extension of the democratic revival that had begun in the later 1930s and continued into the postwar years.[69]

Some white Americans joined in this rhetorical campaign of the civil rights movement, most notably progressive politicians like Fiorello LaGuardia, Helen Gahagan Douglas, and Henry Wallace.[70] In formal letters of greeting to the 1946 Urban League conference, even President Truman and that illustrious citizen of the world, Albert Einstein, each said in his own words that America could not properly assume international leadership until it solved its own racial problems. When the NAACP solicited the letter from Truman, Walter White advised the president and his aides concerning its content.[71]

A wave of postwar lynchings gave particular urgency to the need to set a better example for the eyes of the world. This need was felt by the Truman administration and the white press as well as the African American community. In a speech to the California State Bar Association, U.S. Attorney General Tom Clark declared that the lynchings damaged international confidence in American leadership and urged his audience to help put a stop to such crimes. In November 1946, a *Collier's* editorial condemned the "recent resurgence of lynching and mob violence" in the South, less because of its own inherent evil than because it provided the basis for "anti-American propaganda" directed by Moscow. "We could best spike this particular Communist propaganda gun by just dropping what remains of our lynch habit," the editorial argued. The reformist end was justified by a more twisted logic than that employed in the African American press, but the aim was nonetheless advanced. In calling for congressional passage of an anti-lynching bill in March 1947, *The Crisis* too framed its arguments in international terms, but it rooted them in morality rather than propaganda battles: "Is it too much to ask that after a global holocaust of blood and death, with the peoples of the world yearning for life and peace, that the United States of America enact legislation to outlaw and punish the crime of lynching?"[72]

This global perspective on American race relations was just one example of the postwar tendency to view national and international issues as two halves of the same walnut (to borrow a phrase President Truman would later use to characterize his most celebrated foreign-policy initiatives, the Truman Doctrine and the Marshall Plan). As a June 1946 *Life* editorial put it, "It is fatal to suppose that foreign and domestic policy can ever be two different and separate things."[73] In January 1946, in a major radio speech on the problems of postwar economic reconversion, President Truman told the nation that failure to achieve "full production and full employment" in the U.S. would bring serious consequences, not only for the American people but for "our position as a leader among the nations of the world." This speech focused on domestic problems but framed them in international terms. Beyond creating better lives for U.S. citizens and better markets for U.S. business, Truman stressed, a full-production, full-employment economy in America "means world confidence in our leadership." Conversely, "Stable world relationships require full production and full employment in the United States." Seeking leverage against political opponents in Congress, Truman concluded by invoking once again the burdens of global responsibility: "We cannot shirk our leadership in the postwar world."[74]

To more jaded ears of the post-Vietnam, post-Watergate age, these phrases may sound like "mere rhetoric," but in the wake of World War II's horrors they carried resonance and weight for many Americans. One "busy housewife" wrote the president on behalf of a group of neighbors to express their "hope to see this country prosper equally and progress in the manner befitting its position among the leading nations of the world!" Another woman responding to Truman's speech looked forward "to a better world in which all will enjoy the blessings and benefits of American democracy" and concluded that "our house should be in good order to receive" the world's representatives to the United Nations. A self-proclaimed member of "the underpaid 'white collar' class" used the same, increasingly commonplace metaphor: "My prayer is that America may first put its house in order, for then we can see clearly to lead the world away from war . . . to perfect and if possible everlasting peace. My wish is that history may award you this honor."[75]

The labor movement, too, linked domestic and international issues. With its motto that the "UE Fights for a Better America" to achieve the ubiquitous wartime goal of "a better world," the United Electrical workers union implied from its own left-wing perspective that world responsibility begins at home. And Claude Pepper concluded his speech to the UE's 1946 convention by explicitly linking "the liberal battle" in America and "in the world"—prompting a standing ovation from the union's delegates.[76]

In the UAW, both outgoing president R. J. Thomas and president-elect Walter Reuther tied their domestic agendas to the international scene. With the victory over Fascism and Nazism, Thomas told the delegates to the union's 1946 convention, "we have another fight to win, a fight over the same element that we had to fight on an international scale." The new fight was at home, Thomas asserted, against the National Association of Manufacturers and its Congressional allies— reactionary forces out to smash the UAW and organized labor. Thomas's concern with reaction paralleled that of Thurgood Marshall and Walter White in the NAACP. Like other American liberals in the period before the Truman Doctrine speech, these labor and civil rights leaders felt more threatened by "home-grown Fascism" than by international Communism. Thomas, in fact, was supported by the Communist Party within the UAW. But in 1946 Thomas was eclipsed, both in his rhetorical invocation of the war and in the convention's voting, by the anticommunist, former Socialist Walter Reuther.[77]

In his acceptance speech after defeating Thomas for the UAW presidency, Reuther spoke of the power of a labor movement dedicated to "the welfare of the people at large," rather than simply its own material interests. In Reuther's vision, the UAW, would be more than just a bread-and-butter trade union in the established American grain: "There is much work to be done in the world. We won the war. The task now is to win the peace. We have the job of mobilizing America, the labor and progressive forces, so that we can be certain there will be just as determined a fight on the homefront to make the peace secure as was demonstrated by our boys on the battlefield to make victory possible."[78] Reuther's ascendancy seemed an auspicious moment for the noncommunist and anticommunist left, black and white alike. In his *Chicago Defender* column, Walter White hailed Reuther's victory as a potential turning point. Did Reuther represent the emergence of "a new and distinctively American leadership" that could guide labor and other progressive forces? "On the answer to that question," White wrote, "hangs the future of America and perhaps the world."[79] Once again, the stakes were global.

Between late 1945 and early 1947, the only pronounced dissent from the idea of U.S. global responsibility came from a shrinking number of "isolationists," who sought to minimize the nation's overseas commitments. But these critical voices — including, most prominently, the voice of Senator Robert A. Taft — grew increasingly marginalized and delegitimized. Moreover, the isolationist tag had become a brush with which to tar political opponents, a form of vilification and ad hominem attack. If individuals, publications, or organizations were "isolationist," if they questioned the notion that the United States held global responsibilities, then whatever they said about world affairs did not merit serious attention.

For the most part, consequently, public debate over the basic purposes of U.S. foreign policy was limited to discussion concerning the nature and content of the nation's worldwide obligations. The most fundamental question within this discourse was whether the United States was morally and economically prepared to meet the challenges of world stewardship and world leadership. Did the United States really have the economic strength to feed the earth's starving millions and rebuild the world economy? Did it have the moral strength to provide the postwar world with vision, hope, and guidance?

The idea of world stewardship struck deep chords in many U.S. citizens, but hardly all. Many people were concerned that the postwar U.S. economy could not sustain the burden; others believed it would require too much sacrifice in terms of U.S. living standards, including their own. And African American leaders and commentators often expressed wariness about aiding Europeans who were in turn suppressing other dark-skinned peoples struggling for freedom.

The idea of world leadership also raised the question of whether the United States was morally prepared to lead, whether it was capable of providing a model of democracy at home that justified its moral preachments. Espoused most vociferously by the African American community and the civil rights movement, but also advanced by organized labor and liberal politicians like Helen Gahagan Douglas and Claude Pepper, the view that world leadership must begin at home was hardly a form of "isolationism" or "America-Firstism," since it accepted the idea of global responsibility as its basic premise. But since the United States was obliged to accept world moral leadership, in this view, it had to reform its own social, political, and economic life to achieve the moral and economic strength necessary for the task. To lead the world, the United States would have to set a moral example the world could follow; it would have to practice at home what it preached abroad.

Throughout this period, the actual goals of U.S. world leadership remained abstract, vaguely defined, and highly contestable. Particularly concerning issues like colonialism and the political and economic rights of common people everywhere, large questions remained open — in the public arena, if not in the councils of state: World leadership for what? For an unbridled capitalism or a global New Deal? For the end of colonialism or for its preservation? A Jim Crow world of democracy for whites only, or a world of racial equality and justice?

The two poles were perhaps best symbolized by the slogans associated with Henry Luce and Henry Wallace. These two men represented respectively the right wing and the left wing of "liberal internationalist" thought — the principal limits of American nationalist globalism. The United States was poised to launch a new epoch of world history, in keeping with its own special destiny. Was it to be the American Century or the Century of the Common Man? In the former, American supremacy was paramount, and it would spread the blessings of American prosperity and democracy throughout the world. In the latter, the needs of common, working people were paramount, regardless of their nationality or race, and because of its wealth, power, and democratic traditions, the United States was in a position to help meet those needs. Despite Wallace's lapses into millennialism, these differences of emphasis were more than semantic.

Throughout this period also, the Truman administration was developing its own language for explaining and justifying its globalist foreign policies, a language that resonated with many citizens but not with all. But like its foreign policy, the administration's public discourse had yet to take final form; it was still evolving. The next step in this evolution, the next step in the cultural and ideological origins of the cold war, developed from the notion that the United States, as world steward and world leader, was obliged to serve as world peacekeeper as well. Again, large questions remained, in the public sphere, between late 1945 and early 1947: How to keep the peace? Through the United Nations or through U.S. military preparedness? Through Big Three unity or by standing tough against Soviet aggression? In One World, or two? By March 12, 1947, these open questions would be closed.

VISUAL ESSAY: THE GLOBE AS AMERICAN ICON

Images of the globe in corporate advertising and editorial cartoons proliferated at the end of World War II and in the immediate postwar years, providing a potent iconography of America's new global supremacy. These images frequently conveyed a sense of racial hierarchy in the U.S.-led, postwar world order. (Copies of all illustrations reproduced here were provided courtesy of General Research Division, The New York Public Library, Astor, Lenox and Tilden Foundations.)

With advertising imagery like this, aircraft manufacturers sought to dramatize the global reach of air power, and the resulting importance of maintaining strong U.S. air forces in the postwar period. (Consolidated Vultee Aircraft Corporation ad, *Saturday Evening Post*, August 18, 1945, 16)

One-System Highway of the Air

AIR TRAVEL between any two places on earth provides an entirely new transportation pattern.

The American Airlines System has received government authorization to operate a single, unified service from North America to transatlantic nations. You will soon be able to enjoy the same

Flagship accommodations between your home town and the cities of Europe as you now can between cities within the United States.

Utilization of global air transportation makes a closer cultural relationship among all peoples not only possible but *imperative.* As distances grow shorter by

air and frequency of international contact increases, the ability to be a "good neighbor" is acquired with more convenience and growing satisfaction. Your use of overseas air transportation will implement our nation's foreign policy: "To live together in peace with one another as good neighbors."

AMERICAN AIRLINES *System*

THE NATIONAL AND INTERNATIONAL ROUTE OF THE FLAGSHIPS

Civilian airlines also used the globe as an advertising icon, to convey both the image of a newly unified world and the sense that the entire planet was at the disposal of the American consumer. (American Airlines System ad, *Saturday Evening Post*, November 10, 1945, 92; Trans World Airline ad, *Collier's*, March 30, 1946, 65)

TWA—FIRST TO PUT THE CONSTELLATION INTO THE SKIES

— AND THE WORLD AT YOUR FEET

*High in these heavens, there's gentle adventure unknown
to earth-bound things. There are clouds to race with, and
gorgeous skies to see, and now and then a passing fellow
traveler to salute. To this TWA seeks to add, through
skilful piloting and hospitable attention, that kingly
feeling of complete contentment that makes you want to
fly when you travel—and travel TWA when you fly.*

TRANS WORLD AIRLINE

Step right up, amigos ... Have a Coke

...Yank friendliness comes back to Leyte

Naturally Filipinos thrilled when their Yankee comrades-in-arms came back to the Philippines. Freedom came back with them. Fair play took the place of fear. But also they brought back the old sense of friendliness that America stands for. You find it quickly expressed in the simple phrase *Have a Coke.* There's no easier or warmer way to say *Relax and be yourself.* Everywhere *the pause that refreshes* with ice-cold Coca-Cola has become a symbol of good will—an everyday example of how Yankee friendliness follows the flag around the globe.

*   *   *

Our fighting men meet up with Coca-Cola many places overseas, where it's bottled on the spot. Coca-Cola has been a globe-trotter "since way back when".

"Coke" = Coca-Cola
You naturally hear Coca-Cola called by its friendly abbreviation "Coke". Both mean the quality product of The Coca-Cola Company.

Coca-Cola ran an extensive ad campaign in 1945 featuring the company's trademark red bottle cap converted into a global map, along with diverse "local" scenes that conveyed the worldwide reach of Coke and American culture. The slogan, "Coca-Cola—the global high-sign," suggested that the archetypal American soft drink signaled to people everywhere that the world was safe again. (Coca-Cola ad set in Leyte, the Philippines, *Collier's,*

Now you're talking...Have a Coca-Cola

...or tuning in refreshment on the Admiralty Isles

When battle-seasoned Seabees pile ashore in the Admiralty's, one of the world's longest refreshment counters is there to serve them at the P. X. Up they come tired and thirsty, and *Have a Coke* is the phrase that says *That's for me*—meaning friendly relaxation and refreshment. Coca-Cola is a bit of America that has travelled 'round the globe, catching up with our fighting men in so many far away places —reminding them of home—bringing them *the pause that refreshes*—the happy symbol of a friendly way of life.

* * *

Our fighting men meet up with Coca-Cola many places overseas, where it's bottled on the spot. Coca-Cola has been a globe-trotter "since way back when".

-the global high-sign

You naturally hear Coca-C called by its friendly abbreviati "Coke". Both mean the quality pr uct of The Coca-Cola Compa

November 3, 1945, 31; ad set in the Admiralty Isles, *Saturday Evening Post*, October 13, 1945, inside back cover. "Coca-Cola" and "Coke" are registered trademarks of The Coca-Cola Company.)

This glossy color advertisement encouraged consumer patience with continuing gasoline rationing during the war's closing stages by representing the United States as a Knight in Shining Armor, spinning the globe on its axis and exploding gasoline-filled incendiary bombs around the world. (Ethyl Corporation ad, *Saturday Evening Post*, April 1945, inside front cover)

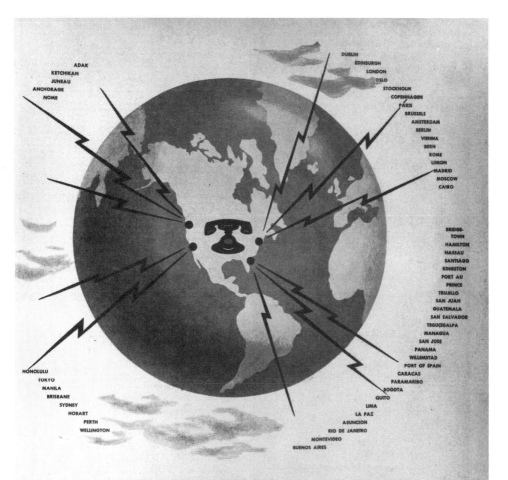

THE WORLD'S IN REACH AGAIN

Today, nearly all our former radiotelephone circuits—and many new ones—are in operation to Europe, South America, Central America and the Far East.

We have more than twice as many direct circuits operating to overseas areas today as we did in 1939. Through them you can reach some 60 countries, territories and dominions throughout the world.

Rates are lower, too. A three-minute call from any place in the United States to most any overseas point—including all of Europe—now costs no more than $12. To many nearby countries it is even less.

 BELL SYSTEM OVERSEAS TELEPHONE SERVICE

This Bell System ad illustrated the new connectedness of the postwar world. Not surprisingly, it portrayed a global communications system centered on the United States. (Bell System Overseas Telephone Service ad, *Collier's*, November 16, 1946, 46)

Editorial cartoons, such as these two from *Collier's*, frequently portrayed U.S. global responsibility quite literally, often using Uncle Sam, one of the core symbols of American nationalism. ("World War and World Peace" editorial cartoon, Fitzpatrick in *Collier's*, November 24, 1945, 94; "Uncle Sam as World Leader" editorial cartoon, Fitzpatrick in *Collier's*, March 23, 1946, 90)

NOW LET'S SEE, WE PROMISED TO STRAIGHTEN YOU OUT, DIDN'T WE?

Political cartoonists frequently personified the war-torn world as a banged-up, globe-headed vagabond dependent on U.S. assistance. ("Doc Byrnes and Patient" editorial cartoon, Duffy in the *Baltimore Sun*, as published in the *New York Times*, August 19, 1945, Sec. 4, 10—reprinted with permission from the *Baltimore Sun*, SunSource; "Now Let's See. We Promised to Straighten You Out, Didn't We?" editorial cartoon, Duffy in *Saturday Evening Post*, January 22, 1949, 10)

COULD BE HE CAN'T USE THE STUFF.

This racialist variant of the imagery in the two preceding illustrations was a clear swipe at President Truman's Point Four plan for economic assistance to Asia, Latin America, and Africa, the point being that economic aid would be wasted on the world's nonwhite peoples. ("Could Be He Can't Use the Stuff" editorial cartoon, Duffy in *Saturday Evening Post*, July 9, 1949, 10)

"THE STATE OF THE WORLD"

In 1947 especially, political cartoons showed the world splitting in two. ("The State of the World" editorial cartoon, Fitzpatrick in the *St. Louis Post-Dispatch*, as published in the *New York Times*, July 6, 1947, Sec. 4, 3; "Two Worlds" editorial cartoon from the *Richmond Times-Dispatch*, as published in the *New York Times*, October 12, 1947, Sec. 4, 3—reprinted with permission from the *Richmond Times-Dispatch*)

"TWO WORLDS"

FRED O. SEIBEL.

Burck in The Chicago Sun-Times

"I do solemnly swear to uphold . . ."

Commenting on Truman's inauguration in January 1949, this cartoon illustrated America's global responsibilities quite earnestly. ("I do solemnly swear to uphold . . ." editorial cartoon, Burke in the *Chicago Sun-Times*, as published in the *New York Times*, January 23, 1949, Sec. 4, 3—reprinted with special permission from the *Chicago Sun-Times*, Inc. © 1999)

Yardley in The Baltimore Sun

"Uncle Atlas hasn't much choice."

This cartoon image of Uncle Sam as Atlas conveys the standard, benign view of American power—and the standard, malign view of the alternative should the U.S. fail to meet its responsibilities to all the quaintly costumed peoples of the world. ("Uncle Atlas hasn't much choice" editorial cartoon, Yardley in the *Baltimore Sun*, as published in the *New York Times*, July 31, 1949, Sec. 4, 5—reprinted with permission from the *Baltimore Sun*, SunSource)

4 FROM ONE WORLD INTO TWO

Tensions between the United States and the Soviet Union developed gradually during and after World War II. Within U.S. public discourse, mounting discord between these wartime allies eventually forced a redefinition of America's worldwide duties. The deepening conflicts between the United States and its only conceivable rival made it increasingly difficult to talk about a unified world under U.S. leadership, particularly in matters of war and peace. By 1947, the wartime dream of "one world" had faded, U.S. global responsibility was redefined in terms of the anticommunist containment policy, and the world was once again divided into two.

The Truman Doctrine speech of March 12, 1947, which publicly codified these shifts, succeeded in reshaping U.S. foreign-policy discourse because it tapped into the mixture of nationalist and universalist values that already shaped much of that discourse. By incorporating deep-seated strains of American anticommunism into the emerging ideology of nationalist globalism, with its basic precepts of national greatness and global responsibility, Truman's speech gave that ideology added potency. The new vision of a divided world helped to explain the turmoil and complexities of the postwar era in a way that the ideas of national greatness and global responsibility alone had failed to do. The image of Soviet communism as a threat to the United States and the world it sought to build helped to explain why the responsibilities of world stewardship, leadership, and peacekeeping were so urgent, so extensive, and so sure to require long-term commitments.[1]

Although the Truman Doctrine speech codified this redefinition of U.S. global responsibility and thus solidified the ideology of the Cold War in essentially its final form, public discussion of the nation's role as international peacekeeper, particularly in the mainstream press, had been moving toward a similar view for at least a year. The Truman Doctrine speech was indeed a critical moment in the history of U.S. foreign-policy discourse, and of postwar history in general, but it is important to note that the administration's new formulation fell upon decidedly fertile ground.

Wartime propaganda persistently pegged hopes for peace on the creation of the new United Nations Organization and the continuation of "Big Three" unity between the United States, Great Britain, and the Soviet Union. But these popular hopes were quickly ensnared in the complexities of postwar international politics. A series of editorial cartoons illustrates the changes that took place. The first, appearing in the liberal *St. Louis Post-Dispatch* in September 1945, showed two monsters representing Germany and Japan (the former an oafish-looking thug wearing a swastika armband, the latter a slanty-eyed, buck-toothed gorilla, typical of the racialist symbolism of the war) struggling in vain against the three mighty bars of their prison-cell windows. Under the caption "the necessary bars," the bars themselves spelled out "Big," "Three," "Unity." That December, as the Big Three foreign ministers convened in Moscow, the same cartoonist drew the British, U.S., and Soviet flags flying together above the Kremlin walls, but under a cautious, questioning title: "Meeting with Christmas Spirit?" By February 1946, a cartoon in the *Louisville Times* entitled "New World Symphony" showed the Big Three each playing its tune: John Bull, on flute, whistled "pastoral dreams of empire"; Uncle Sam, on tuba, thundered "atomic blasts"; and Joe Stalin, on bass drum, banged out "booming nationalism." No doubt the result was a frightening cacophony.[2]

Even by late 1945, the American media often presented the United States itself, rather than the U.N. or the Big Three, as the main buffer between war and peace. An editorial cartoon in *Collier's*, illustrating an editorial entitled "World War and World Peace," exemplifies this view. It portrays two human figures pushing a huge globe up a slight incline. One's back bears the word "Patience"; the other's, "Teamwork." With patience and teamwork, this sketch suggested, the United States could move the earth toward peace and away from war. The accompanying text commented on the often rancorous conference of foreign ministers then underway in London, emphasizing the benefits of openly airing the differences between the Big Three now that the war was over. To succeed in its role as world peacekeeper, *Collier's* argued, the United States needed greater public appreciation of the limits of Big Three unity.[3]

The nation's capacity for patience and teamwork remained question marks from the end of the war through 1946. Yet most Americans desired peace more than anything else, and throughout 1946 many continued to believe that international cooperation, especially with the other major powers, through the United Nations and eventually through world government, was the only path to peace.[4] Labor spokesmen, like many observers, stressed Big Three unity as the key to lasting peace. At the 1946 UE convention, Jack Kroll, director of the CIO's Political

Action Committee (CIO-PAC) argued that Britain, Russia, and the United States needed to work together because no one of them was always right or always wrong. When Kroll proclaimed, "we don't want a third world war," the delegates interrupted him with applause. A third world war would be an atomic bomb war, Kroll added, which would mean the end of "civilization as we know it." It is striking that this phrase, a recurring theme of the nuclear age, was already current in 1946. That same convention unanimously approved a foreign-policy resolution that called on President Truman to seek a meeting of the Big Three aimed at halting the breakdown of the world into hostile blocs and the consequent drive toward war. At the 1946 UAW convention, both UAW president R. J. Thomas and CIO president Philip Murray similarly emphasized working-class desire for international cooperation.[5] The civil rights movement also expressed the common desire for peace as a paramount goal — a prerequisite to survival.[6]

The internationalist approach still had its critics. The *New York Daily News,* for example, equated "internationalism" with "interventionism," and expected more major wars as a result. One *News* editorial equated "One Worldism" with the "principle that we are obligated to mind everybody else's business and remake every other government which we don't like" even if its own people do. Unfortunately, according to the *News,* voters chose that course by reelecting Franklin Roosevelt in 1944. The United States was now mired "in the UNO sludge," with no choice but to establish a worldwide spy network and maintain a state of constant military readiness. After all, the editorial concluded, "it looks as if our armed forces will be more than busy, all over the world, for a long time to come." The same editorial page presented a letter from a Bronx reader, identified as "Ye Olde Isolationist," questioning whether the winning of the war was worth the price, whether the world was any better off, and whether the problems of racial hatred and rivalry had been solved. "If Hitler was a menace," the letter asked in its closing sentence, "is Stalin a lesser menace?"[7]

While Big Three unity was hardly accepted everywhere as a panacea in early 1946, the possibility of constructive relations among all the major wartime allies was not yet ruled out of acceptable discussion, even in the mass media. Many observers believed that rising world tensions resulted from conflicts between the British Empire and the Soviet Union, and that U.S. policy should aim to ameliorate those tensions. In a January 26 feature article for *Collier's,* entitled "U.S.A.: Peacemaker among the Powers," Walter Lippmann, the enormously influential newspaper columnist who later helped affix the "Cold War" label to the postwar era, argued that the United States alone could mediate in the conflicts between Britain and the Soviet Union. Lippmann asserted that Americans were "anxious and unhappy" because they lacked a clear vision of the nation's world role. Many, he warned, feared that victory in the Second World War would prove as futile as in the First. Yet he saw no chance of a public turn toward isolationism. "The question is not whether we shall participate in world affairs," Lippmann wrote, "but in what way we shall participate."

Lippmann liked to present himself as a dispassionate "realist" regarding international affairs, but this essay presented a more romantic view of the nation's new role, casting it as a matter of historical necessity, even national destiny. Because "the United States is not a military power in the most seriously disputed and unsettled regions of the Old World," Lippmann argued, international realities "require us to assume the role of conciliator, mediator, and peacemaker" between the British and the Soviets.

The United States could use its great power successfully, according to Lippmann, only by promoting "a righteous peace." Any efforts at conquest or domination of other nations would only weaken and impoverish the United States. This situation made the present moment historically unique. "Hitherto a world in which all peoples were under a common law has been the aspiration of the weak nations," Lippmann argued. "But now there is a great power in the world, second to none in its military might, which has every reason for making this great cause its own." To achieve this goal would fulfill "the deepest and oldest American belief that the world can be made a better place" in which people live together in peace, with greater justice than ever before. Destiny offered the present generation of Americans the opportunity to be "the peacemaker among the powers, and to labor as guardian and protector, champion and promoter of the effort to organize the world for peace and to institute a regime of law." Surely, Lippmann concluded, Americans would like nothing more than to meet this challenge: "If we embrace our destiny, we shall find in the grand purpose which it gives us, peace in our own souls, zest and high spirits to overcome all the obstacles in our path, seeing always before us proudly the wide horizon and the splendor of those who live greatly in a great time." [8] The editors of *Collier's* shared Lippmann's grand vision of the United States as mediator between Great Britain and the Soviet Union, reiterating this theme frequently throughout most of 1946. Well to Lippmann's left, liberals like Senator Claude Pepper shared it too. No anti-Soviet consensus yet existed.[9]

CHURCHILL'S "IRON CURTAIN" SPEECH AND U.S. FOREIGN-POLICY DISCOURSE

In March 1946, against this backdrop, former British prime minister Winston Churchill traveled to Fulton, Missouri, to deliver a speech at Westminster College. President Truman accompanied him on the long train ride from Washington and on the podium at Westminster. The small, little-known liberal arts college was accorded this honor because one of Truman's Missouri pals was an alumnus and because its name evoked the cultural ties between Great Britain and the United States. The speech Churchill delivered there on March 5 would become one of the most famous utterances of the postwar era. It represented only the views of one individual, not the policies of any government. Yet Truman introduced Churchill and sat behind him as he spoke, lending an official air and implicit sanction to the speech. Churchill's main substantive proposal, a call for an Anglo-American alliance against the Soviet Union, garnered little popular support in the United States. Indeed, it provoked substantial criticism and protest. But by dramatizing the division of Europe with a stark new metaphor, Churchill had a significant impact on U.S. foreign-policy discourse. "From Stettin in the Baltic to Trieste in the Adriatic," Churchill declaimed, "an iron curtain has descended across the continent." The "iron curtain" phrase, which Churchill had used in writing previously but which gained its vogue through this one well-publicized speech, resonated widely. The tenor of his speech, its alarmist tone, of which the dramatic metaphor was just one component, helped to alter U.S. public talk about U.S.-Soviet relations and the U.S. world role in general.

The Fulton speech instantly created a stir. "U.S. British Tie, Churchill Aim," proclaimed the banner headline that dominated the late edition of the *New York Daily News.* While the paper made clear that Truman never explicitly endorsed Churchill's policy proposals, it reported that Churchill told the crowd that the president had "traveled a thousand miles to dignify and magnify" their gathering. The *News* reported that Truman followed Churchill with an extemporaneous speech of his own, warning of "perilous times" that required an unprecedented "moral awakening" of the American people. (Not coincidentally, the president reiterated those themes the next day in a speech to the Federal Council of Churches.) The *News* article on the Fulton speeches was illustrated with a map of Europe, its eastern half shaded darkly. Interestingly, the darkened half already included Czechoslovakia, where two years later a Communist coup nonetheless caused a war scare.[10] The *News*'s March 7 editorial sniped at Churchill for being one of those orators who start wars and leave them for ordinary soldiers to finish. Yet the editorial concluded that if Churchill's speech pointed the way U.S. foreign policy was heading, then the nation had best "get back to war strength" as quickly as possible. Like others on the political right, however, the *Daily News*'s Washington columnist John O'Donnell was far more skeptical. In his view, the Fulton speech was merely a clever ploy to secure the proposed British loan.[11]

The big weekly magazines were more openly receptive to Churchill's message. A *Saturday Evening Post* editorial in the last week of March suggested that the Fulton speech had contributed to a "new groundswell of opinion" that finally made clear to most Americans "the incredible folly of Yalta." The editorial called for renewed efforts to seek out a settlement with Russia. But it also called for a firm stand on behalf of western democratic principles in the face of "Soviet imperialism."[12] While *Life* took no clear stand on Churchill's call for an Anglo-American military alliance, it applauded his ideological emphasis—the "crusading note" that set his speech apart from previous "get tough with Russia" speeches—a note that had been "curiously lacking" in U.S. policy and rhetoric. What the United States needed, according to *Life,* was a renewal of its traditional missionary sense. Yet that renewal was already underway.

Borrowing words from John Foster Dulles, *Life*'s editorial writers suggested that in the glory days of the 1890s, "We acted under a sense of moral compulsion, as a people who had a mission to perform in the world. . . . We sought, through conduct, example and influence, to promote everywhere the cause of human freedom. We availed of every opportunity to spread our gospel throughout the world." Never mind that the American imperialism of the 1890s had been hotly contested by a vibrant anti-imperialist movement, that it had been imbued with racism and accompanied by heightened racial oppression domestically, or that it culminated in a long, brutal war of conquest in the Philippines. Dulles, Luce, and other ideologues of American nationalist globalism in the 1940s were the ideological heirs of late-nineteenth-century imperialists like the Reverend Josiah Strong.

Life proposed two steps the United States could take to restore this missionary sense to its foreign policy. First, the editors proclaimed, America had to supply the United Nations Organization with the "spiritual drive" it needed to become a "positive force for human welfare." Second, "America has a special duty to hasten progress toward self-government among the dependent peoples of the world." Liberation movements in India, Indonesia, and elsewhere were more properly America's business than Russia's, *Life* argued, because "their slogans are those of Jefferson, Lincoln and Wilson, not Karl Marx." The United States should welcome this new evidence that people "still seek liberty and justice above all things."[13]

In June, one of *Collier's* main foreign-affairs correspondents assessed Churchill's impact. The Fulton speech, wrote Frank Gervasi, "contributed to the tension with the Soviet Union" and "aroused a storm of argument for and against Russia but had the effect of clearing the air. The country knew, after the Churchill speech, just how bad relations with Moscow had become." Gervasi cited State Department public opinion polls showing that "American confidence in Russia's desire to cooperate with the democracies in the preservation of peace had sunk to a new low."[14]

But that confidence had fallen sharply even before Churchill's speech. In May 1945, shortly after V-E day, a Gallup poll found that 45 percent of those surveyed believed Russia could be trusted to cooperate with the United States after the war.

In a poll taken the week that the United States bombed Hiroshima and Nagasaki and clinched its great moment of total victory, that figure increased to 54 percent. But by the beginning of March 1946, just before the Fulton speech, only 35 percent of those surveyed believed that Russia would cooperate with the United States in world affairs. By December 1946, eight months after the Iron Curtain had been christened, that figure actually rebounded to 43 percent.[15]

Churchill's speech generated criticism from both the left and the right.[16] In his ABC broadcast that same day, the liberal radio commentator Raymond Gram Swing criticized Churchill's Fulton speech as "one that spoke darkly of a divided world." Swing himself held firmly to the "one world" vision, and claimed that the youth of America and other countries did as well — or wanted to. He concluded that the threat of atomic war "makes the whole speech really meaningless," since war between great powers had become unthinkable.[17] The following day, Methodist Bishop G. Bromley Oxnam, president of the Federal Council of Churches, speaking to the closing session of the council's conference, refused to accept Churchill's stark moral dichotomy. Oxnam presented both the Soviet and the western models of society as having positive attributes as well as moral failings. "We refuse to identify the Christian gospel with an economic order," the bishop said. By refusing to sanctify western capitalism, Oxnam suggested that the churches sought a moral high ground and political middle ground on which to nurture peaceful coexistence and creative solutions to the world's ills.[18]

Negative reaction to the Fulton speech complicated the rest of Churchill's trip in the United States. The CIO veterans committee organized picket lines during Churchill's stay in New York City, where he was scheduled to speak at a dinner in his honor on March 15. On the 14th, the State Department announced that Undersecretary of State Acheson had canceled plans to attend the dinner, ostensibly detained by pressing business back in Washington. But it seemed the Truman administration was distancing itself from Churchill.[19] The president himself continued to avoid any public confrontation with the Soviets and publicly downplayed the alleged dangers of the current international scene. The *Daily News* even ran a full back-page photo of Truman smiling broadly and strolling casually on the White House lawn, with the caption headlined "Grounds for Optimism."[20]

The black press presented a more critical view of the Fulton speech than the mass media generally did. Leery of Churchill's imperialist background and racist views, African American commentators generally emphasized the racialist overtones of his call for an Anglo-American alliance, a theme the white-controlled mass media ignored. An American Negro Press service news story stressed that Churchill's plea for brotherhood did not apply to colonial peoples. In an editorial, the *Pittsburgh Courier* castigated the speech as an "invitation to imperialism." In his *Courier* column, sociologist and political commentator Horace Cayton likened Churchill to Hitler and argued that the real conflict in the world lay between Britain and Russia, not between Russia and the United States.[21] Months later, an editorial in *Ebony* magazine similarly linked Churchill's call for "unity of the two great Anglo-Saxon civilizations for world leadership" with Hitler's notion of "Aryan supremacy."[22]

In his *Chicago Defender* column, the N A A C P's Walter White criticized President Truman's role in introducing Churchill at Westminster College as a shabby way of showing "that the United States is backing the kind of imperialistic program Churchill advocates." Churchill's speech itself, White wrote, demonstrated "abject fear on the part of the so-called Anglo-Saxon English-speaking white people of the world." With the British Empire in ruins and the United States "materially prosperous but morally and intellectually bankrupt," White asked, "is there any wonder then that paralyzing fear of any power so great as is Russia's should grip the white Anglo-Saxon nations?"[23]

Of the *Pittsburgh Courier*'s numerous columnists, representing a range of African American opinion, only the cantankerous, conservative George Schuyler found any redeeming value in Churchill's speech. But, like many old isolationists, Schuyler was caught between his anti-interventionism and his anti-Soviet sentiments. Schuyler initially complained that Churchill's call for an Anglo-American alliance sounded "like the fight against Hitler all over again." The next week, however, he wrote that the movement of Soviet troops through Iran threatened not only British oil interests but the outbreak of World War III. "Unless the Russians are bluffing," Schuyler concluded, "it seems that Churchill's warning is justified despite the screams of his critics."[24]

Despite those screams, from white and black critics alike, Churchill's iron-curtain metaphor proved resonant. Churchill did not invent the division of Europe, but he named it in more compelling terms than anyone had before. By late 1945, the *Saturday Evening Post* reported, the western border of the Russian zone of Germany had come to be known, throughout western Europe, as the "asbestos curtain." CBS news analyst Eric Sevareid used this phrase in his evening broadcast days after the Fulton speech, perhaps as a barb against Churchill.[25] But this metaphor never caught on in the United States. As a fire-retardant material, asbestos had positive qualities; the phrase "asbestos curtain" might suggest that the Soviet Union benevolently sought to protect its zone from dangerous elements outside. The "iron curtain," by contrast, was more generally impenetrable; it also had more alarming, militarist undertones, conjuring as it did memories of the "Iron Cross," which symbolized German militarism during the First World War.

After Churchill's Fulton address, the iron curtain metaphor appeared frequently in U.S. public discussion; the "asbestos curtain" was absent. Henry Luce's *Life* did more than its share to popularize the new term, beginning with a featured photo-essay in April 1946, the month after the Fulton speech, entitled simply "The Iron Curtain" and subtitled "Behind It Russia Controls Destiny of All Nations of Eastern Europe." Later that spring, noted commentators like Joseph and Stewart Alsop and John Foster Dulles used the phrase as the easiest shorthand for Soviet domination of Eastern Europe. *New York Times* correspondent Brooks Atkinson called it "a marvelously apt phrase," then proceeded to use it as a regular term needing no further clarification.[26] Thanks to the enthusiasm of influential opinion leaders like the Alsops, Dulles, Luce, and Atkinson, Churchill's phrase seems to have become part of common speech almost instantaneously.

PREPAREDNESS AS THE PATH TO PEACE

Army Day celebrations were held around the country on April 6, 1946, in the first postwar spring, reminding communities throughout the United States and the world of the military strength that had won the war. Everywhere the message from government and military leaders was clear: only the strength that won the war could win the peace. The United Nations could not be relied on; Big Three unity could not be assumed.[27]

President Truman's Army Day speech was a major salvo in his administration's campaign for continued military preparedness. Delivered in Chicago before a huge crowd after a major military parade and broadcast nationwide over all the major radio networks, the speech took as its premise the notion that the United States held major responsibilities for keeping the peace. News coverage showed Truman as commander-in-chief reviewing a massive display of troops and military hardware. The United States, according to the president, could meet its responsibilities as world peacekeeper only if it remained militarily strong. Toward this end, Truman called for a temporary extension of the draft, a program of universal military training (though this text omitted the word "military"), and unification of the armed services. He asserted that the United States would uphold the peace unilaterally through its own military might, rather than through the United Nations and without undue regard for Big Three unity. As the *New York Daily News* put it in its front-page banner headline: "U.S. to Enforce Peace: Truman."[28]

Truman's Army Day speech generated a sharply divided response among those citizens who felt compelled to write to him after hearing it. Many reveled in the glory of world leadership through military might; others protested the president's hawkishness, chastising him for subverting the United Nations and his own moral claims by choosing to rely on unilateral force.[29]

The favorable responses show that Truman's rhetoric struck a deep chord of patriotism in many citizens. "You are leading America to the destiny for which she is intended," wrote one World War II combat veteran, "the only destiny that can justify the dead of America whom we left on foreign battlefields." In the same vein, Myron H. Luria of Cleveland expressed confidence that under Truman's guidance the United States would "maintain our place in the world as the leading nation for years to come." Flavel E. Jenkins of Hammond, Indiana, wrote that he prayed for God's blessing and wisdom for the president and the nation's military and civilian leaders "in guiding our Great nation and the rest of the world to an everlasting peace," presumably to be based on the everlasting power of the United States. And one writer, a World War I veteran whose only son died in combat in Europe in World War II, supported the president's proposals but urged him "to issue a *world* Monroe Doctrine" to keep the peace. (Since the historical Monroe Doctrine was based on the division of the globe into two distinct hemispheres, it is hard to imagine what a more globalized version would look like. Presumably the author had in mind the prevalent popular conception of the Monroe Doctrine embodied in what is commonly called the Roosevelt Corollary to the Monroe Doctrine. Under that corollary, the United States arrogated to itself the right to act as an international police power throughout the western hemisphere. A globalized version of this idea would give the United States the right to act as an international police power anywhere in the world. That is precisely what critics later charged the United States with attempting.)[30]

Citizens who wrote to protest President Truman's call for preparedness also employed the language of world leadership and responsibility. Several urged the president to concentrate on rebuilding the war-torn countries rather than building up the U.S. military machine. As Jerry Cohen of Brooklyn put it, Truman's emphasis on conscription and armaments made little sense "at this time when we are supposed to be leading the world to permanent peace. We would do better to help feed the devastated countries rather than to terrorize them further with our might."[31] Others believed that the United States should exercise its leadership responsibilities by advocating worldwide disarmament rather than national preparedness.[32]

Many Americans saw peacetime conscription and universal military training as hallmarks of the militarism the United States had fought against in both world wars.[33] In early 1946, servicemen stationed in Manila and Paris had organized mass protests against their continuing deployment overseas, and popular demands to "bring the boys home" had resounded throughout the nation since the end of the war.[34] After Truman's Army Day speech, a number of citizens wrote Truman to express support for calls by General Douglas MacArthur and Senator Millard Tydings for U.S. leadership toward the worldwide abolition of military conscription.[35] Voicing a widely-shared concern, Mrs. Ruth H. Ashby of Wabash,

Indiana, asked plaintively whether conscription and military training were really "the way to promote a peaceful world."[36]

Finally, some citizen critics suggested that the president's emphasis on military preparedness undermined any moral credibility the United States possessed. "America has no right to lead the world," wrote Mrs. H. Hanfrecht of Manhattan: "The big three must lead the world." Similarly, Richard R. Braddock, also of Manhattan, argued that maintaining a vast U.S. military force would make the United States rather than the United Nations "the rulers of the world." Braddock and many other Americans believed that was wrong. Mrs. Marcia J. Lyttle of Chicago protested pointedly that Truman's hawkish Army Day speech could not possibly be reconciled with his speech to the Federal Council of Churches a month earlier, in which he invoked the Golden Rule as the guiding principle of U.S. foreign policy.[37]

The media frequently presented military preparedness as part of America's global mission. According to the *New York Daily News,* for example, U.S. military power represented the best available form of "anti-war insurance."[38] A *Life* photo-essay on the Army's "shocking disintegration" quoted General Eisenhower telling Congress that any "gamble with the national security of the United States at this time is a gamble with the peace and security of the world."[39] World security meant U.S. national security, and vice versa. Army recruiting ads featuring photos of President Truman and General Eisenhower promised "one of the world's best jobs," dedicated to upholding the nation's "solemn obligation . . . to safeguard the victory." In a most suggestive example of the blurring of American nationalism and American globalism during late 1946 and early 1947, the featured slogan in these ads sold enlistment as a way to serve humanity, not just country: "Your regular army serves the nation and mankind in war and peace — choose this fine profession now."[40] An ad for the U.S. National Guard put matters bluntly: "In this new era of world uncertainties, peace cannot be preserved by wishful thinking. The basic insurance against future war is national preparedness."[41] "Wishful thinking" meant the untested agency of the United Nations, which the government now felt it had oversold, during the war, as a means of ensuring the postwar peace.

In the media as elsewhere, air power constituted a potent symbol of the nation's new world role and global predominance.[42] In late 1946, the aircraft industry, its future largely dependent on military procurement, launched renewed advertising campaigns advocating continued U.S. air supremacy. "Our country's ability to help keep the peace, at any time," implored one ad for the United Aircraft Corporation, "depends largely on our air superiority at that moment. So, as a citizen and taxpayer, you have a personal interest in the task of keeping this country strong in the air."[43] As a taxpayer, of course, that meant paying for your share of air supremacy. By early 1947, however, *Collier's*, which supported air power with particular vigor, published a two-part feature series entitled "Will Russia Rule the Air?" These articles raised the possibility of the United States losing its predominance in the air to the Soviet Union, a possibility that was previously inconceivable. The race for supremacy in air power was on, proclaimed *Collier's* correspondent W. B. Courtney. Victory would "gain for the winner moral, economic and political world leadership." Preparedness would have a big payoff indeed, although the connection between air power and morality was unclear. Most ominously, Courtney asserted that "the United States is no longer running in first place." If the United States was to have influence in the world, he concluded, "its citizens must learn to share" the burdens of competing to win "the crucial race for control of the world's air."[44]

After August 1945, however, the symbolic significance of air power was simultaneously augmented and superseded by atomic power. One *Life* editorial suggested that all the major postwar problems were symbolically embedded in the atomic bomb: "Food, Russia, strikes, UN, colonies and everything else on the public conscience are inseparably threaded on this bomb, swinging like pendulums in unison between idealism and blue funk."[45] For the *New York Daily News*, support for maintaining the U.S. atomic monopoly constituted a sign of national loyalty. The *News* lumped atomic scientists campaigning against an incipient arms race together with " 'liberals,' Communists and fellow travellers" whose calls for sharing atomic information with the Soviet Union merely demonstrated their treachery. All were cast beyond the pale of legitimate opinion. In a March 14, 1946, editorial, the *News* singled out Secretary of Commerce Henry A. Wallace for holding this position. The accompanying cartoon depicted an effete man with a thin moustache, oversized glasses, and balding pate, the words "American 'liberal' " tagged on the lapel of his double-breasted suit, holding a flag aloft in each hand, pinkies extended. His left hand held a tiny American flag, down near shoulder level. His right hand held the Soviet hammer and sickle up above his head, as he gazed at it mistily. The caption read: " 'My countries 'tis of thee.' "[46]

In her *Ladies' Home Journal* columns, Dorothy Thompson expressed views the *Daily News* editors would find dubious at best. Thompson implored American women to realize that the atomic bomb had destroyed more than "landscapes, buildings, and populations" in Japan; it had also destroyed the United Nations Charter "as an instrument for preventing aggression and keeping peace." The United States and its atomic partners, Thompson wrote, were now "masters of the globe." She also recognized that the world was evolving into two competing power systems centered in the United States and the Soviet Union. This much the *News* would find reasonable. But Thompson deplored the drift toward yet another major war and thought she recognized in the bomb's awesome power a glimmer of hope. The Anglo-American atomic monopoly, Thompson argued, gave the American, British, and Canadian people "the brief opportunity to dictate peace to the world." She urged her readers, whom she addressed as the mothers and future mothers of America, to call on their government to exchange the atomic monopoly for the world rule of law, including international control of atomic energy but going far beyond it. The U.N. was obsolete, but American women could seek to advance the creation of "a super-authority governing and controlling all armaments and reducing their use to the enforcement of the law."[47]

The series of bomb tests held in the Bikini atoll in the Pacific in the summer of 1946 served as a reminder of both the bomb's awesome power and America's professed benevolence. A *Life* photo-essay on the removal of Bikini's human inhabitants, for example, explained that "the natives agreed to give up Bikini because the Navy told them the United States wanted the atom bomb to be used for the good of mankind." In early June, a few weeks before the tests' scheduled start, *Collier's* featured a long article by Vice Admiral W. H. P. Blandy, the officer in charge of the tests, laying out the government's public rationale for "the most stupendous military experiment in history." Until peace could be guaranteed by law, the admiral argued, the U.S. armed forces "have a very grave responsibility" to insure "that all aspects of the use of any weapon are fully explored." The test results would help to assess the bomb's effects "on American Sea Power, Air Power and Ground Power — the spearheads on which the security of our nation still depends."[48]

Similarly, the Truman administration and the mass media presented the Baruch Plan for international control of atomic energy as a sign of the nation's benevolent assumption of global responsibilities. In presenting the plan to the United Nations, Bernard Baruch himself spoke in the language of American nationalist globalism, invoking the nation's "heavy obligations" to the world to tame the new force it had unleashed. *Life* magazine embraced the plan in Baruch's own terms, as disinterestedly internationalist and beneficent: "The U.S., possessing for the moment a weapon of apparently absolute military power, offered to turn its secret over to the world — if only the world would agree to a practical and enforceable way of removing the weapon forever. It was an offer without precedent in the history of nations." It was also an offer to dictate unilaterally the terms of international control, but that was left unsaid. *Life* added that Russian acceptance of the plan, in good faith, would require the lifting of the "iron curtain," though under scrutiny this fact showed the plan was hardly disinterested and perhaps disingenuous. Two weeks later *Life* published two letters to the editor written in response to this article. Both writers criticized the Baruch plan from right-wing perspectives. One called it a form of appeasement, arguing that the bomb's "secret should never be shared," because "God has given it to a peace-loving nation that the peace of the world may be preserved."[49] The *New York Daily News* was also among the plan's many media boosters, further demonstrating its essentially unilateralist nature.[50]

Despite the media barrage, public opinion polls consistently showed that majorities of up to 70 percent or more believed the United States should keep its atomic information to itself. The propaganda for the Baruch plan never really sought to dissuade people from this view. The government and the media presented the issue of international control within the ideological frame of American nationalist globalism. In that view, the United States would maintain a benevolent stewardship over its "atomic secrets" until it made the world safe for them. Predictably, Soviet rejection of the Baruch plan led a growing number of Americans to view the Soviet Union as an aggressor state interested in world conquest rather than international cooperation.[51]

SHIFTING VIEWS ON BIG THREE RELATIONS

Even in the commercial media, resistance to the idea of a divided world persisted in the spring of 1946, but this resistance was beginning to fade. A month after Churchill's "Iron Curtain" speech, the editors of *Collier's* still argued that the role of conciliator between Britain and Russia remained "our chief duty in the great task of averting World War III."[52] In May, *Collier's* included a cartoon that captured the confused state of Big Three relations. It depicted a scene of pandemonium in New York's Times Square, much like New Year's or V-J Day. A man emerging from the subway stared in befuddlement at a beat cop, who explained the cause of the excitement. "Someone started a rumor," said the cartoon's caption, "that we made peace with our allies."

In June, *Collier's* foreign-affairs writer Frank Gervasi published a balanced, two-part series on Soviet foreign policy, arguing that it was rooted in the traditional objectives of czarist foreign policy, rather than any desire for world conquest. The Soviets, Gervasi emphasized, did not seek war with the United States. He even suggested that the United States and the Soviet Union engaged in a kind of negative mirror-imaging: "Each side sees in the pattern of whatever the other says and does a plot to dominate the world and annihilate the opponent. Both are often right and as often both are tragically wrong." In keeping with the *Collier's* editorial line, Gervasi concluded that the British-Russian conflict—not Soviet Communism—lay at the source of "the present chaotic state of world affairs." Both those powers were responsible for the current situation, he argued, adding that the United States shared responsibility "for having failed, thus far, in exerting that strong leadership necessary to avert catastrophe."[53]

Demaree Bess, a *Saturday Evening Post* contributing editor and one of its leading foreign-affairs writers, offered similar arguments. Months after Churchill's Fulton speech, Bess suggested that America's mission was "to break down the growing hostility between the British and Russian empires," not to engage in ideological crusades of its own. "Our job," he continued, was "to convince the Russians that we will not try to impose our brand of capitalism where it is not wanted, provided they do not persist in imposing Russian communism upon reluctant peoples." The United States still needed to bring the Soviet Union "back into the 'family of nations,'" as Franklin Roosevelt had said. But Bess lamented that the world seemed to be "dividing into two distinct parts," one dominated by Russia, the other dependent on the United States. Bess also expressed a fundamental belief in American exceptionalism, a belief central to the larger constellation of U.S. foreign-policy ideology. The United States was "unique among nations in its ability to produce a superabundance of food and all the other things which men most desire." As a result, "the entire world turns to us — not to Russia — to save its people from starvation and general disintegration." While arguing that the United States should perform the role of mediator, Bess seemed to believe that America was destined to be the world's savior as well.[54] Less than two months later, Bess wrote ominously about how the Soviet Union had tricked the United States into giving it control of the Danube River and all countries bordering it. Only American economic aid, he argued, could prevent the Austrians and others from making "their own arrangements, however reluctantly, with the great, expanding Russian empire." Bess no longer called on the United States to settle Russian-British disputes. He now found the United States and the Soviet Union "engaged in a disturbing war of nerves" in Central Europe.[55]

Two feature articles on Korea, published five months apart in the *Saturday Evening Post,* illustrate dramatically the changing views of U.S.-Soviet relations represented in that magazine between spring and late summer of 1946. In the March 30 issue, *Post* contributing editor Edgar Snow called for early, unified elections and the withdrawal of both U.S. and Soviet troops. In twenty years' time, Snow argued, that course could create "a democratic progressive republic friendly to both Russian and American, and reconciling within itself good features of both systems." Snow believed a middle way was still possible in Korea, and in the world. In the August 31 issue, by contrast, the title of another *Post* feature article called the 38th parallel separating north and south Korea "Our Most Dangerous Boundary," as though it represented a border between the United States and the Soviet Union. The article's lead caption framed a sharp dichotomy between American beneficence and Soviet aggressiveness: "Far from home and not happy about it, a few Americans trying to bring freedom to miserable Korea are being shoved around by the Russians." The Soviets aimed at Communist control of all Korea, while the United States sought only to bring "freedom" to all Korea. But the prospects for freedom looked bleak. "It is difficult to imagine any long-range situation here," the article concluded, "in which the Russians won't win out."[56]

The view of U.S.-Soviet relations presented on *Life*'s editorial page underwent a similar shift during the spring of 1946. *Life* led the way in reshaping public opinion concerning the Soviet Union after the war.[57] Yet its April 29 editorial expressed hope that the Paris foreign ministers meeting might yet conclude a general peace treaty, obviating the need for a "separate peace" made without Russia—a peace that would be inherently less secure. "If grasped," *Life* argued, "this opportunity can bring new hope to a world whose peace aims are drifting into war talk." Just four weeks later, though, the magazine's editorial page was devoid of such hope. "Why Kid Around?," the May 27 editorial headline asked rhetorically. The subhead laid the cards out on the table: "There is no 'misunderstanding' between Russia and the West. There is a conflict." That conflict existed, moreover, "in all parts of the world." U.S. global responsibility faced a global challenge, which strengthened the claims of American globalism both at home and abroad.[58]

Between March and June of 1946, *Life* featured a series of essays by prominent figures espousing a firmer U.S. policy toward the Soviet Union. Under the title "The U.S. and the World," Joseph P. Kennedy, former U.S. ambassador to Great Britain, advocated military preparedness, close cooperation with Great Britain, and development of an anti-Soviet bloc as the best means to keep the peace.[59] In the May 20 issue, Joseph and Stewart Alsop proposed a four-point "liberal program" for U.S. foreign policy, based on support for the United Nations, internationalization of the atomic bomb, greater firmness toward the USSR, and "the broadest effort of relief and reconstruction all over the world." The aim of such a program was "both to deflect Soviet policy and to improve world conditions" so that the United States and the Soviet Union could coexist peacefully without an upward spiral of tension and mutual suspicion. To the Alsops, the "tragedy of American liberalism" lay in the failure of American liberals to "face the facts" about the Soviet Union. The Alsops proposed to overcome the tragedy by combining central elements of the agenda of liberal internationalism with a call for a stronger stance against the Soviets.[60]

In June, *Life* published a two-part series on Soviet foreign policy by John Foster Dulles. Dulles argued from the premise that Soviet policy was global—that it aimed to create "one world" based on the Soviet model of a single-party, anticapitalist state. He denied that the United States pursued its own global agenda while warning that the liberal dream of One World could become the nightmare of a Pax Sovietica. Yet he believed the Soviet challenge might revive the traditional sense of national mission within the United States. "As the full implications of the Soviet system come to be better understood by the American people," Dulles wrote, "it will revive in them the spirit which led their forebears to pledge their lives, their fortunes and their sacred honor to secure their personal freedoms."[61] The growing Soviet threat would give new meaning to the ancestral sense of national mission.

According to Dulles, the corporate lawyer and Republican foreign-policy adviser, Russia's global ambitions threatened the core values of the American heritage, rather than America's own global ambitions or the material interests of corporate capital. The program he proposed in response was framed in ideological terms. It featured five steps to show "that our society of freedom still has the qualities needed for survival": (1) rededication of traditional American religious faith; (2) demonstration that traditional American "political and religious faith" could solve the nation's domestic problems; (3) maintaining military strength to show Soviet leaders that U.S. citizens valued the American way of life; (4) using economic aid to promote human freedom around the world; and (5) using de facto military control—as in occupied Germany, Japan, Italy, Austria, China, and southern Korea—to promote the Four Freedoms and the Atlantic Charter conception of justice, "for which we fought."

It was up to the United States to defend freedom from the global designs of the Soviet Union, Dulles argued. But the American public had to be taught to accept the necessary sacrifices: "Our people's apparent recklessness in the use of their freedoms and apparent apathy to the cause of world-wide freedom are primarily due to the failure of those in authority to see the true nature of the present world crisis, to tell it simply to the American people, and to propose, with foresight, policies which measure up to the need. That should be corrected in order that the American people should, by their conduct, make it clear beyond peradventure that they are prepared to accept personal sacrifice to help keep freedom alive in the world." Dulles's critique of current policy had a sharp partisan edge, calling the Democratic administration to task from the perspective of a Republican internationalist. Yet he called for something very much like the Truman Doctrine and the policies it helped to justify, such as the Marshall Plan and the North Atlantic Treaty Organization (NATO), nine months before President Truman proclaimed the doctrine in his famous speech of March 12, 1947. A year later, George Kennan used rhetoric strikingly similar to Dulles's in the closing passage of the famous "X" article on "The Sources of Soviet Conduct." Kennan, of course, served in the Democratic administration that Dulles criticized. But that only shows that a common view was shared widely in the foreign-policy establishment.

Public statements like this by prominent opinion leaders like Dulles helped to prepare the ground for the Truman Doctrine. By March 1947, the field was well tilled and fertilized. The view that the United States could mediate between the British and the Soviets fell from favor as commentators increasingly saw America locked in a global struggle with Russia. As Dulles put it, accommodation between the two nations was impossible until Soviet leaders "abandon their grandiose program and accept a world in which the Soviet Union will be one of many nations, each representing a distinctive way of life." Yet Dulles and others who held this view hardly treated the United States as simply "one of many nations," but rather as the standard-bearer and guarantor of human freedom.[62] In such discourse, all attributes of U.S. policy that might be seen as meddlesome, provocative, or over-reaching were effectively projected onto the image of the adversary. This ideological emphasis served to obfuscate the global reach of U.S. economic and security interests.[63]

THE "LIQUIDATION" OF HENRY WALLACE AND THE MARGINALIZATION OF DISSENT

In this atmosphere, Secretary of Commerce Henry A. Wallace, last of the New Deal liberals in Truman's cabinet, continued to believe in the long-term goal of a unified, open-door world and in the consequent need for the United States and the Soviet Union to coexist peacefully. On September 12, 1946, at a progressive political rally in New York City's Madison Square Garden, Wallace criticized the trend toward a policy of confrontation with Russia. Wallace's speech was balanced and moderate in both substance and tone. The left-wing crowd even hissed at him, saving its cheers for the more hard-hitting denunciations of U.S. foreign policy offered by Senator Claude Pepper and Paul Robeson, the dissident African American singer, actor, and activist. President Truman later called Wallace a Communist dupe, but the Communist Party's *Daily Worker* newspaper fiercely denounced Wallace's Madison Square Garden remarks.

Wallace's speech nonetheless caused a major controversy, dominating the national news for over a week and culminating in Wallace's forced resignation from the cabinet. Most daily newspapers firmly backed Secretary of State Byrnes and his policy of "getting tough" with the Soviet Union. The mainstream media closed ranks behind the secretary of state, often dismissing Wallace's approach without examining his ideas. The African American press, however, showed greater appreciation for Wallace's views, singling out his statement that lynchings in the American South posed a major threat to international peace, a statement the white-owned media essentially ignored. *Pittsburgh Courier* columnist Marjorie McKenzie expressed a view shared by many of her colleagues when she lamented "the liquidation of Henry Wallace from the cabinet." By the end of the Wallace affair, the range of public discussion concerning U.S. foreign policy had narrowed considerably.[64]

Wallace had been the last dissenter from a policy of confrontation with the Soviet Union within high government circles, the last advocate for the possibility of either cooperation or productive competition between the United States and the Soviet Union. With his departure from the government, discussion within the Truman administration about the basic underpinnings of U.S. foreign policy came to an end. Within the public sphere, the dissenting perspectives that Wallace represented lost considerable legitimacy. In response, dissenters, including Wallace himself, grew increasingly shrill and strident, which did little to increase the popular appeal of their views. In a Gallup poll conducted between September 27 and October 2, 1946, 76 percent of those who said they had followed the Byrnes-Wallace debate favored Byrnes's ideas over Wallace's; 50 percent believed Wallace favored a policy of appeasement, while 17 percent thought he was pro-Soviet or even a Communist himself. Yet many American liberals saw Wallace as FDR's true and martyred heir, and he maintained a certain stature and a considerable following. Both would decline precipitously over the next two years.[65]

By late September 1946, in the wake of "L'affaire Wallace," as it was dubbed, opposition to the emerging policy of containment persisted only at the margins of the public sphere. Discussion of the basic ideological assumptions and goals of U.S. foreign policy continued only among the left wings of both the labor and liberal movements, the members of a small but vigorous peace movement, a handful of old isolationists, and the African American community.[66] In the white-controlled commercial press, favorable representations of the Soviet Union, or of the possibility of cooperation or productive competition between the two emerging great powers, grew rare. The media increasingly presented the Soviet Union as an aggressor state analogous to Nazi Germany, making a U.S.-Soviet conflict seem inevitable.[67]

Writing in *Life* in late October 1946, Reinhold Niebuhr, the leading liberal exponent of this anti-Soviet view, argued that the United States was responsible for preventing a Soviet conquest of Western Europe, especially Germany. Niebuhr provided a potent rationale for continuing U.S. commitments in Western Europe, asserting that Russia aimed to conquer the entire continent, not just to build a zone of buffer states. For the liberal Niebuhr, as for the Republican Dulles, Soviet ideology was "universalist, rather than nationalist." Niebuhr consciously framed his argument in opposition to Wallace's recent speech and the viewpoint Wallace represented—a sentimental liberalism, in Niebuhr's thinking, that ignored "the tragic aspects of human existence," particularly the evil embodied in the Soviet system. Like Dulles, the Alsops, and other established commentators, Niebuhr proposed a two-pronged policy—"strategic firmness" against the USSR and "affirmative economic reconstruction for Western Europe." Ever the pragmatist, though, Niebuhr emphasized the limits of American power in relation to the Russian sphere in Eastern Europe. The United States, he warned, should make "no demands in words that cannot be carried out short of war." However, when

Reader's Digest reprinted Niebuhr's article for its millions of readers in January 1947, it deleted this eminently diplomatic caveat.[68]

In the *Saturday Evening Post* a month and a half later, Joseph and Stewart Alsop presented similar arguments to explain "Why We Changed Our Policy in Germany." The Alsops, like so many other observers, presented U.S. global policy as the necessary response to Soviet actions. The pressures of Soviet policy, they claimed, were forcing Secretary of State Byrnes to transform U.S. policy "from negative to positive, with all the long-range commitments abroad which this implies."[69] Here as elsewhere by late 1946 and early 1947, the image of Byrnes's personal toughness served as a kind of symbol of America's international responsibility in the face of Soviet truculence. As a profile in the January 4, 1947, issue of the *Saturday Evening Post* put it, "the small figure of Jimmy Byrnes has become a focus of the hopes and fears of mankind." Through the long, tough negotiations with the Russians, Byrnes worked on, "and as long as he is in the struggle, so is the power of America."[70] Ironically, President Truman named George Marshall to replace Byrnes as secretary of state just days after these lines appeared in print. But the general-turned-statesman, whom Truman called the greatest living American, provided an even stronger symbol of U.S. power and responsibility. An editorial cartoon from the *New Hampshire Morning News* showed an Olympian Marshall striding confidently from a globe labeled "World War II" to another labeled "World Peace Problems." The caption, "Two Worlds," suggested that if General Marshall could make this transition successfully, perhaps the division of the world into warring blocs could be prevented. According to a Gallup poll taken in early February, 64 percent of the public approved of Truman's appointment of Marshall—and 51 percent thought the new secretary should "be firmer with Russia than Mr. Byrnes was." By October, 63 percent of those polled thought Marshall had been handling the Soviets well.[71]

By October 1946, following the Wallace flap and Yugoslavia's downing of two U.S. military planes, *Collier's* finally abandoned its opinion that the United States should serve as mediator between Britain and Russia. This turnabout came with a vengeance. The Yugoslavian incident, the *Collier's* editors asserted, showed that Russia's was "a gangster government" directed by "religious fanatics, whose religion is communism, and who are gunning for the British Empire and the United States, most likely in that order." The best U.S. course, therefore, was "to remain stronger than Russia . . . to refuse steadfastly to give in to any Russian demands that impinge on our vital interests anywhere in the world, and to crack down on the Russian fifth column in this country." The editors still claimed to believe that war was not inevitable, but the tone of this editorial makes it hard to tell why. A week later, *Collier's* ran a cartoon depicting a woman in a liquor store saying to the clerk: "I don't think *I'll* use any more vodka until we get a more definite foreign policy." President Truman had yet to enunciate a clear anti-Soviet line, but the mass media were now clamoring for one.[72]

Like its competitors and like the Truman administration, the *Saturday Evening Post* took an increasingly tough stand against the Soviet Union in late 1946 and early 1947.[73] Yet in February and March, the *Post* published a remarkable three-part series by Edgar Snow that attempted to explain the reasoning behind Soviet actions. The magazine's editors made clear that the views Snow presented did not reflect *Post* editorial views, but they also emphasized the importance of Snow's aim. As Snow himself put it, Hitler's failure to understand the Soviet Union largely determined his defeat, so the United States had best improve its understanding of that nation. Setting out to achieve an empathetic understanding of Soviet foreign policy, Snow interpreted Stalin's February 1946 "election day" speech as a political ploy for domestic consumption, not the aggressive call to arms that many commentators, including the influential Walter Lippmann, had taken it to be. Snow's explication of that speech and of Soviet policy generally was coherent and compelling, but his *Post* series presented a view completely at odds with the dominant public discourse of early 1947.[74]

From a Russian perspective, Snow told his *Post* readers, U.S. foreign policy hardly seemed so morally pure, nor Soviet foreign policy so purely immoral, as the U.S. media suggested. For example, Snow argued, the average Russian could see little difference between U.S. policy in Latin America and Soviet policy in Eastern Europe. Similar points were made at this time by left-wing critics of Truman administration foreign policy, such as Claude Pepper and members of the United Electrical workers, but seldom by this time were such critical comparisons of U.S. and Soviet policies made by mainstream journalists writing in mass-circulation periodicals. In late February and early March 1947, Snow was swimming directly against the tides of both public opinion and government policy. He mocked the self-righteousness that dominated U.S. foreign-policy discourse: "We know absolutely that 'there is no Anglo-American bloc,' as the *New York Times* says, 'there is only a fraternal association.' But something in the Moscow air prevents the Russians from seeing the fundamental difference." Snow also satirized influential writers like Reinhold Niebuhr and Brooks Atkinson of the *Times*. In doing so, he revealed the extent to which U.S. actions looked threatening to Russian eyes and the dangers of denigrating the Russian perspective on world affairs.[75]

In the article "Stalin Must Have Peace," which concluded the series in the *Post*'s March 1 issue, Snow argued that Stalin sought peaceful cooperation with the United States, and that war was the last thing the Soviets wanted. Snow's articles prompted a favorable response from *Post* readers.[76] But by this time U.S. policymakers and opinion leaders had essentially abandoned the idea of peaceful cooperation. Less than two weeks after "Stalin Must Have Peace" appeared,

President Truman enunciated the doctrine of global anticommunism that would come to bear his name. With the lines of battle at last drawn clearly, what would soon be known as the Cold War then began in earnest.

U.S. GLOBALISM TRIUMPHANT

Ironically, as the world was dividing, politically and discursively, from one world into two, U.S. government and opinion leaders asserted the notion of U.S. global responsibility more forcefully than ever. The world might be divided, but the United States was still responsible for the peace and well-being of the whole. Rather than receding before an international system that was not so easily unified, pacified, or reconstructed, the discourse of American nationalist globalism grew ever more pronounced.

Well before the Truman Doctrine speech, the president himself led this rhetorical charge. Speaking to the opening session of the United Nations General Assembly in New York City on October 23, 1946, Truman proclaimed that the United States was dedicated to realizing the four freedoms throughout the world. The threat or use of force anywhere, he asserted, directly concerned the American people. In keeping with the tradition of nationalist ideas about America's mission, Truman once again construed the United States as the agent of historical providence. "The course of history," he said, "has made us one of the stronger nations in the world. It has therefore placed upon us special responsibilities to conserve our strength and to use it rightly." The American people, Truman added, accepted their special responsibilities to secure a lasting peace; and the nation would do its best to meet them.[77]

In his 1947 State of the Union address, Truman again stressed the theme of peace through strength: "We live in a world in which strength on the part of peace-loving nations is still the greatest deterrent to aggression. World stability can be destroyed when nations with great responsibilities neglect to maintain the means of discharging those responsibilities." Once again, those responsibilities were global. "We have a higher duty and a greater responsibility than the attainment of our own national security," said the president: "Our goal is collective security for all mankind." Truman stressed that the United States would never "retreat into isolationism," but even the New York Daily News found his State of the Union pronouncements on foreign affairs and national defense to be "eminently sensible." The News's isolationism and the Truman administration's internationalism converged in a shared commitment to unilateral U.S. action.[78] Moreover, the News, like the administration, saw U.S. national security concerns as global in scope. American nationalism and American globalism reinforced each other and blended together.

No voice in the country proclaimed the triumph of globalism in U.S. foreign-policy discourse more emphatically than *Life* magazine. In January 1947, *Life* published a series of three editorials reexamining the foundations of U.S. foreign policy and arguing that the United States alone bore responsibility for world peace and prosperity. As a great power, the United States had to maintain dual foreign-policy objectives — "a permanent choice of routes." In 1947, the twin goals of U.S. policy were simple: "1) to prevent the next war; 2) to win it." That war, if it came, would be against the Soviet Union. In 1946, *Life* argued, the United States had focused on the second, negative aim — "the soldier's half." In 1947 and beyond, the task was to catch up on the more positive aim "of preventing war by building a true world community." The meaning of "world community" and the steps involved in building it remained vague. The real question, according to *Life*, was whether Americans could "summon enough coolness and resolution" to work diligently toward building that community, rather than simply blaming the Russians or dreaming of world government.[79]

Life's editors saw few if any limits to the reach of U.S. power. Although they believed the state department needed to develop "some long-term strategic ideas to match those of the Kremlin," they argued in the second installment of the series that "there have seldom been so many ready-made opportunities for America to exert her influence for the better." Under the closing subhead "The Entire World," this second editorial quoted General Marshall, the newly named Secretary of State, as saying that U.S. strategic interests were no longer limited to the Western Hemisphere and that "we are now concerned with the entire world." To *Life*, reshaping Europe and Asia constituted valid and viable aims of U.S. policy. Even when treating the planet in terms of "its old-fashioned geographical parts," *Life*'s editorial writers concluded, "it seems to be a series of prepared positions where the U.S. can win diplomatic triumphs if it will. So is it with the two worst trouble spots, Europe and China; so is it all around the globe. Everywhere the risks are great, the stakes high, the challenge not to be refused."[80]

The concluding editorial of the series laid out the task of U.S. foreign policy in both ideological and economic terms. "Russia is an idea as well a country," *Life* argued: "To prevent and win the war we must win the billion-odd people in the grandstand to our side by a demonstration that ours is the better idea, the better system." The way to do that was for "the No. 1 nation" to transform "the prewar pattern of nationalism and poverty" by promoting "freer world trade." In this effort, *Life* suggested, the American businessman held the key to the future well-being of humanity. By going abroad "as wealth-creators," American businessmen would win multitudes to capitalism and build strong allies for the United States. In the concluding paragraph of the series, *Life* defined America's "special destiny" in the crucial postwar decade in a manner that clearly invoked nationalist myths of manifest destiny and providential mission: "This is the special destiny of America in the next decade: to break the old patterns, to share not its wealth but its talent for creating wealth, to help the world breathe freely once again. It is the least soldierly part of George Marshall's new job to see and promote this destiny. But it is also the part where foreign and domestic policies join hands; where Americans, going abroad, can be most themselves."[81] This joining of the traditional American nationalist theme of a uniquely grand and benevolent national destiny with the new conceit that U.S. interests now encompassed "the entire world" provides a potent example of the postwar ideology of American nationalist globalism. In this manner, nationalist ideas were called upon to advance a globalist foreign policy.[82]

In his new role as leading critic of U.S. foreign policy from outside the government, Henry Wallace voiced globalist sentiments that shared ideological guideposts with Henry Luce and Harry Truman. Wallace had become editor of the elite liberal weekly *The New Republic* in December 1946, and he used its pages to espouse his foreign-policy views. In a December 16 piece entitled "Jobs, Peace, Freedom," he proclaimed both globalist scope and nationalist sentiments. "My field is the world," Wallace wrote, in tones that made Marshall's look low-keyed: "My strength is my conviction that a progressive America can unify the world and a reactionary America must divide it."[83] In January 1947, Wallace voiced perhaps the most extreme, messianic form of American nationalist globalism of any influential figure. "By reason of history, geography and sheer economic strength," he wrote, "America has it in her grasp to furnish that great and last [*sic*] peace which the prophets and sages have preached for thousands of years."[84] Wallace's difference with the dominant view primarily concerned methods of dealing with the Soviet Union, and his emphasis on the welfare of the "common man" at home and abroad. He shared with Truman, Luce, and other Cold Warriors the basic preconception that the purpose of U.S. foreign policy was to reshape the world.

TOWARD THE TRUMAN DOCTRINE, AND
THE END OF ONE WORLD

The Truman Doctrine speech of March 12, 1947 has generally been treated as a major turning point in postwar U.S. history—as a major reformulation not just of U.S. policy but of America's world role and national purpose.[85] Yet while the new doctrine did mark a momentous change, the ideology it embodied did not spring out of the blue in response to the perceived crisis in the Mediterranean in early 1947. Nor did it spring solely from the minds of policymakers who imposed it upon a recalcitrant public. What I want to argue, rather, is that when viewed in the context of U.S. public discourse in early 1947, Truman's most famous speech codified shifts that had been taking shape since the end of the war. It fused the emergent ideology of nationalist globalism with the increasingly prominent sentiments of global anticommunism. This fusion created a potent ideological mix that both explained current international crises and justified U.S. global activism. This new ideological potion served as the glue holding together a Cold War consensus from 1947 until the collapse of the Soviet Union in 1991 and even beyond. The Truman Doctrine speech did not create a new worldview and foist it upon the American people and their congressional representatives. Rather, it encapsulated and reified ideological beliefs that were already widely shared, and it used them to mobilize support for the Truman administration's major foreign-policy objectives.

The stage was set for the Truman Doctrine speech on February 21, 1947, when the British government informed the U.S. government that it could no longer carry its financial and military burdens in Greece and Turkey. According to one influential account, State Department officials realized in a flash "that Great Britain had within the hour handed the job of world leadership, with all its burdens and all its glory, to the United States." [86] But the U.S. government had been actively assuming the burdens and glory of world leadership for some time. And, as should be clear by now, both the government and the commercial mass media had been encouraging the American people to accept those burdens and enjoy the glory. Much of the U.S. public, in short, was well prepared for the crises of February and March 1947, and for the doctrine formulated to resolve them. [87] By January 1947, as shown above, the demand for a clearly articulated, globalist foreign policy responding to Soviet aggression had already become a dominant theme in U.S. public discourse. In March 1947, President Truman met this demand by enunciating such a policy in boldly ideological terms.

The mainstream press helped to advance the Truman administration's viewpoint. In its February 24th editorial on "The British Crisis," *Life* argued that Britain's long-term economic troubles concerned the United States as well, and that "the U.S. should assume more of the military load" to aid Britain in its current travails. If Britain could no longer manage her empire, the United States might have to pick up the slack by "policing Palestine, Greece, India or other hot spots" and adopting policies there which "may in most cases parallel the previous British policy." As always, *Life*'s full-page editorial appeared opposite its full-page "Picture of the Week." Most suggestively, that week's picture showed President Truman receiving a ceremonial kiss on the brow from Archbishop Athenagoras, spiritual leader of the Greek Orthodox Church in the United States. The *U.S. News and World Report* declared that Americans could no longer "indulge in armchair sharpshooting at British imperialism." As the *Saturday Evening Post* made clear, the Mediterranean crisis was not just a matter of maintaining the British Empire, but of maintaining order in the world and thereby preventing World War III. A *Post* editorial quoted Secretary of State Marshall, who had likened the current situation to the fall of Athens in the Peloponnesian War and the fall of Rome: "The development of a sense of responsibility for world order and security, the development of a sense of the overwhelming importance of this country's acts, and failures to act, in relation to world order and security—these in my opinion are great 'musts' for your generation."[88] Great crises brought great challenges. A great nation would meet them.

In a piece published ten days before the Truman Doctrine speech, the *New York Times* correspondent Hanson Baldwin drew an equally stark historical metaphor. The United States, Baldwin wrote, "far more than any single factor, is the key to the destiny of tomorrow; we alone may be able to avert the decline of Western civilization, and a reversion to nihilism and the Dark Ages." Baldwin's words echoed those of a recent press briefing by Assistant Secretary of State Dean Acheson. The Truman administration fueled crisis reporting of this sort, and in doing so helped create a public atmosphere in which the Truman Doctrine would find a favorable reception. By March 12, anything less would have prompted criticism concerning the administration's continuing irresolution.[89]

On March 6, 1947, at Baylor University in Waco, Texas, President Truman delivered a foreign-policy speech with a domestic political thrust, aiming to promote a bipartisan approach to foreign economic policy. Beyond economics, this speech contained an important ideological message. At Baylor, the president no longer spoke of the Four Freedoms of the war years, positing instead only three forms of freedom, reconfigured so as to change the meaning of the word itself. From the earlier quartet, freedom of worship and freedom of speech remained, but freedom from fear and freedom from want, with their socialistic overtones, were now replaced with freedom of enterprise. "It must be true," the president asserted, "that the first two of these freedoms are related to the third."[90] In this manner, Truman conflated freedom and capitalism, a conflation with deep roots in U.S. political culture, no doubt, but one which now served as an explicit underpinning of U.S. foreign policy.[91] In the Cold War, unlike in World War II, freedom of enterprise became elevated to the level of a fundamental freedom upon which all other freedoms ultimately depended. The radicalism of the Depression years was now receding. So were early postwar fears of another economic collapse and the tenuous U.S. commitment to social democracy. The belief that all freedom depended on freedom of enterprise would serve as perhaps the most potent rationale for global anticommunism. It was a rationale first made explicit in Truman's Baylor speech, just six days before he officially declared the nation's commitment to the emerging global struggle between freedom and tyranny. There is apparently little surviving mail to the president concerning this speech. But, suggestively, the favorable responses that still exist came disproportionately from business-men and elite figures, including Chester Bowles, former isolationist and adver-tising mogul turned wartime price-control chief turned postwar liberal politi-cian.[92] Perhaps less elite, less business-oriented Americans were still concerned with freedom from want and freedom from fear.[93]

The Truman Doctrine speech itself built on the foundation laid in the Bay-lor speech, redefining the ubiquitous but abstract conception of global respon-sibility into a policy of direct, bilateral economic and military assistance to "free peoples" everywhere.[94] In Truman's March 12 usage, and in the dominant U.S. foreign-policy discourse from that day until the collapse of Soviet Communism in 1991, "free" essentially meant noncommunist, pro-capitalist, and preferably anticommunist. As demonstrated by friendly U.S. relations with authoritarian regimes in Spain, Iran, South Korea, South Africa, and elsewhere, it certainly did not mean democratic. The power of Truman's speech came from its combina-tion of limited policy proposals with a universalist framework for global policy justified in terms of traditional nationalist values and hatreds. Ideologically, the new doctrine explained the international situation in terms of a conventional morality of good versus evil, while also providing a seemingly clear guide for U.S. action in a troubled world. Politically, Truman asked for little — less than $400 million in aid to Greece and Turkey. In the long run, acceptance of the univer-sal doctrine would prove far more important, far more dangerous, and far more costly than that initial appropriation.

The effectiveness of the Truman Doctrine has been explained alternately in terms of its appeal to universal values or to nationalist values. My point, how-ever, is that it tapped into the existing fusion of universalist and nationalist values that already shaped much public discourse concerning America's role in the post-war world — the ideology of American nationalist globalism. It incorporated the principle of global anticommunism within this ideology along with the principles of national greatness and global responsibility in a manner that gave new mean-ing to both and new potency to the whole mixture. The Truman administration hardly created anticommunism. Rather, it attempted to harness the rising yet still largely latent forces of popular anticommunism behind its major foreign-policy objectives.[95] By redefining the nation's global responsibilities to mean the respon-sibility to prevent the expansion of communist power anywhere and everywhere, a move that much of the mass media had been clamoring for, President Truman completed the division of "One World" into two. Under the Truman Doctrine, the United States would be "the leader of the free world," but not the whole world.

5 DEFINING "FREE WORLD" LEADERSHIP

By the spring of 1947, the United States was "the No. 1 nation" in a world divided into hostile blocs. Resuscitating the wartime metaphor for the struggle against the Axis dictatorships, the United States called its side "the free world" and set about the business of leading the cause of "freedom" in the new global struggle. The cultural historian Daniel T. Rodgers has argued that freedom was the key word of the entire postwar era in American politics, the word for which the struggles of both the Cold War and the civil rights movement were waged. Building on Rodgers's insight, I want to argue that the idea of free-world leadership became the controlling metaphor in U.S. foreign-policy discourse throughout the postwar period. Most Americans have lived inside this metaphor for so long it may be difficult to recognize its metaphorical function. But the idea of "two worlds" is clearly a metaphor for a bipolar system of international politics, and the idea that the U.S.-dominated bloc constituted the realm of freedom is similarly a discursive construction. The Free World, in this view, was a metaphor, depending on one's viewpoint, for the capitalist world-system or the anticommunist bloc. Within this construction, freedom was indeed linked preeminently to freedom of enterprise and to private property rights. To illustrate the metaphorical rather than literal nature of the Free World idea, one has only to note the inclusion of apartheid South Africa, the Shah's Iran, and Chiang Kai-shek's China, among other dictatorships and autocracies, as valued members of this self-designated sphere of liberty.[1]

The notion that America's national purpose was "to lead the free world" emerged gradually between 1947 and 1950. From 1950 on, it became reified; the image of the United States as Leader of the Free World served as the central trope in U.S. foreign-policy discourse at least until the collapse of the Soviet Union in 1991. From the beginning of this period, however, the meaning of freedom was the focal point of considerable contention within U.S. public culture, even as the range of the foreign-policy debate narrowed. And domestic politics, including the politics of the labor and civil rights movements, were bounded by the terms of the Free World metaphor. Contrary to the popular slogan that "politics stops at the water's edge," domestic interests have long played a crucial role in U.S. foreign policy. What is less commonly noted is that foreign policy — or, more accurately, a nation's position in the international system — sets the parameters within which domestic political struggles take place. In the early postwar years, the politics of race and class were intimately bound up with the politics of foreign policy. The indisputable emergence of the United States as a hegemonic power set the context within which labor and civil rights leaders operated. African Americans and organized labor held subordinate positions in the U.S. political economy, and most observers tended to view them as narrow interest groups focused on domestic concerns. But in the 1940s each had strong international commitments as well, and each played a significant role in the public politics of foreign policy after the war. The meaning of freedom lay at the center of their efforts. Key elements of the African American community and the labor movement attempted to contest the meaning of free-world leadership and to appropriate it for their own ends. But those attempts must be understood in the context of the predominant interpretations espoused by the White House and the mass media.

In the official discourse of the Truman administration, and in much of the commercial mass media, freedom was equated with capitalism, and communism was deemed a new slavery. In 1947 and 1948, policymakers and opinion leaders gradually came to speak of "a democratic world" or "a free world" when discussing either the American-led bloc or the ultimate aim of U.S. leadership. The definite article was not yet regularly attached to these phrases. Only in 1949 and 1950, with the formation of NATO, the advent of Communist rule in China, the explosion of the first Soviet atom bomb, and the ever-rising pitch of U.S. anticommunism, did the notion of "*the* Free World" come into widespread usage as a proper noun. Only as the leader of a new military alliance, seemingly locked in mortal combat with Kremlin-controlled world communism, did the United States come to call itself "the leader of the free world." That "world" often featured anticommunist ideology and capitalist economics more than political liberty, but the U.S. government was primarily concerned, after all, with rebuilding a capitalist world economy ravaged by depression and war of unprecedented magnitude.

As the political historian Richard Freeland and others have argued, the Truman administration willingly exaggerated the Communist threat to gain public support for its primary international objectives and manipulated domestic anticommunism to undermine left-wing critics of its foreign policy. Yet Truman and his advisers believed Soviet power constituted a genuine threat to what the diplomatic historian Melvyn Leffler has termed the "preponderance of power" that the United States needed to maintain if it was to accomplish its global mission. They saw Russia as the fountainhead of a unified, worldwide anticapitalist movement that directly opposed their own plans for U.S.-led world economic expansion. In this view, widely shared by influential members of both the foreign-policy and media elites, Communist movements everywhere were deemed to be controlled by Moscow.[2]

The anticommunist mood unleashed by the Truman Doctrine and the administration's efforts to discredit its left-wing critics as Soviet stooges placed significant new limits on the possibilities of effective foreign-policy dissent. With the national purpose clearly defined by the image of global struggle against Soviet-controlled world Communism, openly anti-capitalist critics like W. E. B. Du Bois, Paul Robeson, or the left-wing leaders of the UE, and even pro-capitalist critics like Henry Wallace and many of his supporters, were all too easily painted red, their views dismissed on the basis of perceived disloyalty. Others accepted the rhetorical framework established by the Truman administration and sought to present their critiques within its constraints. On one level, these more moderate critics, most notably Walter White of the NAACP and Walter Reuther of the UAW, simply sought to keep a foot in the door, both with the administration and in the public foreign-policy debate. At the same time, they held anticommunist sentiments of their own, developed through years of political experience within their own movements.

To most African Americans in the late 1940s, the division between free and unfree, globally as well as domestically, still fell along the color line more than the Iron Curtain. Freedom meant racial equality and liberation from racial and economic oppression more than opposition to communism. Freedom from fear and freedom from want — the increasingly forgotten half of the Four Freedoms — still seemed more fundamental to many black Americans than did freedom of enterprise. Yet sharp disagreements arose among African American leaders over the linked questions of communism and U.S. foreign policy.

The labor movement tore itself apart over these same questions, dividing fiercely over the meaning of freedom and the nation's claims to free-world leadership. Within the UE, the right wing accepted the definition espoused by the government while the left wing continued to define freedom in terms of the full Four Freedoms, emphasizing freedom from want and freedom from fear. In the UAW, Walter Reuther largely supported Truman's foreign policy while still asserting the claims of freedom from fear and want along with more traditional political freedoms. In short, the discursive politics of leading the free world helped to shape the trajectories of both the civil rights and labor movements and, indeed, of U.S. public life generally, in the later 1940s.

THE TRUMAN DOCTRINE AND THE CIVIL RIGHTS MOVEMENT

Most African American commentators, from George Schuyler on the right to W. E. B. Du Bois on the left, responded critically to the Truman Doctrine. Both Schuyler and Du Bois bitterly satirized the administration's claims to be intervening on behalf of freedom and democracy, which in their view existed in Greece and Turkey no more than in Mississippi. *Pittsburgh Courier* executive editor P. L. Prattis called the United States "an aggressor Nation, sending its money and its force far beyond the confines of its true national interest." Prattis rejected isolationism, but he also rejected the notion that the United States possessed a special destiny to lead the world. "We should help where we are asked and are truly wanted," he wrote. "But we should not be deluded into believing that it is necessary for America to have armed bases all over the world and to rush into every country to prevent the spread of communism." Such meddling, he argued, would only provoke war. Other African American leaders shared Prattis's sentiments; Howard University president Mordecai Johnson even called the Truman Doctrine speech a declaration of war. These critics condemned Truman for tying the United States to a tottering British Empire weighed down with racist, imperialist baggage. Shortly after the speech, the State Department exacerbated African American antipathy to the Greek-Turkish aid program by rejecting Haiti's request for a modest $20 million loan. But African American criticism of the Truman Doctrine persisted well after its initial enunciation.[3]

NAACP executive secretary Walter White took a rather complicated stand on the Truman Doctrine, endorsing its ostensible goal of supporting democracy while criticizing its universalist logic, unilateral method, and reliance on military aid. White argued that a solution to the Mediterranean situation should have been sought first through the Big Four meeting underway in Moscow, second through the United Nations, and third through renewed U.S. funding for UNRRA, which would then have administered nonmilitary aid. This position was similar to the counterproposal advanced by the leading congressional dissidents, Claude Pepper and Glen Taylor. No doubt the administration was alarmed when the Gallup poll reported, just over two weeks after Truman's speech, that 63 percent of those surveyed thought "the problem of aid to Greece and Turkey should be turned over to the United Nations" — just as critics like Pepper, Taylor, and White urged. Yet the NAACP leader sought to position himself as a friendly critic rather than an opponent of the Truman administration's foreign policy. While claiming not to question Truman's goal, White noted that to embark on the path laid out by the Truman Doctrine the United States would set itself on a bitterly ironic course: "Having failed miserably to assure democratic elections in Mississippi and Georgia, we will have set out to assure them all over the world outside of the United States." White opposed unilateral U.S. military intervention, but by endorsing the ostensible goal of assuring democratic elections everywhere, he sought to increase the pressure toward assuring them in his native South.[4]

White muted his criticism of the Truman Doctrine for another, related reason as well: He wanted Truman to speak at a mass rally at the NAACP's annual conference that June. No U.S. president had ever before addressed the NAACP. A presidential speech would vastly expand the Association's audience at home and abroad, both through live radio broadcasts and subsequent press coverage. Its leaders saw this as a major opportunity to advance their cause.

In early April, White met with Truman at the White House and secured the president's tentative agreement to speak at the planned event at the Lincoln Memorial that June. At Truman's request, the NAACP executive secretary discussed the event in detail with David Niles, one of the president's most liberal aides. In an April 11 letter, White assured Truman that this would be a great event in the NAACP's history "and one in which your address will have not only nationwide but world-wide significance."[5]

Through Niles, the White House consulted with the NAACP concerning the tone and content of the president's speech. When Niles suggested that Truman speak to the Lincoln Memorial audience "as an American audience rather than a preponderantly Negro one," the Association's leadership responded enthusiastically. That manner of address would place the president's rhetoric in line with the NAACP's long-standing strategy of emphasizing that Negroes simply sought their full birthright as Americans. White suggested to Niles that the president emphasize the importance of "the so-called race question" internationally as well as nationally: "Every failure to live up to the highest ideals of democracy creates dangerous disunity at home at a period of the greatest peril our nation has ever known and at the same time damages tragically our influence abroad. Frank recognition of this would not only hearten those who battle for democracy at home but would also demonstrate to the peoples of the world who are being propagandized by America's enemies that the United States frankly recognizes its shortcomings but at the same time is working to correct them." White further suggested that Truman make this principle concrete by endorsing specific "remedial measures," some of which he had already expressed support for, including federal anti-lynching legislation, the establishment of the President's Committee on Civil Rights, abolition of the poll tax and the ending of disfranchisement, and the extending of federal assistance for education and health. "A strong, clear statement by the President at this critical juncture would be an historic event," White noted.[6]

Truman's decision to speak at the NAACP rally was part of a calculated effort to court the Negro vote, as several historians have argued; but the speech he actually delivered reflected the administration's concern with the international ramifications of "the so-called race question."[7] The NAACP's message had registered at the White House, a point the Association stressed in its publicity materials.[8] Since its founding, the NAACP's political strategy had been to underscore the discrepancy between America's professed creed of democracy and freedom for all and its actual record of racial injustice. In 1947, the Truman administration's rhetoric of world leadership in the name of freedom and democracy lent added power to that strategy. Walter White realized this acutely and sought to capitalize on the situation. The president's agreement to speak to the nation's largest civil rights organization just three months after enunciating the Truman Doctrine gave the Association an unparalleled opportunity to place its message at the center of the nation's public life.

As in the preceding years, the global nature of the color line was a major theme at the NAACP's 1947 Annual Conference, which culminated with Sunday's mass rally at the Lincoln Memorial. On a scorchingly hot summer day in Washington, the crowd of about 10,000 fell far short of the 75,000 who had gathered at the same site in 1939 to hear Marian Anderson sing, an event White helped to organize and which he hoped this gathering would surpass in size and significance. But the event gained extensive and prominent press coverage, and the featured speeches, by Eleanor Roosevelt and Senator Wayne Morse as well as Walter White and President Truman, were broadcast nationwide on all the major radio networks. The State Department recorded Truman's speech for broadcast overseas. If the size of the crowd disappointed the organizers, the president's message and the attention he attracted surely met or even surpassed their brightest hopes.[9]

In introducing Truman, White delivered essentially the same message he had espoused in his speech to the Association's 1946 annual conference but in far more moderate tones. Invoking a key phrase from the American rhetorical tradition as well as past struggles against slavery and fascism, White declared that the NAACP operated according to the proposition "that no nation can exist half-free, half-slave." To the foreign ambassadors whose presence the Association had sought for symbolic reasons, White said that U.S. democracy was imperfect, but that the present gathering showed that many Americans were determined "to make our nation truly a 'government of the people, by the people and for the people.' " He emphasized the importance the American struggle for racial equality held for "the two-thirds of the world's people whose skins are colored." In concluding his remarks right before introducing President Truman, White declared, "We welcome to this struggle, whose outcome will help to determine the future of mankind, every citizen who believes the Bill of Rights means what it says."[10]

To a remarkable extent, the president did indeed join the struggle by operating within its rhetorical framework, following the main theme that White had suggested to Niles. At the outset, Truman said the subject of his speech was "civil rights and human freedom." The nation stood at a turning point in its long-standing efforts "to guarantee freedom and equality" to all citizens, the president declared, pairing the key word of his own foreign policy discourse with the word

African Americans most generally paired it with as well. "Recent events in the United States and abroad have made us realize that it is more important today than ever before to insure that all Americans enjoy these rights," he continued, emphasizing that when he said *all* Americans he meant *all* Americans but never singling out Negroes as a special group. The postwar period brought new urgency to the need to remedy the evils of racial intolerance and prejudice, Truman said, sounding a recurrent refrain of postwar civil rights rhetoric:

> The aftermath of war and the desire to keep faith with our nation's historic principles makes the need a pressing one.
>
> The support of desperate populations of battle-ravaged countries must be won for this free way of life. We must have them as allies in our continuing struggle for the peaceful solution of the world's problems. Freedom is not an easy lesson to teach, nor an easy cause to sell, to peoples beset by every kind of privation. They may surrender to the false security offered so temptingly by totalitarian regimes unless we can prove the superiority of democracy.

To advance the strongest possible case for democracy, the president argued, echoing any number of speakers at NAACP meetings before him, the United States would have to show the world "that we have been able to put our own house in order." Because of these international pressures, Truman asserted, the federal government now had to take the lead in extending and defending the civil rights of all Americans. While the speech advanced no specific policies toward that end, no U.S. president had ever before made such a pledge. The head of state had publicly accepted the principal claim of the emerging postwar civil rights movement: if it was to lead the free world, the United States would have to ensure the freedom of its own citizens.[11]

In his thorough study of Truman's presidency, the journalist and historian Robert J. Donovan suggests that with this speech civil rights emerged as "suddenly a factor in the cold war" for President Truman. My point here is that this emergence was hardly as sudden as Donovan and other observers have believed. The linkage between civil rights and the cold war emerged neither out of thin air nor out of purely electoral considerations. It was largely the result of the consistent and penetrating rhetorical pressure that the civil rights movement brought to bear, in the courts of both world opinion and domestic opinion, on a glaringly weak point in the administration's international posture. And it was a central aspect of the struggle over the meaning of freedom, which lay at the heart of U.S. public culture in the 1940s.[12]

The NAACP's national leadership viewed Truman's Lincoln Memorial speech as a major triumph. When ABC radio commentator Martin Agronsky suggested that Truman's "fine sounding phrases" might be merely "a political gesture," White disagreed vigorously. While he had often had differences with Truman, White wrote Agronsky, he found the Lincoln Memorial speech to be "by far the most forthright any American President has ever made on this subject. And the frank admission that there are woeful wrongs in this country and that we must do something about them, now and not at some future date, means more, I believe, than a political gesture." The July issue of the *Crisis,* the NAACP's official publication, ran "Truman's Address" on its editorial page — in lieu of any other editorial comment. In August, the journal's lead editorial hailed the speech as "the most comprehensive and forthright statement on the rights of minorities in a democracy, and on the duty of the government to secure and safeguard them that has ever been made by a President of the United States."[13] Friends and colleagues, including NAACP assistant secretary Roy Wilkins and Essie Robeson, Paul Robeson's wife, thought the event was one of the great moments of White's career and of the civil rights movement.[14]

Newspapers across the country covered the event on their front pages, and newsreels replayed it in the nation's movie theaters. The press generally emphasized the connection between civil rights and foreign policy that formed the hub of the president's message. Many papers featured photographs of Truman speaking from the steps of the Lincoln Memorial to the throng of both black and white Americans below. Editorial pages nationwide echoed the NAACP's central postwar themes, which the president had essentially expressed as his own and broadcast to the world. A *Detroit Free Press* editorial praising Truman's speech was illustrated with a cartoon of Uncle Sam standing with his back to a mirror, captioned " — As the World Sees Us." Facing forward, Uncle Sam looked clean and sharp, but the back of his jacket, reflected in the mirror, was in tatters, covered up with patches labeled "abuse of minorities," "race bias," and "hate." As the editors of the Catholic weekly *America,* put it: "American democracy, as Mr. Truman made clear, is on trial before the world. We are holding out our way of life as the world's best hope." Therefore, as the president said, we must " 'put our own house in order.' "[15]

Truman's mail concerning the speech was overwhelmingly favorable, but the NAACP had hardly moved to the top of his agenda. When White wrote the president about the enthusiastic response to his Lincoln Memorial speech, Truman simply passed it on to David Niles, asking him to acknowledge it. On an earlier note from White, Truman had written, "I don't care for this white negro and I am always doubtful of anything he says." Despite this personal distaste, however, the president had to respond to the political pressures that White represented.[16]

Having secured the president's rhetorical commitment, the NAACP's relationship to the Truman administration proceeded along two quite different fronts through the rest of 1947 and into early 1948. Like most of the African American community, the Association awaited the report of the President's Committee on Civil Rights and hoped it would mark a significant step toward fulfilling the promise of Truman's Lincoln Memorial address. At the same time, it prepared a petition to the United Nations Human Rights Commission protesting the violation of the human rights of African Americans within the United States.

As the NAACP's director of special research, charged primarily with international affairs, W. E. B. Du Bois had proposed the idea of petitioning the United Nations in August 1946. Inspired by the model of the brief petition submitted to the UN that June by the left-wing National Negro Congress, Du Bois believed the NAACP should put its prestige behind a more expansive and thoroughly documented statement of grievances to the world organization on behalf of Americans of African descent.[17] In September, the Association's board of directors gave him a green light and a budget for the project. Du Bois and his colleagues completed the petition in January 1947, and from January to October, the Association sought unsuccessfully to have it placed before the UN General Assembly, but without making the document public. On October 11, the NAACP finally released copies to the press, under the title "An Appeal to the World." Thanks largely to U.S. government efforts to block it, the UN never took action concerning the petition, but the U.S. press generally gave it favorable coverage, particularly concerning its central thrust, which pointed to the gap between noble ideals professed abroad and harsh realities lived at home. In this manner, the petition succeeded in placing added pressure on the Truman administration to act on the president's expressed commitment to civil rights for all Americans.[18]

"An Appeal to the World" was not uniformly well received in the United States. Some white southerners criticized the NAACP and its leadership for giving ammunition to the Soviet Union in the worldwide ideological struggle. Within the African American community, the cantankerous and increasingly conservative George Schuyler attacked the petition as proof that the NAACP had become a Communist-front group. In a February 28, 1948, *Pittsburgh Courier* column, as war hysteria began to percolate in the United States over the Communist takeover in Czechoslovakia, Schuyler wrote that the relatively favorable views that certain Negro intellectuals held of the Soviet Union, combined with their criticism of the United States "at a time when the U.S. and the U.S.S.R. are on the verge of open warfare," only raised questions about the loyalty of Negro citizens.[19]

In what seems more than a coincidence, the President's Committee on Civil

Rights released its report, "To Secure These Rights," six days after the NAACP released its petition. In December 1947, the *Crisis* published a condensed version of the petition and an editorial praising the Committee's work.[20] Supporting the report as "a good start" while pressing grievances before the world provided the NAACP with a double-edged sword, which allowed it to encourage the administration's initial steps while dramatizing the gravity of the problems to be overcome and threatening to weaken the main thrust of the administration's foreign policy. The report's rhetoric, like Truman's earlier civil rights speech, fit well with the NAACP's basic strategy of invoking the conscience of the nation within the moral framework established by the Declaration of Independence and the Gettysburg Address, as well as the legal framework of the Constitution. The report spoke the same Myrdalian language as the NAACP leadership, emphasizing both the moral imperative of the American Creed and the diplomatic imperative of world leadership.[21] As P. B. Young Sr., editor and publisher of the *Norfolk (Va.) Journal and Guide*, put it, "the declarations of the committee are in truth but a *reaffirmation of faith* in all of those things we call 'the American way' of life." In Young's words: "If this country now rejects and repudiates such a reaffirmation of faith in democratic living, after fighting two wars in one generation to preserve and spread democracy, it will make itself morally defenseless against the criticism and propaganda of other nations and peoples, thus weakening its useful influence in the world at a time when that influence is critically needed if the world, and itself, are not to be engulfed by chaos." For Young, and for the NAACP leadership, the key issue in "To Secure These Rights" was the same issue raised by "An Appeal to the World."[22] An influential segment of African American opinion was coming to accept the professed foreign-policy goals of the Truman administration and then using them as leverage to advance domestic civil rights reforms. W. E. B. Du Bois, the primary architect of the NAACP's UN petition, however, did not subscribe to that segment of opinion.

In September 1948, two months before the first postwar, post-Roosevelt presidential election, the NAACP board dismissed Du Bois as director of special research, and Du Bois charged White with linking the Association to Truman's foreign policy.[23] The seemingly abrupt and unceremonious dismissal of the most eminent living African American intellectual caused an uproar within the black community. Many Americans, white as well as black, interpreted the firing as evidence that the nation's red-baiting epidemic had infected the NAACP as a result of its erstwhile dalliance with the Truman administration. Paul Robeson, Henry Wallace, and Du Bois himself all expressed this view.[24]

Du Bois's dismissal stemmed from several difficulties between Du Bois and White, including differences over relations with the Truman administration and the press and acrimonious personal relations between the two men. Their final falling out was sparked by their conflicting positions on Henry Wallace's campaign in the 1948 presidential election. Du Bois publicly supported Wallace while White, despite his high regard for Wallace, opposed him on the ground that a third-party candidacy was doomed and would only serve to elect a reactionary Republican. Du Bois's vehement opposition to White's strategy concerning Truman's foreign policy and the 1948 election transformed a tenuous relationship into an unworkable one. But the immediate cause for his dismissal was his criticism of White for agreeing to serve as a consultant to the U.S. delegation to the UN General Assembly meeting in Paris. Ironically, Du Bois and White had served together as consultants to the U.S. delegation at the UN's founding conference in San Francisco in 1945; but much had changed since 1945. In a September 7, 1948, memorandum to White and the NAACP board, Du Bois charged White with tying the Association to "the reactionary, war-mongering colonial imperialism of the recent administration." The press somehow got hold of the memo before the board could discuss it. The board concluded that Du Bois had been insubordinate, first in refusing to cooperate with White in preparing for the Paris meeting, then in making the internal dispute public. Du Bois denied responsibility for the leak.[25]

The split between White and Du Bois signaled White's efforts to position the NAACP within the emerging currents of "vital center" liberalism, and to anchor its claims ever more firmly in the rhetoric of American nationalism, which further served to protect the movement from charges of disloyalty.[26] As part of these efforts, White would continue to profess acceptance of the administration's stated foreign-policy goals, presenting often penetrating critiques and fundamental alternatives as though they were merely tactical matters. This approach allowed the Association to be heard within the mainstream of public discourse, and it afforded considerable leverage for the movement's domestic agenda. Yet, as several scholars have argued, it watered down the anticolonial, anti-imperialist thrust of the African American critique of U.S. foreign policy. But contrary to Du Bois's claims, which seem to have influenced some of the subsequent scholarship on this question, the Association never wholly endorsed cold war diplomacy in this period.[27]

FOREIGN AID AND RACIAL INJUSTICE: FROM THE MARSHALL PLAN TO "POINT FOUR"

From the moment it was proposed in June 1947, the Marshall Plan, or European Recovery Program, was widely hailed by the mainstream media, organized labor, and white liberals as precisely the kind of clear, forward-looking foreign policy that the American public could both understand and support. After three years of crisis and emergency relief, here at last was a coherent proposal for economic reconstruction. Many Americans who criticized the Truman Doctrine as negative and militaristic welcomed the Marshall Plan as a positive, peaceful alternative. The two initiatives were part of a single, overarching foreign policy ("two halves of the same walnut," Truman said), but few Americans saw them as such at the time.

The African American press, however, voiced skepticism about the Marshall Plan. In September 1947, for example, one *Pittsburgh Courier* article said that the Marshall Plan could not assure a democratic Europe because U.S. racial practices had made Europeans leery of American-style democracy. In July 1948, another *Courier* article emphasized the apparent contradiction between the U.S. government's strong efforts to rebuild the economies of Western Europe and its neglect of "economic slums" in the United States.[28] By 1949, several African American columnists argued that the Marshall Plan's results were the opposite of its supposed aims.

Pittsburgh Courier executive editor and columnist P. L. Prattis criticized the Marshall Plan repeatedly, employing a spate of arguments against it. In February 1948, as Congress debated the plan, Prattis argued that Truman's recent civil rights pronouncement showed that the president and some of his advisers knew that "greater democracy at home" was at least as important to the effort to contain communism "as the spending of seventeen billion dollars in Europe." That July, Prattis wrote a column suggesting that the Marshall Plan was merely a scheme to create markets for U.S. corporations, using a speech by Senator Glen Taylor, Henry Wallace's vice presidential running mate and a leading foreign-policy dissident, as his main source. Following this line of reasoning in a July 1949 column, Prattis argued that the erstwhile European Recovery Program had precipitated Britain's economic decline by making it financially dependent upon the United States. Yet by March 1950 he asserted that the Marshall Plan undermined U.S. economic interests by building up ungrateful economic competitors who turned around and took customers away from U.S. business.[29]

The gravest concern African Americans expressed about the Marshall Plan was that it might serve to perpetuate European colonialism and imperialism (two words that African American commentators used more or less interchangeably).[30] Both George Schuyler and Horace Cayton, for example, attacked Marshall Plan financing of French imperialism and military suppression of liberation struggles in Indochina. The *Crisis* first mentioned the Marshall Plan in a piece on the British colonies and their importance as a source of raw materials for the United States. When Secretary of State George Marshall unveiled the new program in his much-

heralded commencement address at Harvard, the *Pittsburgh Courier* editorialized that economic aid to Europe might simply enable European powers to perpetuate their overseas empires:

> Since the United States must put up the money, enemies of imperialism in
> this country must insist that along with these loans there must be assurance of
> social and economic democracy in the colonies.
>
> If this is not done, the United States will be in the unenviable position of
> financing imperialism, and thus negating all of the high principles which its
> spokesmen are forever propounding.[31]

The NAACP took a more ambiguous position, endorsing the Marshall Plan but
with caveats and proposed amendments. Testifying before the Senate Foreign Relations Committee in February 1948, Walter White said the NAACP supported U.S.
aid to Europe but also urged assistance to all peoples in need, particularly to those
of Africa, Asia, and the Caribbean. White argued that the United States should use
the European Recovery Program as a lever toward ending colonialism by requiring all beneficiaries to assist less fortunate nations and grant self-determination
to their colonies. A resolution adopted at the NAACP's 1949 annual conference
took essentially the same position. In effect, the Association attempted to use its
endorsement of the Marshall Plan to advance its anti-imperialist agenda.[32]

In December 1948 and January 1949, the Dutch attack on the newly independent Republic of Indonesia reinvigorated African American criticism of the
Marshall Plan. To the NAACP leadership, the Indonesian case provided an important test of U.S. intentions toward the nonwhite world. In a December 23 press
release, the NAACP reported that White had telegraphed Marshall Plan director Paul Hoffman urging the immediate withdrawal of all Marshall Plan aid to
the Netherlands "in the interest of humanity and the extension of democratic
ideals" throughout Asia. "This desperate attempt of The Netherlands government," White argued, "cannot be sustained without American aid." When informed that funds destined for use in Indonesia had been suspended, the NAACP
declared that this move failed to meet its demands. Even if no Marshall Plan
monies were used directly in the Indonesian invasion, White argued in a second
telegram to Hoffman, as the NAACP reported in a December 30 press release, "such
funds made available to the Netherlands government enable that government to
release other funds to carry on the war against the Indonesian people."[33] In a *Chicago Defender* column, White cast the matter in a cold war context but concluded
that colonialism, not communism, posed the most egregious problem: "For if
the Dutch are not stopped in their insane course, revolt which will play directly
into the hands of Russia, will sweep throughout Asia, Africa and other parts of

the world where men are robbed for the benefit of absentee landlords in Europe and other places. This is an even larger issue than 'containing Communism.' It is one of stopping greed based on racial arrogance." The *Crisis* framed the question still more starkly in a January 1949 editorial: "The eyes of all Asia are upon the Indonesian situation. Does the Western world mean what it says it means about self-determination, independence, freedom?"[34]

In the *Pittsburgh Courier,* writers ranging from the conservative George Schuyler to the progressive Horace Cayton criticized Marshall Plan funding of the Dutch move to reconquer Indonesia. Cayton's position roughly paralleled White's. He supported the Marshall Plan "if it is used for its avowed purpose, the bolstering of the democratic force of the world," but not if it financed the brutal suppression of colonial peoples. Cayton concluded that not even the communist bogey could change his mind. Bolstering the world's democratic forces required ending colonialism more than containing communism. To Cayton and other African American observers, the idea that European imperial powers were the core of "the free world" was clearly a sham, however democratic they might be at home. In his column the following week, Cayton wrote that despite advance warning of the Dutch invasion, "our military men, being imperialists at heart themselves, winked at the whole affair." By June 1950, Cayton argued that the Marshall Plan was propping up European colonialism beyond its natural life span.[35]

In his January 1949 inaugural address, President Truman called for "a bold new program" of economic and technical assistance to the non-European world. This idea seemed designed in part to meet such criticisms of the Marshall Plan as African Americans had raised.[36] Yet "Point Four," as the program was known, received mixed reviews in the African American community. In its editorial commenting on Truman's inaugural address, the *Pittsburgh Courier* interpreted Point Four solely as a sign of "the intensification of the so-called cold war" which required "a continuation of peace-time gifts of our natural resources to numerous nations outside the Soviet orbit." Rather than praising the idea of aid to non-European peoples, the *Courier* emphasized that "the President's world program" meant military assistance to Western Europe. Some writers saw racism at work in the Point Four proposal. George Schuyler, for example, initially interpreted Truman's inaugural address as auguring the president's intention "to save everybody in the world . . .—except the Africans," probably because he simply could not believe Africa would be included. Despite his own, often vituperative anti-communism, he remained an iconoclastic critic of American globalism. Later in the year, however, Schuyler charged that congressional opposition to Point Four was racially motivated. "Billions for Europe is okeh," he wrote fliply, "but nothing must be spent on the Caribbean, South America, Asia and Africa, else dark people might get a break." In May 1950, *Courier* correspondent Trezzvant W. Anderson commented that "colored peoples are going slow on biting what's on this 'Point Four' hook. They want to know more about what Unc has on his mind before going along with the program."[37]

At the NAACP's annual conference in July 1949, Rayford Logan, professor of history at Howard University and the Association's top foreign-affairs consultant following Du Bois's dismissal, encouraged NAACP members to "help to push through an effective Point IV." Logan's comments on Point Four provide a useful example of how African American leaders attempted to advance an African American foreign-policy agenda within the parameters established by the Truman administration. Logan scoffed at Truman's request to Congress for $45 million in aid to the nonwhite world. As Logan put it, those who initially hoped that the president's "bold new program" would be "a large scale undertaking for the backward areas comparable to the billions being spent under the Marshall Plan for Western Europe now see Point IV in its proper perspective." The "bold new program" called for less than one-twentieth of a billion for all of Africa, Asia, and Latin America. Worse still, the journalistic "spokesmen for Big Business" were already attacking the proposal, suggesting that giving any aid to the "backward" regions was like throwing money down a sewer. Paraphrasing a famous line from American diplomatic history, Logan wrote that the corporate-controlled media had proclaimed that the United States should spend "billions for Western Europe, but not one cent for Africa and other underdeveloped areas." Logan offered his own keen explication of a derogatory cartoon in the *Saturday Evening Post* which "caricatures the 'underdeveloped areas' as a flat-footed, big-mouthed, bread-nosed imbecile with rings in his ears and arms reaching below his knees. The imbecile is also baldheaded. Uncle Sam is holding a bottle in his hand labeled 'Bold New Plan' Hair Tonic. The cartoonist, in order to make crystal clear his meaning, explains: 'Could be he can't use the stuff.'"

Logan urged NAACP supporters to advocate several basic principles to amend Truman's proposal. Aid workers and technical advisers should have "the proper attitude toward the peoples with whom they are going to work" and should be chosen on a nondiscriminatory basis; labor should be accorded the same protection as capital; U.S. labor unions should assume responsibility for developing labor unions in the recipient areas; and the recipient peoples should be afforded avenues for participating effectively in developing and carrying out the program, probably through associate membership in the United Nations and the appropriate UN agencies. In other words, the aid should be administered through the United Nations rather than unilaterally by the United States. Logan hoped these ideas could be advanced through testimony before the Senate Foreign Relations and House Foreign Affairs Committees, and through the NAACP's regular participation in State Department foreign-policy discussion groups for voluntary associations.[38]

The NAACP continued to lobby for such reforms after the Point Four program was in place. In 1952, the Association proposed amendments to the House Foreign Affairs Committee that would extend aid directly to dependent areas rather than through the controlling European powers. The NAACP's rhetoric remained staunchly anticolonial and antimilitarist, critical of NATO as well as colonialism. As an Association press release quoted Walter White,

> most areas under the rule of major powers can receive assistance from the United States only in connection with plans for defense of the North Atlantic Area.
>
> This means that the colonial people in Africa and Asia come in solely as fifth wheels to the European war machine.
>
> The colonial people of the world are determined to have freedom and they may become the enemies of anyone who even appears to stand between them and liberty.

The Association's Point Four amendments, White said, "would help to show clearly that the United States does not intend to have its foreign aid program used to support the colonial system."[39]

FREEDOM AT HOME, FREEDOM ABROAD

Government efforts to hold up American democracy as a model for the world received constant critical scrutiny in the African American community. In April 1947, for example, the *Crisis* lambasted Secretary of State George Marshall, and James Byrnes before him, for trying to define democracy for the world while the United States continued to deny democracy to Negroes at home. That both men were white Southerners served to highlight the contradiction. To the NAACP, the way to resolve this dilemma was to fulfill the ideals, not to stop preaching them; official foreign-policy rhetoric provided leverage for civil rights claims.[40]

By contesting rather than rejecting the official rhetoric of world leadership in the name of peace, democracy, and freedom, African Americans gained a strengthened position from which to advance the cause of racial justice within U.S. public life. As one speaker at the NAACP's 1948 annual conference argued, the United States could "lead the world to a new era of peace and prosperity and freedom," but only "if we can make democracy work fully and effectively right here in America." That same year the NAACP adopted a Declaration of Principles, which called the civil rights movement "our great crusade for the redemption of democracy." America could lead the world toward freedom, but only if the NAACP first redeemed the soul of America. This redemption motif, concerning American democracy and the new, worldwide significance of U.S. racism, was also employed both explicitly and implicitly in the African American press and by activists like Bayard Rustin not associated with the NAACP. In the 1960s, the Reverend Martin Luther King Jr. would use the theme of national redemption more potently than any of his predecessors. But he built upon the rhetorical tradition of the NAACP. In an article on Congress's failure to adopt strong anti-lynching legislation, *Pittsburgh Courier* staff writer Trezzvant Anderson argued that "only the passage of firm anti-lynching laws can put this Nation in a position to redeem itself in the eyes of the world." For Anderson and other black journalists, hypocrisy served as a key word linked to the concept of American democracy.[41]

The gap between foreign-policy preachments and domestic social realities received perhaps its most ironic dramatization in January 1949 at the hands of Eva Peron, the wife of Argentine dictator Juan Peron, in a story well told by *Pittsburgh Courier* columnist Horace Cayton. Instead of begging for U.S. dollars, like Madame Chiang Kai-shek or the British and Dutch Empires, Mrs. Peron donated clothing for 600 poor children in Washington, D.C. "We could play God for the rest of the world," Cayton wryly observed, "but could not clothe our poor children" in the would-be capital of the free world. Although Peron had embarrassed the State Department "in the cold war of nerves" with Russia, Cayton implied that she may have done the United States a favor by helping to air "the evils of our maladjusted economic system and lack of civil rights." He even suggested that the next time she wanted publicity the dictator's wife should send a check to the NAACP.[42]

As the Cold War intensified, the African American press scrutinized the underrepresentation of blacks in the U.S. diplomatic corps. Eliminating the color barrier in the State Department, as elsewhere, wrote Horace Cayton, was necessary "to save America and the world for democracy." In the spring of 1950, when Secretary of State Dean Acheson declared the need for "total diplomacy" in the world struggle with the Soviet Union, Rayford Logan retorted that " 'total diplomacy' requires total democracy in the United States," including equality of opportunity within the State Department.[43]

Within this context, the nation's most prominent African American diplomat, Ralph Bunche, became the focus of extensive attention. Tellingly, Bunche worked for the United Nations by the late 1940s, not the United States. He achieved international renown for mediating the Arab-Israeli settlement talks in 1949, receiving the Nobel Peace Prize the following year. In 1949 and 1950, the *Courier* campaigned for Bunche's appointment as U.S. ambassador to the Soviet Union. Placing a black American in such a high-profile Cold War post would be a powerful way of preaching what former secretary of state Marshall called the "gospel of freedom." This "crusade" gained support outside the African American community, most notably from *Collier's* magazine, but the appointment never materialized. Bunche spent the rest of his life working for the UN Trusteeship Division, toward the end of dismantling colonialism.[44] Bunche saw colonialism as the antithesis of freedom. In accepting the NAACP's Spingarn Award in 1949, Bunche invoked Lincoln's words when he asserted that "the world cannot exist half colonial and half free."[45] Like other African American observers, Bunche appropriated the metaphor that defined the Cold War and used it to assert that the color line, not the Iron Curtain, remained the locus of the worldwide struggle for freedom.[46]

As it sought to maintain an effective working relationship with the Truman administration, the NAACP's anticolonialist voice was muted to fit the Cold War context, but it was not silenced.[47] For example, the Association never explicitly opposed the North Atlantic Treaty Organization but never endorsed it either. Restoring Europe's economic stability and military security was unobjectionable, but restoring Europe's colonies was unacceptable. Walter White argued that the Atlantic Pact should include guarantees that "Western Europe will not be economically restored and militarily armed at the expense of colonial peoples of Asia, Africa and other parts of the world."[48] In March 1949, the NAACP urged that the treaty be amended to preclude NATO's use against colonial liberation movements. In 1949 the Association was especially concerned with Italy's efforts to regain control of its African colonies, efforts that were settled by the UN General Assembly that November. The UN settlement provided for Libyan independence by 1952, an investigatory commission on Eritrea, and a UN trusteeship for Somaliland (as Somalia was then called) under Italian administration. The NAACP was not fully satisfied, particularly because of the role the UN allowed Italy in Somalia, but still saw the settlement as "a partial victory" for its program.[49] If it had opposed the pact explicitly, or if it had rejected any consultative relationship with the U.S. government, the NAACP would have been locked out of the prevailing discourse and could have made no effective anticolonial demands at all.

"FREEDOM" AND FOREIGN POLICY IN THE LABOR MOVEMENT

Like the civil rights movement, social democratic and left-wing segments of organized labor attempted to use the main themes of postwar foreign-policy discourse as a fulcrum to advance both their domestic agendas and their own international concerns. But this strategy was less effective for the labor movement, partly because it was far more divided, largely because racial inequality, rather than class conflict, emerged as the most acute dilemma in American public life in the emerging Cold War context. For many union members and leaders, moreover, as for many African Americans, foreign-policy issues were closely linked to sentiments of patriotism and national loyalty.

In 1946 and early 1947 the more conservative and fiercely anticommunist AFL was already bound up with the Truman administration's overseas efforts, while the CIO seemed to many a bastion of foreign-policy dissent, but that would soon change. These developments in labor's foreign-policy discourse are well illustrated in the cases of the United Electrical Workers and the United Automobile Workers. By 1949, the UE and other left-wing, Communist-linked unions were expelled from the CIO, largely over foreign-policy issues; if its dissenting voice was not altogether silenced, it was in effect left howling in the desert. The UAW, meanwhile, had come to endorse most of the Truman administration's foreign-policy initiatives.

In 1947, the Truman Administration moved against Marshall Plan opponents in the CIO's left wing, and the CIO's leadership moved to keep in step with the administration. CIO president Philip Murray invited Secretary of State George Marshall to speak for the plan at the organization's 1947 convention. But administration opponents, including Communists, still had the strength to block full CIO endorsement of the Marshall Plan. Instead, the convention adopted a compromise resolution that supported the program's basic ideas without specifically endorsing it. The compromise could not hold, however, and the CIO subsequently underwent a protracted struggle that led to a purge of Communist Party activists and left-wing unions by 1948 and 1949. The 1948 CIO convention not only endorsed the Marshall Plan explicitly but also attacked its critics. That convention similarly pledged support for the United Nations while condemning the perceived Soviet abuse of its Security Council veto power. The CIO purge was partly motivated by the leadership's desire both to enhance labor's legitimacy in the eyes of the U.S. public and to curry favor with the Truman administration. Like their NAACP counterparts, the national CIO leadership believed that its cause required a friendly federal government. Along with the Truman administration's internal security program and the mounting anticommunist mood in the country, the CIO's move contributed to the growing tendency to equate foreign-policy dissent with fundamental disloyalty to the nation and its values. Since the CIO had previously seemed like the strongest organizational base for foreign-policy dissent, its entry into the emerging Cold War consensus was doubly significant. Yet given CIO president Phil Murray's long-standing anticommunism, his abiding patriotism, and his belief that labor's position in the United States was extremely vulnerable and dependent on federal government support, this development was not surprising.[50]

As two of the largest and most progressive unions in the country, the UE and the UAW stood at the center of these developments, but the controversies played out very differently in the two organizations. The anticommunist Walter Reuther had captured the UAW presidency in 1946 and secured control of its executive board the following year, while the UE leadership remained, at the very least, sympathetic to party activists and opposed to anticommunism of any kind. Under Reuther the UAW accepted the main direction of U.S. foreign policy between 1947 and 1949 and kept internal dissent over international matters to a minimum.[51] The UE, by contrast, grew increasingly divided over political matters, particularly concerning the Marshall Plan, Henry Wallace's 1948 presidential campaign, and the increasingly ubiquitous questions of Communism and the Soviet Union. UE president Albert Fitzgerald and his left-wing colleagues in the union's national headquarters opposed the Marshall Plan, supported Wallace, fought red-baiting, and continued to advocate U.S.-Soviet cooperation. Former UE president James Carey led the so-called "right-wing" opposition that supported the Marshall Plan, attacked Wallace, condemned all traces of Communist influence as un-American, and endorsed the Truman administration's policies for containing Soviet influence. By 1949 the UE split in two, with Carey as the head of the new, CIO-sponsored International United Electrical Workers (IUE). Not surprisingly, the Truman administration worked against the UE leadership and supported the formation of Carey's dual union.[52]

The political cultures of the UE and the UAW differed in many significant ways, reflecting larger divisions within the labor movement and the American left.[53] Reuther's UAW pursued a strategy of vital center liberalism, albeit of a markedly social democratic cast. Reuther sought, in many ways, to act as the left wing of the vital center, contradictory as that may seem. The underlying belief was that to be politically effective you had to fit your ideas within the spectrum of acceptable debate.[54] The UE leadership eschewed such strategies of moderation and refused to surrender to the swelling anti-Communist tide. Although the UE never actually endorsed the Progressive Party in 1948, it supported the party's right to participate in that year's presidential campaign, and UE president Fitzgerald chaired its first national convention, which nominated Henry Wallace. As early as late 1947, by contrast, Reuther called Wallace "a lost soul."[55] The foreign-policy differences between the two unions were even evident in the invocations given at their national conventions. At the UE's 1948 convention, Rabbi Louis Newman sought divine blessings on the United States "in consonance with the patriot's words: 'My country, if right to be kept right; my country, if wrong, to be set right.'" At the UAW's 1947 convention, the Rev. George G. Higgins gave no indication that the nation might need to be set right in international matters. Instead, he asked divine blessings for the president, the cabinet, and Congress in their efforts "to carry out wisely and intelligently the enormous responsibilities which, in Your Divine Providence, have been placed upon their shoulders at this critical moment in the history of our beloved country and in the history of the world" and for "the efforts of our nation toward the establishment of a just and lasting peace" and in the cause of human freedom.[56] As in the official justifications for the new containment doctrine, the myth of providential destiny framed the discussion.

HENRY WALLACE, THE MARSHALL PLAN, AND THE PURGING OF THE UE

Nineteen-hundred forty-seven was a pivotal year in the histories of U.S. foreign policy and the American labor movement. Symbolizing the growing division within organized labor, Secretary of State George Marshall delivered the featured speech at the 1947 CIO convention, while Henry Wallace delivered the keynote address at the UE's convention that year. Though he had been a featured speaker himself at the past two UE conventions, CIO president Murray did not even attend the Electrical Workers 1947 gathering. Murray thought well enough of Wallace, but like many liberals he opposed the idea of a third-party presidential campaign in 1948 on the grounds that it would only insure a Republican victory. Wallace had not yet declared his candidacy, but Murray wanted to discourage it. He was already leading the CIO in a direction at odds with Wallace's foreign-policy views, particularly concerning the Marshall Plan, which became a sort of litmus test of labor's loyalty.[57]

Wallace's speech emphasized foreign affairs, and most UE delegates responded enthusiastically, with intermittent applause, cheers, and two standing ovations. As in 1946, Wallace asserted that the United States and the Soviet Union could exist together in a single, peaceful world; those who denied this view were criminally "preaching the inevitability of war." He attacked Truman for putting U.S. foreign policy in the hands of Wall Street and the military and for exploiting international issues to obfuscate domestic problems like inflation. The Truman Doctrine, Wallace charged, "calls for guns to arm undemocratic governments and for food only for the countries opposed to the Soviet Union." Wallace called instead for a foreign policy that would "hold out the hand of friendship to the distressed people all over the world" with no such strings attached. Truman's militaristic, interventionist foreign policy was already causing inflation and unstable production, he asserted, and would eventually cause unemployment and war if not stopped. "You cannot separate foreign and domestic issues," Wallace declared to the delegates' applause, adding that "though there are attempts to divide it in two, this is truly One World." Nonetheless, Wallace's campaign, which garnered only about one million votes in November 1948, would mark that slogan's death knell.[58]

Like Wallace, the UE's majority-report foreign-policy resolution that year set the debate in populist terms, as a struggle between the interests of Wall Street and the common people. It implied that the Marshall Plan merely advanced U.S. financial interests while rejecting the claim that the Truman administration sought to promote freedom abroad. A dissenting minority-report proposal, by contrast, accepted the claims of U.S. world leadership toward "the extension of economic and political democracy." The minority report supported the general contours of Truman's foreign policy, particularly concerning economic aid. But it also urged express refusal to condone antidemocratic governments of the right as well as the left, and called for labor representation in the administration of overseas aid programs.[59] Whereas the majority report appealed to a sense of international working-class solidarity, the minority report appealed to patriotism. Opponents of the majority resolution sought to frame the debate in nationalist rather than populist terms, most notably by raising the question of Communist Party influence within the UE. Its proponents responded by accusing their critics of red-baiting. Clearly, the divisions within the UE were well established before this debate, and the Communist Party held considerable influence within the union's left wing. Yet the floor debates reflected serious disagreements over international affairs.

The left's strongest argument lay in the idea that foreign and domestic policies were "two sides of the same coin." Delegate William Sheehan of Local 1154 framed this position well in a rhetorical question: "Can you expect the guy that tried to chisel you, to speed you up, to break your labor unions, that throws your representatives in jail because they help out on a strike—can you expect that those same people . . . are going to carry on a foreign policy which is for the benefit of the common people throughout the world?" Of course not, Sheehan answered. Wall Street interests merely sought to whip up war hysteria to take people's minds off domestic problems, and to exploit workers abroad just as they did at home. "If we want to go back to peace and security," Sheehan argued, "we are going to have to do the political action job, to see that our representatives . . . are going to carry out a decent domestic policy." Only then would the United States have a decent foreign policy as well.[60]

In response, the anticommunist minority argued that the majority resolution sounded like a brief for the Soviet Union while simply obscuring the ideological conflict between the United States and the Soviet Union. To Delegate Drohan of Local 1102, the majority report seemed to imply that the world's problems could be resolved "by calling the Red Army over here to deliver us from the hold we are in from this Wall Street crowd." Instead, Drohan argued, the UE was in a position to help direct the vast power of the United States "in the field of good." "What we need," Drohan asserted, "is a policy on the part of our government which will take the wrinkles out of the bellies of the people in Europe and give them coal and steel and food and clothing in order to help them from their devastation and their wants in order to put them on their feet." That sounded a lot like the Marshall Plan. While Drohan added that this "should be done on the basis of need" and without attention to politics and ideology, the minority report made the same point. So did the Truman administration.[61]

When Henry Wallace returned to the UE convention in 1948 as the Progressive Party's presidential candidate, he reiterated the themes he had espoused a year earlier. But now he criticized labor leaders—including the top CIO leadership—who supported Truman and the bipartisan foreign policy symbolized most potently by the Marshall Plan, noting, "Wherever the bi-partisan foreign policy has been most active," as in Greece or nationalist China, "the trade unions have been among the first victims." To Wallace, the foreign policy of Truman and Marshall "aimed at increasing the world-wide profiteering of the same trusts which are profiteering at the expense of the American people at home." The Progressive Party, by contrast, stood for "good relations with the common people all over the world."[62]

The Marshall Plan remained the central point of contention at the 1948 UE convention. This time both the proposed foreign-policy resolutions and the delegates discussed it explicitly. The left-wing majority report, approved by a substantial majority, called for "a foreign aid program which would direct itself to improving the conditions of the people, not to increasing the profits and possessions of big business." It demanded that aid be administered through the United Nations and without interference in the economic and political affairs of recipient nations. Moreover, it argued that the European Recovery Program (ERP) violated these principles. The right wing's minority report, by contrast, pledged full support for the ERP. In doing so, it endorsed the ultimate aim of spreading America's "democratic way of life" and providing "the people of other lands" with the same freedoms assured under the U.S. political system. Most significantly, the minority endorsed the CIO's declared opposition to totalitarianism, a position directed at the Soviet Union and which the UE's left-wing national leadership refused to support.

The floor debates on foreign policy and on peacetime conscription and universal military training echoed the previous year's. The left-wing presented the Marshall Plan as "an international Taft-Hartley [Act]," inherently antilabor. The right wing meanwhile backed CIO president Philip Murray in his support of Truman administration foreign policy, with the aim of securing public support for organized labor from the White House.[63] In general, the right wing argued that U.S. foreign policy advanced the cause of human freedom, while the left wing argued that it merely advanced the interests of U.S. capital. In a sense, the question concerned capitalism's ability to advance human freedom. Both sides understood that the Marshall Plan was designed to rebuild the economies of Western Europe on the model of mid-twentieth-century, U.S. corporate capitalism. To James Carey and his supporters, that was a worthy aim so long as organized labor played a sufficient role to insure the rights of working people; the only alternative seemed to be totalitarian communism and the eclipse of freedom. To UE president Albert Fitzgerald, James Matles, and others on the UE left, the expansion of corporate capital was simply inimical to the well-being of common people everywhere.

By 1949, the UE had become so fractious that no foreign-policy resolutions even made it to the convention floor, and the right-wing broke off to form its own dual union, with Phil Murray's support. Under James Carey's leadership, the new International Union of Electrical workers (or IUE) blandly supported virtually all of the Truman administration's foreign-policy initiatives. With its expulsion from the CIO that year, the UE was effectively defined as a Communist Party front and a mouthpiece for Soviet foreign policy. As such, it lost any public legitimacy it had as a trade union, let alone as a voice on foreign-policy matters. The IUE supported NATO, Point Four, U.S. intervention in Korea, and the general tenor of the Truman administration's foreign policy in 1949 and 1950. The old UE did not, but few outside its ranks seemed to care. Over time, the divided electrical workers would lose much of their once considerable clout within their industry.[64]

FREEDOM WITH SECURITY: FOREIGN POLICY IN THE UAW

The politics of foreign policy played out quite differently in the UAW. Firmly under Walter Reuther's leadership after the fierce struggles of 1944 through 1947, the UAW aimed to be more than just a bread-and-butter trade union. It aimed to be a force for social justice in the United States and beyond. As Reuther expressed this vision at the close of the organization's 1947 convention, "We are the vanguard in America in that great crusade to build a better world. We are the architects of the future."[65] Like Walter White of the NAACP, Reuther was active in the formation of Americans for Democratic Action. Both anticommunism and American nationalism were central themes in his rhetoric, which now dominated the union's discourse.[66]

On foreign affairs, Reuther spoke the language of American nationalist globalism at least as fluently as Harry Truman. But he consistently spoke it in the name of an ardently progressive social and economic agenda. Like civil rights leaders, Reuther accepted the claims of U.S. world leadership in the name of freedom but emphasized the struggle for freedom and justice on the home front. In Reuther's laborite version of nationalist globalism, America had a special role in the world, organized labor had a special role in America, and the UAW had a special role in organized labor. In his view, the union's ultimate purpose was "to save and make democracy work in the world."[67] As Reuther told the union's 1947 convention, people all over the world wanted the same things that UAW members wanted—"an opportunity to live with freedom and justice in human dignity, without fear of tomorrow." The "whole world" looked to the UAW, Reuther asserted, for the answer to the problem of meeting basic human needs without sacrificing human freedom. "We want economic security in the world," he said, "but we don't want to pay the price of human freedom to get that security. We want freedom with security in the world, and that is the thing we are fighting for." The task as he painted it was nearly messianic:

> we are building the kind of labor movement that will remake the world where the working people will get the benefits of their labor. . . .
> . . . we have got the tools for the first time in the history of civilization to conquer poverty and human insecurity. All we have to do is learn to use those tools. That is the great job in America.[68]

Reuther's brother Victor, director of the union's education department, reiterated this theme at the 1949 UAW convention. To its millions of friends around the world, he insisted, the UAW was "more than just a Union; it is a new kind of force that is not concerned alone with higher wages and better working conditions, important as they are, but it is a Union that is in tune with the needs of the people throughout the whole world for not only greater personal freedom, but for greater security as well, and they look to the UAW to spearhead their fight for a better and a more secure world."[69]

Yet this new force for security and freedom was securely tied to the Truman administration's foreign policy of free-world leadership. For all the utopian globalism of their rhetoric, the Reuthers' fight was a fight for America, not just against social and economic injustices but against anyone attempting "to sell the membership, the Union, or our country down the river to any foreign power in the world."[70] Unlike the UE leadership's, or the UAW's own left wing, Walter Reuther was also fighting against communism. Having come to power by fighting Communist Party members within the UAW, Reuther had no qualms about lining up behind the anticommunist aims of Truman's foreign policy.[71]

Once in power, Reuther exerted tight control over the union's conventions, often dominating discussions himself and leaving little room for the kind of raucous foreign-affairs debates that characterized the UE. In 1947, his nominal opponent for the UAW presidency, Delegate John DeVito, tried to contest Reuther's claims to represent the cause of freedom, either in the union or in the world. DeVito invoked his own experience fighting for freedom in the war, then accused Reuther of using excessive, demagogic red-baiting as a tactic to force his way of thinking on the UAW membership. Those charges did not get DeVito very far, however, and Reuther was reelected easily. The anti-Reuther forces used the rhetoric of freedom elsewhere as well, but with little success.[72]

Reuther dominated the proceedings so thoroughly that CIO president Philip Murray was the only other speaker to discuss foreign policy at the union's 1947 convention. Murray spoke in support of the Marshall Plan, of course, though without mentioning it by name. To Murray, economic aid was bound up with national loyalty. Declaring himself a patriotic American who believed the United States "to be the best country in the whole wide world today," the CIO president pledged to support fully "every possible effort made by the American people and by our Congress to provide every grain, every solitary grain of food and other kinds of economic aid to the despairing people of the world." In a remark clearly directed at Henry Wallace, Murray denounced the charge "that this great nation of ours wants war." Murray argued that the democratic process protected the United States from being a warlike country because the people would always find the nation's warmongers and "kick them to hell out of whatever places they might be in." Murray hoped and prayed that "peoples in other lands may be provided the same opportunity" to correct such abuses. Where Wallace saw U.S. foreign policy as a threat to world peace, Murray argued that the nation's political culture and economic strength served as bulwarks against war.[73]

Like Murray's CIO, the UAW ardently supported the Marshall Plan, though Walter Reuther emphasized that the United States had to provide the world with a working model of democracy as well as economic aid. In his opening speech to the 1949 UAW convention, Reuther told a story about his recent travels in Western Europe. European workers he had spoken with praised the ERP, but they said they needed America to give them hope as well as material aid. When Reuther asked how America could give them hope, they answered, "You can give the hungry people of Europe hope by proving that American democracy has the moral strength and political know-how to solve the everyday problems of its people. . . . out of that will flow the kind of hope that will inspire the people of the world in their struggle to climb back out of the dark pits of destruction of war."[74] That, Reuther said, was the UAW's job.

The Reuther forces managed to silence most outright opposition to the Marshall Plan within the UAW, at least at their national conventions, mainly by linking such opposition to the Communist Party. The party did oppose the Marshall Plan, of course, but that did not necessarily mean that all who opposed it were simply following the party line. At the 1949 convention delegate Ellis of Local 453 protested that it was all too easy "to throw everybody into the Communist line that disagrees with you." Declaring himself an ordinary progressive follower of Roosevelt and Wallace, he said that he and others opposed the plan because it undermined the best interests of both U.S. workers and recipient nations. He suggested that the Marshall Plan had caused an economic crisis in Britain and contributed to U.S. unemployment by limiting trade with Eastern Europe. But Reuther cut Ellis off before he could develop this point further, saying that his time was up, and the next speaker castigated Ellis as one of "these Party boys." In a way, that proved Ellis's point, whether he was a Party affiliate or not. It certainly foreclosed a fair hearing of his views on the Marshall Plan.[75]

The same convention adopted an International Relations Program that endorsed the Truman administration's main foreign-policy initiatives and goals while expressing ideals at odds with, and to the left of, the administration's.[76] It supported "constant vigilance" against Soviet aggression and "equally constant readiness to cooperate with the USSR" on practical matters involving no sacrifice of principle. It supported the UN, but viewed the international organization as an initial step toward the goal of world government. It backed the Marshall Plan, but underscored the importance of working with European social democrats and supported efforts toward the public ownership of German industry. While endorsing the Atlantic Pact, the union stressed that U.S. security efforts "must place ever-increasing emphasis on programs of social reconstruction and less on military plans." The administration by this time was moving in the opposite direction.

Concerning Point Four, the UAW enthusiastically endorsed President Truman's call for "a bold new program" of U.S. capital aid and technical assistance to the underdeveloped areas of Latin America, Asia, Africa, and the Near East. Like the rest of the CIO, the UAW emphasized that the "technical know-how" to be provided should include labor organizations, collective bargaining, and fair labor standards. The union construed Point Four as a weapon in the Cold War, "a dramatic and telling opportunity to convince the world that America's interest in progress derives neither from the urge toward profits nor the urge toward imperial domination" and "our most eloquent possible reply to both the libels and the activities of Communist imperialism." The resolution insisted, however, that such aid should support the world's democratic forces in struggles against dictatorships of the right as well as the left, rather than to blindly oppose communism without regard to democracy.

The Marshall Plan, as a key symbol of America's emerging role as leader of the free world, also had to be protected from antidemocratic taints. The union's foreign-policy program opposed any and all U.S. encouragement of Franco's Spain, particularly the possibility of extending Marshall Plan aid. Support for Western Europe's sole surviving dictator might prompt European workers "to doubt our sincerity in giving aid to free peoples."

The floor debate over this foreign affairs program was limited to a brief exchange between UAW president Reuther and Delegate Paul Boatin of Local 600, one of the left-wing's floor leaders and generally acknowledged as a member of the Communist Party.[77] Boatin's objections paralleled the foreign-policy views espoused more widely in the UE. He chastised the resolution for failing to criticize "the policy of our American bankers and . . . the way they try to boss the world," charging that the UAW seemed to "forget in the main that the foreign policy of this country is dominated by the same bankers who dominate the domestic policy." Through their control of U.S. foreign policy, U.S. financial interests were now "going abroad and trying to make big profits out of the people of Europe, and the people of Asia and the people of Africa and other countries" just as they did at home. To Boatin, Point Four was just one more method of using the U.S. government as an agent of U.S. capital, seeking to exploit the labor and resources of Africa and Asia. In this context, he argued, the Atlantic Pact's pledge to protect peace meant that sometimes "we will have to send troops to protect the investments of bankers." Reuther answered these charges by asserting that the UAW and the CIO had criticized U.S. foreign policy when warranted, most notably by condemning improved relations with Franco's Spain. "We are opposed to imperialism," he proclaimed, "whether it comes from Wall Street or the Kremlin," implying that Boatin criticized only Wall Street. Reuther asserted that the UAW supported U.S. foreign policy whenever it strengthened the world's democratic forces. But he never responded to Boatin's contention that overseas economic expansion combined with formal alliances would lead to overseas military intervention.

For all their anticommunism, Reuther and his UAW followers consistently emphasized that the key to "free-world victory," to borrow Henry Wallace's wartime phrase, lay in demonstrating that U.S. democracy could meet basic human needs while maintaining fundamental freedoms. Ultimately, Reuther argued, that meant reasserting "the sovereignty of people above profits in America." He decried the moral double standard of a nation that could spend $400 billion for war while denying adequate medical care to its own citizens who "happen to be born on the wrong side of the railroad tracks."[78] Like numerous African American commentators, Reuther invoked the image of the United States standing trial before the international community: "The world is going to judge America, and we must judge ourselves, not by our technical progress, not by our ability to split the atom or make a jet ship go 700 miles an hour. We have got to judge ourselves as the world would judge us, by our ability to translate technical progress into human progress, human security, human dignity and human happiness."[79] Reuther simply focused this rhetorical device on the purposes of the U.S. economic system rather than on the injustices of U.S. race relations.

Indeed, the national leaders of both the NAACP and the UAW were involved in something of a partnership, and their two projects fit hand in glove. This partnership had been forged in the wake of fierce conflicts between rank-and-file UAW members and nonunion black workers in Detroit in the 1930s. By the postwar era, both organizations sought significant domestic reforms. Both believed their aims ultimately depended on the support of the federal government. And both expressed their common goals through their own versions of the language of nationalist globalism. As NAACP assistant secretary Roy Wilkins put it in an official greeting to the UAW's 1949 convention, both organizations were "dedicated to the purpose of making this nation the finest example of democracy that the world has ever seen."[80]

When speaking about civil rights, Reuther employed the same rhetoric as African American leaders. "Civil rights is a must in America," he told the UAW's 1949 convention. "How can we sell American democracy to the world when we don't practice what we preach at home?"[81] Another speaker at that convention, the black civil rights activist Anne Hedgeman, called the 1948 report of the President's Committee on Civil Rights the most significant document — "to America and to the whole world" — since the U.S. Constitution. The struggle for civil rights, Mrs. Hedgeman said, was "a battle for democracy" — a critical battle in the nation's "declared war on totalitarianism." Immediately after Mrs. Hedgeman's speech, Reuther declared that the UAW understood fully "that freedom in the world is indivisible, that nobody is truly free as long as there are other people who are not free."[82] Elsewhere Reuther's discussion of freedom seemed to reflect the ideas of Reinhold Niebuhr, but in this instance it seemed more in the tradition of Eugene Debs and American socialism, which is after all the tradition Reuther came from.

The 1949 UAW convention adopted a resolution on "Civil Rights and Human Freedom," the same phrase that President Truman had used to name the theme of his 1947 speech to the NAACP. Like Truman's speech, the UAW resolution emphasized connections between the international situation, America's world leadership, and domestic civil rights questions: "We cannot maintain our position as the leader of world democracy if we have not placed our own house in order. A nation with a vast sense of guilt lacks the inner sureness and unity for the role of a leader. We are going to suffer from that inner uncertainty until democracy begins to work for all the people. . . . our job ahead in this field is to wipe out the deficit in human rights that threatens to drag us down into moral bankruptcy in the eyes of the free world."[83] These words reminded one UAW delegate of a recent visit to the Statue of Liberty, and of the inscription at its base, about America's lamp of love for the world's oppressed masses "who yearn to be free." To Delegate Szluk of Local 600, the UAW's civil rights resolution could "make those words ring a true meaning of democracy throughout the world. It is one thing to talk about it, it is one thing to brag about it, but another thing to demonstrate it."[84] To lead the free world, the United States would have to stop bragging and make itself a free society in ways it had never been before, providing economic security along with political freedom for all its citizens.

CONCLUSION

Between 1947 and 1950, the notion that the United States was "the leader of the free world" began to emerge as the dominant trope to explain America's hegemonic role in a divided world. The meaning of free world leadership was contested in significant ways by the African American community and elements of organized labor, but the range of foreign-policy debate grew increasingly constricted in these years. These rhetorical struggles helped to shape the subsequent development of both the civil rights and labor movements and of U.S. public culture generally, not just in the late 1940s but throughout the Cold War era.

Freedom had been a key word for African Americans since the days of slavery, so its emergence as the key word first of World War II and then the Cold War gave the civil rights movement a strong rhetorical hand. Under the leadership of Walter White, the NAACP played that hand skillfully, participating in public discourse on U.S. foreign policy to advance its own domestic and international goals of ending racial injustice and colonialism. To participate in that discourse, it had to operate within the dominant terms of the debate — American national greatness, global responsibility, and global anticommunism in the name of freedom and democracy. By the late 1940s, these ideological constructs were linked tightly together under the rubric of leading the free world. Left-wing dissidents who rejected these terms, including most notably W. E. B. Du Bois and Paul Robeson, were effectively branded as Communist dupes and barred from the debate.

By and large, however, the civil rights movement accepted the claims of America's free world leadership and used these claims to argue that such leadership required racial equality at home and the end of colonialism abroad. Domestically, this strategy helped spur significant developments in U.S. race relations, including the desegregation of the armed forces, Truman's 1947 speech to the NAACP, and the 1954 Supreme Court decision in *Brown v. Board of Education of Topeka, Kansas*. These developments, in turn, set the stage for the mass civil rights struggles of the later 1950s and 1960s, which eventually brought an end to the Jim Crow system of legal segregation in the South. Internationally, the NAACP's strategy did not prevent the U.S. government from taking up the interests of European colonial powers — most notably, and most tragically, in Southeast Asia. Nonetheless, it enabled the Association to express clear dissent in specific cases, such as *in* Indonesia and *in* Italy's former colonies in Africa, without being dismissed as traitorous. More generally, the African American argument that a free world that included colonialism was not worthy of the name helped to complicate the Cold War definition of freedom as simply anything that was not Communism. If African American foreign-policy dissent became more muted after 1947, at least it persisted. That persistence is particularly notable in an era when more fundamental, strategic dissent seldom escaped repression.[85]

Various segments of organized labor also approached foreign-policy issues in conjunction with their own domestic concerns. The AFL had long supported the main contours of U.S. foreign policy as a way of allying itself with the federal government. In the 1940s, the CIO came to pursue a similar strategy. By 1949, the UE and other elements of the CIO that opposed the Marshall Plan were expelled from the mainstream of the labor movement. The UAW, meanwhile, offered tactical criticism of the Truman administration's foreign policy but accepted its main goals. Like the NAACP, the UAW sought to ally itself with the Truman administration and to use the prevailing discourse on U.S. foreign policy to advance its own domestic agenda. But the issues of class and property rights that Reuther raised did not carry the same weight as issues of race on the scale of the American Creed. During the 1950s and 1960s, organized labor would achieve significant economic gains for union members but few of its broader social and political goals.

Labor's relative inability to advance its larger domestic agenda or dissenting foreign-policy views within the dominant discourse stemmed in part from its own internal strife and fragmentation, particularly concerning communism, foreign policy, and national loyalty. While the dissenting foreign-policy views expressed by the left within the CIO were often penetrating, they all too often came from union activists with ties to the Communist Party.[86] When Phil Murray finally moved to purge Communist influence in the CIO after the 1948 election, he did so by quashing any elemental foreign-policy dissent within the organization. The subsequent tactical dissent expressed by the UAW was severely limited and largely rhetorical. Walter Reuther tried to argue that the United States would have to build a viable social democracy at home if it was to meet its responsibilities as leader of the free world. But the increasingly conservative ethos of postwar America made this argument untenable.

The greater success of the NAACP's strategy, considered over the entire period from the late 1940s to the mid-1960s, stemmed largely from its ability to focus most dramatically on the hypocrisy of U.S. claims of promoting democracy abroad while it denied democracy at home on the basis of race. The NAACP had always been dedicated to achieving the full rights of U.S. citizenship for African Americans. In the early postwar years, more incisively than ever before, the Association eloquently proclaimed its devotion to the American Creed embodied in the Declaration of Independence, the Bill of Rights, and Lincoln's Gettysburg Address, while challenging the nation to live up to this creed. Walter Reuther and the UAW attempted a similar strategy. But Reuther's challenge to the nation included a challenge to the rights of private property, which were as fully sanctified as any ideal in the American Creed. Indeed, in the Cold War, "free enterprise" was increasingly accepted as the most fundamental, most American form of freedom. As a result, Reuther's challenge to economic injustice could not strike the same nationalist chords as the NAACP's challenge to racial injustice. Over the years, Reuther's UAW achieved great success as a bread-and-butter trade union, but not as the vanguard of the new, social democratic America he had sought.

In the mid-1940s, the CIO and the NAACP both stood for an antimilitarist, anticolonial, multilateralist foreign policy based upon international cooperation; by 1950 both organizations supported the main elements of the Truman administration's foreign policy, which was increasingly militaristic, hegemonic, and unilateralist. Top national labor and civil rights leaders — including most notably the CIO's Philip Murray, the UAW's Walter Reuther, and the NAACP's Walter White — believed that their movements needed the federal government, and especially the executive branch, as an ally. Supporting the Truman administration's foreign policy became an important method of securing that alliance and demonstrating national loyalty without giving up their own domestic demands. Yet by accepting the main goals of U.S. foreign policy, both the NAACP and the CIO helped to cement the Cold War consensus as the new foundation of U.S. public culture, which ultimately limited the range of debate on domestic as well as foreign-policy issues. Under markedly different circumstances — without such intense anxieties over communism and national loyalty, without the division of the left-liberal community prompted by the 1948 Wallace campaign — these major organizations might together have formed the base for a popular movement against the emerging Cold War.[87] By the end of the 1940s, however, that potential was clearly lost, as fundamental foreign-policy dissent became a sign of essential disloyalty to the nation.

6 LIMITED WAR, GLOBAL STRUGGLE —
THE MEANING OF KOREA

By the time North Korean forces invaded South Korea in June 1950, prompting full-scale U.S. military intervention, the ideology that would underpin the Cold War consensus — and dominate U.S. foreign-policy discourse throughout the postwar era — was fully in place. The ideology of American nationalist globalism filtered perceptions of events in Korea throughout U.S. public culture, both among policymakers and among the citizenry. The consensus emerging around that ideology severely constrained the debate over U.S. intervention; former leading foreign-policy dissenters such as Claude Pepper and Henry Wallace supported Truman's move in Korea and accepted the rationale provided by the new ideology. Those who continued to oppose the fundamental direction of U.S. foreign policy — such as W. E. B. Du Bois, Paul Robeson, and the leaders of the United Electrical Workers — were now thoroughly marginalized and delegitimized.

Over the course of its duration, the Korean War would not be the most popular of wars, but the initial response to Truman's decision to intervene was overwhelmingly positive. The State Department reported survey results showing that three out of every four Americans supported sending U.S. troops into Korea. Moreover, Americans generally interpreted the events of June 1950 through the ideological prism of American nationalist globalism. "We are fighting the second team," said Secretary of State Dean Acheson, the man primarily responsible for the U.S. decision to intervene, "the real enemy is the Soviet Union."[1] By June 1950, it was difficult for most Americans to think otherwise.

NSC-68 AND KOREA: THE PUBLIC FACE OF A SECRET PLAN

To the president and other policymakers, to much of the media, and to broad sections of the public, Korea seemed less the site of one nation's civil war than the locus of the global struggle between the United States and the Soviet Union — between "the free world" of U.S.-led international capitalism and "the slave world" of Soviet-led international communism. In the view of the Truman administration, North Korea had little if anything to do with the movement of its troops across the 38th parallel on June 25, 1950. Most Americans viewed the North Korean move as an unprovoked attack that ignited the war suddenly. The media sometimes compared it to a Nazi blitzkrieg. Yet some 100,000 Koreans had already died — before the June 1950 invasion — in an ongoing civil war that began in 1946. The Truman administration nonetheless operated on the assumption that, as Secretary of State Acheson later said, "It isn't a Korean war on either side." [2]

That assumption was firmly rooted in the ideology of nationalist globalism, which undergirded the administration's worldview. That worldview had received its fullest exposition that spring, in a document that came to be known as NSC-68 (for National Security Council Memorandum Number 68). During the fall of 1949, in the wake of the apparent "loss" of China to Communist control and the United States' loss of its atomic monopoly when the Soviet Union exploded its first nuclear bomb, President Truman had launched the process of developing a comprehensive, long-range plan for U.S. global policy. That process produced NSC-68, which was written during the first four months of 1950 and approved by President Truman in April.

Though NSC-68 presents itself as an authoritative policy statement, it has a strongly ideological tone. It is a primal text of American nationalist globalism. The document operates within an explicitly globalist framework, taking the entire world as the necessary unit of analysis for considerations of U.S. national security. Its vision of a rigidly bipolar world is presented in starkly Manichaean rhetoric. That rhetoric described a terrifying new world of "continuing crisis" and mounting disorder — a world in which "the polarization of power" between the United States and the Soviet Union "inescapably confronts the slave society with the free." The Soviet Union, it proclaimed, was "animated by a new fanatic faith, antithetical to our own" and was intent on securing "domination of the Eurasian land mass" and expanding its absolute authority indefinitely.[3] This global menace posed a fundamental challenge to the United States both as a world leader and as a nation: "We must lead in building a successfully functioning political and economic system in the free world. It is only by practical affirmation, abroad as well as at home, of our essential values, that we can preserve our own integrity, in which lies the real frustration of the Kremlin design." [4] By way of "practical affirmation," NSC-68 disallowed negotiations with the Soviets and proposed a demanding program for waging sustained, total cold war. That program included development of the hydrogen bomb; a rapid, large-scale buildup of U.S. conventional forces; construction of a strong, U.S.-led alliance system throughout the noncommunist world; and heavy tax increases to pay for these measures. It also included greater efforts by the government and the media to mobilize and sustain public support for the Cold War struggle. As NSC 68 made clear, the nation's top foreign-policy makers were concerned that the American people might not be prepared to make the sacrifices needed to maintain national unity in pursuit, once again, of free-world victory.[5]

NSC-68 remained a highly classified document for decades, but its central tension—between the need for an ambitious, comprehensive, long-term plan for U.S. global policy and the need to ensure public support for that policy—was central to U.S. public culture even as it was being written. Indeed, that tension was the dominant theme of two major studies of public opinion published in 1949 and 1950.

In *Public Opinion and Foreign Policy,* a study sponsored by the Council on Foreign Relations, a team of scholars and journalists headed by Lester Markel of the *New York Times* warned against the public's "dark areas of ignorance" and apathy concerning foreign affairs. The authors view domestic public opinion as an "instrument" of foreign policy, a tool to be manipulated by policymakers and take the position that the public's proper role is not to inform government officials but to support them. Markel advocated a combination of education and propaganda to ensure that support, emphasizing that such efforts had to be based on a broad, cohesive program that could be presented clearly to the public.[6]

In his influential study, *The American People and Foreign Policy,* political scientist Gabriel Almond made a similar argument in more elaborate form. Influenced by the national-character studies approach that had developed in the United States during World War II, Almond worried that isolationism was deeply embedded in the American character, as a kind of foreign-policy corollary to individualism.[7] In this view, Americans had an almost inborn tendency to withdraw from public, idealistic pursuits into private, selfish ones. If that was the case, the public's apparent acceptance of America's global responsibilities in the postwar period might prove transitory at best. Almond argued further that "American foreign policy moods" tended to be highly unstable. In a "mass democracy" faced with long-term global challenges, therefore, the "American foreign policy mood" required constant management by the governing elites. Since the end of World War II, he argued, only the perception of a fundamental threat, in the form of Soviet communism, had held the isolationist impulse in check. While Almond found the national mood of 1950 to be "plastic," "passive," and "permissive," he saw no guarantee that it would continue to support long-range, activist foreign policies "in the absence of a clear threat." The key, then, was to make sure the threat remained clear.

The hyperbolic rhetoric of NSC-68 revealed the foreign-policy elite's anxieties concerning the public's willingness to go along with its ambitious plans, but Almond offered assurances: "The American foreign policy mood is permissive;

it will follow the lead of the policy elites if they demonstrate unity and resolution. The decline of isolationism has widened the scope of discretion of the policy and opinion elites. The problem of contemporary American foreign policy is not so much one of mass traditions and resistances as it is one of resolution, courage, and intelligence of the leadership."[8] NSC-68 embodied the efforts of the foreign-policy leadership to demonstrate its own resolution, courage, and intelligence — to itself. The highly classified document was intended only for a select audience of insiders; it is more a rallying cry, or a call to battle, than a serious analysis of the world scene. Paul Nitze, the new director of the State Department's policy planning staff, had produced just what his boss, Secretary of State Dean Acheson, had ordered: a statement clearer than truth. In the late spring and early summer of 1950, even Acheson, with his air of infinite self-assurance, had doubts as to how the public would be brought along on the enormous undertaking outlined in NSC-68. But then, as Acheson later said, while the nation's foreign-policy leaders grappled with this question, "Korea came along and saved us."[9]

The outbreak of full-scale war in Korea "saved" Acheson, Truman, and company by providing a ready-made justification for the vast global initiatives called for in NSC-68. Although there was no public consensus in support of those initiatives before June 25, 1950, the ideology around which that consensus would be forged was already operative. Looking through the ideology of American nationalist globalism, Acheson and Truman instantly viewed the Korean situation as part of the global struggle between the United States and the Soviet Union. So did millions of other Americans, for whom nationalist globalism provided the only means of making sense of the news that U.S. armed forces would again face combat overseas. In the days, weeks, and months ahead, the media only amplified that view.

EXPLAINING INTERVENTION: PRESIDENTIAL RHETORIC, PUBLIC RESPONSE

In his initial statements explaining developments in Korea in the summer of 1950, President Truman hardly mentioned the state of North Korea. Without naming the Soviet Union as the aggressor, he intimated that the dark forces of international communism had invaded the independent Republic of Korea. Three years after the Truman Doctrine speech and just months after Senator Joseph McCarthy launched his own demagogic anticommunist crusade, most Americans viewed those forces as monolithic and ineluctably in the service of the Kremlin. President Truman and his advisers shared that ideological conception of a unified world communist movement directed from Moscow. But as Bruce

Cumings, the leading historian of the origins of the Korean War, has pointed out, the administration's worldview obfuscated the great irony of this supposed act of international aggression: Koreans—not Russians, not Chinese—had invaded Korea.[10] Yet Truman likened this act of "Communist totalitarianism" to Nazi aggression in Europe at the beginning of World War II, particularly when he invoked the negative images of appeasement in a September 1 broadcast speech. In Truman's public utterances, only the defenders south of the 38th parallel were Korean; the invaders from north of the 38th were simply communists. Thus the U.S. forces he brought to bear on the Korean conflagration were not intervening in a civil war, but were acting to uphold the international rule of law and to defend the freedom of the Republic of Korea and by extension of "free peoples everywhere," to use the language of the Truman Doctrine.

Truman's initial public statements, issued to the press on June 26 and 27, referred to "forces from North Korea" but spoke of the Republic of Korea—that is, South Korea—as the only Korean government, lawful or otherwise. Moreover, the president situated the fighting in Korea within a Manichaean global struggle against international communism rather than a civil war between left-wing and right-wing Koreans: "The attack upon Korea makes it plain beyond all doubt that communism has passed beyond the use of subversion to conquer independent nations and will now use armed invasion and war."[11] In his press conference of June 29, moreover, Truman said that the Republic of Korea had been "unlawfully attacked by a bunch of bandits which are neighbors of North Korea." So without naming the Soviet Union or China, he implied that they stood behind the southward movement of North Korean troops.[12]

On July 19, in his first speech broadcast to the American people concerning Korea, the president again framed the conflict as an international matter of communism versus freedom rather than an internal matter among Koreans: "By their actions in Korea, Communist leaders have demonstrated their contempt for the basic moral principles on which the United Nations is founded. This is a direct challenge to the efforts of the free nations to build the kind of world in which men can live in freedom and peace."[13] The president implicitly invoked the lessons of Pearl Harbor as well as Munich in arguing that the Communist invasion of Korea "is a warning that there may be similar acts of aggression in other parts of the world. The free nations must be on their guard, more than ever before, against this kind of sneak attack." Consequently, Truman called for stepped-up U.S. military preparedness and strengthening of the common defenses of the free world.[14]

Truman also implied that the invasion of South Korea signaled a threat to the security and freedom of the United States itself—that ultimately Korea was simply a part of the struggle between American freedom and communist tyranny. As the president put the matter bluntly in his July 19 radio address, the American people are unified in their belief in democratic freedom. We are united in detesting Communist slavery.

We know that the cost of freedom is high. But we are determined to preserve our freedom — no matter what the cost.

This assertion of national unity was quickly reified by the media. A *March of Time* newsreel, for example, interspersed clips of Truman uttering these lines with dramatized scenes of American families (all middle-class and white) tuned in to the president's words, all looking extraordinarily dour yet anxious as well. There was no question now, in time of war, of needing to put the national house in order. Instead the president declared that the United States "stands before the world as an example of how free men, under God, can build a community of neighbors, working together for the good of all," and that it sought to build such a community "not only for ourselves, but for all people." The United States was intervening in Korea and embarking on a new round of global militarization in the name of peace and freedom for all humanity.[15]

Truman reiterated these themes in a second broadcast report to the American people concerning the Korean situation on September 1, 1950. Two months after his initial decision to intervene, the president explained that U.S. forces were in Korea to defend "the cause of freedom in the world" and that the freedom of the United States itself was bound up with the freedom of South Korea. More starkly than he had before, Truman emphasized the indivisibility of freedom, proclaiming, "We cannot hope to maintain our own freedom if freedom elsewhere is wiped out." In this speech, the president never referred to the U.S. military intervention as a "police action," although that was the term used to justify it under UN auspices without Congress declaring war. Rather, Truman declared that "the battle in Korea is the frontline in the struggle between freedom and tyranny." That larger struggle was worldwide, of course, and events in Korea demonstrated that expanded military capabilities would be required in the global struggle for freedom, peace, and justice against the threat of Communist imperialism. As he had on other occasions, Truman invoked the notion that the United States had been called by providence to lead the free world in this struggle:

> At this critical hour in the history of the world, our country has been called upon to give of its leadership, its efforts, and its resources to maintain peace and justice among nations. We have responded to that call. We will not fail.
>
> . . . We pray God to give us strength, ability, and wisdom for the great task we face.

These words were not "mere rhetoric" designed to justify the administration's policies and mobilize consent behind them. Here and elsewhere, Truman's public discourse reflected the ideological framework within which high policy was made. That ideological framework also shaped the public response to the Korean situation. Consequently, the president's rhetoric tapped the sentiments of a wide range of citizens who viewed the situation similarly. Not all Americans supported Truman's decision to intervene, of course, but, according to public opinion polls, an overwhelming majority did, and a large majority probably shared the administration's basic outlook on the Korean conflict. It was, after all, a quintessentially "American" outlook, embedded in the prevailing nationalist ideology of the time.

In the months after the United States entered the war in Korea, public opinion polls showed high levels of support for the administration's defense buildup; they also suggest that most Americans viewed the Korean situation in global terms. In a Gallup poll taken between July 9 and 14, 53 percent thought Congress should draw up plans for total mobilization in the event of a major war. More significantly, 70 percent responded that they were willing to pay higher taxes for a larger army and a larger navy; 72 percent were willing to accept tax hikes to pay for a larger air force. In the same survey, 68 percent said it was more important to stop Soviet expansion in Europe and Asia than to keep the United States out of a major war. Fully 79 percent responded that they thought the United States should "go to war with Russia if Communist troops attack the American zone in Germany," though only 15 percent thought the United States should declare war on the Soviet Union immediately.

In another Gallup survey three weeks later, 57 percent said they thought "the United States is now actually in World War III." Only 28 percent thought the fighting in Korea would stop short of another full-scale global conflagration. (In November the same question elicited similar results.) In this same survey, over 70 percent favored U.S. steps to build up the armies of West Germany and Japan to prepare against possible communist attacks. And 78 percent favored Universal Military Training (UMT), marking an increase from favorable ratings of 65 to 70 percent for UMT in polls over the preceding several years. (Again, UMT was one central military initiative that Truman pressed for but never achieved; it was blocked, however, by concerted congressional opposition, not by mass public opinion.)

In a November Gallup survey, nearly four months after the U.S. entry into the Korean War, 81 percent of those polled thought Russia was "trying to build herself up to be the ruling power of the world." In response to a question about the administration's decision to double the size of the U.S. armed forces to some 3 million men, 50 percent thought that figure was "about right" — while 33 percent thought it was too low. When China entered the war late in the year, a development that would prolong the war beyond Truman's presidency and help bring his popularity ratings to record lows, the Gallup poll found that 81 percent of those surveyed thought the Chinese had acted "on orders from Russia." The same poll found that 73 percent approved the administration's proposed doubling of U.S. defense expenditures in 1951 over 1950 levels. Most of those people were willing to pay higher personal income taxes to pay for that buildup.[16]

Even more revealing than the polling data, however, is the qualitative evidence provided by the letters ordinary citizens sent to President Truman in response to his initial statements on Korea. Those letters vividly show how the main themes of Truman's discourse, and thus the ideology of nationalist globalism, resonated powerfully with a wide range of American citizens.

Of those Americans who wrote to Truman in response to his statements concerning Korea in the summer of 1950, the overwhelming majority wrote in support of his decision to intervene.[17] Like the president, those supporting the intervention generally saw the Korean conflict as an expression of the global struggle between Communism and freedom, which dominated public discourse in the period before June 25, rather than of civil strife between Koreans, about which most Americans knew little if anything. In response to the president's initial statement of June 27, for example, the crew of the SS *African Moon,* all members of the National Maritime Union, telegraphed the president from New York City to endorse Truman's stand in Korea and pledge their support for "complete victory in defeating any form of Communism throughout the world and to preserve the American way." Similarly, the day the president announced his decision to send U.S. air and naval forces to aid South Korea, an American Legion post in Denver unanimously endorsed Truman's move "to check the advance of Communism in the Far East" and pledged its support for any and all measures the government deemed necessary "to terminate for all time the threat of communism to our freedom."[18]

The mail responding to Truman's July 19 radio address was overwhelmingly positive. It included strongly supportive telegrams from such influential figures as Paul Bissinger, president of the San Francisco Chamber of Commerce, and David Sarnoff, chairman of the board of RCA, who pledged his corporation's "fullest cooperation in the national effort," emphasizing that the National Broadcasting Company was an RCA subsidiary.[19] A telegram from Michael Francis Doyle of Philadelphia nicely summed up the general response, telling the president that "your clear understandable address this evening will more firmly than ever unite our people in defense of civilization and freedom everywhere."[20] Lasalle Nolin of Woonsocket, Rhode Island, asserted explicitly that the United States was at war not with North Korea but with Soviet-controlled international communism as a whole, just as Truman suggested. Like other ardently anticommunist letter writers, Nolin called for measures outlawing the Communist Party in the United States and detaining all party members. One man supported Truman's decision "to oppose Moscow in Korea," but asked when the administration would "start to oppose Moscow in our own country" by putting U.S. Communists "out of circulation or out of business."[21]

Truman's speeches, which justified overseas military intervention in the name of worldwide freedom, peace, and civilization, struck patriotic chords in many hearts. In the view of Joseph M. Gantz of Cincinnati, Truman's September 1 speech "lives up to the highest ideals and traditions of our country" and would not only inspire "all good Americans" but provide "a beacon of hope, to all the peoples of the world." James Valfriend wrote Truman to praise his actions and his "masterful address" of July 19 and to express his own "proud faith in the American tradition of freedom for all mankind." One man applauded Truman's September 1 speech and told the president that he was "the sole hope for a free world."[22]

To Mrs. Edward H. Allen, the wife of a Navy veteran who had recently volunteered to return to active service, the president's July 19 speech "must have been a great comfort to free peoples everywhere." In three long, well-written, and well-typed paragraphs, however, Mrs. Allen never even mentioned Korea. Instead, she wondered "how any grown person who has read the newspapers for the last few years can possibly doubt the seriousness of this fight for the survival of our Western Civilization." Indeed, the evidence suggests that only those who were extremely skeptical about what they read in the mainstream press or heard on the air could sustain such doubts by mid-1950. Americans should all join together, Mrs. Allen concluded, as "a nation united with a determination that our strength will deter Russia from any future agression [sic] anywhere on the globe." The National Security Council couldn't have said it better. In response to Truman's September 1 speech, Mr. and Mrs. U. L. Hobbs of Chicago, Illinois, wrote a similarly long letter that also failed to mention Korea itself. The Hobbses concurred that the struggle was a worldwide one between freedom and communism, but they stressed their own, and what they regarded as Truman's, concern for "the basic aspirations towards a better material life among the backward peoples of the earth — freedom from want as well as freedom from fear — . . . if we are to take the lead away from communist imperialism." A rather different approach was recommended by John Alva Bell of Laguna Beach, California, who concluded his September 4 telegram to the president by asserting that since "this world cannot exist half slave and half free," the time was ripe for "a war of aggression for peace." Others told the president that the solution to the Korean crisis lay in dropping atomic bombs on the Kremlin.[23]

Many citizens linked their support for Truman's statements on Korea to religious concerns. Responding to Truman's September 1 speech, Rev. Thomas Grice, past national chaplain of the American Legion, offered the president God's blessings "for the finest and most complete statement of American policy and idealism ever given to the world." In a telegram praising the president's July 20 speech, Frank Smathers Sr. of Miami told Truman that he prayed "that God may guide and strengthen your resolve to mobilize and employ American moral and material might to insure the peace, freedom and happiness of all mankind." Rabbi A. M. Herschberg, president of the Federated Rabbinical Colleges of Chachmey Lublin in Chicago, offered Truman the prayers of his constituents and expressed their hope that the Communist forces who fought against the power and spirit of God would be defeated. Irvi Meserth of Cincinnati gave perhaps the most forthright expression of American holy nationalism, in a telegram telling the president that his July 19 radio message would "unify our nation for years to come in our God given duty to maintain world peace."[24]

Some Americans wrote Truman to express their willingness to sacrifice their own lives or the lives of their children for the cause of freedom as the president defined it. Charles Varga, writing from Philadelphia's Germantown neighborhood, told the president that he and his three sons stood behind him, ready to fight in Korea "to make this world a better place to live in." Men well beyond fighting age similarly expressed their willingness to give their lives for their country, and many younger men did in fact volunteer in the period immediately after the United States entered the war. Women rang variations on these themes. Mrs. Alice Newquist of Molina, Illinois, was prepared to see her three sons join the military to fight and possibly die in Korea because she knew, paraphrasing Truman, "that the price of freedom is expensive." The wife of a Philadelphia jeweler wrote the president that at his command she and her husband would "surrender to your leadership, the dearest possession of our lives, our nineteen year old son." To nineteen-year-old Barbara J. Bushie of Mohawk, New York, her own life "would not be enough to give so that my younger sisters could live in freedom and peace."[25]

Not all Americans were so enthusiastic about the advent of the Korean War. Most grassroots critics who wrote President Truman to oppose intervention argued that military action hardly promoted the administration's professed aims of peace, freedom, and democracy. Some argued that it subverted the principle of self-determination; others argued that Truman seemed to be supporting anti-democratic, right-wing regimes in the name of democracy; and still others argued that Truman's approach was overly militaristic. Others focused on domestic ramifications, questioning the constitutionality of Truman's executive decision and the long-term costs of global interventionism.[26]

While the Truman administration and most of the mass media seemed unable to view the Korean situation as a civil conflict between Koreans, some U.S. citizens, mainly women, did manage to understand it in those terms. "If we are to intervene in every civil war in the world," wrote Mrs. A. A. Gajcwski from Alexander, North Dakota, "what future has our youth? Surely constant war is not peace and freedom." Mrs. Ingrid Stoetzer of Cleveland believed the Koreans were engaged in a conflict comparable to the American Civil War, and that surely no nation had a right to intervene in that great affair. "Are we not trying to play God, Mr. President?" she asked. Marion Sternbach of Los Angeles wrote that the American Revolution itself would be judged subversive by 1950 standards, adding that "it seems to me we stand in the same relation to the people of Korea, China, Malaya and Indo China (not to mention Greece) as Great Britain did to us on that occasion." Mrs. L. Weisman of Manhattan cited a different kind of parallel: "If our country could not intervene in the Spanish civil war when such intervention might have prevented World War II," she asked, "why are we interfering in this civil war, when we know full well this interference can cause a World War III?"[27]

Other grassroots critics of the Korean intervention argued that armed might alone could not ensure peace, freedom, and democracy. Some stressed that the United States would have to ensure improved living conditions throughout the world to achieve its professed aims. Others advanced pacifist arguments. A World War II veteran from Illinois wrote the president on personal stationery bearing the motto "America is my home, and the world is my country." "Freedom and democracy," he proclaimed, "cannot be taught at the point of a rifle — or with tanks bombers and warships. . . . We destroy a democratic freedom with every bullet we fire; and we sow an acre of totalitarian seed with every bomb we drop."[28] A Baltimore couple declared that most Americans knew "that war is always wrong and futile," even when disguised as a UN police action. Yet, as they wrote to Truman, "in this war hysteria nearly everyone who advocates peace seems to be automatically labeled a 'Communist' so that most American citizens are frightened and confused into supporting your war in Korea and your preparations for bigger and more deadly wars."[29]

THE MEDIA SHARE THE MESSAGE

The mass-circulation weeklies all endorsed Truman's decision to intervene, presenting it in terms of the now official ideology of nationalist globalism even while criticizing the administration for having bungled its way into the new crisis. *Life,* the *Saturday Evening Post,* and *Collier's* all treated the intervention in Korea as a necessary stand against the Soviet Union and international Communism, as though the Koreans themselves had little to do with the situation. To the editorial writers, as to the secretary of state, it was not really a Korean war on either side. As the *Saturday Evening Post* expressed the prevailing view in its July 22 editorial, "Despite Moscow's scrupulous care to keep Russian forces out of the Korean fracas, it is plain that the attack represents a Red challenge to western efforts to block the spread of Russian imperialism in Asia." A truth so plain needed no evidence.[30]

To *Life*'s editors, Truman's decision marked a courageous turnaround after five years of failed policy toward Asia. But its July 10 editorial quickly turned that endorsement into an argument for full support of Chiang Kai-shek, whom publisher Henry Luce had long trumpeted, against all evidence and argument to the contrary, as the key to a democratic, noncommunist Asia. In *Life*'s view, the United States had assumed the twin tasks of protecting all noncommunist Asian nations against external Communist aggression and of developing stable political economic orders within these countries, to protect them from domestic turmoil and rebellion. In performing this admittedly "mighty job," the editorial concluded, the United States stood to gain more than it would give: "We shall gain in the broadening of our participation in the whole human adventure."[31] It was still the American Century after all.

Despite its special interest in China, *Life* viewed the Korean hostilities primarily through a global lens. A July 17 editorial argued that public support for Truman's decision to intervene gave the United States a renewed opportunity to take the initiative in the global Cold War struggle: "The popular response to the Korean crisis definitely proves that there is a will in the U.S. to support *any* action that may be necessary to check the spread of the Soviet cancer. Since this will palpably exists, U.S. policy is hobbled only by the current defects of American military posture. These defects can and will be eradicated." Truman's surprising resolve in Korea marked a moment of spiritual awakening which, according to *Life*, had "restored the U.S. position all over the free world." In declaring that the national will would support "*any* action," the editorial writers effectively reified the activist consensus they sought to promote. *Life* urged the United States to press for implementation of the Schuman Plan to integrate the French and German steel industries and creation of a European union; to pursue improved relations with India, Indo-China, and the Philippines; and to strengthen all potential allies, both militarily and economically. Again singling out China, *Life* asserted that Chiang Kai-shek should be made "a full partner in the cold war." Finally, *Life* called on the administration to make clear to Stalin that it would intervene in response to any Soviet moves against Yugoslavia and Iran.[32] This last point reflected a frequently voiced concern that the perceived Soviet aggression in Korea was merely a prelude to similar acts elsewhere, possibly including Germany, Japan, Formosa, India, and Indo-China as well as Yugoslavia and the Middle East. In September, a *Collier's* editorial treated the invasion of South Korea as simply one step in the Kremlin's "blueprint for world conquest." A *March of Time* newsreel entitled "As Russia Sees It" portrayed the Korean War in a similar light, complete with images of the globe and the various countries Stalin had supposedly considered attacking before settling on Korea, as well as those he might attack next.[33]

In September 1950, two in-depth reports in the *Saturday Evening Post* purported to present the underlying significance of the Korean situation. The first, by Joseph and Stewart Alsop, was entitled "The Lesson of Korea"; the second, by Demaree Bess, was entitled "How Long Will This War Last?"

According to the Alsops, "The lesson of Korea is grimly simple. Despite innumerable warnings, we did not do enough to deter Soviet aggression or to contain Soviet imperialism." Korea showed once and for all that the Soviets were intent on enslaving the entire world. Korea was the opening salvo of a campaign to bring all of Asia and Europe into the Soviet Empire, but the ultimate aim of this campaign was even more insidious than that. "The real Kremlin goal," the Alsops claimed, "is to make the living death of the slave society the universal condition of mankind, from the shores of the Atlantic to the islands of Japan, from the icy cliffs of Spitsbergen to the bright sands of Cape Comorin." By presenting their dramatic analysis as a matter of inside information, the Alsops freed themselves from the need to present any empirical support for their assertions: "In Korea, the Kremlin meant to start something exactly like the furious gnawing of a flood. Surrender was to lead, by easy stages, to surrender. Victory in Korea was to be the prelude to victory everywhere. This was emphasized and re-emphasized in every analysis of the Korean attack by the State Department experts. And it was for this reason, and this reason only, that the president gave the order to fight for Korea, which the armed services held long ago to be militarily valueless." Like President Truman himself, the Alsops invoked the Munich analogy, embellishing it by suggesting that the situation in the 1950s was far more perilous than that in the 1930s and that "the Kremlin plays the power-and-terror game upon a larger stage than Hitler ever dreamed of" — a stage where the next scenes might be set in Iran, Burma, Indo-China, Berlin, Vienna, and Belgrade.

The Alsops asserted that the Soviet Empire now held military predominance over the United States and "the free world," and that the entire Soviet strategy for world conquest was based on this fact. The United States would therefore have to rebuild Western military strength. In the Alsops' view, Secretary of Defense Louis Johnson was the principal culprit, both for "economizing" when he should have been pursuing maximum preparedness and for claiming that the military was more fully prepared than it was. U.S. foreign and military policy had to be cut loose from all fiscal constraints because the very survival of human freedom was at stake. This required not just rebuilding U.S. military strength but building up the strength of all U.S. allies and potential allies as well, particularly in Europe. At bottom, the lesson of Korea was that Americans had only themselves to blame for the grave situation they now faced: "We and the whole free world are in most dreadful danger because we, as leaders of the free world, have ignored the inherent menace of Soviet war preparation. . . . Everything that can conceivably contribute to the strength of the free world must now be done without hesitation, without question, without regard to politics or cost." Americans had to accept heavy personal sacrifices to ensure the security of the free world. National survival required an unwavering consensus. The alternative, the Alsops concluded, was "to indulge ourselves for a fugitive instant and then to see the totalitarian silence and the night of the soul close over this world of ours."[34] The lesson of Korea seemed to combine the lessons of Munich with the lessons of Orwell's *1984*, or at least with certain elements of its rhetoric.

Still, the Alsops reported that the Soviets sought to avoid total war with the United States, seeking instead to vanquish the forces of freedom piece by piece, and that point provided the main thesis of Demaree Bess's "How Long Will This War Last?" Bess concluded that the hot war in Korea signaled the end of the cold war as such, and that henceforth the United States should prepare for a series of future Koreas, because Russia had embarked on a strategy of lighting such fires around the globe. The good news was that total war seemed unlikely; the bad news was that Korea marked simply the beginning of a ceaseless string of limited conflicts at locations around the globe. The article's concluding paragraph offered a gloomy answer to the title's question: "The American people are confronted with the dreary and painful job of learning how to fight the kind of piecemeal war which the Russians have planned and begun. Nobody in Washington will even venture a guess about how long this kind of war will last. But some people there recall that Europeans once fought a Thirty Years' War and even a Hundred Years' War."[35] With these two articles by the Alsops and Bess, both claiming to base their assessments on privileged inside information, the *Saturday Evening Post* provided high-powered publicity for the State Department's new grand strategy—for the worldview expressed behind the scenes in NSC-68. Korea gave that worldview the best publicity that money, or lives, could buy, which is essentially what Acheson meant when he later said that "Korea came along and saved us." The media portrayed the outbreak of the Korean War as the opening volley of a long, drawn-out world war that might last for generations. The official ideology of American nationalist globalism provided the most potent explanation for such a dreadful situation, while also providing moral clarity about the righteousness of the cause.

Life's editorial writers took this worldview to the extreme. In the Lucean outlook expressed on *Life*'s editorial page, the United States held responsibility for "bringing order and security to Korea, China and to all the people beyond Eboli, where (they say) Christ stopped."[36] As a missionary nation, Henry Luce's America had to complete Christ's unfinished work, no matter the cost. An August 14 *Life* editorial endorsed "A Program for America" recently proposed by Senator Styles Bridges of New Hampshire. This program included the following steps: calling up of the National Guard for federal service; mobilizing around-the-clock military production; establishing a civil defense program; abolishing all "handout programs" and "pork barrel grabs" to free monies for defense spending; requiring registration of all U.S. Communists; and mobilizing anticommunists everywhere, including Chiang Kai-shek's Formosa and Franco's Spain.[37] This last proposition prompted one *Life* reader to point out that "Hitler too opposed Communism. By the same process of reasoning we should support Hitler — if he were rising to power now." Another reader bluntly accused *Life* of trying to "sprinkle fascism with the holy water of your supposed program for freedom."[38] But to *Life*'s editors the struggle was on, to the death, throughout the world. Mistakes in response to the Korean crisis "meant slavery — no less — for all the world, including the people of the U.S."[39] So the United States would have to lead the world to its own salvation: "We have to mobilize effectively not only ourselves but all of the more than one billion people outside the Iron Curtain who, under inspiring leadership, will work and fight for the total defeat of World Communism."[40] The Iron Curtain was no longer merely a European phenomenon. At home, all the vast resources of the United States were now required for the global struggle: "It was American Freedom by which and through which this amazing achievement of wealth and power was fashioned. And it is to the defense of Freedom and to the proclamation of Freedom throughout the earth that all this wealth and power will be dedicated."[41] This was a call for total cold war, as envisioned in NSC-68. Like NSC-68, *Life* omitted any blemishes (such as slavery and other forms of exploitation) from the American narrative. American society was poised to become a vast Gideon's Army, doing battle for the Lord. The worldwide "proclamation of Freedom" would be predicated on the worldwide projection of U.S. power.

ACCEPTING INTERVENTION: THE *DAILY NEWS* AND SENATOR TAFT

The *New York Daily News* engaged in no such ideological cheerleading, but its response to Truman's intervention in Korea showed at least a reluctant acceptance of the nationalist-globalist definition of international reality. Editorially, the *Daily News* greeted the North Korean invasion of South Korea as a sign of disarray in the Truman administration's Asia policy. But while the paper generally made clear that the attackers were North Koreans, not Russians, its headlines routinely referred to them as "Korean Reds" or just plain "Reds," and its editorial writers referred to the Soviet Union as North Korea's "puppet-master." In news articles, moreover, the administration viewpoint came through loud and clear. On June 26, for example, the headline above a United Press wire story proclaimed:

"Korea War Called 2d Thrust for Red Asia." The lead reported that government experts "described the Korean war as the second stage of a Russian campaign to subjugate the entire Far East by means of puppet regimes." The "first stage," of course, had been "the conquest of China" by the Soviet Union. That would have been startling news to the Chinese, but to most Americans it was an accepted fact. With their move in Korea, the report continued, "the Russians are pushing out from China to a two-pronged pincers movement against other Asiatics." Despite its editorial skepticism concerning Truman's foreign policy, the *News* actually helped to project the administration's basic explanation of the Korean conflict.[42]

Truman's June 27 decision to send U.S. forces into Korea prompted banner headlines and a certain amount of grudging respect from the *News'* editorial writers. "U.S. PLANES, SHIPS FIGHTING IN S. KOREA," ran the front-page headline, with a terse subhead: "Stop Reds, Guard Formosa: Truman." Below the headline, the tabloid featured a photograph of "a serious-visaged" Truman along with his "grim" defense secretary, Louis Johnson, and Attorney General J. Howard McGrath. Inside, the news story on Truman's decision appeared under the title "President's Order: Save Korea!" The paper's lead editorial called the move "Truman's Greatest Gamble," a gamble that might lead to World War III if Stalin responded by sending in Soviet troops behind "his North Korean puppets" rather than backing down as he had in Berlin. The editorial said Truman deserved credit for acting swiftly and decisively, but it hedged its bets on the president's wager. The closing sentence simply urged readers to hope, "for the sake of the nation — for the sake of the world," that the president had walked in "with his eyes open and a fair chance to win." The *News's* Washington commentator, John O'Donnell, expressed similar sentiments.[43]

O'Donnell and the *News* editorial writers also called for Dean Acheson's resignation as secretary of state, as did Senator Robert A. Taft, whose views O'Donnell especially identified himself with. Taft's June 28 speech in Congress was featured prominently in the *Daily News* and amplified in both O'Donnell's column and the newspaper's editorial. The senator backed Truman's Korean decision and accepted his rationale for intervention, although he criticized the president for usurping congressional authority over the use of the armed forces. In Taft's view, Truman was finally drawing a clear line against the Communist threat — a line that should have been drawn much earlier. The senator also emphasized the need for "unstinted support" of the U.S. troops in Korea, and warned that the "de facto war" in North Korea could lead to a full-scale war with the Soviet Union. But he argued that the president had reversed Acheson's policies, which Taft believed had actually encouraged Communist aggression in Asia. Acheson "had better resign," said Taft, "and let someone else administer the program to which he was, and perhaps still is, so violently opposed." The irony here is twofold. First, Acheson played a central role in Truman's decision to "draw the line" and intervene in Korea. Second, and more important, Taft's comments show that by 1950 the conservative, formerly anti-interventionist or "isolationist" wing of the Republican Party was actually demanding that the globalist framework of the Truman Doctrine be applied equally in Asia as in Europe, even if it meant expanded military expenditures and overseas commitments.[44]

Sharing Taft's conservative position, the *Daily News* now accepted the global nature of the cold war conflict and restricted its criticism of the Truman administration to tactical matters. The *News* continued to cast a skeptical eye toward both the United Nations and the United States' "alleged allies" in Europe. It also continued to lambaste Acheson and to suggest that the Truman administration had, at best, blundered its way into the Korean conflagration. Above all, it stressed the need to "keep tabs" on the profligate, big-government Democrats as the necessary military buildup proceeded. But by mid-1950 it seemed to accept, somewhat grudgingly, the basic framework that shaped the administration's foreign policy.

To the *News*'s editorial writers, President Truman's July 19 speech presented a blueprint "for U.S. policing of the earth until such time as world Communism either dies on the vine or crawls back into its original hole" in Russia. The editorial rightly viewed this plan as "an expansion of the original Truman Doctrine." While voicing a note of complaint in reporting that the president had asked Congress for some "drastic measures" (including an initial $10 billion to pay for the intervention alone, consumer credit controls, and possible price controls), the *News* never said those measures were uncalled for. Rather, it endorsed the joint statement issued by Taft and Republican House leader Joseph W. Martin, which declared that Republicans would "scrutinize carefully each measure proposed by the administration to make sure it is actually necessary to mobilize the nation's resources, and not merely to serve as a step toward permanent government controls." If Walter Reuther expressed a social democratic variant of American nationalist globalism, the *Daily News* now clearly expressed a conservative brand. The paper was prepared to "embark with Harry on this undertaking to police the world." It simply urged its readers "to keep relentless tabs on the President" and to guard against creeping totalitarianism at home. "It would be a grim joke," the editorial concluded, if in the struggle against communist dictatorship "we should let ourselves be razzle-dazzled into dictatorship in our own country." That was a sober assessment from an editorial page that often sounded flippant.[45]

In September, the *News* criticized Truman's next major speech concerning the Korean situation for employing "high-sounding sentiments" about fighting in Korea to preserve peace for all time. To the *News*'s editors, that sounded too much like the rhetoric that Woodrow Wilson and Franklin Roosevelt had used in dragging the United States into two previous world wars. But that editorial still did not criticize Truman's basic foreign-policy strategy. The range of debate was narrowing dramatically as events in Korea seemed to confirm the nationalist-globalist view.[46]

COLD WAR, HOT WAR, COLOR LINE

The African American press generally supported Truman's decision to intervene in Korea, though it did so in rather less sanguine, less hyperbolic terms than the popular white-controlled magazines did. (One correspondent, however, had repeatedly predicted the outbreak of World War III by mid-1950 and consequently greeted the Korean conflict as the opening skirmish in a general war.) African American commentators often viewed the intervention within the context of race relations as well as U.S.-Soviet relations. But the significant progress made toward desegregating the military during the later 1940s helped to buttress African American support for the war, even while it heightened black demands for the end of all segregation in the U.S. armed forces, a matter in which the Army lagged far behind the Air Force and the Navy. Historically, blacks had tended to see military service as an opportunity to demonstrate their loyalty to the flag and strengthen their claim to full citizenship rights; military desegregation powerfully reinforced this view. During the Korean War, the black press regularly celebrated the role of black servicemen in combat. The African American pilots who flew combat missions in Korea were presented as a particular source of racial pride. The "Tan Yanks" were "our GIs" in a way that the white Yanks obviously weren't. As *Pittsburgh Courier* columnist Marjorie McKenzie put it, "Almost nothing could give Negroes a greater sense of belonging to this nation than the right to die for it on a basis of equality and dignity." Their palpable patriotism in the Korean crisis, wrote her colleague Henry Bibb, "should muzzle the Dixiecrats."[47] *Ebony* magazine's editorial page expressed similar arguments, concerning both Korea and the ever-heightening "world struggle for democracy" of which Korea was, in its view, but a part. Such commentary was gauged not simply as a response to the outbreak of war but as a refutation of Paul Robeson's earlier controversial comment that blacks would not fight for the United States against the Soviet Union.[48]

The African American response to the outbreak of the Korean War was sharply polarized between Robeson's dissidence and an uncritical patriotism. One letter to the editor of the *Pittsburgh Courier* expressed frustration at the black press's heavy emphasis on "the well-known fact that the Negro will . . . fight for America without question." The writer, Rev. William Marion of Evanston, Illinois, argued that the African American press would better serve its readers by examining the basis for "the United Nation's intervention into Korean affairs," to determine whether it was justified, "rather than whoop up the Negro's willingness to plunge into the conflict." Rev. Marion concluded by suggesting that the UN flag in Korea should have been given to Ralph Bunche rather than Douglas MacArthur—presumably because Bunche was a man of peace as well as a man of color, and perhaps also because he headed the UN's Trusteeship Division, charged with overseeing the process of decolonization. But the kind of critical reflection the Rev. Marion called for was largely missing from the black press now that the nation—and African American troops—were at war.[49]

In its first editorial on the Korean situation, the *Courier* called the conflict a civil war and said that all Americans wondered whether it would ignite into a third world war. Yet the same editorial applauded the United States for acting through the United Nations, endorsed the UN for condemning "the aggression against the southern Korean republic," and suggested that other nations should join the United States in backing up the UN's authority with military force. A month later, another *Courier* editorial elaborated the paper's position and showed that its editorial writers now operated clearly within the framework of American nationalist globalism, a significant shift from its earlier, more critical position. This piece argued against the notion "that this is a war of American 'imperialism' against colored people across the Pacific." Instead, the *Courier* argued, the Korean conflict was a war to halt the spread of Communist totalitarianism, which the paper now deemed a form of "slavery worse than chattel slavery on every count." Evidently, the *Courier* now saw the Iron Curtain as a greater barrier than the Color Line.[50]

Several *Courier* columnists even implied that the U.S. intervention could help to erase certain parts of the color line. With a touch of irony, Marjorie McKenzie argued that the Korean War actually enhanced the prospects of peace, because it forced America to focus its attention on the nonwhite world. To meet the challenge posed in Korea, McKenzie concluded, the United States would have to abandon its racist assumptions. Uncharacteristically, though, McKenzie never critically examined the nature of the challenge in Korea.[51]

NAACP Secretary Walter White pursued a similar tack. In his *Chicago Defender* column, White wrote that "Korea has brought the United States face to face with the global race question far sooner than even the best informed Americans believed would be the case." War against a nonwhite nation, under the banner of freedom and democracy, left U.S. race prejudice even more painfully exposed than it had been before. Dixiecrat white supremacists had become the State Department's greatest public relations liability. Yet against "Communist propaganda of a 'race war'" between the white and nonwhite worlds, White asserted that "the Korean struggle is one between an aggressive totalitarianism and an imperfect democracy whose most grievous weaknesses are the sins of colonialism and race." White thus accepted the administration's formulation of the issue: the real protagonists were the Soviet Union and the United States. To White, Indian and Pakistani support of the U.S.-UN intervention belied the notion of a "race war." The NAACP leader now endorsed the view that the Soviet Union sought to conquer all of Asia one nation at a time, from Southeast Asia to India. To defeat this strategy and "avert destruction of us all," White argued, the United States would have to gain the support of the nonwhite peoples of Asia, Africa, and Latin America, all of whom "regard as the barometer of white sincerity the treatment of Negroes in the United States." In enlightened self-interest, therefore, the United States had no choice but to treat its African American citizens on a basis of equality. White's anticommunism was no doubt sincere, and stemmed in part from NAACP dealings with the U.S. Communist Party dating back to the 1930s, but his ability to turn issues of global anticommunism into arguments for domestic racial equality was uncanny.[52]

As an organization, the NAACP's initial response to the Korean conflict was multifaceted, reflecting concern with racism and the legacy of colonialism as well as with communism. The Association's 1950 annual conference concluded the same day that North Korean forces crossed the 38th parallel, so the membership never had a chance to consider the opening phase of the war. An editorial in the August–September 1950 issue of *The Crisis* simply accepted "the hot war in Korea" and treated U.S. victory there as a certainty. But the NAACP's official publication questioned whether the United States possessed the vision or understanding necessary to respond adequately to the economic and political problems of an emerging postcolonial Asia. A purely military and simplistically anticommunist approach would prove insufficient, it argued, and continued racism would doom U.S. relations with nonwhite peoples. As the editorial concluded: "We cannot win Asia to our side by backing reactionaries like Bao Dai in Indochina, Chiang Kai-shek in Formosa, or Rhee in South Korea. And we will never win the political war in Asia as long as Koreans and Asiatics are 'gooks' in the eyes of our fighting men. Whether we know it or not, Asia is in revolution. Her people fight for nationhood. Here is America's opportunity to live up to her own revolutionary past by helping the struggling masses of Asia to economic security and political independence."[53] Shortly after this editorial went to press, however, the NAACP's board of directors voted at its September 14 meeting to support "the efforts of the United States and the United Nations to halt Communist aggression in Korea." Ironically, those efforts included support for Syngman Rhee's authoritarian regime in South Korea.

The NAACP board's resolution combined arch anticommunist rhetoric with a plethora of civil rights demands. "Victory over disruptive and sinister Communist forces" required the support of noncommunist Africa and Asia, the resolution argued, and to win such support, the United States would "have to demonstrate that democracy is a living reality which knows no limitation of race, color or nationality." Beyond military victory in Korea, but toward the goal of victory in the global struggle against communism, the resolution called for "prompt and effective action to end all forms of racial discrimination and segregation in our military and civilian life." Specifically, the NAACP board's endorsement of the Korean war provided a vehicle for demanding "the abolition of separate Army units, the removal of barriers to employment opportunities, the end of segregation in education, the lifting of all barriers to housing, the elimination of all Jim Crow restrictions in travel, recreation and public accommodations generally, and the outlawing of outmoded patterns of segregation in the Nation's Capital."[54] These were strong demands in 1950, yet they were couched in militant Cold War rhetoric, in a document fully supporting both U.S. military intervention in Korea and the official justification of that intervention. Like much of the African American community, for which it remained the most influential voice, the NAACP had moved securely within the Cold War consensus. The hot war in Korea helped redraw the lines of the Cold War debate in the United States, promoting national unity and strengthening the administration's hand.

J. A. Rogers, whose idiosyncratic historical scholarship always informed his iconoclastic newspaper writings, offered perhaps the most consistently critical perspective on the beginnings of the Korean War of any African American columnist. In his July 15 column, Rogers argued that the United States was simply getting itself stuck on an interventionist treadmill: "All history shows one war leads inevitably to another, therefore Americans may never again know real peace, never again be free from taxation for war, war, war." He asserted, moreover, that "Asia, Communist or not, intends to be free of white dominance." Rogers again pierced the prevailing discourse the following week, insisting that South Korea was a police state, not a democracy, and that although "the news of the invasion was carried as if it were another Pearl Harbor, both sides had been fighting on the border for years." He blamed the current crisis on U.S. diplomatic bungling at Yalta, which had produced the "unnatural" division of the country. In his July 29 column, Rogers argued that Koreans on both sides of the 38th parallel wanted rice and land more than democracy. The Koreans, he added, had never known "real democracy" throughout their long history, and democracy was a slow process for any country to develop, as U.S. history clearly showed. So, for Rogers, the claim that the UN and the United States were intervening in the interest of democracy in Korea held little credence. The only certain thing, he concluded, was that more such wars of intervention would follow. Rogers was prophetic, as were those few others who expressed similar views. But they were voices crying out in the wilderness.[55]

In keeping with their closely linked political strategies, the UAW's response to the Korean War partly paralleled the NAACP's. UAW president Walter Reuther supported Truman's decision to send U.S. forces to South Korea from the beginning.[56] The union did not convene in 1950, but in his opening remarks to its 1951 convention, Reuther discussed the crisis in terms of the larger global struggle and in keeping with his own social democratic version of nationalist globalism: "The struggle between tyranny and freedom, between Communism and Democracy, is a struggle for men's minds, their hearts and their loyalties, and you cannot win that struggle if you fight only on the battlefield. If we are going to make freedom secure in the world and really stop the forces of Communist tyranny, then we have to fight against poverty and hunger and insecurity in the world with the same devotion with which we fight against Communist aggression on the battlefronts." Reuther proclaimed that "the free labor movement," and especially the UAW, was the bulwark in the fight to use the world's unprecedented productive capacity "to abolish poverty and hunger in the world." The peoples of Asia, Europe, South America, and Africa were struggling for freedom and social justice, and the United States had to prove to them "that in the kind of world we are fighting to build, it is possible to have both bread and freedom." The labor movement understood that fight far better than "the Wall Street boys," Reuther said, despite their claims to the contrary. Echoing the "Double V" campaign of the African American community during World War II, Reuther declared that "this is a two-front fight. We will fight the Commies on the battlefront and we will fight the profiteers on the home front." In other speeches to the UAW's 1951 assemblage, CIO president Philip Murray and former congresswoman Helen Gahagan Douglas also discussed the current crisis in terms of a global struggle between freedom and tyranny.[57]

That same UAW convention overwhelmingly approved a resolution on Korea that not only supported U.S. intervention but compared the invasion of South Korea to the Nazi aggression against Austria, Czechoslovakia, and Poland and the Soviet aggression against Finland "that together launched World War II," as well as to the Japanese attack on Pearl Harbor. It presented the situation in Manichaean terms, and held Moscow fully responsible for initiating this latest aggression as part of "its program of world domination."

A handful of delegates dissented, however, arguing that the situation in Korea was more complicated. While disclaiming any intention of defending the Communist role in Korea, for example, Delegate Anderson of Local 15 argued that it was in fact a Korean war: "This Korean War is not just inspired by Soviet agents as the public press would have us believe, but it is to a large extent a civil war, a revolutionary war such as the American people fought back in 1776, and our American Civil War, because it is largely between the property classes of Korea and the workers of Korea." Delegate Arnoff of Local 195 argued that the uncritical anticommunism reflected in the resolution ultimately contributed to a fascist resurgence. In response to such criticism, Reuther announced that the resolutions committee proposed to amend the resolution to state that the UAW opposed "the corrupt reactionary regime of Syngman Rhee" as well as "the totalitarian aggression of Communist tyranny." Still, Reuther himself insisted that the question under debate was whether the Soviet Union or the United Nations was responsible for aggression in Korea; like Dean Acheson, Reuther seemed to think it was not a Korean war at all. By a show of hands, in the end, the UAW convention adopted the amended resolution all but unanimously, with fewer than twenty delegates voting against it.[58]

At the 1950 conventions of the two electrical workers' unions, discussions of the Korean War followed markedly different lines. The new International Union of Electrical Workers (IUE) never really discussed the war. But, without discussion, its delegates voted unanimously to adopt a resolution on the "Korean Crisis and Patriotism" that presented a classic Cold War view of the conflict. In this document, the crisis had been sparked simply by "Communist aggression in Korea." Neither North nor South Korea was mentioned at all. The underlying conflict was between the United States and the Soviet Union, hence the emphasis on patriotism. In the name of patriotism, the IUE proclaimed its unqualified "support for American leadership in the struggle for a free and democratic Korea." Of course, the struggle was not really about Korea, and it would not end once that nation was "free and democratic," whatever that might mean: "The United States is locked in combat with a ruthless and cunning enemy. The outcome of this struggle may well decide the future course of the whole free world. Americans realize that, now that we have taken up arms in the defense of freedom, we shall not lay down those arms until the issue has been settled in complete victory for the free world." Patriotism compelled unquestioning devotion to a war without end. Playing on the adage that eternal vigilance is the price of peace, the IUE resolution declared that "the price of freedom is hard work in producing the weapons of war and the tools of peace and the will to use these weapons and tools to achieve our goals." The text pointed out that IUE members were "the producers of vital weapons needed" in the quest, and closed by pledging "their sweat and toil, their hearts and loyalties, to the patriotic duty of defending our country and the free world."[59]

At the 1950 UE convention, by contrast, criticism of the U.S. "war economy" reverberated throughout the delegates' discussions of economic and trade union issues as well as foreign policy, even though UE members too were heavily employed in war industries.[60] The UE once again adopted a foreign-policy resolution thoroughly critical of the Truman administration's programs. Although the resolution itself never mentioned Korea by name, the Korean conflict dominated the ensuing floor debate.

Leftist UE members demonstrated a subversive understanding of how the ideology I call American nationalist globalism controlled the country's public discourse. Delegate Sandra Waite spoke of employers attempting to use the wartime call for national unity to block workers' demands for wage increases. She then urged members to turn the tables and question the patriotism of the companies that were so committed to fighting communism. Delegate David Minton told his fellow UE members that when American soldiers in Korea used the word "Gook" it meant "I am an American; I'm superior to anyone in the whole world; I am superior to the colored people of Asia." He warned that this attitude was antithetical to the nation's democratic claims and would provoke extensive hatred toward the American people. Other delegates complained that any criticism of the administration's foreign policy was all too promptly branded "un-American."[61]

Most incisively of all, delegate William Smith of Chicago Local 108 decried what he saw as the widespread American tendency to support the government "right or wrong" without criticizing it when it was wrong. If the American people failed to break this habit, he asserted, then "we have got a long, vicious fight against the people who are fighting for freedom in this world." Smith prefaced this remark by saying that when he woke up that morning he heard on the radio that Red China was moving into Indochina in support of the Viet Minh. "The first thing that occurred to me," Smith related to the convention, "is that now our troops also will be moving into Indo-China." Perhaps Smith and his brothers and sisters in the post-purge UE really were all Communist Party members or fellow travelers. But they understood a thing or two about their own country and the dangerous track it was on.[62]

In his opening remarks earlier in the convention, UE president Albert Fitzgerald claimed that the union still contained "shades of opinion that go all the way from 'Pull the troops out of Korea!' to 'Drop an atom bomb on Russia!'" Fitzgerald urged members to pursue a middle ground of supporting the troops while reserving the right to criticize the government's foreign policies. After lengthy debate, the delegates voted to adopt the proposed foreign-policy resolution. Ironically, the organization that had been expelled from the CIO as a Communist front group contained a greater range of free expression than the supposedly democratic union created to replace it in the CIO fold. Yet the dissent expressed within the UE was now so thoroughly painted with the red brush that it mattered little in the public sphere outside the convention hall.[63]

CONCLUSION

By mid-1950, the range of public debate concerning U.S. foreign policy had narrowed considerably since the end of World War II and even since 1947 and 1948. The world in which Americans stood proudly triumphant in 1945 had come to seem a tumultuous and dangerous place by 1947, and it seemed even more so by 1950. But when another war broke out, the result was not increased confusion but heightened clarity in public discussion of world affairs. The ideology of American nationalist globalism offered a simple explanation for events in Korea, in the United Nations, in the world at large. The Truman administration operated within the framework of that ideology in formulating its policies, and the president used it in justifying those policies to the American people. The foreign-policy and opinion-shaping elites were worried by the problem of securing and maintaining a public consensus behind an ambitious policy of global activism. But the initial response to the Korean War suggested that such a consensus was at hand, not because the general public understood all the details or nuances of complex policy issues, but because most Americans had come to share the ideological perspective that guided the policymakers themselves and because ideological dissent had been delegitimized or repressed. As the realities of the war grew more complicated, as more Americans died in Korea, and as the aims of U.S. policy came to seem unclear, the Truman administration's conduct of the war would come under increasing criticism. But the ideology of nationalist globalism would remain in place to offer a ready explanation for unsettling developments in a tumultuous world and to justify future interventions.

CONCLUSION

By 1950, the ideology of the Cold War had come to dominate public life in the United States. It was an ideology of American nationalist globalism, in which the United States was seen to be locked in global struggle with forces of international communism, controlled by a Soviet government intent on world conquest. That struggle was believed to threaten fundamental American values, most notably freedom of enterprise and freedom of religion, and the possibility of spreading those values, which were deemed universal, to the rest of the world, which longed for them. Within this ideology, virtually all international problems or crises were seen as part of the overarching conflict between the United States and the USSR — between their competing ideologies and ways of life. Within this framework, a threat to "freedom" anywhere in the world was deemed a threat to the American way of life. This provided a simple, dichotomous view that seemed to many if not most Americans to explain the often frustrating and infinitely more complex developments of the postwar world. The roots of this ideology lay in a tradition of thinking about America's national mission and destiny, a tradition reaching back to the seventeenth century. Key elements of this ideology were in place at the end of World War II; some developed during the war, and others preceded it. The final pieces fell into place between 1945 and 1950. Throughout those years, the range of U.S. foreign policy discourse grew increasingly narrow.

Still, even in 1949 and 1950, policymakers and students of public opinion worried that full public support for expanded global commitments would be difficult to come by. Influential studies by the political scientist Gabriel Almond and by a team of authors working under the aegis of the Council on Foreign Relations argued that the general public was woefully ignorant about details of U.S. foreign policy and apathetic about world affairs unless they clearly threatened the well-being of the United States. With NSC-68, the Truman administration prepared to embark on an astonishingly ambitious, long-term program to rebuild the world's political and economic system while combating and ultimately defeating the alleged global threat of Soviet-controlled international communism. That report called for extensive efforts to mobilize public support for waging sustained, total cold war, while its authors displayed significant anxieties about whether such support could be achieved or sustained. When the United States intervened in the Korean War in June 1950, Truman administration officials were pleasantly surprised to find that public response to the key programs they now proposed was strongly positive.

Perhaps the general public was as ignorant and apathetic about world affairs as the experts believed at the time; or perhaps that view was simply a projection of the anxieties of an elite intent on demonstrating its own self-assurance, as embodied in Truman's feistiness, Marshall's calm countenance, and Acheson's Olympian arrogance. But by 1950 the general public, powerfully influenced by the Truman administration and the mass media, tended to share the same ideological outlook on world affairs as the foreign-policy elite. Within that view, the Korean situation made sense only as a manifestation of the U.S.-Soviet conflict. Indeed, few alternative interpretations were readily available, particularly to U.S. citizens who did not wish to be branded disloyal. The potency of American nationalist globalism as an ideological lens that helped to make sense of a chaotic world had been growing consistently since the end of World War II, as it was projected constantly by the government and by much of the mass media. With the intervention in Korea, nationalist globalism secured near-total hegemony in U.S. public culture. Americans who believed that the Korean War had its primary roots in Korea rather than in the global struggle between American freedom and communist tyranny were a tiny minority with virtually no political relevance. But the roots of the dominant ideological view predated the resurgence of popular anticommunism in the later 1940s.

The U.S. victory in World War II had been widely viewed as a sign of America's greatness as a nation. Within the emerging ideology of nationalist globalism, as espoused by the Truman administration and within the mass media, that greatness was seen to entail global responsibilities. As the world's foremost power, the United States was obliged to maintain the peace, to rebuild the world economy, and to provide moral leadership so that America's universalistic values could be realized throughout the world. Certain segments of the American public, most notably within organized labor and the African American community, held visions of America's world responsibilities that differed in significant ways from ideas put forward by the Truman administration and the commercial mass media. But they still operated within the framework of national greatness and global responsibility. Views that opposed such global commitments were deemed "isolationist" and were largely excluded from the acceptable range of public debate.

Between 1945 and 1947, however, mounting tensions between the United States and the Soviet Union led to the breakdown of the vision of a unified postwar world under U.S. leadership. The idea of One World united around American values gave way to the image of a world divided in two. By 1947, in fact, the wartime metaphor of two worlds, free and unfree, locked in mortal combat, had returned to the center of U.S. foreign-policy discourse. Originally used to describe the condition of total war against fascism and Nazism, this metaphor was resuscitated to describe the emerging cold war against the Soviet Union.

The ideology around which the Cold War consensus was forged from 1947 on consisted of three main constructs: national greatness, global responsibility, and anticommunism. Anticommunism was the last leg of this ideological triad to fall into place. By explaining why the United States was having such a difficult time meeting its global responsibilities while simultaneously buttressing the nation's claims to greatness, anticommunism put the whole ideology in working order. The third leg enabled the triad to stand. But the essential ideology was one of American nationalist globalism, not anticommunism. In itself, anticommunism was hardly new to U.S. political culture in 1947. But with the Soviet Union sitting astride Eastern and Central Europe, global anticommunism now became a defining element in U.S. foreign-policy ideology as represented in public discourse. The perception that the communist menace was worldwide received significant amplification in 1949, with the "loss" of China to Mao's army and the Soviet Union's explosion of its first atomic device.

The idea of the Soviet threat proved salient precisely because it threatened the idea of the American Century. Global anticommunism fit powerfully into the existing mixture of national greatness and global responsibility—American nationalism and American globalism—because this mixture had already begun to function as an ideology of nationalist globalism that helped many Americans make sense of their nation's dominant place in the postwar world. Global anticommunism lent increased potency to this ideological vision. The appeal of global anticommunism—and especially the impact of the Truman Doctrine speech of March 12, 1947—must be understood in that context.

In 1947 the Truman Doctrine provoked far-reaching debate, though it clearly carried the day. In 1950 the application of that doctrine to Asia provoked overwhelming support. After the enunciation of the Truman Doctrine and the Marshall Plan in the first six months of 1947, and especially after congressional approval of the Marshall Plan in the wake of the Czech coup in February and March of 1948, the range of acceptable public debate about the basic objectives of U.S. foreign policy had grown increasingly constricted. To a certain extent, Henry Wallace attempted to make these objectives a central question of the 1948 presidential campaign. But Wallace and the foreign-policy questions he sought to raise were painted with a red brush that left them beyond the pale of acceptable public discussion. Certain elements of the civil rights and labor movements attempted to express dissent over U.S. foreign-policy initiatives in tactical terms, but to do so they accepted the terms of the debate as established by the Truman administration's stated global objectives. In so doing, groups like the NAACP and the UAW sought to gain both government and public support to advance their own domestic agendas. While both organized labor and African Americans gained certain objectives as a result, their acceptance of the official objectives of U.S. foreign policy contributed to the narrowing of public discourse concerning both national and international issues.

In late 1948 and 1949, systematic dissenters who forthrightly opposed the basic foreign-policy strategy of the Truman administration, such as W. E. B. Du Bois, Paul Robeson, and Henry Wallace, found themselves more marginal than ever. The UE and other left-wing unions that opposed the Marshall Plan were expelled from the CIO, which in effect took away their status as respectable American trade unions. These dissenters had stepped outside the bounds of legitimate discourse as defined by the prevalent notions of national greatness, global responsibility, and anticommunism. Wallace certainly preached his own doctrine of national greatness and global responsibility, but his failure to accept global anticommunism nonetheless placed him beyond the pale.

As I have sought to demonstrate, most national leaders of the civil rights and labor movements, most notably of the NAACP and the UAW, chose to operate within the boundaries established by the government and the mass media. In 1945 these organizations had been far to the left of the Truman administration. But between their own anticommunism, their desire to demonstrate their own national loyalty, and their belief that their own domestic agendas depended on friendly relations with a Democratic administration, they came increasingly to support the main contours of Truman's foreign policy. The NAACP and the UAW continued to offer tactical criticisms, but in the absence of any sustained public debate about the fundamental, strategic, and ideological assumptions guiding U.S. foreign policy, such tactical dissent had little effect.

On the right, the conservative, "isolationist" opposition to American globalism had been essentially undermined by the entire experience of World War II, from Pearl Harbor to Hiroshima and Nagasaki. After the war, nonetheless, the *New York Daily News* and other unilateralist voices — including, most notably, Senator Robert A. Taft — joined in the choruses of American national greatness yet remained skeptical about the notion of global responsibility. From 1947 to 1950, however, their staunch anticommunism forced a growing, though never complete, convergence with the dominant ideology of nationalist globalism. By 1950, they essentially accepted U.S. global responsibility as a consequence of the nation's greatness and its commitment to global anticommunism.

The lack of fundamental public debate about the nature and purposes of U.S. foreign policy after 1950 contributed to the development of an increasingly militarized foreign policy controlled by narrow ideological blinders that obscured fundamental international realities. "The so-called Cold War," in the words of Joyce and Gabriel Kolko, "was far less the confrontation of the United States with

Russia than America's expansion into the entire world — a world the Soviet Union neither controlled nor created."[1] The ideology of American nationalist globalism, which defined international reality in terms of a Manichaean struggle between the U.S.-led "free world" and Soviet-controlled communist totalitarianism, served to justify the expansion of U.S. power throughout the world while obfuscating the enormous complexities of a world experiencing the final collapse of European colonialism. It enabled most Americans to feel pride in being citizens of a great nation that wanted only to protect its own way of life and to defend "free peoples everywhere" from totalitarian aggression. The absence of debate about the underlying assumptions of U.S. foreign policy throughout most of the Cold War era served to reify that ideological conception.

Since the fall of the Berlin Wall in 1989 and the collapse of the Soviet Union two years later, the ideological foundations of American nationalist globalism have been loosened but not undone. There is no longer an interventionist consensus, because there is no longer a predominant perception of a single, overarching threat to the United States. But most Americans are quite sure that their country won the Cold War and that they are citizens of the world's number-one nation. As the Persian Gulf War demonstrated, national greatness and global responsibility can mobilize a potent public consensus behind large-scale intervention without anticommunism playing a role. Until we have a more thoroughgoing debate over the nature and purposes of our nation's foreign policy in a complex, rapidly changing world, we remain in danger of falling back into an ideological definition of international realities. If that should happen — especially if it should happen in combination with declining U.S. global hegemony, domestic economic travails, and the persistence of awesome U.S. military power — it could pose a grave new threat itself, both to the health of the republic and to the safety of the world.

NOTES

DN: New York Daily News
HST: Harry S. Truman
HSTL: Harry S. Truman Library, Independence, Mo.
NAACP: Records of the National Association for the Advancement of Colored People, Library of Congress, Washington, D.C.
NUL: Records of the National Urban League, Library of Congress, Washington, D.C.
OF: President's Official Files, Harry S. Truman Library, Independence, Mo.
PC: Pittsburgh Courier
PP: Public Papers of the Presidents of the United States, Harry S. Truman, 1945–1950
PPF200: President's Personal Files, File 200, Harry S. Truman Library, Independence, Mo.
SEP: Saturday Evening Post
UAW: United Automobile, Aircraft and Agricultural Implements Workers of America
UE: United Electrical, Radio and Machine Workers of America
Vital Speeches: Vital Speeches of the Day

PREFACE

1. See L. Hunt, *New Cultural History;* and Fox and Lears, *Power of Culture.*
2. Anderson, *Imagined Communities.* My view of public culture owes much to Bender, "Wholes and Parts." See also Habermas, "The Public Sphere."
3. See Rodgers, *Contested Truths.* My approach to public discourse has also been influenced by Foucault's *The Archeology of Knowledge and the Discourse on Language,* esp. the appended essay, "The Discourse on Language," 215–37.
4. For more detailed citation of many of these sources, see my doctoral dissertation (Fousek, "To Lead the Free World").
5. See Sussmann, *Dear FDR;* McElvaine, *Down and Out in the Great Depression;* and esp. Brinkley, *Voices of Protest.*
6. In December 1945, 81 percent of U.S. adults surveyed had never seen a television set in operation. In May 1949, 44 percent of those polled had seen a television program, but only 4 percent had a set in their home. By May 1950, 62 percent had seen a television program, but still only 10 percent had a television in their home. Gallup, *Gallup Poll,* 1:551, 2:821, 2:921. Also see Diggins, *Proud Decades.*
7. Detailed accounts of the communist issue in the U.S. labor movement, both of which provide extensive discussions of the UE and the UAW in the immediate postwar years, are given by Cochran, *Labor and Communism;* and Levenstein, *Communism, Anticommu-*

nism, and the CIO. The importance of international issues within the UE is discussed by Schatz, *Electrical Workers,* 167–221, esp. 184, 193–95, and 215. For a more general discussion of organized labor and early Cold War foreign policy, see Radosh, *American Labor and U.S. Foreign Policy,* 304–47 and 435–52, esp. 435–37.

INTRODUCTION

1. Gaddis, *U.S. and the Origins of the Cold War,* 351; LaFeber, "American Policy-Makers, Public Opinion, and the Outbreak of the Cold War"; Paterson, "Presidential Foreign Policy, Public Opinion, and Congress: The Truman Years"; and Kofsky, *Truman and the War Scare of 1948.*
2. For the sharpest and most detailed argument along these lines, see Freeland, *Truman Doctrine and the Origins of McCarthyism.*
3. Vaughn, *Holding Fast the Inner Lines.* Alexander's *Nationalism in American Thought* remains perhaps the best synthetic study of this neglected theme in the middle decades of the twentieth century, and it ends with World War II. For one exception, which explicitly treats American nationalism as a major theme in postwar diplomatic history, see McLean, "American Nationalism, the China Myth, and the Truman Doctrine."
4. Hutchinson and Smith, *Nationalism.* Two relatively recent but highly idiosyncratic studies treating American nationalism in the twentieth century as well as earlier, both of which have helped to inform my own thinking, are O'Brien, *God Land: Reflections on Religion and Nationalism,* and Zelinsky, *Nation into State: The Shifting Symbolic Foundations of American Nationalism.* However, these two works preceded the general resurgence of nationalism, both as a social force and as an object of study, triggered by the collapse of the Soviet empire.
5. Dunn, *Contemporary Crisis of the Nation State,* 3, 8; A. D. Smith, *Nations and Nationalism,* 56–57; Anderson, *Imagined Communities,* 6.
6. Anderson, *Imagined Communities,* 1–7; A. D. Smith, *Nations and Nationalism,* 55.
7. Greenfield, *Nationalism,* 3–4.
8. Kohn, *American Nationalism,* esp. 3–4, 8–10.
9. Weinberg, *Manifest Destiny;* Stephanson, *Manifest Destiny;* Tuveson, *Redeemer Nation.* This tradition also figures in M. H. Hunt's treatment of "national greatness" in his *Ideology and U.S. Foreign Policy,* 19–45. The significant persistence of this tradition in the post-1945 era is treated broadly in Baritz, *Backfire.* It is also referred to in passing by Ambrose, *Rise to Globalism,* 109–10; and Paterson, *On Every Front,* 73. However, none of these works examines it systematically or in detail.
10. See "Ideology as a Cultural System," in Geertz, *Interpretation of Cultures,* 193–233, esp. 218–20 and 232. See also Gleason, *Speaking of Diversity,* 153–228; and Susman, "The Culture of the Thirties," in his *Culture as History,* 150–83.
11. See Ambrose, *Rise to Globalism;* and Divine, *Second Chance.*
12. See, for example, Ambrose, *Rise to Globalism,* 109–10; Gleason, *Speaking of Diversity,* 189–91, 199; Paterson, *On Every Front,* 72–74; Reinig, "America Looking Outward," 166; and Ekirch, *Decline of American Liberalism,* 319, 333.
13. Michael H. Hunt's book *Ideology and U.S. Foreign Policy* demonstrates the significance of an ideological analysis of foreign-policy discourse and provides a provocative survey, but because of its chronological breadth, it develops no detailed examination of the

post-1945 years. And although Hunt elucidates many continuities in U.S. foreign-policy ideology over the course of the nation's history, he does little to illuminate the significant tensions and discontinuities of the post-1945 period.

14. See Kohn, *American Nationalism*, 3–37; Gleason, *Speaking of Diversity*, 139, 154, 166–67, 172, 176, 196; and Russel B. Nye, "The American Sense of Mission," in his *This Almost Chosen People*, 164–207.

15. Quoted in Gardner, *Architects of Illusion*, 205.

16. Quoted in LaFeber, *Origins of the Cold War*, 156.

17. On the popular rejection of Wilson and the mood of the period, see Leuchtenburg, *Perils of Prosperity*, esp. 50–65 and 84–85; and the more recent survey of the interwar years, Parrish, *Anxious Decades*, esp. 3–16. On continuing international involvements, see Williams, "Legend of Isolationism"; and Costigliola, *Awkward Dominion*.

18. The following discussion draws on Richard M. Ketchum's vivid narrative history of the period, *The Borrowed Years, 1938–1941: America on the Way to War*.

19. See Barnet, *The Rockets' Red Glare*, 188.

20. On postwar isolationism, see Doenecke, *Not to the Swift*; Radosh, *Prophets on the Right*; and Henry W. Berger, "Senator Robert A. Taft Dissents from Military Escalation," in Paterson, *Cold War Critics*, 167–204.

21. See Gleason, *Speaking of Diversity*, 164–67 and 188–201, esp. 189–97.

22. Tellingly, in a recent book series on twentieth-century U.S. history, Michael Parrish's book on the interwar years is called *Anxious Decades*, while John Patrick Diggins's book on the 1940s and 1950s is called *The Proud Decades*.

23. See Warren I. Susman, "Culture of the Thirties," in Susman, *Culture as History*, 154, 157–58, 160, and 164; and Alexander, *Nationalism in American Thought*.

24. Henry R. Luce, "The American Century," *Life*, February 17, 1941. Luce's essay was also published, with commentaries, in booklet form (Luce, *American Century*). See also Baughman, *Luce and the Rise of the American News Media*, 130–33, 136; and Blum, *V Was for Victory*, 284–85.

25. On the concept of dominant *ethnie* exerting hegemony in nationalist formations, see A. D. Smith, *Nations and Nationalism in a Global Age*, 57–60. On the concept of the "hegemonic bloc" and its applicability to recent U.S. history, see Lears, "Concept of Cultural Hegemony"; and Lears, "A Matter of Taste," esp. 51.

26. On militarization and national security, see Sherry, *In the Shadow of War*, as well as his earlier work, *Preparing for the Next War*. See also Kofsky, *Truman and the War Scare of 1948*.

27. Ferguson, "Industrial Conflict and the Coming of the New Deal."

28. See, for example, Isaacson and Thomas, *The Wise Men*. The term "wise men" also appears in Leffler, *A Preponderance of Power*, 499–502, where the author employs it as a significant analytical device.

29. On the cultural and ideological context of that episode, see LaFeber, *The New Empire*, 62–101; Hofstadter, "Cuba, the Philippines, and Manifest Destiny" (1965), which remains provocative and engaging; and Weinberg, *Manifest Destiny*, 252–323.

30. X [George F. Kennan], "The Sources of Soviet Conduct," *Foreign Affairs* 25 (July 1947): 582; reprinted in *Life*, July 28, 1947, 53–63.

31. Henry A. Wallace, "The Enemy Is Not Each Other," *New Republic* 116 (January 27, 1947): 25. Quoted in Reinig, "America Looking Outward," 380.

32. See Lewis, "Origins and Causes of the Civil Rights Movement," esp. 7–8 and 10; and Gleason, *Speaking of Diversity*, 165.

33. See Gerstle, *Working-Class Americanism*, 153–95, 278–309.

34. Markel, *Public Opinion and Foreign Policy*.

35. See Freeland, *Truman Doctrine and the Origins of McCarthyism*; and Markel, *Public Opinion and Foreign Policy*, 117, 215.

36. See Larson, *Origins of Containment*. More traditional diplomatic histories that provide insight concerning elite ideas and ideology include Gardner, *Architects of Illusion*; Yergin, *Shattered Peace*; and Leffler, *A Preponderance of Power*.

37. Boyer, *By the Bomb's Early Light*; Sherry, *In the Shadow of War*. See also Whitfield, *Culture of the Cold War*, which focuses mainly on the 1950s.

38. Fukuyama, "The End of History?"

CHAPTER ONE

1. This interpretation parallels that put forward by Sherry, *Rise of American Air Power*, 355. For public opinion polling data, see Gallup, *Gallup Poll*, 1:527; and Hadley Cantril, *Public Opinion, 1935–1946* (Princeton, 1951), 20–24 (cited by Sherry, *Rise of American Air Power*, 420 fn. 150). See also Boyer, *By the Bomb's Early Light*, 22–24, esp. 24, where Boyer points out that the percentage of those viewing the bomb as "a good thing" declined (from 69 percent in August 1945 to 55 percent in October 1947), "as the wartime climate faded and people turned increasingly to thoughts of the future."

2. Boyer emphasizes the apprehensiveness provoked by the bomb at the moment of victory. See Boyer, *By the Bomb's Early Light*, 7. That apprehensiveness formed a very important part of U.S. reactions to the bombing of Hiroshima and Nagasaki. My aim here, however, is to emphasize that the bomb also signified U.S. power, if not omnipotence. Both "readings" of the bomb shaped U.S. foreign-policy discourse, the latter more overtly than the former. The apprehensiveness persisted primarily as subtext.

3. Compare Truman's remarks with those of Churchill and Stalin. See *Vital Speeches* 11 (May 1, 1945): 418; and *Vital Speeches* 11 (May 15, 1945): 450–54.

4. See Wittner, *Rebels Against War*; and Doenecke, *Not to the Swift*.

5. Both quotations are from "Statement by the President Announcing the Use of the A-Bomb at Hiroshima," August 6, 1945, *PP, 1945*, 197.

6. Ibid., 198.

7. Ibid., 198.

8. Ibid., 199. See also the discussion of this sentence and Truman's other initial statements concerning the atomic bomb in Sherry, *Rise of American Air Power*, 349–50. Sherry notes that these statements, like the decision to use the atomic bomb, "had been substantially worked up in advance by others," not by Truman himself. Yet, he argues, "taken together, they neatly parroted the war's diverse and conflicting rationales for air power." By examining the rise of the idea of war from the air and its transformation from "unimaginable horror" to "distant commonplace," Sherry's brilliant and disturbing book provides an important context for Truman's statements (see 316 and passim).

9. See Sherry, *Rise of American Air Power*, 350–55; and Boyer, *By the Bomb's Early Light*, 3–26.

10. *DN*, August 7, 1945, 1.

11. *New York Sun* correspondent Phelps Adams, as quoted in Boyer, *By the Bomb's Early Light*, 7. (Boyer cites Adams's observation as "quoted in 'The Atom Bomb,' *Catholic World*, September 1945, p. 452.")

12. *Life*, August 20, 1945, 25–31.

13. Ted Lewis, "Cosmic Missile Believed Truman's Ace at Potsdam," *DN*, August 7, 1945, 2.

14. *DN*, August 8, 1945.

15. Reprinted in the *New York Times*, Sunday edition, August 12, 19, 1945.

16. See *DN*, August 7–14, 1945, for more detailed evidence on this point.

17. It is worth noting here that Truman's "public approval rating" stood at 87 percent in mid-1945, although it would fall to 32 percent after the midterm election of November 1946. See LaFeber, *American Age*, 449.

18. See O'Brien, *God Land*, esp. 40–42.

19. See Weinberg, *Manifest Destiny*.

20. *PP, 1945,* 207.

21. The most thorough study of this tradition remains Tuveson's 1968 *Redeemer Nation*.

22. *PP, 1945,* 211.

23. Ibid.

24. Ibid., 212–13.

25. Ibid., 213.

26. The president also expressed this view in his August 6 statement announcing the bombing of Hiroshima. See *PP, 1945,* 197. Sherry points out that Truman's references to the role of Providence in giving the U.S. the bomb rather than Germany distinguished his statements from previous statements rationalizing the use of air power during the war. See Sherry, *Rise of American Air Power,* 349.

27. *PP, 1945,* 213–14.

28. F. C. Walker to Truman, August 9, 1945; Charles B. Whiddon, Chattahoochee, Fla., to Truman, August 10, 1945; and Walter H. Hellman, Portland, Oreg., to Truman, August 10, 1945 — all in PPF200. Unless otherwise noted, all citizen letters to President Truman cited in this chapter are from PPF200.

29. W. T. McKinley, Albuquerque, N.Mex., to Truman, August 9, 1945; Mr. And Mrs. T. Byron, Chicago, Ill., to Truman, August 10, 1945; Julius Rasmussen, Marshfield, Wisc., to Truman, August 10, 1945; Ignatius Szper, New York, N.Y., to Truman, August 10, 1945.

30. Harris Wofford Jr. to Truman, August 10, 1945; E. F. Hutton to Truman, August 17, 1945.

31. Fully entitled "The Atomic Age: That Flash Showed Where Man's Real Problems Are: Not Under the Bed But in the Cellar," *Life*, August 20, 1945, 32. The meaning of the subtitle is at best difficult to construe.

32. See also Editorial, "We Aren't God," *DN,* August 14, 1945, 17; and Editorial, "A Time for Patience," *SEP,* September 8, 1945, 112.

33. *DN*, August 10, 1945, 1, 3, 17.

34. On the nation as an "imagined community," see Anderson, *Imagined Communities*. On the role of land in the conception of national identity, see O'Brien, *God Land*.

35. This and the other quotations from the editorial on Truman's Potsdam broadcast are from "Truman's Wise Speech," *DN,* August 11, 1945. The newspaper further developed its points concerning the need for the U.S. to develop both its atomic arsenal and its international spy network in another editorial two days later; see "Two Bombs For One — Two Spies For One," *DN,* August 13, 1945, 15.

36. This point was reiterated and amplified in a subsequent *News* editorial, "We Aren't God," *DN*, August 14, 1945, 17.

37. *DN*, August 11, 1945.

38. *DN*, August 15, 1945, 13.

39. Margaret McKenzie, "Pursuit of Democracy," *PC*, August 11, 1945. The belief that the USSR had largely abolished racial discrimination was widespread in 1945, but to fully appreciate McKenzie's irony here, one must note that her postwar columns do not seem to reveal any particular sympathy for the Soviet Union.

40. J. A. Rogers, "Rogers Says," *PC*, August 18, 1945, 7. As a newspaper correspondent, Rogers had covered the Italian invasion of Ethiopia in 1935 and 1936. In the 1940s and 1950s, he devoted numerous volumes to tracing the African ancestry of "great men" and examining interracial sexual liaisons in world history. For some background on Rogers and a generally positive appraisal of his scholarly work, see John Ralph Willis, review of *World's Great Men of Color,* by J. A. Rogers, in the *New York Times Book Review,* February 4, 1973, 21.

41. George S. Schuyler, "Views and Reviews," *PC*, August 18, 1945, 7. Schuyler's long journalistic and literary career followed an often tortuous path from A. Philip Randolph's socialist journal *The Messenger* to the John Birch Society's arch-conservative *Review of the News.* By the mid-1940s, he was well on his way to the latter position. For useful background and an incisive assessment of Schuyler's neglected but important place in black letters and U.S. intellectual and cultural history generally, see Henry Louis Gates Jr., "A Fragmented Man: George Schuyler and the Claims of Race," *New York Times Book Review,* September 20, 1992, 31, 42–43.

42. The process by which this acquiescence occurred over the course of World War II is a central theme of Sherry, *Rise of American Air Power.* As Sherry notes, this process was generally both ignored and inculcated by the press.

43. See Dower, *War Without Mercy,* esp. chap. 4, "Apes and Others," 77–93.

44. Marjorie McKenzie, "Pursuit of Democracy," *PC*, August 18, 1945.

45. See Blum, *V Was For Victory,* 208.

46. For a good discussion of the FEPC, see Polenberg, *War and Society,* 117–23.

47. "A Permanent FEPC," editorial, *Crisis,* September 1945, 249.

48. Quoted in "Real Victory to Come with FEPC Passage," *PC*, August 25, 1945, 5. See also front-page news story on FEPC in the same issue of the *Courier.*

49. *PC*, August 18, 1945, 1, 4.

50. Ibid., 10.

51. "The President's News Conference of August 14, 1945," *PP, 1945,* 216–17.

52. See "Statement by the President Commending Federal Employees." August 14, 1945, *PP, 1945,* 219. For the general public response, particularly photographic representations thereof, see various articles and "centerfolds" in *DN*, August 15–17, 1945, and the extensive photo-essay, "Victory Celebrations," in *Life,* August 27, 1945, 21–33.

53. "Cheers of Thousands Greet Truman," *DN*, August 15, 1945, 10.

54. *PC*, August 25, 1945, 9.

55. Toki, " 'The Prayers of the Righteous Bear Rich Fruit!' " *PC*, August 25, 1945, 10.

56. "Toki Types," *PC*, August 25, 1945, 10. In the same issue, see also O. J. Cansler, "Kolumn Komments" (on Dallas) and Roy Leeland Hopkins, "Toppin' the Town" (on Los Angeles), both on page 14.

57. "Proclamation 2660: Victory in the East — Day of Prayer. August 16, 1945," *PP, 1945,* 223.

58. *PP,* 1945, 254–57.

59. Ibid., 256.

60. Ibid., 256.

61. See Kohn, *American Nationalism,* esp. 3–37.

62. *PP,* 1945, 256–57.

63. Ibid., 257.

64. *Life,* August 27, 1945, 34.

65. See Baughman, *Henry R. Luce and the Rise of the American News Media,* 103–28, 130–33, 136, 160. Baughman suggests that Luce saw himself as a kind of unofficial propaganda minister for U.S. world leadership. From 1940 on, Baughman argues, the publisher believed his "purpose" as a public man was to articulate the idea of "American mission" for the general public (128).

66. Ben Hibbs, signed editorial, "A Time for Patience," *SEP,* September 8, 1945, 112.

67. See note 64 above. Lincoln was a favorite source for both magazine editorial writers and presidential speech writers at the end of World War II, as he had been for Franklin Roosevelt in the 1930s as well. Yet the war-end appropriations of Lincoln's rhetoric lost his tragic tone, substituting the smug hubris of triumphalist nationalism, even when counseling "patience."

68. "Rogers Says," *PC,* August 25, 1945, 7. Also see *DN,* August 15, 1945, 13.

CHAPTER TWO

1. See Blum, *V Was For Victory,* 301–2 and passim.

2. Gallup, *Gallup Poll,* 1:514, 497.

3. In discussing Roosevelt as a foreign policy leader, the historian Robert Dallek does not analyze the role of Roosevelt's rhetoric in shaping public debate on U.S. foreign relations. Rather, Dallek writes that "external events played a central part in helping Roosevelt bring the country through the war in a mood to take a major role in overseas affairs. Much of Roosevelt's public diplomacy during the war was directed toward this goal: The portraits of an effective postwar peace-keeping body, of a friendly Soviet Union, and of a peaceful China had as much to do with creating an internationalist consensus at home as with establishing a fully effective peace system abroad. Principally influenced by Pearl Harbor, which destroyed isolationist contentions about American invulnerability to attack, and by the country's emergence as the world's foremost Power, the nation ended the war ready to shoulder substantial responsibilities in foreign affairs." See Dallek, *Franklin D. Roosevelt and American Foreign Policy, 1932–1945,* 529–38, esp. 537–38. My own emphasis on discourse and ideology is not meant to deny the importance of either "external events" or the United States's objective "emergence as the world's foremost Power" in shaping public opinion about the nation's world role. Rather it is intended as a means of reconstructing, at least partially, the ways in which these and related developments were perceived and discussed in the public sphere at the time.

4. Sherry, *In the Shadow of War,* 29–44.

5. "Annual Message to Congress, January 6, 1942," in Roosevelt, *War Messages,* 27–28.

6. Rosenman, *Public Papers of Franklin D. Roosevelt,* 10:192, cited in Rodgers, *Contested Truths,* 250 fn. 4.

7. Wallace, "Price of Free World Victory," 369.

8. Wallace explicitly invoked the analogy between 1862 and 1942, asserting that the world of the 1940s, like the United States of the 1860s, "could not remain half slave and half free" (ibid.). The proposition that this dichotomy provided "the controlling metaphor of the Cold War" is put forward in Rodgers, *Contested Truths*, 215. I am also indebted to Rodgers for pointing out that "freedom" came to prominence in the 1940s precisely as a war word. The centrality of this metaphor in the postwar period is often pegged to the Truman Doctrine; for just one recent example, see Walter LaFeber, "American Empire, American Raj," in Kimball, *America Unbound*, 69. On *Prelude to War*, see Dower, *War Without Mercy*, and Koppes and Gregory, *Hollywood Goes to War*, as well as the film itself.

9. Raymond Swing's Broadcast, Tuesday, May 8, 1945, Swing Papers, Library of Congress. Concerning Nazism, note that most Americans refused to believe reports of the "final solution" until near the end of the war. See Wyman, *Abandonment of the Jews: America and the Holocaust, 1941–1945*.

10. Blum, *V Was for Victory*, 8–9, emphasizes FDR's efforts to distance himself from Wilson. See also Polenberg, *America at War*, 173; Dallek, *Franklin D. Roosevelt*, esp. 7–20, 361, 440–41, 484; and Kimball, *The Juggler: Franklin Roosevelt as Wartime Statesman*, 63–64, 93–94, 102–5, 109, 120, 128, 185–91.

11. See Franklin D. Roosevelt, "American Foreign Policy," speech to the Foreign Policy Association, New York City, October 21, 1944, as published in *Vital Speeches* 11 (November 1, 1944): 38. For FDR's use of the ostrich metaphor, see *Vital Speeches* 11 (March 1, 1945): 290. For Wilson's use, see John Bartlett's *Familiar Quotations*, 16th ed. (Boston, 1992), 572.

12. *Vital Speeches* 11 (November 1, 1944): 37. See also Roosevelt's Speech to Congress, March 1, 1945, *Vital Speeches* 11 (March 15, 1945): 325.

13. *Vital Speeches* 11 (November 1, 1944): 38.

14. Franklin D. Roosevelt, "Inaugural Address, January 20, 1945," *Vital Speeches* 11 (March 1, 1945): 290. On the conception of American history and national purpose as an experiment or test, as opposed to a matter of destiny, see Arthur Schlesinger Jr., "The Theory of America: Experiment or Destiny?" in his *Cycles of American History*, 5–22, esp. 12 on Lincoln's treatment of the Civil War as a test of whether the republic could endure. It is interesting to note that Roosevelt's speech was clearly modeled after Lincoln's classic Second Inaugural Address, at least in terms of its self-proclaimed brevity. By bringing Providence to bear on the nation's test, Roosevelt's own speech does not fit neatly into Schlesinger's dichotomous model of experiment versus destiny.

15. *New York Times*, April 15, 22, 29, 1945.

16. See Leuchtenburg, *In the Shadow of FDR*, 1–40; Hamby, *Beyond the New Deal*, 53–85 and 87–119; on Rosenman, see Donovan, *Conflict and Crisis*, 8–115, esp. 109–10. For some examples of Truman's reiteration of FDR's ideals, see items on the following pages in *Vital Speeches*: 11 (May 1, 1945): 418; 11 (May 15, 1945): 450, 454; and 11 (June 15, 1945): 514.

17. On FDR as nationalist, see Kimball, *The Juggler*, 185–200, esp. 185. On Truman, see Hamby, "Mind and Character of Harry S. Truman," esp. 52; and Hamby, *Beyond the New Deal*, 115–16. See also "Truman's First Hundred Days," *Life*, August 6, 1945, 19.

18. This significant alteration in presidential rhetoric is particularly striking in Truman's first speech to Congress as president, the day after Roosevelt's burial, and in his V-E Day remarks, which mention only America and Americans, in sharp contrast to Churchill and

Stalin, who used the occasion to praise their Allies as well as their own countries. See *Vital Speeches* 11 (May 1, 1945): 418; and *Vital Speeches* 11 (May 15, 1945): 450–54. See also Donovan, *Conflict and Crisis,* xvi–xvii; and Hamby, "Mind and Character of Harry S. Truman," esp. 52.

19. "Address Before a Joint Session of the Congress. April 16, 1945," *PP, 1945,* 1–6 (quotation on 2).

20. Truman used this phrase with startling frequency during his now legendary railroad campaign trips in 1948. See *PP, 1948.* For the contrast between Roosevelt's cosmopolitanism and Truman's provincialism, compare Dallek, *Franklin D. Roosevelt,* and Hamby, "Mind and Character of Harry S. Truman."

21. On the long-standing belief in U.S. national greatness as a central element in the ideology of U.S. foreign policy throughout the nation's history, see M. H. Hunt, *Ideology and U.S. Foreign Policy,* 19–45. For related themes, see Woodward, "Irony of Southern History," esp. 188–93 and 209–10. For Luce, see Henry Luce, "The American Century," *Life,* February 17, 1941, 61–65; Baughman, *Henry R. Luce and the Rise of the American News Media,* 130–33, 136; and Blum, *V Was for Victory,* 284–85.

22. *New York Times,* May 13, 1945.

23. See Chapter 1 above for a discussion of this theme with regard to the atomic bomb and the end of the Pacific War.

24. Editorial, "Moods of Victory," *Life,* May 14, 1945, 40; Fulbright, *Arrogance of Power.*

25. "The War Ends in Europe," *Life,* May 14, 1945; Editorial, "Moods of Victory," *Life,* May 14, 1945, 40.

26. Editorial, "The Fourth of July," *Life,* July 2, 1945, 22.

27. See Weinberg, *Manifest Destiny;* Tuveson, *Redeemer Nation;* and Stephanson, *Manifest Destiny.*

28. See "Remarks Upon Receiving an Honorary Degree From the University of Kansas City. June 28, 1945," *PP, 1945,* 149–52.

29. Editorial, "America and Russia: To Equal the Communist Talent for Persuasion We Must Develop Persuasiveness of Our Own," *Life,* July 30, 1945. See also Demaree Bess, "Can We Live With Russia?" *SEP,* July 7, 1945, 87.

30. Russell W. Davenport, "Germany—Our Greatest Gamble," *Collier's,* July 7, 1945. On Davenport's background, see Ketchum, *Borrowed Years,* 413–20, 518, 777–78; and *U.S.A.: The Permanent Revolution* (New York, 1951), cited in Lichtenstein, "Labor in the Truman Era," 150–51.

31. See Todorov, *Conquest of America;* and R. B. J. Walker, *Inside/Outside.*

32. The following discussion focuses on articles appearing in the *Saturday Evening Post,* but for an example of the same themes in another magazine, see the editorial entitled "The Old-Time (U.S.) Religion," *Collier's,* August 11, 1945, 82. See also James Marshall, "American Mission: A world culture through education," *Vital Speeches* 11 (January 1, 1945): 185–89; and the General Motors advertisement headlined "Journey into Tomorrow" in *Collier's,* November 3, 1945, 70.

33. *SEP,* April 21, 1945, 44. Interestingly, the poem shared its page with part of an article entitled "Do We Want the West Indies?" which suggested that both the U.S. and the West Indies would be better off if the U.S. took charge of the islands from the British, Dutch, and French after the war.

34. I am indebted to Walter LaFeber for pointing out the parallels with Turner. For an excellent discussion of Turner's thought within the context of U.S. foreign-policy ideology, see LaFeber, *The New Empire*, 63–72, 95–101.

35. Richard Coudenhove-Kalergi, "American Optimism vs. European Pessimism," *SEP*, September 15, 1945, 17, 101.

36. S/Sgt. Jameson G. Campaigne, USMC, "What's the Matter With the U.S.A.?" *SEP*, November 3, 1945, 34, 128.

37. Hal Borland, "Sweet Land of Liberty," *SEP*, December 22, 1945, 9, 37.

38. See Editorial, "Americans Hope for U.S. of Europe," *SEP*, April 7, 1945, 112; George Creel, "The United States of Europe," *Collier's*, December 22, 1945; Editorial, "Did Wisdom Die in 1787?" *SEP*, December 29, 1945, 84; Editorial, "On the Edge of a New Evolution," *SEP*, August 18, 1945; and Secretary of War Robert P. Patterson, "Four Planks for Peace," *Collier's*, November 24, 1945, 60. Also see various speeches by Roosevelt and Truman, particularly Truman, "Address in San Francisco at the closing Session of the United Nations Conference, June 26, 1945," *PP*, 1945, 139; and Boyer, *By the Bomb's Early Light*, 33–45.

39. On Arabs, see the photo-essay "Middle East Oil," in *Life*, June 11, 1945, 25–37, esp. 36–37, where the headline "Americans Bring Their Comforts and Culture to Saudi Arabia's Desert" appears opposite a full-page photograph of Arab boys playing baseball. On Russians, see Edgar Snow, "Russia Still Suspects Us," *SEP*, November 17, 1945, 9–10 and 98, where Snow says that the Russian people, at least, like Americans and admire America's productive powers. On Pacific Islanders, see "Okinawa Now," *SEP*, November 17, 1945, 26–27, "a Post Picture Story"; and "Guam: U.S. Makes Little Island into Mighty Base," *Life*, July 2, 1945, 63–75, an extensive photo-essay.

40. Ben Hibbs, "Journey to a Shattered World," *SEP*, June 9, 1945, 84; William Walton, "The People of Pilsen," *Life*, June 25, 1945, 14; and Ernest O. Hauser, "Italy's Black Shirt Fades to Red," *SEP*, September 1, 1945.

41. See Dower, *War Without Mercy*, 34–37, 48–52, 140; and M. H. Hunt, *Ideology and U.S. Foreign Policy*, 46–91.

42. See Hutchison, *Errand to the World*, esp. 1–14; and Twain, "To the Person Sitting in Darkness."

43. Brigadier General Carlos P. Romulo, "Asia Must Be Free," *Collier's*, October 20, 1945, 12. Romulo was then resident commissioner of the Philippines to the United States and would later serve as president of the Philippines.

44. The quotation is from Editorial, "The Little Brown Brother Has Earned a Break," *SEP*, August 11, 1945, 100, which provides an archetypal example of U.S. paternalism.

45. Clark Coleman, American Negro Press, "Jim Crow Hits Philippines," *PC*, October 13, 1945, 20.

46. See, for example, Roi Ottley, "Democracy (American Style) Goes to Germany: Same Nazis Who Killed Jews Now Taught To Hate Negroes," *PC*, December 22, 1945, 13; J. A. Rogers, "Rogers Says," *PC*, August 18, 1945, 7; and P. L. Prattis's column, *PC*, August 25, 1945, 7.

47. Jekeais, "Psalm from the Islands," *SEP*, June 16, 1945, 34 and 79.

48. Sherry, *In the Shadow of War*.

49. See Gallup, *Gallup Poll*, 1:490, 501–2, 509, 516, 539.

50. *DN*, August 3, 1945, 21; John O'Donnell, "Capitol Stuff," *DN*, December 25, 1945, 4. See also United Press, "Japan's Death Blow Due: Mac," *DN*, August 2, 1945, 20; "Strong Air

Force Top Defense, Says Arnold," *DN*, August 2, 1945, 2; and Editorial, "Does Might Make Right? Sure, In War," *DN*, August 4, 1945, 11.

51. Robert P. Patterson, Secretary of War, "Four Planks for Peace," *Collier's*, November 24, 1945, 15. See also Editorial, "Let's Not Go Back to Bed," *Collier's*, December 15, 1945, 98, which presents military preparedness as a matter of "life and death for the United States as a free nation"; W. B. Courtney, "Air Power — Today and Tomorrow," *Collier's*, September 15, 1945, 30; and the four-part series by Wesley Price, "Birth of a Miracle," which appeared in consecutive issues of the *SEP* beginning August 25, September 1, 8, 15, 1945.

52. For examples, see Editorial, "Scientific Research Is Our First Defense," *SEP*, August 25, 1945, 108; International Trucks advertisements in *Life*, August 27, 1945, 107, *SEP*, November 24, 1945, 71, and *Collier's*, December 1, 1945, 24; Truman, "Address Before a Joint Session of the Congress on Universal Military Training. October 23, 1945," *PP*, 1945, 405; Editorial, "Let's Not Go Back to Bed," *Collier's*, December 15, 1945, 98, illustrated with a striking cartoon of Uncle Sam curled up asleep beneath a blanket of American soil under a tree; and North American Aviation ads in *Life*, August 13, 1945, 91; and *SEP*, August 11, 1945, 37.

53. American Airlines advertisement, *Collier's*, April 21, 1945, 75; and *SEP*, April 21, 1945, 73.

54. See Goodyear Aircraft ads: *Life*, September 3, 1945, 56–57; and *Life*, December 10, 1945, 68–69.

55. Goodyear Aircraft ad, *Life*, September 3, 1945, 56–57.

56. Goodyear Aircraft ad: *SEP*, April 14, 1945, 56–57; *Collier's*, May 12, 1945, 44–45.

57. See, for example, the following: Boeing ads in *SEP*, August 25, 1945, 43, and *Life*, November 26, 1945, 123; Consolidated Vultee Aircraft Corp. ads in *SEP*, June 16, 1945, 64–65, August 18, 1945, 62–63, and November 10, 1945, 76–77, and in *Life*, July 30, 1945, 52–53; North American Aviation ads in *SEP*, August 11, 1945, 37, and *Life*, August 13, 1945, 91; Aircraft War Production Inc. ad, *Life*, July 9, 1945, 60; and Oldsmobile Division of General Motors ad, *Life*, July 9, 1945, 15. For a sea power parallel, see Dodge Division of Chrysler Corporation ads in *Life*, July 23, 1945, 40–41, and *SEP*, August 25, 1945, 50–51. The political economy of the postwar aircraft industry is discussed by Kofsky, *Harry S. Truman and the War Scare of 1948*, 11–82.

58. Divine, *Second Chance*, 313; *PP*, 1945, 404–5, 411, 431–38. See also the "Con" letters in response to the "10-27-45 Speech" in PPF200.

59. "A Better World" was a popular internationalist slogan of the day, which the United Electrical workers played on with their own slogan, "For a Better America," a sentiment echoed in other unions too.

60. With its large Canadian membership, the UAW usually sang "O Canada!" as well. It otherwise operated within the contours of U.S. public culture.

61. Because of travel restrictions in the immediate aftermath of the war, national union conventions were not held in 1945. The discussion here draws on material from 1944.

62. FDR to UAW president Addes and UAW, in UAW, *Proceedings, 1944*, 76; see also, in the same source, Sidney Hillman's ardently pro-Roosevelt speech, 237–44. On Hillman, see Fraser, "Sydney Hillman: Labor's Machiavelli."

63. UAW, *Proceedings, 1944*, 4, 251.

64. UAW, *Proceedings, 1944*, 364.

65. UAW, *Proceedings, 1944*, 112.

66. Ibid., 112; UE, *Proceedings, 1944*, 80. On Murray, see Schatz, "Philip Murray and the Sub-

ordination of the Industrial Unions to the United States Government." On Wallace, see Ronald Radosh and Leonard P. Liggio, "Henry A. Wallace and the Open Door," in Paterson, *Cold War Critics,* 76–113; and J. S. Walker, *Henry A. Wallace and American Foreign Policy.*

67. UE, *Proceedings, 1944,* 91, 126.
68. UAW, *Proceedings, 1944,* 128. On Africa and the administration's shifting rhetoric, see Borstelmann, *Apartheid's Reluctant Uncle,* 15–17. On Roosevelt's personal opposition to colonialism, see also Kimball, *The Juggler,* 127–57.
69. UAW, *Proceedings, 1944,* 11–12, 402–3.
70. UE, *Proceedings, 1944,* 29.
71. UE, *Proceedings, 1944,* 64–65.
72. UE, *Proceedings, 1944,* 32. On Murray's full support of the war effort, including the no-strike pledge, see Schatz, "Philip Murray," 246–49.
73. Lichtenstein, *Labor's War At Home,* 202.
74. See Howe and Widick, *UAW and Walter Reuther,* 120–25, for a classic account of the politics of the no-strike pledge at the 1944 UAW convention, esp. 123 for the flag-waving incident. See also Barnard, *Walter Reuther and the Auto Workers,* 87–88; and Levenstein, *Communism, Anticommunism and the CIO,* 174–78.
75. UAW, *Proceedings, 1944,* 102, 106.
76. Ibid., 106–7, 115.
77. Ibid., 165–66.
78. UE, *Proceedings, 1944,* 68.
79. UAW, *Proceedings, 1944,* 154, 158.
80. Ibid., 164–65.
81. See Levenstein, *Communism, Anticommunism, and the CIO,* 176–77; and Howe and Widick, *UAW and Walter Reuther,* 120–25, esp. 123.
82. Levenstein, *Communism, Anticommunism, and the CIO,* 176.

CHAPTER THREE

1. For related interpretations on this point, see D. White, "Nature of World Power in American History" and "History and American Internationalism."
2. Cartoon by Duffy in the *Baltimore Sun,* as published in the *New York Times,* Sunday edition, August 19, 1945.
3. Sherry, *In the Shadow of War.* See also his earlier work, *Preparing for the Next War.*
4. Yergin, *Shattered Peace,* esp. 12–13; and Leffler, *Preponderance of Power.* Note, however, that what Akira Iriye has called the "globalizing of America" began earlier (see Iriye, *Globalizing of America*).
5. Tuveson, *Redeemer Nation;* Miller, *Errand to the Wilderness.*
6. Yergin, *Shattered Peace,* 171, 443–44 fn. 26; Hamby, *Beyond the New Deal,* 12–15; Francis Spellman, Archbishop of New York, "Wisdom — Not Weapons of War," *Collier's,* January 5, 1946, 11–13; "Trouble Spots Plague the World," *Life,* September 2, 1946, 29–34; editorial, *Life,* January 21, 1946, 30.
7. See Radosh, *Prophets on the Right;* Paterson, *Cold War Critics;* Doenecke, *Not to the Swift;* Doenecke, "Strange Career of American Isolationism"; and Green, *Shaping Political Consciousness,* 171–80. On Wallace's role, see Chapter 4.

8. Milton MacKaye, "Things are Different in the White House," *SEP,* April 20, 1946, 12; Robert M. Yoder, "Are You Smart Enough To Be a Citizen?" *SEP,* September 21, 1946, 19, 98, 102. Cartoon by Low, *New York Times,* Sunday edition, September 9, 1945. For concern with "normalcy," see "U.S. Normalcy: Against the Backdrop of a Troubled World 'Life' Inspects An American City at Peace," *Life,* December 3, 1945, 27–35; editorial, "One Year After V-J Day," *Collier's,* August 24, 1946, 82; and editorial, "Politicians and Peace," *Collier's,* September 7, 1946, 90. *Life's* tenth anniversary issue (November 25, 1946) ardently celebrated the triumph of internationalism over isolationism between 1936 and 1946.

9. *Collier's,* April 6, 1946, 70; *SEP,* November 16, 1946, 78.

10. "Taft and Vandenberg," *Life,* October 7, 1946, 102–14 (quotations on 108, 114).

11. For quotation, see Arthur M. Schlesinger Jr., "His Eyes Have Seen the Glory," *Collier's,* February 22, 1947, 39; see also Robert A. Taft (as told to James C. Derieux), "No Substitute for Freedom," *Collier's,* February 1, 1947. On Taft's growing difficulty in communicating his ideas against the tide of the dominant public language, see Green, *Shaping Political Consciousness,* 171–80.

12. For a plethora of evidence, see Ashby, "Shattered Dreams."

13. See any number of Truman speeches from 1945–46. The quotations are from Editorial, "The Choice is Ours," *Collier's,* March 9, 1946, 82. See also Editorial, "Shall We Have a Depression?: There are plenty of signs that we will, but the decision is still up to us," *Life,* October 7, 1946, 32; and Frank Gervasi, "This Is Your Business," *Collier's,* September 14, 1946, 18–19, 35–37. The *Life* editorial is "The Green Curtain: It hangs between us and a sales opportunity for democracy in Latin America," *Life,* March 10, 1947, 34. See also John Lear, "They're Learning About Us the Hard Way," *SEP,* January 4, 1947, 20, 44–47; Editorial, "Economic Civil War," *DN,* May 25, 1946, 13; and Editorial, "U.S. Foreign Policy, III: Its most hopeful project depends for success on the American businessman," *Life,* January 20, 1947, 34.

14. Editorial, "The World and John L.," *Life,* May 20, 1946, 22; Editorial, "Economic Civil War," *DN,* May 25, 1946, 13. For Truman, see "Radio Address to the American People on the Railroad Strike Emergency, May 24, 1946," *PP, 1946,* 276; "Special Message to the Congress Urging Legislation for Industrial Peace, May 25, 1946," *PP, 1946,* 277–78; and "Veto of the Price Control Bill, June 29, 1946," *PP, 1946,* 327. See also Editorial, "We Can Still Lick This Thing: Common-Sense Pricing, Working, Buying Will Beat Inflation and Start Our Economy Rolling," *Life,* July 8, 1946, 28.

15. Editorial, ". . . As Others See Us," *Life,* March 4, 1946, 38 ("oasis" quote). For a vivid portrayal of Europe's plight and America's consequent responsibilities, see story by John Dos Passos, *Life,* January 7, 1946, 21–24; see also letter to editor concerning this piece, *Life,* January 28, 1946, 5, 7. On refugee children, see, for example, "Europe's Children: Christmas brings joy and sadness," *Life,* December 30, 1946, 22–23; and United Jewish Appeal ads in *Life,* February 17, 1947, 103, and March 3, 1947, and in *SEP,* February 22, 1947, 135. On food relief, the quotation is from "World Relief Is America's Job," *SEP,* December 22, 1945, 112; see also "We Won't Let Europe Starve," *Collier's,* November 10, 1945, 90; Editorial, "The World and U.S. Food," *Life,* February 25, 1946, 34; lead photo-essay, "The Harvest That Saved the World," *Life,* July 29, 1946, 21–25 (Kansas farmers quote); Clinton P. Anderson, Secretary of Agriculture, "One Hungry World," *Collier's,* May 18, 1946, 18–19, 45–46; and General Mills advertisements framed around the question "Why do

the hungry ask first for bread?" in *SEP*, January 11, 1947, back cover; and *Life*, January 20, 1947, 54.

16. On the belief in the U.S. as world redeemer, see Tuveson, *Redeemer Nation;* and H. N. Smith, *Virgin Land.* Quotes are from Truman, "Address in Columbus at a Conference of the Federal Council of Churches, March 6, 1946," *PP, 1946,* 141, 143. Truman invoked the Golden Rule in the same manner on other occasions too; see *PP, 1945,* 380–81, 435, and *PP, 1947,* 165. Citizens' letters responding to this speech, both favorably and skeptically, are in PPF200. For Dulles's view, see John Foster Dulles, "The Churches and World Order," *Life*, March 18, 1946, 34.

17. Editorial, "We Can't Turn Down the British Loan," *SEP*, April 13, 1946, 136 (quotations); Truman, "Radio Appeal to the Nation for Food Conservation To Relieve Hunger Abroad, April 19, 1946," *PP, 1946,* 215; see also *PP, 1947,* 149–50, 159–60. One study of cold war attitudes as expressed in a variety of U.S. magazines, including elite liberal publications such as the *Nation* and the *New Republic* as well as the mass-circulation magazines examined here, found that the elements of self-interest and altruism in U.S. foreign policy "were viewed as complementary and not paradoxical" (Reinig, "America Looking Outward," 170). For a related thought expressed by a member of the policymaking elite, see LaFeber, *America, Russia, and the Cold War,* 51.

18. United Jewish Appeal ad, *SEP*, March 29, 1947, 133 (Eisenhower quote, italics in original). On the spiritual dimension generally, see Editorial, "Few of Us Give Till It Hurts," *SEP*, August 31, 1946, 120. The quoted phrases are from Editorial, "Just Give Us the Food Facts," *Collier's*, June 29, 1946, 82; and Editorial, "Roll Out the Food," *Collier's*, January 19, 1946, 78. See also Elsie Thomas Culver, "America Gives Again," *Collier's*, March 23, 1946, 80; and Francis Cardinal Spellman, "Resurrection," *Life*, April 22, 1946, 27, a poem broadcast nationwide on Easter Sunday.

19. "U.S. Seeks Wheat for the Starving," *Life*, May 6, 1946, 27–34 (photo-essay). See also Editorial, "Greed On the Farm," *Life*, May 6, 1946, 36; Editorial, " 'Eat Less' — Sure, Why Not?" *Collier's*, April 20, 1946, 94; Editorial, "Let 'Em Eat Carrots," *Collier's*, May 11, 1946, 90; and Editorial, "July — Worst Food Month," *Collier's*, July 20, 1946.

20. Dorothy Thompson, "A Call to American Women," *Ladies' Home Journal*, August 1945. On Thompson, see Kurth, *American Cassandra.*

21. Cartoons from the *New York Times*, February 10 and March 3, 1946, and September 23, 1945. For a useful analysis of Uncle Sam as a visual symbol of American nationalism, see Zelinsky, *Nation into State.*

22. Eric Sevareid News Analysis, March 9, 1946, Columbia Broadcasting System, in Sevareid Papers, Library of Congress.

23. Gallup, *Gallup Poll,* 1:569, 582; see also 1:500, 510, 562, 571, 574, 576. By October 1947, only 22 percent of those surveyed approved renewed rationing, although 60 percent were willing to keep meatless Tuesdays, as the government urged (see 1:681–82, 686). See also *Collier's*, May 25, 1946, 90; June 1, 1946, 8; June 8, 1946, 8; June 15, 1946, 8; and *Life*, August 19, 1946, 4; "Got Any Old Clothes For Our Allies Today?" *DN*, January 4, 1946, 11. For views of men and women on the street, see "The Inquiring Fotographer," *DN*, March 15, 1946, and May 8, 1946, 33.

24. W. B. Courtney, "UNRRA: First Gravestone of Peace," *Collier's*, October 12, 1946, 22–24, 74–76 (quotation on 24); Randolph McPherson, letter to editor, *Collier's*, November 23, 1946, 93.

25. "Statement by the President Announcing Emergency Measure To Relieve the World Food Shortage, February 6, 1946," *PP, 1946,* 107–8 (quotation on 108). Citizens' letters responding to this statement are in PPF200. The surviving letters in the Truman Library are overwhelmingly "Pro"; there is only one thin folder of "Con" letters.

26. Miss Elizabeth Boyd Disbrow, 221 Clinton Ave., New Rochelle, N.Y., to HST, February 27, 1946; John H. Drew, 26 Stevens St., Oceanside, Long Island, N.Y., to HST, February 27, 1946; and R. K. Kuhl, 1338 South Hudson Ave., Los Angeles, Calif., to Rep. G. L. McDonough, February 7, 1946; Lewis Elvin Hamby, 111 Emerson Circle, Oak Ridge, Tenn., to HST, February 12, 1946. See also J. Vogel, Newark, N.J., to HST, February 27, 1946. All letters are in PPF200. Unless otherwise noted, all citizen letters to President Truman cited in this chapter are from PPF200.

27. Lois S. Vaught and Arnold B. Vaught, Hudson View Gardens, W. 183rd St. and Pinehurst Ave., New York, N.Y., to HST, February 9, 1946; Miss Nora M. O'Brien, 369 Armory St., Springfield, Mass., to HST, February 10, 1946; Mrs. N. H. Vreeland, R.D. 2, Trenton, N.J., to HST, March 13, 1946.

28. Marshall D. Ulm, Methodist Minister, Murrayville, Ill., to HST, February 16, 1946. The surviving letters supporting Truman's February 6, 1946, statement on world food relief include a large number of letters from clergymen, with Methodists particularly well represented, a fact easily explained by that sect's traditional emphasis on "good works." One suspects that these themes appeared, from time to time at least, in Sunday sermons throughout the country during the period covered in this chapter. For similar thoughts expressed on behalf of a nonreligious civic association, see Mildred A. Guttwillig, Chairman, New York City Consumer Council, Long Island City, N.Y., to HST, February 8, 1946.

29. Lucille Forbes Milton [or Millon] (Mrs. Tiaferro Milton), 1234 Bryn Mawr Ave., Chicago, Ill., to HST, February 6, 1946. For another letter expressing both these points, see Abbie S. Olds and Raymond F. Olds, Gould Farm, Great Barrington, Mass., to HST, February 8, 1946.

30. Aldo M. Marcucci, 1st LT., INF., Takoma Park, Md., to HST, February 7, 1946.

31. Editorial, "Get a Horse: UNRRA's End Still Leaves Americans Faced with the Big Job of World Rehabilitation," *Life,* December 30, 1946, 18. *Life* presented this theme repeatedly from late 1945 to early 1947; see, for example, Editorial, "The Trouble With UNRRA . . . ," November 5, 1945, 48; Reinhold Niebuhr, "The Fight for Germany," October 21, 1946, 70; Editorial, "What Are We Waiting For?" November 4, 1946, 36; and "Marshall Flies Home to His New Job," January 20, 1947, 32.

32. Editorial, "They Are Desolate in the Streets," *SEP,* May 11, 1946, 148.

33. Editorial, "Contented Voters — A Scarcity Item," *SEP,* July 20, 1946, 124. See also Editorial, "It's Time We Declared Peace," *SEP,* June 15, 1946, 144. For a related point, see Editorial, "How Much Famine is 'Policy Made'?" *SEP,* May 25, 1946; *SEP,* May 11, 1946, 148.

34. See Gallup, *Gallup Poll,* 1:530, 535–36, 549–50; Editorial, "We Can't Turn Down the British Loan," *SEP,* April 13, 1946, 136; "Truman Signs British Loan," *Life,* July 29, 1946, 28–29.

35. See "The U.S. in Germany," *Life,* January 28, 1946, 32; Demaree Bess, "How Long Will We Stay in Germany?" *SEP,* February 2, 1946, 17, 97–98; Drew Middleton, *Collier's,* February 9, 1946, 12–13, 64–65; "Occupation Etiquette," *Collier's,* February 16, 1946, 90; Julian Bach Jr., "America's Germany," *Life,* May 13, 1946, 104–14, excerpted from a book of the same title, "the first book by an American on the progress of the U.S. occupation"; " 'Our

Germans,'" *Life*, November 11, 1946, 34; Quentin Reynolds, "Experiment in Democracy," *Collier's*, May 25, 1946, 12–13, 41–42; Ernest O. Hauser, "The Germans Resist 'Liberation,'" *SEP*, August 10, 1946, 17, 121–22; "Byrnes on Germany," *Life*, September 23, 1946, 42; and "Occupied Germany," *Life*, February 10, 1947, 85–103. For justifications of the policy shift, see Demaree Bess, "How We Botched the German Occupation," *SEP*, January 26, 1946, 9–10, 34, 37; Joseph and Stewart Alsop, "Why We Changed Our Policy in Germany," *SEP*, December 7, 1946, 12–13, 38–43; Reinhold Niebuhr, "The Fight for Germany," *Life*, October 21, 1946, 65–72; and Editorial, "Realism on Germany a Long Time Coming," *SEP*, January 18, 1947, 132. For contrary views from ordinary citizens, see the letter from an ex-POW supporting the Morgenthau plan, *DN*, September 17, 1946; and J. Anthony Marcus, Rye, N.Y., to *Life*, March 3, 1947, 7.

36. The quotation is from Noel F. Busch, "A Report on Japan," *Life*, December 2, 1946, 105–27. See also "Hirohito and MacArthur," *DN*, January 3, 1946; Mark Gayn, "Our Balance Sheet in Japan," *Collier's*, March 23, 1946, 12–13, 81–82; and Edgar Snow, "What the Jap is Thinking Now," *SEP*, May 11, 1946, 9–11, 36, 39.

37. Frederick W. Branch, "Air-Line Timetable," *SEP*, May 11, 1946, 70. On the notion of "the Air Age" as an inherently global age, see Schulten, "Transformation of World Geography in American Life." For sample ads, see those for Douglas Aircraft in *SEP*, October 12, 1946, 116–17, and January 11, 1947, 60–61; and *Life*, January 13, 1947, 62–63; and those for Lockheed Aircraft Corporation in *SEP*, March 2, 1946, 95; *Collier's*, March 9, 1946, 79; and *Life*, February 3, 1947, 49. On the aircraft industry, see Yergin, *Shattered Peace*, 341–43; and Kofsky, *Harry S. Truman and the War Scare of 1948*, 11–82.

38. See Pan American World Airways ads in *SEP*, October 26, 1946, 80–81, and *Life*, February 3, 1947, 43–44; joint airlines ad in *Collier's*, May 11, 1946, 10. American Airlines ads in *SEP*, April 6, 1946, 100–101; *Life*, April 8, 1946, 50–51; and *Collier's*, April 13, 1946, 48–49. Northwest Airlines ads in *SEP*, September 14, 1946, 142; October 21, 1946, 153; November 9, 1946, 129; December 7, 1946, 75; January 25, 1947, 112; and February 22, 1947, 112. The quoted TWA ad is in *Collier's*, March 30, 1946, 65.

39. On the concept of the "visual cliché" as a prevalent and potent tool in advertising, see Marchand, *Advertising the American Dream*, 234–39, 248–55. On "capitalist realism," see Schudson, *Advertising, The Uneasy Persuasion*, 209–33; and Marchand, *Advertising the American Dream*, xviii. For the Goodyear ads, see, for example, *SEP*, May 25, 1946; *Collier's*, January 4, 1947, 52; and *Life*, November 11, 1946, 74–75. Bell System ads in *Life*, November 11, 1947, 3; *SEP*, November 30, 1946, 159; and *Collier's*, November 16, 1946, 49. Canadian Club ads, *Life*, December 9, 1946, inside back cover; and *Collier's*, December 21, 1946, 99. See also Caterpillar Tractor Company ad, *Collier's*, March 8, 1947; Revere Copper and Brass ad, *SEP*, January 11, 1947, 122; Clark Bar ads, *SEP*, February 1, 1947, 12, February 15, 1947, 112, and March 1, 1947, 111; Schlitz Brewing ad, *Collier's*, January 26, 1946, 38–39. This iconography of world leadership itself merits further explication.

40. See Rankin in *Congressional Record*, December 18, 1945, 12283, cited in Doenecke, "Strange Career of American Isolationism," 80; Bruce Hutchinson, "Is the U.S. Fit to Lead the World?" *Reader's Digest*, 48 (May 1946): 1–5, cited in Reinig, "America Looking Outward," 212; and Dorothy Thompson, "Wanted: Leadership," *Ladies' Home Journal*, March 1946.

41. Editorial, by Robert Strausz-Hupé, "Foreign Policy Begins At Home," *SEP*, February 23, 1946, 140.

42. *Collier's*, March 23, 1946.

43. Letter, *Life*, June 3, 1946, 8. See also *Life*, July 22, 1946, 19, 95.

44. Editorial, "Human Rights and the Law," *Life*, July 1, 1946. For other discussions of U.S. world leadership in *Life*, see Editorial, "What's the Score?" September 9, 1946, 36; Editorial, "U.S. Foreign Policy, II," January 13, 1947; "Marshall Flies Home to His New Job," January 20, 1947; "Democracy," February 17, 1947, 28; and Editorial, "The Green Curtain," March 10, 1947, 34. See also "World Freedom of News," *Collier's*, April 13, 1946, 94.

45. John B. Allen to HST, January 1946; Letter to the editor, *New York Sunday News*, September 22, 1946, 51.

46. Paul Phillip, "Lessons in Community Organization and Group Work Learned from War Experiences," paper presented to National Urban League Annual Conference, 1946, in NUL, IX, Box 14. Keynote address by Archibald J. Carey Jr., 2, 5, NAACP, II, Box A31, "1946 Speeches" folder.

47. The first two quotations are Walter White's, from a radio script publicizing the NAACP's 1946 annual conference, "Program: Headline Editions, American Broadcasting System, Wednesday, June 26, 7:00 P.M., EDST," NAACP, II, Box A30. Other quotations are drawn from Editorial, "Happy New Year," *Crisis*, January 1947, 9; and Horace Cayton, "Diplomats," *PC*, March 8, 1947, 7.

48. United Association of Journeyman Plumbers and Steam Fitters of the United States and Canada, "Proceedings of the 1946 Convention," published in the *Journeyman Plumbers and Steam Fitters' Journal*, 1946, 14–16, 90–91. On Meany's long-standing anticommunism, which grew sharper during and after World War II, see Zieger, "George Meany: Labor's Organization Man," 331–32, 337–38. For "rank-and-file" examples, see David L. Aaron to HST, January 7, 1946; and Dr. George Rosen, Cazenovia, N.Y., to *Collier's*, July 13, 1946, 80–81. For background, see Radosh, *American Labor and U.S. Foreign Policy*.

49. UE, *Proceedings, 1946*, 122–23 (UE quotes), 56 (Fitzgerald quote). On the WFTU, see Weiler, "United States, International Labor, and the Cold War," esp. 19.

50. UAW, *Proceedings, 1946*, 96.

51. Ibid., 3, 31–32.

52. UE, *Proceedings, 1946*, 131–32.

53. UE, *Proceedings, 1946*, 131–44. For background on Pepper's views, see Hamby, *Beyond the New Deal*, 104–5; and Thomas G. Paterson, "The Dissent of Senator Claude Pepper," in Paterson, *Cold War Critics*, 114–39.

54. UE, *Proceedings, 1946*, 229–30, 225 (Asher quote).

55. On the African American community and U.S. foreign policy in the postwar era, see Solomon, "Black Critics of Colonialism and the Cold War"; Roark, "American Black Leaders"; Horne, *Black and Red*, esp. 19–82; Plummer, "Evolution of the Black Foreign Policy Constituency"; and, most importantly, Plummer, *Rising Wind*, far and away the most thorough treatment of the subject.

56. Edgar Snow, "The Philippines Cry for Help," *SEP*, March 16, 1946, 14–15, 36, 39 (quotation); and Editorial "State of Hawaii?" *DN*, January 10, 1946.

57. Photo-essay, "New Republic Is Born in Philippines," *Life*, July 22, 1946, 19–25; Paul C. McNutt, "Democracy's Child Is 21," *Collier's*, July 6, 1946, 24, 67–69. See also Editorial, "Farewell to the Philippines," *Collier's*, July 13, 1946, 86; Jack Belden, "Independence Has Its Headaches," *Collier's*, March 29, 1947, 85–89; and, for Truman's official statements, *PP*, *1946*, 337–38.

58. Harold L. Ickes, "The Navy at Its Worst," *Collier's*, August 31, 1946, 22–23, 67. For letters responding to this article (two favorable, one critical), see *Collier's*, October 12, 1946, 69.

59. Mrs. Gertrude Avers, 162 So. Haysworth St., Los Angeles, Calif., to HST, January 4, 1946; Pvt. Peter Agoston, Camp Crowder, Mo., to HST, January 3, 1946; and letter, "Must Be Freedom for All," from "A Reader," *PC*, March 16, 1946, 6.

60. Editorial, "The Burdens of Empire," *DN*, December 27, 1946, 23; Edgar Snow, "Secrets from Siam," *SEP*, January 12, 1946, 12–13, 37–41 (quotation on 12); Editorial, "A Spectre Haunts the Empire Builders," *Ebony*, July 1946, 40.

61. Edgar Snow, "No Four Freedoms for Indo-China," *SEP*, February 2, 1946, 20, 82–84 (quotations on 83, 84).

62. George Padmore, "Trusteeship: The New Imperialism," *Crisis*, October 1946, 302; George Schuyler, "The World Today," *PC*, March 16, 1946, 1; George Schuyler, "Views and Reviews," *PC*, October 6, 1946, 7. On Indonesia, see, for example, Editorial, "Lidice and Bekasi," *PC*, December 29, 1945, 6; Kumar Goshal, "As an Indian Sees It," *PC*, December 29, 1945, 7; Horace Cayton, "Cayton Says," *PC*, December 22, 1945, 7, and December 29, 1945, 7; Ralph Coniston, "Time Bomb in Asia," *Collier's*, January 26, 1946, 26–30; and photo-essay "Revolt in Java: The Richest East Indies Colony tries to throw off Dutch rule," *Life*, January 28, 1946, 77–85.

63. Editorial, ". . . And a Child Shall Lead Them," *Ebony*, December 1945, 28; "Liberian Minister Says: Opportunity For All Is Real Need," *PC*, March 23, 1946, 15. Weaver's speech, along with others using similar themes, is in NUL, IX, Box A14. See also "The House We Live In," *Ebony*, January 1946, 20; and Walter White, "Race and the Hope of Peace," radio broadcast manuscript, Station WLW (NBC) in Cincinnati, 6/28/46, 12:00–12:15 P.M. EDT, in NAACP, II, Box A30, "1946 Publicity" folder.

64. "Address of Walter White," in NAACP, II, Box A31, "1946 Speeches" folder; Walter White, column manuscript dated September 14, 1946, and marked "printed 9/21/46," in NAACP, II, Box A74, "Articles — Walter White/Chicago Defender/Columns 1946" folder. For related discussions of the South Carolina connection, see W. E. B. Du Bois column manuscript dated April 20, 1946, also for publication in the *Chicago Defender*, in NAACP, II, Box A68, "Articles/WEB Du Bois/Newspaper Articles/1945–47" folder; American Negro Press service article, "At Peace Conference: Russian Writer Observes 'Anglo-Saxon Hypocrisy,'" *PC*, October 5, 1946, 3; and Editorial, "Democratic Elections — In Poland," *Crisis*, March 1947, 73.

65. Walter White, column manuscript "printed 11/23/46," in NAACP, II, Box A74, "Articles — Walter White/Chicago Defender/Columns 1946" folder; White quoted in "Negro Veterans Disillusioned, Speaker Tells NAACP Conference," *Cincinnati Times-Star*, Wednesday, June 26, 1946, 21, clipping in NAACP, II, Box A30, "1946 Publicity" folder.

66. "Acceptance speech of Thurgood Marshall, Springarn Medalist at the NAACP Conference, June 28, 1946, Cincinnati, Ohio," in NAACP, II, Box A31, "1946 Speeches" folder. Extensive material in the "1946 Publicity" folder in NAACP, II, Box A30 suggests that many of the conference's key speeches were broadcast nationally on the major radio networks.

67. "Address of Walter White," in NAACP, II, Box A31, "1946 Speeches" folder.

68. Horton, "Comment," 135. "Address of Walter White," 6, in NAACP, II, Box A31, "1946 Speeches" folder. On Myrdal's impact, see Lewis, "Origins of the Civil Rights Movement."

69. "Report of the Executive Secretary to the Annual Conference of the National Urban

League, St. Louis, Missouri, Wednesday, September 25, 1946 — 8:00 P.M.," in NUL, IX, Box A14. See my analysis of this democratic revival in the Introduction.

70. Fiorello LaGuardia, speech to 1946 NAACP conference, esp. 2, 7, 8, in NAACP, II, Box A31, "1946 Speeches" folder; "Helen Douglas Speaks on U.S. Foreign Policy," *PC,* March 23, 1946, 3; and Henry Wallace quoted in "Eliminate Racism," *PC,* September 21, 1946, 4.

71. Urban League press release, NUL, IX, Box A14; Truman to NUL [National Urban League], reprinted in conference program, NUL, IX, A32A. For the background of Truman's letter to the 1946 NAACP conference, and the letter itself, see Memorandum, Walter White to Miss Wasem, NAACP, II, Box A30; White to Truman, May 13, 1946, NAACP, II, Box A31, "1946 Speakers, L–V"; Truman to White, conference greetings, June 11, 1946, NAACP, II, Box A29, "1946 Greetings" folder, with brief response from White to Truman. See also Mary L. Dudziak, "Desegregation as a Cold War Imperative," *Stanford Law Review* 41 (November 1988): 78.

72. "Atty. Gen. Clark: Nations Watch U.S. Lynchings," *PC,* October 5, 1946, 3; Editorial, "Ammunition for the Russians," *Collier's,* November 2, 1946, 102; Editorial, "Lynching No. 1," *Crisis,* March 1947, 73. For an excellent analysis of the postwar lynching wave, see Shapiro, *White Violence and Black Response,* 355–77.

73. Editorial, "Mr. Byrnes's New Hand: He Has Some New Cards for the Paris Game But Still Needs Harder Work at Home to Back Him Up," *Life,* June 17, 1946, 34; Editorial, "Send Them Here! Europe's Refugees Need a Place to Go and America Needs to Set a World Example," *Life,* September 23, 1946, 36.

74. "Radio Report to the American People on the Status of the Reconversion Program. January 3, 1946," *PP, 1946,* 2, 8.

75. On the importance of "mere rhetoric" in foreign-policy ideology, see M. H. Hunt, *Ideology and U.S. Foreign Policy,* 16. Mrs. E. H. Allen et al., 3232 Benda St., Los Angeles, Calif., to HST, January 4, 1946; Meta Axelrod (Mrs. Nathan Axelrod) to Hon. Peter A. Quinn, January 16, 1946, PPF200; and A. P. Adair, 84 Downing St., Sea Cliff, N.Y., to HST, January 4, 1946.

76. UE, *Proceedings, 1946,* 23, 143.

77. The factional politics of the UAW in this period have been widely studied. My own interpretation has been influenced by the accounts provided by Barnard, *Walter Reuther and the Auto Workers;* Howe and Widick, *UAW and Walter Reuther;* and Levenstein, *Communism, Anticommunism, and the CIO.* Other useful accounts, marred by their own factional partisanship, are Cochran, *Labor and Communism;* and Keeran, *Communist Party and the Auto Workers Union.*

78. UAW, *Proceedings, 1946,* 6, 218–19.

79. White, column manuscript, June 8, 1946, in NAACP, II, Box A74, "Articles/Walter White/Chicago Defender/Columns 1946" folder.

CHAPTER FOUR

1. On the pre–Cold War roots of American anticommunism, see Fried, *Nightmare in Red,* 3–58; and Heale, *American Anticommunism.*

2. From the *New York Times,* Sunday editions, September 23, 1945, December 23, 1945, and February 24, 1946.

3. *Collier's,* November 24, 1945, 94.

4. See Ashby, "Shattered Dreams." On the world-government movement, see Boyer, *By the Bomb's Early Light,* 27–45.

5. UE, *Proceedings, 1946,* 69, 229–34 (Kroll quotes); UAW, *Proceedings, 1946,* 8, 96.

6. See, for example, the resolution "On World Peace" of the 1946 Annual Conference of the National Urban League, in NUL, IX, A14; and Walter White, "Race and the Hope of Peace," radio manuscript, Station WLW (NBC) in Cincinnati, Ohio, June 28, 1946, 12:00–12:15 P.M. EDT, in NAACP, II, 1946 Annual Conference files.

7. Editorial, "Spies/Spain," *DN,* March 6, 1946, 29, with cartoon and letter, under headline "Uneasy about Victory," on same page; see also Editorial, "V-E Day," *DN,* May 8, 1946, 33.

8. Walter Lippmann, "U.S.A.: Peacemaker Among the Powers," *Collier's,* January 26, 1946, 16–17, 65–69 (quotations on 16, 17, 69).

9. See Pepper to UE convention in UE, *Proceedings, 1946,* 143.

10. *DN,* March 5, 1946, 1; *DN,* March 6, 1946, 2, 28. On Truman's Federal Council of Churches speech, see Ted Lewis, "Churches Should Back His Program: Truman," *DN,* March 7, 1946, 2, 26.

11. Editorial, "Britain — U.S. — Russia," *DN,* March 7, 1946, 27. John O'Donnell, "Capitol Stuff," *DN,* March 8, 1946, 4.

12. Editorial, "We Won't Get Peace by Ducking Facts," *SEP,* March 30, 1946, 120.

13. " 'Getting Tough' with Russia," *Life,* March 18, 1946, 36.

14. Frank Gervasi, "What's Russia Up To?" *Collier's,* June 22, 1946, 12–13, 52–54 (quotations on 52).

15. Gallup, *Gallup Poll,* 1:508, 523–24, 565, 617.

16. Key excerpts of the speech are presented in LaFeber, *Origins of the Cold War,* 135–39. For context, see Donovan, *Conflict and Crisis,* 190–92; and LaFeber, *America, Russia, and the Cold War,* 38–39. Contrasting interpretations of the speech's impact on U.S. public opinion include Freeland, *Truman Doctrine and the Origins of McCarthyism,* 64; Gardner, *Architects of Illusion,* 104–5; and, for the most convincing view that the speech initially received a mixed response but ultimately "pointed the way for public opinion," Yergin, *Shattered Peace,* 174–78 (quotation on 178). For public opinion data, see *Public Opinion Quarterly* 10 (Summer 1946): 263–65.

17. Raymond Swing, broadcast manuscript, March 5, 1946, WMAL, ABC, in Raymond Gram Swing Papers, Box 29, in the Library of Congress, Manuscript Division. On Swing's support for the idea of world government, see Boyer, *By the Bomb's Early Light,* 31–33, 36–37.

18. Associated Press news story, "No Holy War Against Isms, Bishop Warns," *DN,* March 8, 1946, 6.

19. "CIO Left Wingers Call 5,000 to Picket Winnie," *DN,* March 15, 1946, 3, 24; and Associated Press news story, "He Won't Be There, Acheson Decides," *DN,* March 15, 1946, 24.

20. *DN,* March 16, 1946, 28.

21. American Negro Press news story, datelined Fulton, Mo., " 'Churchill the Talker!' 'Brotherhood' Plea Not Meant for Colonials," *PC,* March 16, 1946; Editorial, "Invitation to Imperialism," *PC,* March 16, 1946, 6; Horace Cayton, "Shows Hand," *PC,* March 16, 1946, 7, and "War Threat Remote: We Can Get Along with Russia But the British Can't," *PC,* March 23, 1946, 7. Excellent context is provided in Plummer, *Rising Wind,* 169.

22. Editorial, "A Spectre Haunts the Empire Builders," *Ebony,* July 1946, 40.

23. Walter White, column manuscript, dated March 8, 1946, in NAACP, II, Box A74, "Articles — Walter White/Chicago Defender/Columns 1946" folder.

24. George Schuyler, "The World Today," *PC*, March 16, 1946, 1, and March 23, 1946, 4. On Schuyler's political trajectory, see Henry Louis Gates Jr., "A Fragmented Man: George Schuyler and the Claims of Race," *New York Times Book Review*, September 20, 1992, 31, 43.

25. For the "asbestos curtain" phrase, see Ernest O. Hauser, "Red Hamburg Calls the German Tune," *SEP*, November 24, 1945, 17; and Eric Sevareid, new analysis, March 9, 1946, Columbia Broadcasting System, in Sevareid Papers, Library of Congress, Manuscript Division.

26. "The Iron Curtain," *Life*, April 29, 1946, 27–35; Joseph and Stewart Alsop, *Life*, May 20, 1946, 69; John Foster Dulles, "Thoughts on Soviet Foreign Policy," *Life*, June 3, 1946, 118–19, 121, 124; Brooks Atkinson, "Russia 1946," *Life*, July 22, 1946, 85–94 (quotation on 86) — originally published in the *New York Times*, July 7, 8, 9, 1946. For other uses of the phrase, see M. W. Fodor, "Trouble Behind the Iron Curtain," *Life*, July 15, 1946, 49–56; and Editorial, "U.S. Foreign Policy, II," *Life*, January 13, 1947, 22; Demaree Bess, "Our Agents Behind the Iron Curtain," *SEP*, August 24, 1946, 18–19, 117–18; and Editorial, "How Much Can You Inspect through an Iron Curtain?" *SEP*, January 25, 1947, 124.

27. *New York Sunday News*, April 7, 1946, 2, 36, 46, 48, 49. On international broadcasts of and about Truman's Army Day speech, see William Benton, "Memorandum for the Secretary, Re: President Truman's Army Day Speech," April 11, 1946, PPF200.

28. *PP, 1946*, 185–90; *New York Sunday News*, April 7, 1946, 1.

29. The surviving mail at the Truman Library in response to this speech is more or less evenly divided between pro and con letters. Much of the con mail specifically opposes universal military training and draft extension, which were the most contentious policy proposals advanced in the speech.

30. Alfred B. Stapleton, 140 Claremont Ave., New York, N.Y., to HST, April 7, 1946; Myron H. Luria, 3624 E. 151 St., Cleveland, Ohio, to HST, April 6, 1946; Flavel E. Jenkins, 532 Vine St., Hammond, Ind., to HST, April 6, 1946; Claude R. Myers, Newark, N.J., to HST, April 7, 1946 — all in PPF200. Unless otherwise noted, all citizen letters to President Truman cited in this chapter are from PPF200.

31. Jerry Cohen, 904 De Kalb Ave., Brooklyn, N.Y., to HST, April 12, 1946.

32. See, for example, the following letters: Harper G. Brow, Philadelphia, Pa., to HST, April 10, 1946; Dorothy M. Blackman and Charles L. Blackman, 223 East Dunedin Rd., Columbus, Ohio, to HST, April 10, 1946; and Lowell Heisey, Purdue University, to HST, April 13, 1946.

33. See, for example, the following letters: Christine Burkhard, Trenton, N.Dak., to HST, April 6, 1946; Mr. and Mrs. William H. Johnston, Baltimore, Md., to HST, April 11, 1946; and Earl G. Sours, RR #1, Box 172, Dayton, Ohio, to HST. For background, see Chambers, *Draftees or Volunteers*, 359–424; and Flynn, *The Draft, 1940–1973*, 88–109.

34. Hal Boyle, Associated Press, "Homesick Fever Burns Out Pacific Army Morale" and William C. Wilson, United Press, "2,500 Homesick GIs Parade to Manila HQ," both in *DN*, January 7, 1946, 2; Editorial, "Disorders in Manila," *DN*, January 9, 1946, 27; Gerry Greene, "Truman to Restive GIs: You Must Cinch Victory," *DN*, January 9, 1946, 2; and "We Wanna Go Home," *Life*, January 21, 1946, 36–37. For an excellent analysis, see Ashby, "Shattered Dreams."

35. See Mr. and Mrs. Albert P. Strom, 222 Castlegate Rd., Pittsburgh, Pa., to HST, April, 11, 1946; and Harold Worden Wylie, Minister, Stone Presbyterian Church, Clinton, N.Y., to HST, April 17, 1946.

36. Mrs. Ruth H. Ashby, RR #4, Wabash, Ind., to HST, April 8, 1946. Mrs. Ashby wrote as the mother of three World War II veterans.

37. Mr. H. Hanfrecht, 307 West 102nd Street, New York City, to HST, April 9, 1946; Richard R. Braddock, 412 West 115th Street, New York, N.Y., to HST, April 12, 1946; Mrs. Marcia J. Lyttle, 5729 Dorchester Ave., Chicago, Ill., to HST, April 7, 1946.

38. *DN*, January 2, 1946, 23; for a similar theme represented in an editorial cartoon, see *DN*, March 6, 1946, 29.

39. "The Army," *Life*, April 22, 1946, 29–35 (quotation on 29). For other examples, see "The State of the Armed Forces," *Life*, September 2, 1946, 96–108; Editorial, "Our Wisest Foreign Policy," *Collier's*, May 4, 1946, 86; and Editorial, "Hey! Wait a Minute," *Collier's*, November 16, 1946, 114.

40. See *Collier's*, January 19, 1946, 41; *Life*, February 25, 1946, 70; *SEP*, April 6, 1946, 54; *SEP*, January 18, 1947, 105; *Life*, January 27, 1947, 111; and *Collier's*, March 8, 1947, 60 (all full-page advertisements).

41. *SEP*, March 22, 1947, 76–77; *Collier's*, March 22, 1947, 36–37.

42. For examples of the representation of U.S. air power in the popular media, see photo-essay "U.S. Shows Off New Superplanes," *Life*, July 8, 1946, 23–27; "The State of the Armed Forces," *Life*, September 2, 1946, 96–108; "Kenney Air Planning on Global Scale," *DN*, March 15, 1946, 20; John Kord Lagemann, "The Handwriting on the Ice," *Collier's*, November 16, 1946, 18–19, 39–42; and Charles J. V. Murphy, "The Arctic: It Has Become the Key to World Strategy," *Life*, January 20, 1947, 55–62. For the wartime roots of these advertising motifs, see Sherry, *Rise of American Air Power*. On the relationship between air power and the postwar U.S. global role, see Yergin, *Shattered Peace*, 202–3.

43. Ad, United Aircraft Corporation, *SEP*, November 30, 1946, 74–75. See also Consolidated Vultee Aircraft Corporation ads, *SEP*, November 16, 1946, 145; *SEP*, December 7, 1946, 136; and *Life*, December 16, 1946, 109; and Alcoa ad, *SEP*, October 19, 1946. On the state of the aviation industry, see Yergin, *Shattered Peace*, 6–7 and 11–82.

44. W. B. Courtney, "Will Russia Rule the Air?" *Collier's*, January 25, 1947, 12–13, 59, 61 (first two quotations on 12); and February 1, 1947, 16, 67, 69 (last two quotations on 69).

45. Editorial, "Atomic Spring: After a Winter of Confusion, the Lilienthal Report Is a Warm Ray of Hope," *Life*, April 15, 1946, 36.

46. Editorial, "Soldiers—Civilians—Atoms," and cartoon, *DN*, March 14, 1946, 25. For contrast, compare this view with that expressed by one scientist who called for "a patriotism not to one country but to the human race," in Harold C. Urey, "I'm a Frightened Man," *Collier's*, January 5, 1946, 18–19, 50–51 (quotation on 51).

47. For quotations, see Dorothy Thompson, "Atomic Science and World Organization," *Ladies' Home Journal*, October 1945, 6, 128. She developed some of these ideas further in her *Ladies' Home Journal* columns of February and May 1946.

48. "Atom Bomb Island," *Life*, March 25, 1946, 105–9 (quotation on 107); and Vice Admiral W. H. P. Blandy, U.S.N., "Atomic Test Case," *Collier's*, June 8, 1946, 12–13, 39–44 (quotations on 13 and 44). See also Frank D. Morris, "Cloud of Doom," *Collier's*, September 7, 1946, 13. For a suggestive cartoon, depicting "natives" listening to the radio and commenting on the atomic tests, see *Collier's*, August 17, 1946, 29.

49. "The Baruch Plan for Banning the Atom Bomb," *Life*, June 24, 1946, 34–35 (quotations on 35). The same perspective on the Baruch plan is presented in John K. Jessup, *Life*, November 11, 1946, 77–82, which went so far as to say that the plan "may be the world's last chance" (82). See also letters on "The Atom and Baruch," *Life*, July 15, 1946, 6 (quotes).

50. *DN*, September 18, 1946, 2, 39. See also Joseph and Stewart Alsop, "Your Flesh Should Creep," *SEP*, July 13, 1946, 9, 44, 47, 49–50; Editorial, "We Can't 'File Away and Forget' the Atom Plan," *SEP*, July 20, 1946, 124; Scripps-Howard Newspapers advertisements, *SEP*, August 3, 1946, 87; and *Life*, August 12, 1946, 89.

51. Gallup, *Gallup Poll*, 1:525, 536; and Boyer, *By the Bomb's Early Light*, 56–58. Other polls showed large majorities favoring continued U.S. production of atomic bombs; see Gallup, *Gallup Poll*, 1:578–79, 613, and Yergin, *Shattered Peace*, 240–41.

52. Editorial, "Concerning Russia," *Collier's*, April 6, 1946.

53. In *Collier's*, May 18, 1946, see Editorial, "Bridge of Understanding," 98; Earl of Halifax, "Message to Americans," 15, 60–62; and cartoon, 83. See also Frank Gervasi, "What's Russia Up To?" *Collier's*, June 22, 1946, 12–13, 52–54 (quotations on 53, 54).

54. Editorial, "It's Time We Declared Peace," *SEP*, June 15, 1946; Demaree Bess, "Roosevelt's Shadow Over Paris," *SEP*, June 29, 1946, 9–10, 98, 100–101 (quotations on 101, 10, 100, and 101, respectively).

55. Demaree Bess, "Look What Russia's Doing Now," *SEP*, August 17, 1946, 11, 92, 94, 97–98 (quotations on 98 and 10).

56. Edgar Snow, "We Meet Russia in Korea," *SEP*, March 30, 1946, 18–19, 117–18 (quotation on 118); and Harold J. Noble, "Our Most Dangerous Boundary," *SEP*, August 31, 1946, 20–21, 99–100, 102 (quotations on 20 and 102).

57. See Yergin, *Shattered Peace*, 444 fn. 33; Reinig, "America Looking Outward"; and Baughman, *Henry R. Luce and the Rise of the American News Media*.

58. Editorial, "No Peace Yet," *Life*, April 29, 1946, 36; and Editorial, "Why Kid Around?: There is no 'misunderstanding' between Russia and the West. There is a conflict," *Life*, May 27, 1946, 36.

59. Joseph P. Kennedy, "The U.S. and the World," *Life*, March 18, 1946, 106–18; and Editorial, " 'Getting Tough' With Russia," *Life*, March 18, 1946, 36.

60. Joseph and Stewart Alsop, "Tragedy of American Liberalism," *Life*, May 20, 1946, 68–76 (quotations on 76, 69).

61. John Foster Dulles, "Thoughts on Soviet Foreign Policy and What to Do about It, Part I," *Life*, June 3, 1946, 112–26 (quotation on 126); see esp. 113 on "Pax Sovietica."

62. John Foster Dulles, "Thoughts on Soviet Foreign Policy and What to Do About It, Part II," *Life*, June 10, 1946, 118–30. Two weeks later, *Life* published seven letters to the editor on Dulles's articles, an unusually large number of published letters on a single piece or series. Four strongly supported Dulles's views; two opposed them; one simply called the series "a major declaration and elucidation of U.S. foreign policy." See *Life*, June 24, 1946, 8, 11. On Dulles's role in the efforts of the foreign-policy elite to shape public opinion, see Yergin, *Shattered Peace*, 173–74 and 444 fn. 33. See also Pruessen, *John Foster Dulles*, 264–67, 284–86.

63. Brooks Atkinson, "Russia 1946," *Life*, July 22, 1946, 91, reprinted from the *New York Times*, July 7, 8, 9, 1946. For a related discussion of such "mirror image" thinking, see Reinig, "America Looking Outward," 126–27. For another interesting example of such thinking, see M. W. Fodor, "Trouble Behind the Iron Curtain," *Life*, July 15, 1946, 54, 56.

64. See accounts of the Wallace controversy in Hamby, *Beyond the New Deal*, 128–34; Yergin, *Shattered Peace*, 245–55; J. S. Walker, *Henry A. Wallace and American Foreign Policy*, 149–65; Leffler, *Preponderance of Power*, 138–39; Donovan, *Conflict and Crisis*, 218–28; and LaFeber, *America, Russia, and the Cold War*, 44–45. The McKenzie quotation is from her "Pursuit of Democracy" column in the Pittsburgh *Courier*, September 21, 1946, 6.

65. See Yergin, *Shattered Peace*, 255, 251. For examples of how the mass-circulation print media helped to marginalize Wallace's views by simply dismissing them or by labeling them "isolationist," see Editorial, "War Talk: In a tense situation we need a constructive proposal. Why not a united Europe?" *Life*, September 30, 1946, 34; "Wallace Gets Fired," *Life*, September 30, 1946, 42; Editorial, "Our Left Wingers Go Isolationist," *SEP*, October 12, 1946, 160; and Beverly Smith, "Byrnes Grows Up to His Job," *SEP*, January 4, 1947, 68. For the polling data, see Gallup, *Gallup Poll*, 1:604.

66. On the liberal movement, see Hamby, *Beyond the New Deal*, 87–145. On the peace movement, see Wittner, *Rebels Against War*, esp. 151–81. On the old isolationists, see Doenecke, *Not to the Swift*, 55–72. For two specific examples of dissent in the African American press, see A. J. Siggins, American Negro Press, "Behind the Scenes: Russia Backs Colonials in War Against Imperialist Countries," *PC*, September 21, 1946, 13; and George Schuyler, "The World Today," *PC*, September 21, 1946, 4.

67. See Adler and Paterson, "Red Fascism."

68. Reinhold Niebuhr, "The Fight for Germany," *Life*, October 21, 1946, 65–72. On the deletion in the *Reader's Digest* reprint, see Reinig, "America Looking Outward," 238, citing *Reader's Digest* 50 (January 1947): 69–72. For an incisive discussion of Niebuhr's thought in this context, see LaFeber, *America, Russia, and the Cold War*, 46–47.

69. Joseph and Stewart Alsop, "Why We Changed Our Policy in Germany," *SEP*, December 7, 1946, 12–13, 38–43 (quotation on 13). Similarly, a *Life* editorial in December argued that "Communist messianism" called for a corresponding U.S. response: "In the name of human liberty, America is bound to resist the spread of Communism." Editorial, "Russia by Thirds," *Life*, December 16, 1946, 30.

70. Beverly Smith, "Byrnes Grows Up to His Job," *SEP*, January 4, 1947, 19, 67–68 (quotation on 19).

71. "Byrnes Out, Marshall in as Secretary of State," top story of the day, *DN*, January 8, 1947, 1, 2, 37; lead photo-essay, "Marshall Flies Home to His New Job," *Life*, January 20, 1947, 27–33; Editorial, "U.S. Foreign Policy, III," *Life*, January 20, 1947, 34; Editorial, "Giants in Our Time," *Collier's*, March 22, 1947, 98; John Hersey, "Mr. Secretary Marshall," *Collier's*, March 29, 1947, 11–13, 48, 51. Cartoon reprinted in the *New York Times*, Sunday edition, January 12, 1947. For the polls, see Gallup, *Gallup Poll*, 1:628–29, 679.

72. Editorial, "We Understand Russia Now," *Collier's*, October 19, 1946, 114; for letters responding to this editorial (two pro, one con), see *Collier's*, November 30, 1946, 98. For the cartoon, see *Collier's*, October 26, 1946, 109. For an example of continuing anti-Soviet sentiments on the magazine's editorial page, see Editorial, "Our Dollars; Our Detractors," *Collier's*, December 21, 1946, 98.

73. In addition to material from the *Post* cited above, see the following *SEP* articles: Demaree Bess, "No Peace in Sight," October 19, 1946, 22–23, 141–44; and Martin Sommers, *Post* foreign editor, "Why Russia Got the Drop on Us," February 8, 1947, 25, 89–95; and any number of editorials, including those of March 1 and March 8, 1947.

74. Edgar Snow, "Why We Don't Understand Russia," *SEP,* February 15, 1947, 18–19, 136–40. The Stalin speech is discussed on 138 and 140.

75. Edgar Snow, "How It Looks to Ivan Ivanovich," *SEP,* February 22, 1947, 23, 127–30 (quotation on 128, discussions of Atkinson and Niebuhr on 129).

76. Edgar Snow, "Stalin Must Have Peace," *SEP,* March 1, 1947, 25, 94–96. For published letters responding to the Snow series (six pro, including letters from Raymond Swing and Chester Bowles, and two con), see *SEP,* March 15, 1947, 4, and March 22, 1947, 4, where an editorial note adds that mail concerning Snow's articles "has been 59 per cent favorable." For an interesting letter to Truman aide Charles Ross that cites Snow's articles in arguing against the Truman Doctrine, see Arthur Strawn to Charles Ross, March 15, 1947, in HSTL, PPF200, Box 305, Folder "3/12/47."

77. "Address in New York City at the Opening Session of the United Nations General Assembly," October 23, 1946, *PP, 1946,* 457–63 (quotations on 458 and 462). For coverage of this speech, see *DN,* October 24, 1946, 1, 3, 34–36. For letters responding to this speech, see HSTL, PPF200, Box 303.

78. "Annual Message to the Congress on the State of the Union," January 6, 1947, *PP, 1947,* 1–12, esp. 11–12; Editorial, "Mr. Truman on the Union," *DN,* January 7, 1947, 21 (see also news coverage on 20).

79. Editorial, "U.S. Foreign Policy, 1947: Its successes in 1946 give only part of the key to the enormous job ahead of it," *Life,* January 6, 1947, 18.

80. Editorial, "U.S. Foreign Policy, II: This is the year it can register some triumphs: for example, in China and Europe," *Life,* January 13, 1947, 22.

81. Editorial, "U.S. Foreign Policy, III: Its most hopeful project depends for success on the American businessman," *Life,* January 20, 1947, 34.

82. See also *Life,* January 20, 1947, 30–33. The classic study of "Manifest Destiny" as a theme in American nationalist thought remains Weinberg, *Manifest Destiny* (1935). A more recent, thoughtful synthesis is Stephanson, *Manifest Destiny* (1995).

83. Henry Wallace, "Jobs, Peace, Freedom," *New Republic* 115 (December 16, 1946): 789.

84. Henry Wallace, "The Enemy Is Not Each Other," *New Republic* 116 (January 27, 1947): 25.

85. See, for example, LaFeber, *America, Russia, and the Cold War,* 49; Yergin, *Shattered Peace,* 275–302; and Jones, *Fifteen Weeks,* 171.

86. Jones, *Fifteen Weeks,* 7. See also Gardner, *Architects of Illusion,* 217.

87. See Reinig, "America Looking Outward," 427–28.

88. Editorial, "The British Crisis: We cannot watch with indifference while our closest ally goes down," *Life,* February 24, 1947, 34, and "Picture of the Week," 35; Editorial, "If Britain Gets Out, Who Goes In?" *SEP,* March 29, 1947, 156.

89. *New York Times,* March 2, 1947, quoted in Gardner, *Architects of Illusion,* 219, along with reference to Acheson's press briefing. On the role of crisis reporting, see Reinig, "America Looking Outward."

90. *PP, 1947,* 167–72 (quotations on 167, 169). See also Leffler, *Preponderance of Power,* 161–62; LaFeber, *America, Russia, and the Cold War,* 54–55; and Gardner, *Architects of Illusion,* 219–20.

91. Daniel T. Rodgers has suggested that this conflation of freedom and capitalism was first fully realized in the 1940s, although he makes no specific analysis of the role of Truman's discourse. See Rodgers, *Contested Truths,* 212–17.

92. All the surviving mail concerning this speech at the Truman Library is contained in one folder, labeled "Pro"; a corresponding "Con" folder is marked "empty when received" at HSTL, August 29, 1956. On Bowles, see Hamby, *Beyond the New Deal*, esp. 6, 40, 70–71, 161–62, 165–66; and Doenecke, *Not to the Swift*, 21, 24, 30, 59.

93. Certainly, the theme of the Baylor speech did not come up in the working-class and African American materials I have examined. But one can only speculate, not argue, from such a lack of evidence.

94. Useful interpretations of the Truman Doctrine speech and its impact include Draper, "American Hubris"; Yergin, *Shattered Peace*, 275–302; Gardner, *Architects of Illusion*, 205–25; LaFeber, "American Policy-Makers, Public Opinion, and the Outbreak of the Cold War," 52–55; LaFeber, *America, Russia, and the Cold War*, 49–58; Freeland, *Truman Doctrine and the Origins of McCarthyism*, 84–101, 150–51, 178–79; Paterson, "Presidential Foreign Policy, Public Opinion, and Congress"; and Leffler, *Preponderance of Power*, 121–27, 142–46.

95. For a small sample of public opinion data demonstrating the potency of popular anticommunism before and immediately after the Truman Doctrine speech, see Gallup, *Gallup Poll*, 1:587, 593–94, 640.

CHAPTER FIVE

1. See Rodgers, *Contested Truths*, 212–23.

2. Freeland, *Truman Doctrine and the Origins of McCarthyism*; Leffler, *Preponderance of Power*.

3. W. E. B. Du Bois, "The Winds of Time," *Chicago Defender*, April 26, 1947, clipping in NAACP, II, Box A68, "Articles/W. E. B. Du Bois/Newspaper Articles/1945–47." For Schuyler, Prattis, Johnson, and others, see *PC*, March 15, 22, 29, 1947. On Haiti, see John A. Diaz, "U.S. Rules Out Loan to Haiti," *PC*, March 29, 1947, 1, 4. For examples of persisting criticism, see Marjorie McKenzie, "Pursuit of Democracy," *PC*, June 14, 1947, 6; Horace Cayton, "Truman Needs Help," *PC*, June 14, 1947, 7; and P. L. Prattis, "The Horizon," *PC*, November 20, 1948, 16.

4. Walter White, "The Issue in Greece," column manuscript dated 3/17/47, for 3/20 release; letter to the editor, *New York Times*, clarifying an April 2, 1947, *New York Times* report on White's position; and Claude Pepper to White, April 3, 1947; all in NAACP, II, Box A285, "Foreign Affairs/Greece and Turkey/1947." On Pepper and Taylor, see Paterson, *Cold War Critics*, 114–39 (Pepper) and 140–66 (Taylor). For the polling data, see Gallup, *Gallup Poll*, 1:639.

5. White to HST, April 11, 1947, in NAACP, II, Box A34, "Annual Conference Sunday Meeting/Correspondence regarding/March–May." On Niles, see Donovan, *Conflict and Crisis*, 315–16. See also Berman, *Politics of Civil Rights*, 61–65.

6. White to David Niles, June 3, 1947, NAACP, II, Box A34, "Annual Conference 1947 Sunday Meeting/Correspondence regarding/June–August"; and discussion of "President Truman's Speech—June 29th—Annual Conference" (from Minutes of Committee on Administration 5/26/47), NAACP, II, Box A34, "1947 Speakers."

7. See Berman, *Politics of Civil Rights*, x, 76–77, 79–135, 237–40; Bernstein, "Ambiguous Legacy," 279; Yarnell, *Democrats and Progressives*, 34–35; Divine, "The Cold War and the Election of 1948," 92–93; Sitkoff, "Harry Truman and the Election of 1948."

8. Press releases of May 30 and June 14, 1947, and other items in NAACP, II, Box A33, "1947 Publicity." See also Walter White, column manuscript dated June 14, 1947, in NAACP, II, Box A74, "Articles — Walter White/Chicago Defender/Columns 1947."

9. See the addresses by Helen Gahagan Douglas, W. E. B. Du Bois, and others in NAACP, II, Box A34, "1947 Speeches" file. On White, see his column cited in preceding note, and White, *A Man Called White,* 347-49. On media coverage, see NAACP, II, A33, "1947 Publicity" folder; and Wilkins with Mathews, *Standing Fast,* 198.

10. "Address by Walter White, Secretary of the NAACP, June 29, 1947," in NAACP, II, Box A34, "1947 Speeches."

11. See manuscript in NAACP, II, A34, "1947 Speeches" folder and published text in *PP, 1947.* For the emphasis on "*all* Americans" in Truman's delivery as well as in the text itself, see "Martin Agronsky, Monday, June 30, 1947, To ABC," radio transcript in NAACP, II, Box A34, "1947 Speakers."

12. Donovan, *Conflict and Crisis,* 334.

13. White to Martin Agronsky, July 15, 1947, NAACP, II, A34, "1947 Speakers" file; Editorial, "Truman's Address," *Crisis,* July 1947, 200; and Editorial, "Truman to the NAACP," *Crisis,* August 1947, 233.

14. See Wilkins to White, June 30, 1947; Constance Hazel Daniel to Walter White, June 29, 1947; and Essie Robeson to White; all in NAACP, II, Box A32, "1947 Greetings.

15. See clippings and press releases in NAACP, II, A33, "1947 Publicity" file. See also *DN,* June 30, 1947, 20. For the *Detroit Free Press* editorial, "Rights of All," and cartoon (probably from June 30, 1947), the *America* editorial (July 12, 1947), and other clippings, see NAACP, II, Box A34, "1947 Speakers." On newsreel showings and the NAACP's satisfaction with the event, see "Memorandum to All the Staff: From Mr. White," July 2, 1947, in NAACP, II, Box A34, "Annual Conference 1947, Correspondence regarding, June–August."

16. See Walter White to Harry S. Truman, July 9, 1947; Truman to David K. Niles, memorandum; and miscellaneous correspondence on the June 29, 1947 speech in HSTL, PPF200. On the earlier note and Truman's responding to these political pressures, see Shapiro, *White Violence and Black Response,* 372, 374.

17. On the relationship between the two petitions, see Shapiro, *White Violence and Black Response,* 349-51; for a very different perspective, imbued with Cold War anticommunism, see Record, *Race and Radicalism,* 147-48.

18. See "NAACP Petition to the United Nations/Chronology" and various newspaper clippings in NAACP, II, A637, "United Nations/Petition (NAACP)/1948-49" file. Useful accounts include Dudziak, "Desegregation as a Cold War Imperative," 94-96; Bernstein, "Ambiguous Legacy," 279-80; Berman, *Politics of Civil Rights,* 65-66; Borstelmann, *Apartheid's Reluctant Uncle,* 65-66; Horne, *Black and Red,* 75-82; Roark, "American Black Leaders," 261-62; White, *A Man Called White,* 357-59; and Du Bois, *Autobiography,* 326-39. See also J. A. Rogers, "Rogers Says: Will the Oppressed Peoples Receive a United Nations Hearing?" *PC,* April 23, 1949, 15.

19. Horace Cayton, "Russians: It's Graves, Not Walter White, Who Is Giving Them Their Ammunition," *PC,* February 21, 1948, 7; "Memorandum to Dr. Du Bois From Mr. White," December 16, 1947, in NAACP, II, Box A637, "United Nations/Petition/1947, Nov.–Dec." file; George Schuyler, "Views and Reviews," *PC,* February 21, 1948, 7, and February 28, 1948, 7. For the context, see Kofsky, *Harry Truman and the War Scare of 1948.*

20. W. E. B. Du Bois, "Three Centuries of Discrimination," *Crisis*, December 1947, 362–64, 379–81; Editorial, "A Good Start," *Crisis*, December 1947, 361. On the timing of the report's release subsequent to the NAACP petition, see Bernstein, "Ambiguous Legacy," 279–80; and Borstelmann, *Apartheid's Reluctant Uncle*, 66.

21. On the role of the Gettysburg Address, see Wills, *Lincoln at Gettysburg*, 102–3, 121–47, and passim. On the report's Myrdalian language, see Lewis, "Origins and Causes of the Civil Rights Movement," 8. Useful accounts of the Committee's work include Berman, *Politics of Civil Rights*, 41–78; and Shapiro, *White Violence and Black Response*, 365–73.

22. "To Secure These Rights," *Crisis*, January 1948, 10–11. See also Roy Wilkins's keynote address to the 1948 NAACP Annual Conference, also entitled "To Secure These Rights," in NAACP, II, Box A37, Annual Conference files, "1948 Speeches."

23. In addition to the archival and periodical sources cited below, see Shapiro, *White Violence and Black Response*, 388–91; Horne, *Black and Red*, 97–111; and Record, *Race and Radicalism*, 156–58.

24. See the extensive set of clippings in NAACP, II, Box A240, "Du Bois, William E. B. — Dismissal/Newspapers 1948–49." Numerous letters from NAACP branches protesting Du Bois's dismissal are in NAACP, II, Box A240, "Du Bois, William E. B. — Dismissal/Board of Directors — Branches/1948" and "Du Bois, William E. B. — Dismissal/Board of Directors — Branches/1948–49." Dozens of letters from individuals protesting the firing are in the "Du Bois, William E. B. — Dismissal/Individuals 1948" folder in the same box.

25. See Memorandum to Mr. White from Dr. Du Bois, December 15, 1947; Memorandum to Dr. Du Bois from Mr. White, December 16, 1947; Memorandum to Mr. White from Dr. Du Bois, December 17, 1947; and Memorandum to Dr. Du Bois from Mr. White, December 17, 1947, all in NAACP, II, Box A637, "United Nations/Petition/1947, Nov.–Dec." Also see "Memorandum, W. E. B. Du Bois to The Secretary and Board of Directors of the N.A.A.C.P., September 7, 1948" (which contains the quotation) and "Memorandum to Dr. Du Bois from Mr. White, September 13, 1948," both in "United Nations/Petition (NAACP)/1948–49" folder in same box. See also *Crisis*, October 1948, 302–3; "Dr. W. E. B. Du Bois and the NAACP," in NAACP, II, Box A240, "Du Bois, W. E. B./Biography and philosophy of, 1950"; and the account in Du Bois, *Autobiography*, 326–39. For White's changed position on Wallace's candidacy, see Walter White, "People, Politics and Places," *Chicago Defender*, June 21, 1947, and "Memorandum to Miss Jackson from Walter White," June 23, 1947, in NAACP, II, Box A74, "Articles — Walter White/Chicago Defender/Columns 1947"; and White's address to the NAACP's 1948 annual conference.

26. On White's membership on the official organizing committee of the Americans for Democratic Action, the institutional embodiment of "vital center" liberalism, see Gillon, *Politics and Vision*, 21. For White's participation in an earlier meeting that largely supported Henry Wallace's foreign-policy views, see Hamby, *Beyond the New Deal*, 154–56. The NAACP's concern with charges of disloyalty is emphasized in Record, *Race and Radicalism*, 135.

27. See esp. Horne, *Black and Red*, 56–111, particularly 56, where he refers to a "Faustian bargain" whereby the NAACP's top brass received "a defined attitude and certain civil rights' concessions at home in exchange for steely eyed anti-communism abroad." As I have argued earlier, a significant political exchange between the NAACP and the Truman administration certainly occurred in 1947 and 1948. But Horne's interpretation, like Du Bois's at the time and in his 1968 *Autobiography*, vastly oversimplifies the situation. For a

view that is similar to Horne's but more nuanced, see Von Eschen, *Race Against Empire*. See also Roark, "American Black Leaders," esp. 262–65 and 268. For a related discussion that comes closer to my own interpretation, see Solomon, "Black Critics of Colonialism and the Cold War," esp. 224. Also see Plummer, *Rising Wind*, 167–216, and Plummer, "'Below the Level of Men,'" esp. 644.

28. "'Europeans Are Afraid of Democracy (U.S. Style),'" *PC*, September 13, 1947, 21; "Race Called Scale to Weigh Democracy," *PC*, July 10, 1948, 3. For another example, see P. L. Prattis, "The Horizon," *PC*, February 14, 1948, 7.

29. See Prattis's column, "The Horizon," in the *PC*, February 14, 1948, 7; July 10, 1948, 19; July 23, 1949, 14; and March 18, 1950, 16. See also Horace Cayton's column, "Cayton," in *PC*, February 5, 1949, 15.

30. Horace Cayton, "Dutch Are Using United States Money to Enslave People of Indonesia," *PC*, January 1, 1949, 15; and "Tiny Dutch Nation Defies UN and Gets Away With It," *PC*, January 8, 1949, 15. George Schuyler's position was more satirical and elliptical, even suggesting that U.S. support for the Dutch move should not have surprised anyone; see Schuyler, "The World Today," *PC*, January 1, 1949, 4. (An arch critic of the New Deal, Schuyler also blasted the Marshall Plan as "the International WPA"; see "The World Today," *PC*, January 29, 1949, 4.) On the Indonesian crisis, see also Trezzvant W. Anderson, "Rape of Indonesia Stirs Colored Races," *PC*, January 1, 1949, 1, 4; J. A. Rogers, "Roger Says: The Rape of Indonesia, South Africa, Only Bodes Ill for the Oppressors," *PC*, January 22, 1949, 15; and Joseph D. Bibb, "Subject Dark People," *PC*, April 23, 1949, 14.

31. Editorial, "Financing Imperialism," *PC*, June 7, 1947, 6.

32. "Extend Marshall Plan to Aid Needy in Africa: Walter White Warns That Bias in U.S. Is Hurting Program," *PC*, February 7, 1948, 3; resolution on "International and Colonial Problems" in NAACP 1949 annual conference files. For a dissenting view from one NAACP branch, which took a similar position concerning European colonialism but opposed the Marshall Plan and the Atlantic Pact as well, see the proposed minority "Resolution on the Marshall Plan and the Atlantic Pact" from the Jamaica, N.Y., branch, in NAACP, II, Box A38, "Annual Conference 1949 Resolutions Considered" folder, and in the *Crisis*, June 1949, 185–86. See also Record, *The Negro and the Communist Party*, 263–65.

33. NAACP news releases: "Halt Aid to Dutch, Walter White Urges," December 23, 1948; and "White Repeats Demand: Stop Marshall Plan Aid to Dutch," December 30, 1948, both in NAACP, II, Box A285, "Foreign Affairs/General/1940–49."

34. Walter White, column manuscript, "Sent 12/24/48," in NAACP, II, Box A74, "Articles— Walter White/Chicago Defender/Columns 1948"; Editorial, "Happy New Year," *Crisis*, January 1949, 9.

35. George Schuyler, "The World Today," *PC*, July 23, 1949, 1; Horace Cayton, *PC*, September 3, 1949, 14; "British Colonies and Marshall Aid," *Crisis*, October 1948, 312; and Horace Cayton, *PC*, June 10, 1950, 14.

36. See Borstelmann, *Apartheid's Reluctant Uncle*, 109–13.

37. Editorial, "The President's World Program," *PC*, January 29, 1949, 14; George Schuyler, "The World Today," *PC*, January 29, 1949, 5, and October 8, 1949, 4; and Trezzvant W. Anderson, "World News in a Nutshell," *PC*, May 13, 1950, 7.

38. "Human Rights Through International Agencies," Address by Dr. Rayford W. Logan, July 14, 1949, 40th Annual Conference of the National Association for the Advancement of Colored People, Los Angeles, California, in NAACP, II, Box A39, "Annual Conference

1949 Speeches," 3–6. For background on Logan, see Janken, *Rayford W. Logan and the Dilemma of the African-American Intellectual,* esp. 115–98.

39. Press Release, "Point 4 Aid for Colonies Urged by NAACP Leaders," May 22, 1952, in NAACP, II, Box A617, "State Department/Point IV Programs, 1949–1950."

40. Editorial, "Democracy Defined at Moscow," *Crisis,* April 1947, 105; Editorial, "Foreign Policy and FEPC," *Crisis,* May 1947, 137; see also James Edmund Boyack, "Ambassador Warren R. Austin: 'World Peace Must Be Built on Foundation of Democracy for All,'" *PC,* February 14, 1948, 3; and P. L. Prattis, "The Horizon: The House Told the World That White Americans Are Against Fair Employment," *PC,* March 4, 1950, 16.

41. Speech, NAACP, II, Box A36, Annual Conference Files, "1948 Speakers"; and NAACP Declaration of Principles, NAACP, II, Box A35, Annual Conference Files, "1948 Forms." See also press release, June 27, 1948, "NAACP Delegates Ask Action Now," NAACP, II, Box A36, Annual Conference Files, "1948 Publicity." *PC,* February 5, 1949, 6 (on Rustin); T. V. Anderson, "Congress Winks at Anti-Lynching Bills As Mobs Run Amok," *PC,* June 14, 1947, 13 (quotation). See also P. L. Prattis, "The Horizon: Sight of White Americans Dosing Europeans with Democracy Is Ludicrous," *PC,* April 9, 1949, 14; Editorial, "As We Look to the Japanese," *Crisis,* July 1949, 201; Walter White, *Chicago Defender* columns, August 13 and September 10, 1949, both in NAACP, II, Box A75, "Articles — Walter White/*Chicago Defender*/Columns 1949"; and James W. Ivy, "American Negro Problem in the European Press," *Crisis,* July 1950, 413–18, 468–72.

42. Horace Cayton, "Cayton: Eva Peron Pulls a Fast One and Embarrasses U.S.," *PC,* January 29, 1949, 15; see also J. A. Rogers, "Rogers Says: 'America Is Now the Most Disliked Nation on Earth,'" on the same page.

43. Rayford Logan series on State Department, *PC,* April 15, 1950, 1, 4; April 22, 1950, 1, 4; April 29, 1950, 1, 5; May 6, 1950, 1, 4; May 13, 1950, 1, 4; May 20, 1950, 1, 4. P. L. Prattis, "Marshall Plan Bosses Guilty in Europe of No-Negro Policy," *PC,* February 19, 1949, 7; and Horace Cayton, "Cayton: State Department Making Big Mistake in Ignoring Negroes," *PC,* February 26, 1949, 15.

44. "Russian Embassy Post to Bunche?" *PC,* February 12, 1949, 4; Horace Cayton, "Bunche Proves to World We Can Be Real Diplomats," *PC,* February 19, 1949, 15; "World Hails Bunche," *PC,* March 5, 1949, 1, 5; Joseph D. Bibb, "Some Great Men: Colored Men in High Office Add Honor and Credit to Their Country," *PC,* April 16, 1949, 16; "Dr. Bunche Proposed as Ambassador to Russia," *PC,* June 3, 1950, 1, 5; Horace Cayton, *PC,* June 17, 1950, 14.

45. Ralph Bunche speech in 1949 Annual Conference folder. On the NAACP, see, for example, Resolution on "Colonial Peoples," in NAACP, II, Box A33, "1947 Resolutions"; Resolution on "International Problems," in 1948 Annual Conference file; and Resolution on "International and Colonial Problems" in 1949 Annual Conference file. See also "Address of Dr. W. E. B. Du Bois at 38th Annual Conference, N.A.A.C.P., afternoon of June 26, 1947" in NAACP, II, Box A34, "1947 Speeches"; and "Du Bois Declares Socialism a Haven," *New York Times,* June 27, 1949, clipping in NAACP, II, Box A32, "1947 Correspondence."

46. See esp. Roy Wilkins's speech in "40 Years of the NAACP" in 1949 Annual Conference folder; and Horace Cayton's columns in *PC,* July 3, 1948, 19, and November 13, 1948, 17. For other examples from the *Pittsburgh Courier,* see J. A. Rogers, "Rogers Says," January 22, 1949, 15; Joseph D. Bibb, "Imperialism Doomed: Trouble in Asia and Africa Brewing Over Rotten System of Colonial Tyranny," January 29, 1949, and "Subject Dark People: Im-

perialism Holds Africa, Malaya, Indonesia and Indo-China Under Heel," April 23, 1949; and Trezzvant W. Anderson, "World News in a Nutshell," April 23, 1949, 17, and January 7, 1950, 2.

47. Gerald Horne, by contrast, argues that after dismissing Du Bois, White and the NAACP board abandoned the organization's anticolonial tradition. Yet Horne's own evidence often explodes his interpretation. See Horne, *Black and Red*, esp. 56–73, 89–93, 97–111, 130–31.

48. Secretary to Leslie Perry, Washington Bureau, NAACP, May 2, 1949, NAACP, II, Box A83, "Atlantic Pact (NATO) 1949" folder. On the NAACP's distance from NATO supporters, see letters of July 27, 1949, and September 27, 1949, from Madison S. Jones Jr., NAACP Administrative Assistant, to Frederick C. McKee, Chairman, Committee on National Affairs, in the same folder. For a more explicit critique of NATO from one African American columnist, see Marjorie McKenzie, "Pursuit of Democracy: The Small, Dark Nations Must Deal with Russia by Grace of the West," *PC*, June 10, 1950, 15, which lambastes Acheson's claims that NATO was designed to protect freedom.

49. The quotation is from NAACP press release, March 31, 1949, "NAACP Urges Opposition to Italian Imperialism," in NAACP, II, Box A285, "Foreign Affairs/General/1940–49." See also the discussion of the Italian colonies and NATO in "Report of the Secretary for the April 1949 Board Meeting," with text of the Secretary's telegram to Acheson; NAACP press releases dated April 14, 1949 ("Restoration of Italian Colonial Regime Opposed"), September 15, 1949 ("NAACP Urges State Department Support UN Rule For Colonies"), September 29, 1949 ("NAACP Supports UN Secretary on Trusteeship For Colonies"), and November 23, 1949 ("Colony Settlement 'Partial Victory,' Roy Wilkins Holds"). For discussions from outside the NAACP, see J. A. Rogers, "Rogers Says: U.S. Leaders Want Colonies Returned to Italy; But What About the Colonial People?" *PC*, April 2, 1949, 15; and Editorial, "A 'Liberal' Diplomat Speaks," *PC*, June 14, 1947, 6.

50. See Radosh, *American Labor and U.S. Foreign Policy*, 307–10, 347, 435–38; Schatz, "Philip Murray and the Subordination of the Industrial Unions to the United States Government"; McCormick, *America's Half-Century*, 84–85; Levenstein, *Communism, Anticommunism, and the CIO*, esp. 332–33; and Freeland, *Truman Doctrine and the Origins of McCarthyism*.

51. Bert Cochran (*Labor and Communism*, 277–79) and Harvey Levenstein (*Communism, Anticommunism, and the CIO*, 315) both argue that the UAW became less democratic after Reuther took control. Even Irving Howe and B. J. Widick, whose sympathies clearly lie with Reuther and against his adversaries, Communist and otherwise, conclude that Reuther's more conservative allies gained strength between 1947 and 1949 (Howe and Widick, *UAW and Walter Reuther*, 289).

52. Schatz, *Electrical Workers*, 184. On the Truman administration, see Radosh, *Labor and Foreign Policy*, 436–37.

53. The literature on the UAW is extensive, but see in particular Howe and Widick, *UAW and Walter Reuther;* Barnard, *Walter Reuther and the Auto Workers;* and Lichtenstein, "Walter Reuther and the Rise of Labor-Liberalism." The single most thorough history of the UE is Schatz's *The Electrical Workers,* though Schatz takes a social history approach and does not fully treat certain important issues concerning the union's political culture, such as the role of the Communist Party. Two important studies that focus on the Party and the politics of anticommunism in both the UE and the UAW in the context of the Cold

War are Cochran, *Labor and Communism,* esp. 229–344; and Levenstein, *Communism, Anticommunism, and the CIO,* esp. 167–339.

54. On Reuther's development as a practical politician in this period, see Howe and Widick, *UAW and Walter Reuther,* 200–201, 203–4; and Barnard, *Walter Reuther and the Auto Workers,* 109, and 70–90 for background.

55. Schatz, *Electrical Workers,* 184; Hamby, *Beyond the New Deal,* 263; UE, *Proceedings, 1948,* 25 (on Fitzgerald) and "Resolution on 3rd Party" in same volume. For the Reuther quotation, see Hamby, *Beyond the New Deal,* 207.

56. UE, *Proceedings, 1948,* 8; UAW, *Proceedings, 1947,* 5.

57. See Schatz, "Philip Murray and the Subordination," 244, 252–53; Levenstein, *Communism, Anticommunism, and the CIO,* 208–32, esp. 219–29; and Cochran, *Labor and Communism,* 264–71.

58. UE, *Proceedings, 1948,* 34–41, esp. 37–40. See also Levenstein, *Communism, Anticommunism, and the CIO,* 220–28, 280–83; Cochran, *Labor and Communism,* 298–304; and Markowitz, *Rise and Fall of the People's Century,* 266–97.

59. See UE, *Proceedings, 1947,* 294–305, also 129–70 and 197–217.

60. Ibid., 298–99.

61. Ibid., 301–2.

62. UE, *Proceedings, 1948,* 24–29.

63. Ibid., 189–201 for both reports and the debate, 130–40 for the resolution and debate on UMT and the draft. See also the telegram to Truman from the Yonkers UE local, which supported the UMT in response to his 3/17/48 speeches, in PPF200.

64. See UE, *Proceedings, 1949;* International Union of Electrical, Radio and Machine Workers, *Proceedings,* First Convention, 1949; and Schatz, *Electrical Workers,* esp. 185. See also Cochran, *Labor and Communism,* 272–331, esp. 291–94, 312, 314–15, 317–20; and Levenstein, *Communism, Anticommunism, and the CIO,* 280–302, esp. 294, 300–302, 308–12.

65. UAW, *Proceedings, 1947,* 204. See also Howe and Widick, *UAW and Walter Reuther,* 291; and Barnard, *Walter Reuther and the Auto Workers,* 155.

66. Some historians have argued that the UAW became less democratic after Reuther gained control of the union; see note 51 above. For more sympathetic assessments, see Barnard, *Walter Reuther and the Auto Workers,* 137–55; and Howe and Widick, *UAW and Walter Reuther,* 170, 200–201, 203–4, 235–70, 291.

67. UAW *Proceedings, 1947,* 204.

68. Ibid., 7–9.

69. UAW, *Proceedings, 1949,* 64.

70. UAW, *Proceedings, 1947,* 17.

71. On the role of Communist Party members and of Reuther's anticommunism in UAW politics, see the accounts in Howe and Widick, *UAW and Walter Reuther,* esp. 74, 79–82, 114–17, and 149–71; Barnard, *Walter Reuther and the Auto Workers,* 111–37; Cochran, *Labor and Communism,* esp. 127–95 and 249–96; and Levenstein, *Communism, Anticommunism, and the CIO,* esp. 36–100 and 196–207.

72. UAW, *Proceedings, 1947,* 128–29, 280.

73. Ibid., 64.

74. UAW, *Proceedings, 1949,* 10.

75. Ibid., 74.

76. The following discussion is based on the "International Relations Program" resolution and debate in UAW, *Proceedings, 1949*, 209–13.

77. On Boatin, see Keeran, *Communist Party and the Auto Worker Union*, 260.

78. UAW, *Proceedings, 1949*, 14.

79. Ibid., 16.

80. Ibid., 194; Telegram in NAACP, II, Box A38, "Annual Conference 1949 Greetings" folder. See also greetings from NAACP to Reuther in UAW, *Proceedings, 1947*, 31. For background on the UAW-NAACP partnership, see Meier and Rudwick, *Black Detroit and the Rise of the UAW*, esp. 175–222; and White, *A Man Called White*, 333–35.

81. UAW, *Proceedings, 1949*, 15; see also 145 for similar statements in Reuther's remarks introducing the civil rights activist Anne Hedgeman as a guest speaker.

82. Ibid., 146, 148.

83. Ibid., 227–28.

84. Ibid., 229.

85. See Dudziak, "Civil Rights as a Cold War Imperative"; Dalfiume, *Desegregation of the U.S. Armed Forces*, 2; and Dalfiume, "Forgotten Years of the Negro Revolution," esp. 106.

86. See Levenstein, *Communism, Anticommunism, and the CIO*, 79, 84–90, 150–52, 219–21, 335, 337–39.

87. See ibid., 208–9, 332–33, 335–36; and Horne, *Black and Red*, 19–24.

CHAPTER SIX

1. See LaFeber, "NATO and the Korean War," 473, for both the Acheson quotation and the survey results.

2. See Cumings, *Origins of the Korean War*, Vol. 1, *Liberation and the Emergence of Separate Regimes*, xx–xxiv, xxix; Cumings, *Origins of the Korean War*, Vol. 2, *Roaring of the Cataract*, 625–29 (Acheson quotation on both 625 and 628); and LaFeber, *America, Russia, and the Cold War*, 99–103, esp. 99 for the casualty figure. See also Leffler, *Preponderance of Power*, 361–73. Recent scholarship shows that the USSR did play a significant role in the North Korean invasion (see Weathersby, "New Findings on the Korean War"; Weathersby, "New Russian Documents on the Korean War"; Weathersby, "To Attack or Not to Attack?"; and Cumings and Weathersby, "An Exchange on Korean War Origins"). But Cumings is correct in asserting that the Korean civil war was the key context and that U.S. policymakers were blinded to it by their own ideology, as the Acheson quotations make dramatically clear. In David Holloway's judicious assessment, Cumings "rightly stresses the Korean origins of the Korean war. But the Soviet role is a matter of some moment too" (see Holloway, *Stalin and the Bomb*, 276–83, 428 fn. 28 for quotation).

3. NSC-68, as quoted in LaFeber, *America, Russia, and the Cold War*, 96–97.

4. NSC-68, in Etzold and Gaddis, *Containment*, 389. See 385–442 for the complete text.

5. See LaFeber, *America, Russia, and the Cold War*, 96–98; LaFeber, "NATO and the Korean War," 467–71; McCormick, *America's Half-Century*, 97; and Ambrose, *Rise to Globalism*, 113. See also the valuable and detailed context for NSC-68 developed by Leffler in *Preponderance of Power*, 312–60, esp. 355–60 on the document itself.

6. Markel, *Public Opinion and Foreign Policy*, 3–140, 213–27.

7. For two provocative interpretations of the national-character studies movement in

American social science, which emerged during World War II, see Dower, *War Without Mercy*, 118–46; and Gleason, *Speaking of Diversity*, 123–49, 167–72, 188–201.

8. Almond, *American People and Foreign Policy*, 87–88 and passim.

9. LaFeber, *America, Russia, and the Cold War*, 98, citing Princeton Seminar, July 8–9, 1953, Acheson Papers, Truman Library. See also Cumings, *Origins of the Korean War*, Vol. 2, 434, 761–62 (on NSC-68), and 637–43 (on U.S. public reaction to the outbreak of war).

10. See Cumings, *Origins of the Korean War*, Vol. 2, 619.

11. *PP, 1950*, 491–92.

12. Ibid., 504, 505.

13. Ibid., 537.

14. Ibid., 540.

15. Ibid., 541–42. Also see the newsreel "As Russia Sees It," *March of Time* (1950).

16. Gallup, *Gallup Poll*, 2:929–33, 949, 951–52, 955, 958.

17. In the surviving mail at the Truman Library in response to the president's major radio address of July 19, 1950, "pro" letters outnumber "con" letters by about ten to one. See PPF200 Speeches files, HSTL. Unless otherwise noted, all citizen letters to President Truman cited in this chapter are from PPF200.

18. Frank A. Hellard, recording secretary, and Joseph J. Lashowski, chairman, to the President, July 8, 1950; and Robert E. Lee, Commander, Leyden-Chiles-Wickersham Post No. 1, The American Legion, to The President, June 27, 1950 — both in HST, OF 471-B. Other examples in the same folder include Robert Brown, Secretary of the Active Club of Oakland, Calif., to HST, June 28, 1950; Nile and Mary Adams, Kansas City, Mo., to HST, June 27, 1950; Charles T. Allen, San Antonio, Tex., to HST; William and Eleanore Alesi, Bayville, N.Y., to HST, June 27, 1950; and Sgt. Paul E. Alexander, Skagway, Alaska, to HST, July 9, 1950.

19. Paul A. Bissinger to HST, July 20, 1950; and David Sarnoff to HST, July 20, 1950.

20. Michael Francis Doyle to HST, July 19, 1950.

21. Lasalle L. Nolin to HST, July 20, 1950; and Carl Oerke to HST, July 20, 1950. See also Gustave R. Keane, Huntington, Long Island, N.Y., to HST, 7/19/50; R. R. Yelderman, Omaha, Neb., to HST; Thomas Kannar to HST, 7/20/50; Leo J. Tack, Wichita, Kans., to HST, 7/23/50; Glen Grace, Sacramento, Calif., to HST, 7/19/50; and George Beasley, Gadsden, Ala. to HST, 7/20/50. By occupation, these writers were, respectively, a minister, an electrical worker (and UE-CIO member), a gas service company employee (probably white-collar), a hotel clerk, and chairman of a group called the Old Age Pension Association.

22. Joseph M. Gantz to HST, 9/1/50; James Valfriend, Branford, Conn., to HST, 7/20/50; and Nicholas Biddle to HST, 7/20/50.

23. Hon. John T. Barker to HST, September 2, 1950; Mrs. Edward H. Allen, Waterford, Conn., to HST, July 21, 1950; Mr. and Mrs. U. L. Hobbs to HST, September 3, 1950; and John Alva Bell to HST, [9/1/50]. See also M. S. Stevenson, National Commander of the Disabled Emergency Officers of the World Wars, to HST, July 20, 1950; and A. L. Pulliam to HST, September 4, 1950.

24. Rev. Thomas Grice, Camarillo, Calif., to HST, September 1, 1950; Frank Smathers Sr. to HST, July 20, 1950; Rabbi A. M. Herschberg to HST, [7/19/50]; Irvi Meserth to HST, July 19, 1950. See also Mr. and Mrs. Carl Sartwell, Decatur, Ill., to HST, July 20, 1950; Marilyn Ann Sigoloff to HST [7/19/50]; and Isabelle B. Friedman, Manhasset, L.I., N.Y., to HST, [7/19/50].

25. Charles Varga to HST, July 21, 1950; Barbara J. Bushie to HST, July 19, 1950; John Flood, San Diego, Calif., to HST, July 20, 1950; Harry Goller, aka "Kid Duggan," Chicago, Ill., to HST, [7/19/50]; Edward C. Bernst, Los Angeles, Calif., to HST, July 20, 1950; Mrs. Alice Newquist to HST, July 19, 1950; Marie B. Bachofer to HST, July 21, 1950.

26. For one example of a citizen questioning the constitutionality of Truman's decision to intervene, see Joan Doman, Danbury, Conn., to HST, July 20, 1950. For examples of concern with the costs of intervention, see Harry Swanson, Detroit, Mich., to HST, July 20, 1950; and Horace C. Flanagan, Purchase, N.Y., to HST, July 21, 1950.

27. Mrs. Gajewski to HST, September 5, 1950; Ingrid Stoetzer to HST, July 20, 1950; Marion Sternbach to HST, July 24, 1950; Mrs. L. Weisman to HST, July 22, 1950. For related anti-interventionist sentiment in letters that do not explicitly refer to the Korean conflict as a civil war, see Richard Demming, Denver, Colo., to HST, June 29, 1950, OF 471-B; Robert S. Lathrop Fairfield, Conn., to HST, July 20, 1950; and John H. Proll, Los Angeles, Calif., to HST, July 14, 1950, OF 471-B. For an example of a letter opposing the intervention in Korea as just one example of the United States' supporting undemocratic regimes, see Alexander Zald, Long Island City, N.Y., to HST, September 2, 1950.

28. Joseph A. Prachar, Berwyn, Ill., to HST, July 7, 1950, OF 471-B.

29. Miriam and John C. Paisley, Baltimore, Md., to HST, 8/3/50, OF 471-B. For other examples, see Erling Rohde, National City, Calif., to HST, July 19, 1950; Elsie Johnson, Chicago, Ill., to HST, July 20, 1950; and Olga Forto, Jamaica, N.Y., to HST, July 19, 1950.

30. Editorial, "Moscow Turns On the Heat in Asia, Our Weakest Spot," *SEP*, July 22, 1950, 10. See also Editorial, "We Need Power to Preserve Peace," *Collier's*, August 5, 1950, 74; and the *Life* editorials discussed below. The *Saturday Evening Post*'s editorial cartoons also represented the Korean War through the prism of nationalist globalism; see esp. "Lost in the Red Stars," *SEP*, July 29, 1950, 10; "The Man behind the Smoke Curtain," *SEP*, August 12, 1950, 10; and "A Room with a View," *SEP* September 16, 1950, 10. For editorial criticism of the Truman administration's performance prior to June 27, 1950, see the *Collier's* editorial cited above; Editorial, "We Can't Sell Our Ideals Abroad If They Die at Home," *SEP*, July 29, 1950, 10; Editorials, "Check List of Errors" and "Johnson or Acheson?" *Life*, July 24, 1950, 26; and Editorial, "Johnson vs. Acheson," *Life*, September 25, 1950, 34.

31. Editorial, "A Mighty Job: Action in Korea Involves the Future of Asia's Millions," *Life*, July 10, 1950, 35.

32. Editorial, "A Restored Position: Popular Response to Korea Means the U.S. Has Mobility to Act," *Life*, July 17, 1950, 40.

33. See, for example, "Soviet Germany's Secret Army," *Collier's*, August 12, 1950, 13–15, 70; J. Denson, "Must We Rearm Japan?" *Collier's*, September 9, 1950, 18–19, 69–70; "Is Formosa Next?" *Life*, August 7, 1993, 82–92; Darrel Berrigan, "Will Creeping Communism Engulf India?" *SEP*, September 16, 1950, 42–43, 66–68, 70–72; "Will Stalin Jump Tito Next?" *SEP*, August 5, 1950, 25, 108–10; and Editorial, "We Need Power to Preserve Peace," *Collier's*, August 5, 1950, 74, on Indo-China. The "blueprint" quotation is from Editorial, "Needed: A Vast U.N. Army," *Collier's*, September 30, 1950, 78. Also see the newsreel "As Russia Sees It," *March of Time* (1950).

34. Joseph and Stewart Alsop, "The Lesson of Korea," *SEP*, September 2, 1950, 17–19, 96, 98, 100.

35. Demaree Bess, "How Long Will This War Last?" *SEP*, September 9, 1950, 22–23, 95.

36. Editorial, "Questions from Korea," *Life,* August 7, 1950, 30.

37. Editorial, "Program For America," *Life,* August 14, 1950, 30.

38. Letters to the Editors, from Douglas Straton, Wooster, Ohio, and W. Russell Bowie, South Yarmouth, Mass., *Life,* September 4, 1950, 2, 4. These pages present similarly critical responses from two other readers and vociferous praise from only two others.

39. Editorial, "Questions from Korea," *Life,* August 7, 1950, 30.

40. Editorial, "Targets of Opportunity," *Life,* August 14, 1950, 30.

41. Editorial, "Our Vast Resources," *Life,* August 14, 1950, 30.

42. See, in general, the *DN,* June 26–27, 1950. The editorial is "Truman-Acheson Asia Policy Explodes into Stratosphere," June 26, 1950, 33. The quoted story is in the *DN,* June 26, 1950, 2 and 6, in the first city edition on the reel at the New York Public Library.

43. *DN,* June 28, 1950, 1, 3, 4, 43.

44. *DN,* June 29, 1950, 2, 4, 45, 48, for the news article on Taft's speech as well as the editorial and O'Donnell's column. See also John O'Donnell, "Capitol Stuff," *DN,* June 30, 1950, 4. On Taft's criticism of the president's usurpation of congressional authority, see also Cumings, *Origins of the Korean War,* Vol. 2, 629.

45. Editorial, "Blueprint for Policing the World," *DN,* July 20, 1950, 39. See also the editorials "Nice Gesture for Clemmy," *DN,* July 22, 1950, 15; "The Long, Crooked Road to Korea," *DN,* July 24, 1950, 23; "Acheson on the China Reds," *DN,* September 1, 1950, 31; "Uncle's Muscles—How're They Doing?" *DN,* September 5, 1950, 33.

46. Editorial, "Same Old War to End War," *DN,* September 3, 1950, 25.

47. See Trezzvant Anderson, "World News in a Nutshell," *PC,* March 18, 1950, 6, April 22, 1950, 3, and July 8, 1950, 6; and Dalfiume, *Desegregation of the U.S. Armed Forces; PC,* July 8, 1950, 1. Quotes from Marjorie McKenzie, "Pursuit of Democracy: America Must Realize That Beyond the Atlantic Circle the World Is Yellow, Black," *PC,* July 15, 1950, 14; and Joseph D. Bibb, "If War Comes: America's Darker Minority Can Always Be Depended On to Rally to the Flag," *PC,* July 15, 1950, 15.

48. Editorial, "Is It a War of Color?" *Ebony,* October 1950, 94. See also the *Ebony* editorials "Where Ebony Stands Today," November 1950, 94; and "Brotherhood Becomes Fashionable," December 1950, 74.

49. Rev. William Marion to the Editor, "Bunche, Not MacArthur, Should Carry UN Flag," *PC,* August 5, 1950, 16. For a related view, see also Chester Jones to the Editor, *Ebony,* December 1950.

50. Editorial, "Korea, United Nations, Peace," *PC,* July 8, 1950, 14; and Editorial, "Korea: Background of the War," *PC,* August 12, 1950, 14.

51. Marjorie McKenzie, "Pursuit of Democracy: America Must Realize That Beyond the Atlantic Circle the World Is Yellow, Black," *PC,* July 15, 1950, 14. For similar views, see Joseph D. Bibb, "The Colonies!: The Democracies Are Now in Hot Water Because of Mistreating Their Colonials," *PC,* August 5, 1950, 15; and Horace Cayton, "Cayton: North Koreans Are Not So Undemocratic That We Should Forget Their Racial Problem," *PC,* September 16, 1950, 6.

52. The first quotation from White is from "South Can't Escape Race Showdown—White," *Chicago Defender,* August 5, 1950, clipping; all other quotations are from Walter White, column manuscript marked "sent 8/11"; both are in "Articles—Walter White/*Chicago Defender*/columns 1950" folder, NAACP, II, Box A75. See also Walter White, "Dixiecrats

Keep U.S. Behind International 'Eight Ball,' " *Chicago Defender,* July 8, 1950, clipping, in the same folder.

53. Editorial, "Korean War," *Crisis,* August–September, 1950, 511.

54. Editorial, "Korean War," *Crisis,* October 1950, 586.

55. J. A. Rogers, "Rogers Says" columns, *PC,* July 15, 1950, 15; July 22, 1950, 15; and July 29, 1950, 15.

56. *DN,* July 18, 1950, 8.

57. UAW, *Proceedings, 1951,* 6–7, 64–65, 127–31. For more evidence concerning the rhetorical and political relationship between the NAACP and the UAW, see in the same volume Walter White to Walter Reuther, "Communication" read to the 1951 UAW convention.

58. Ibid., 77–84.

59. International Union of Electrical, Radio and Machine Workers, *Proceedings* (1950), 76–77.

60. UE, *Proceedings, 1950,* 39 and passim.

61. Ibid., 41, 57, 86, 136–37.

62. Ibid., 140.

63. Ibid., 10 (Fitzgerald's remarks) and 169–83 (foreign-policy resolution and debate).

CONCLUSION

1. Kolko and Kolko, *Limits of Power,* 31.

BIBLIOGRAPHY

PRIMARY SOURCES

Manuscript Collections

Library of Congress, Manuscript Division, Washington, D.C.
  Eric Sevareid Papers
  Raymond Gram Swing Papers
  Records of the National Association for the Advancement of Colored People (NAACP)
  Records of the National Urban League (NUL)
Harry S. Truman Library, Independence, Mo.
  President's Official Files
  President's Personal Files

Newspapers and Periodicals

Chicago Defender
Cincinnati Times-Star
Collier's
The Crisis
Ebony
Journeyman Plumbers and Steam Fitters Journal
Ladies' Home Journal
Life
The Nation
New Republic
New York Daily News
New York Sunday News
New York Times
Norfolk (Va.) Journal and Guide
Pittsburgh Courier
Saturday Evening Post
Vital Speeches of the Day

Published Documents

International Union of Electrical, Radio and Machine Workers (IUE-CIO). *Proceedings,* 1949, 1950.
United Automobile, Aircraft and Agricultural Implements Workers of America (UAW-CIO). Convention *Proceedings,* 1944, 1946, 1947, 1949, 1951.

United Electrical, Radio and Machine Workers of America (UE), Convention *Proceedings,*
    1944, 1946, 1947, 1948, 1949, 1950.
U.S. Government Printing Office. *Public Papers of the Presidents of the United States,
    Harry S. Truman, 1945–1950.* Washington, D.C., 1961–1964.

SECONDARY SOURCES

Adler, Les K., and Thomas G. Paterson. "Red Fascism: The Merger of Nazi Germany and
    Soviet Russia in the American Image of Totalitarianism, 1930s–1950s." *American
    Historical Review* 75 (April 1970): 1046–64.
Alexander, Charles. *Nationalism in American Thought, 1930–1945.* Chicago, 1969.
Almond, Gabriel A. *The American People and Foreign Policy.* 2d ed. New York, 1960.
Ambrose, Stephen E. *Rise to Globalism: American Foreign Policy Since 1938.* 5th rev. ed.
    New York, 1988.
Anderson, Benedict. *Imagined Communities: Reflections on the Origins and Spread of
    Nationalism.* Rev. ed. New York, 1991.
Ashby, Steven. "Shattered Dreams: The American Working Class and the Origins of the
    Cold War, 1945–1949," Ph.D. dissertation, University of Chicago, 1993.
Baritz, Loren. *Backfire: A History of How American Culture Led Us into Vietnam and Made
    Us Fight the Way We Did.* New York, 1985.
Barnard, John. *Walter Reuther and the Rise of the Auto Workers.* Boston, 1983.
Barnet, Richard J. *The Rockets' Red Glare: When America Goes to War: The Presidents and
    the People.* New York, 1990.
Baughman, James L. *Henry R. Luce and the Rise of the American News Media.* Boston, 1987.
Bender, Thomas. "Wholes and Parts: The Need for Synthesis in American History."
    Journal of American History 73 (June 1986): 120–36.
Berman, William C. *The Politics of Civil Rights in the Truman Administration.* Columbus,
    Ohio, 1970.
Bernstein, Barton J. "The Ambiguous Legacy: The Truman Administration and Civil
    Rights." In *Politics and Policies of the Truman Administration,* 269–314. Chicago, 1970.
Blum, John Morton. *V Was for Victory: Politics and American Culture During World War II.*
    New York, 1976.
Borstelmann, Thomas P. *Apartheid's Reluctant Uncle: The United States and Southern
    Africa in the Early Cold War.* New York, 1993.
Boyer, Paul. *By the Bomb's Early Light: American Thought and Culture at the Dawn of the
    Atomic Age.* New York, 1985.
Brinkley, Alan. *Voices of Protest: Huey Long, Father Coughlin and the Great Depression.* New
    York, 1982.
Brooks, Thomas R. *Walls Come Tumbling Down: A History of the Civil Rights Movement,
    1940–1970.* Englewood Cliffs, N.J., 1974.
Chambers, John Whiteclay, II, ed. *Draftees or Volunteers.* New York, 1975.
Cochran, Bert. *Labor and Communism: The Conflict That Shaped American Unions.*
    Princeton, N.J., 1977.
Costigliola, Frank. *Awkward Dominion: American Political, Economic, and Cultural
    Relations with Europe, 1919–1933.* Ithaca, N.Y., 1984.

Cumings, Bruce. *The Origins of the Korean War.* Vol. 1, *Liberation and the Emergence of Separate Regimes, 1945–1947.* Princeton, N.J., 1981.

———. *The Origins of the Korean War.* Vol. 2, *The Roaring of the Cataract.* Princeton, N.J., 1990.

Cumings, Bruce, and Kathryn Weathersby, "An Exchange on Korean War Origins." *Cold War International History Project Bulletin* 6–7 (Winter 1995–96): 120–22.

Dalfiume, Richard M. *Desegregation of the U.S. Armed Forces: Fighting on Two Fronts, 1939–1953.* Columbia, Mo., 1969.

———. "The 'Forgotten Years' of the Negro Revolution." *Journal of American History* 55 (1968): 90–106.

Dallek, Robert. *Franklin D. Roosevelt and American Foreign Policy, 1932–1945.* New York, 1979.

Diggins, John Patrick. *The Proud Decades: America in War and Peace, 1941–1960.* New York, 1989.

Divine, Robert A. "The Cold War and the Election of 1948." *Journal of American History* 59 (June 1972): 90–110.

———. *Second Chance: The Triumph of Internationalism in America during World War II.* New York, 1967.

Doenecke, Justus. *Not to the Swift: The Old Isolationists in the Cold War Era.* Lewisburg, Pa., 1979.

———. "The Strange Career of American Isolationism, 1944–1954." *Peace and Change* 3 (Summer–Fall 1975): 79–83.

Donovan, Robert J. *Conflict and Crisis: The Presidency of Harry S. Truman, 1945–1948.* New York, 1977.

Dower, John W. *War without Mercy: Race and Power in the Pacific War.* New York, 1986.

Draper, Theodore. "American Hubris." In *A Present of Things Past: Selected Essays,* 67–96. New York, 1990.

Du Bois, W. E. B. *The Autobiography of W. E. B. Du Bois: A Soliloquy on Viewing My Life from the Last Decade of Its First Century.* New York, 1968.

Dudziak, Mary L. "Desegregation as a Cold War Imperative." *Stanford Law Review* 41 (November 1988): 61–120.

Dunn, John, ed. *Contemporary Crisis of the Nation State.* Cambridge, Mass., 1995.

Ekirch, Arthur A., Jr. *The Decline of American Liberalism.* New York, 1967.

Etzold, Thomas H., and John Lewis Gaddis. *Containment: Documents on American Policy and Strategy, 1945–1950.* New York, 1978.

Ferguson, Thomas. "Industrial Conflict and the Coming of the New Deal: The Triumph of Multinational Liberalism in America." In *The Rise and Fall of the New Deal Order, 1930–1980,* edited by Steve Fraser and Gary Gerstle, 3–31. Princeton, N.J., 1989.

Flynn, George Q. *The Draft, 1940–1973.* Lawrence, Kans., 1993.

Foucault, Michel. *The Archeology of Knowledge and the Discourse on Language.* New York, 1972.

Fousek, John Howard. "To Lead the Free World: American Nationalism and the Ideological Origins of the Cold War, 1945–1950." Ph.D. dissertation, Cornell University, 1994.

Fox, Richard Wightman, and T. J. Jackson Lears, eds. *The Power of Culture: Critical Essays in American History.* Chicago, 1993.

Fraser, Steven. "Sydney Hillman: Labor's Machiavelli." In *Labor Leaders in America,* edited by Melvyn Dubofsky and Warren Van Tine, 207–33. Urbana, Ill., 1987.

Freeland, Richard M. *The Truman Doctrine and the Origins of McCarthyism.* New York, 1971.

Fried, Richard M. *Nightmare in Red: The McCarthy Era in Perspective.* New York, 1990.

Fukuyama, Francis. "The End of History?" *The National Interest* 16 (Summer 1989): 3–18.

Fulbright, J. William. *The Arrogance of Power.* New York, 1966.

Gaddis, John Lewis. *The United States and the Origins of the Cold War, 1941–1947.* New York, 1972.

Gallup, George H., ed. *The Gallup Poll: Public Opinion, 1935–1971.* Vols. 1 and 2. New York, 1972.

Gardner, Lloyd. *Architects of Illusion: Men and Ideas in American Foreign Policy, 1941–1949.* Chicago, 1970.

Gates, Henry Louis, Jr. "A Fragmented Man: George Schuyler and the Claims of Race." *New York Times Book Review* (September 20, 1992): 31, 42–43.

Geertz, Clifford. *The Interpretation of Cultures.* New York, 1973.

Gerstle, Gary. *Working-Class Americanism: The Politics of Labor in a Textile City, 1914–1960.* New York, 1989.

Gillon, Steven M. *Politics and Vision: The ADA and American Liberalism, 1947–1985.* New York, 1987.

Gleason, Philip. *Speaking of Diversity: Language and Ethnicity in Twentieth-Century America.* Baltimore, 1992.

Green, David. *Shaping Political Consciousness: The Language of Politics in America from McKinley to Reagan.* Ithaca, N.Y., 1987.

Greenfield, Liah. *Nationalism: Five Roads to Modernity.* Cambridge, Mass., 1992.

Habermas, Jurgen. "The Public Sphere: An Encyclopedia Article (1964)." *New German Critique* 1 (Fall 1974): 49–55.

Hamby, Alonzo L. *Beyond the New Deal: Harry S. Truman and American Liberalism, 1945–1953.* New York, 1973.

———. "The Mind and Character of Harry S. Truman." In *The Truman Presidency,* edited by Michael J. Lacey, 19–53. New York, 1989.

Heale, M. J. *American Anticommunism: Combating the Enemy Within, 1830–1970.* Baltimore, 1990.

Hofstadter, Richard. "Cuba, the Philippines, and Manifest Destiny." In *The Paranoid Style in American Politics,* 145–87. New York, 1965; reprint, Chicago, 1979.

Holloway, David. *Stalin and the Bomb: The Soviet Union and Atomic Energy, 1939–1956.* New Haven, Conn., 1994.

Horne, Gerald. *Black and Red: W. E. B. Du Bois and the Afro-American Response to the Cold War, 1945–1963.* Albany, N.Y., 1986.

Horton, James O. "Comment on Kenneth J. Kusmer, 'The Black Urban Experience in American History,'" In *The State of Afro-American History: Past, Present, and Future,* edited by Darlene Clarke Hine, 130–35. Baton Rouge, La., 1986.

Howe, Irving, and B. J. Widick. *The UAW and Walter Reuther.* New York, 1949.

Hunt, Lynn, ed. *The New Cultural History.* Berkeley, 1989.

Hunt, Michael H. *Ideology and U.S. Foreign Policy.* New York, 1987.

Hutchinson, John, and Anthony D. Smith, eds. *Nationalism.* New York, 1994.

Hutchison, William R. *Errand to the World: American Protestant Thought and Foreign Missions.* Chicago, 1987.

Iriye, Akira. *The Globalizing of America, 1913–1945* (New York, 1993).

Isaacson, Walter, and Evan Thomas. *The Wise Men: Six Friends and the World They Made.* New York, 1986.

Janken, Kenneth Robert. *Rayford W. Logan and the Dilemma of the African-American Intellectual.* Amherst, Mass., 1993.

Jones, Joseph M. *The Fifteen Weeks (February 21–June 5, 1947).* New York, 1955.

Karl, Barry. *The Uneasy State: The United States from 1915–1945.* Chicago, 1983.

Keeran, Roger. *The Communist Party and the Auto Workers Union.* Bloomington, Ind., 1980.

Kennan, George F. [Alias X]. "The Sources of Soviet Conduct." *Foreign Affairs* 25 (July 1947): 566–82.

Ketchum, Richard M. *The Borrowed Years, 1938–1941: America on the Way to War.* New York, 1989.

Kimball, Warren F. *The Juggler: Franklin Roosevelt as Wartime Statesman.* Princeton, N.J., 1991.

————, ed. *America Unbound: World War II and the Making of a Superpower.* New York, 1992.

Kofsky, Frank. *Harry S. Truman and the War Scare of 1948: A Successful Campaign to Deceive the Nation.* New York, 1993.

Kohn, Hans. *American Nationalism: An Interpretive Essay.* New York, 1957.

Kolko, Joyce, and Gabriel Kolko. *The Limits of Power: The World and United States Foreign Policy.* New York, 1972.

Koppes, Clayton R., and Gregory D. Black. *Hollywood Goes to War: How Politics, Profits, and Propaganda Shaped World War II Movies.* Berkeley, Calif., 1987.

Kurth, Peter. *American Cassandra: The Life of Dorothy Thompson.* Boston, 1990.

LaFeber, Walter. *America, Russia, and the Cold War.* 5th ed. New York, 1985.

————. *The American Age: United States Foreign Policy at Home and Abroad since 1750.* New York, 1989.

————. "American Policy-Makers, Public Opinion, and the Outbreak of the Cold War, 1945–1950." In *The Origins of the Cold War in Asia,* edited by Yonosuke Nagai and Akira Iriye, 43–65. New York, 1977.

————. "NATO and the Korean War: A Context." *Diplomatic History* 13 (1989): 461–77.

————. *The New Empire: An Interpretation of American Expansion, 1860–1898.* Ithaca, N.Y., 1963.

————, ed. *The Origins of the Cold War, 1941–1947.* New York, 1971.

Larson, Deborah Welch. *Origins of Containment: A Psychological Explanation.* Princeton, N.J., 1985.

Lears, T. J. Jackson. "The Concept of Cultural Hegemony." *Journal of American History* 90 (1985): 567–93.

————. "A Matter of Taste: Corporate Cultural Hegemony in a Mass-Consumption Society." In *Recasting America: Culture and Politics in the Age of Cold War,* edited by Lary May, 38–57. Chicago, 1989.

Leffler, Melvyn P. *A Preponderance of Power: National Security, the Truman Administration, and the Cold War.* Stanford, Calif., 1992.

Leuchtenburg, William E. *Franklin D. Roosevelt and the New Deal, 1932–1940.* New York, 1963.

———. *In the Shadow of FDR: From Harry Truman to Ronald Reagan.* Ithaca, N.Y., 1983.

———. *The Perils of Prosperity, 1914–32.* Chicago, 1958.

Levenstein, Harvey A. *Communism, Anticommunism, and the CIO.* Westport, Conn., 1981.

Lewis, David Levering. "The Origins and Causes of the Civil Rights Movement." In *The Civil Rights Movement in America,* edited by Charles W. Eagles, 3–17. Jackson, Miss., 1986.

Lichtenstein, Nelson. "Labor in the Truman Era: Origins of the 'Private Welfare State.' " In *The Truman Presidency,* edited by Michael J. Lacey, 128–55. New York, 1989.

———. *Labor's War At Home: The CIO in World War II.* New York, 1982.

———. "Walter Reuther and the Rise of Labor-Liberalism." In *Labor Leaders in America,* edited by Melvyn Dubofsky and Warren Van Tine, 280–302. Urbana, Ill., 1987.

Luce, Henry R. *The American Century.* New York, 1941.

McCormick, Thomas J. *America's Half-Century: United States Foreign Policy in the Cold War.* Baltimore, 1989.

McElvaine, Robert. *Down and Out in the Great Depression: Letters from the "Forgotten Man."* Chapel Hill, N.C., 1983.

McLean, David. "American Nationalism, the China Myth, and the Truman Doctrine: The Question of Accommodation with Peking." *Diplomatic History* 10 (Winter 1986): 25–42.

Marchand, Roland. *Advertising the American Dream: Making Way for Modernity, 1920–1940.* Berkeley, 1985.

Markel, Lester. *Public Opinion and Foreign Policy.* New York, 1949.

Markowitz, Norman D. *The Rise and Fall of the People's Century: Henry A. Wallace and American Liberalism, 1941–1948.* New York, 1973.

Meier, August, and Elliot Rudwick. *Black Detroit and the Rise of the UAW.* New York, 1979.

Miller, Perry. *Errand to the Wilderness.* Cambridge, Mass., 1964.

Nye, Russel B. *This Almost Chosen People: Essays in the History of American Ideas.* East Lansing, Mich., 1966.

O'Brien, Conor Cruise. *God Land: Reflections on Religion and Nationalism.* Cambridge, Mass., 1988.

Parrish, Michael E. *Anxious Decades: America in Prosperity and Depression, 1920–1941.* New York, 1992.

Paterson, Thomas G. *On Every Front: The Making of the Cold War.* New York, 1979.

———. "Presidential Foreign Policy, Public Opinion, and Congress: The Truman Years." *Diplomatic History* 3 (1979): 1–18.

———, ed. *Cold War Critics: Alternatives to American Foreign Policy in the Truman Years.* Chicago, 1971.

Plummer, Brenda Gayle. " 'Below the Level of Men': African Americans, Race, and the History of U.S. Foreign Relations." *Diplomatic History* 20 (Fall 1996): 639–50.

———. "Evolution of the Black Foreign Policy Constituency." *TransAfrica Forum* 6 (Spring–Summer 1989): 67–89.

———. *Rising Wind: Black Americans and U.S. Foreign Affairs, 1935–1960.* Chapel Hill, N.C., 1996.

Polenberg, Richard. *War and Society: The United States, 1941–1945.* New York, 1972.

————, ed. *America at War: The Home Front, 1941–1945.* Englewood Cliffs, N.J., 1968.

Pruessen, Ronald W. *John Foster Dulles: The Road to Power.* New York, 1982.

Radosh, Ronald. *American Labor and United States Foreign Policy.* New York, 1969.

————. *Prophets on the Right: Profiles of Conservative Critics of American Globalism.* New York, 1975.

Record, Wilson. *The Negro and the Communist Party.* Chapel Hill, N.C., 1951; reprint, New York, 1971.

————. *Race and Radicalism: The NAACP and the Communist Party in Conflict.* Ithaca, N.Y., 1964.

Reinig, Ronald Samuel. "America Looking Outward: American Cold War Attitudes During the Crucial Years, 1945–1947, as Reflected in the American Magazine Medium." Ph.D. dissertation, Syracuse University, 1974.

Roark, James L. "American Black Leaders: The Response to Colonialism and the Cold War, 1945–1953." *African Historical Studies* 4 (1971): 253–70.

Rodgers, Daniel T. *Contested Truths: Keywords in American Politics since Independence.* New York, 1987.

Roosevelt, Franklin D. *The War Messages of Franklin, December 8, 1941 to April 13, 1945.* Washington, D.C., 1945.

Rosenman, Samuel I., comp. *The Public Papers and Addresses of Franklin D. Roosevelt.* Vol. 10. New York, 1950.

Schatz, Ronald. *The Electrical Workers: A History of Labor at General Electric and Westinghouse, 1923–1960.* Chicago, 1983.

————. "Philip Murray and the Subordination of the Industrial Unions to the United States Government." In *Labor Leaders in America,* edited by Melvyn Dubofsky and Warren Van Tine, 234–57. Urbana, Ill., 1987.

Schlesinger, Arthur M., Jr. *The Cycles of American History.* Boston, 1987.

Schudson, Michael. *Advertising, the Uneasy Persuasion: Its Dubious Impact on American Society.* New York, 1984.

Schulten, Susan. "The Transformation of World Geography in American Life, 1880–1950." Ph.D. dissertation, University of Pennsylvania, 1994.

Shapiro, Herbert. *White Violence and Black Response: From Reconstruction to Montgomery.* Amherst, Mass., 1988.

Sherry, Michael S. *In the Shadow of War: The United States Since the 1930s.* New Haven, Conn., 1995.

————. *Preparing for the Next War: American Plans for Postwar Defense, 1941–1945.* New Haven, Conn., 1977.

————. *The Rise of American Air Power: The Creation of Armageddon.* New Haven, Conn., 1987.

Sherwin, Martin J. *A World Destroyed: The Atomic Bomb and the Grand Alliance.* New York, 1975.

Sitkoff, Harvard. "Harry Truman and the Election of 1948: The Coming of Age of Civil Rights in American Politics." *Journal of Southern History* 37 (November 1971): 597–616.

————. *The Struggle for Black Equality, 1954–1992.* Rev. ed. New York, 1993.

Smith, Anthony D. *Nations and Nationalism in a Global Era.* Cambridge, Mass., 1995.

Smith, Henry Nash. *Virgin Land: The American West as Symbol and Myth.* Cambridge, Mass., 1950.

Solomon, Mark. "Black Critics of Colonialism and the Cold War." In *Cold War Critics*, edited by Thomas G. Paterson, 205–39. Chicago, 1971.

Stephanson, Anders. *Manifest Destiny: American Expansion and the Empire of Right.* New York, 1995.

Susman, Warren I. *Culture As History: The Transformation of American Society in the Twentieth Century.* New York, 1984.

Sussmann, Leila A. *Dear FDR: A Study of Political Letter Writing.* Totowa, N.J., 1963.

Todorov, Tzvetan. *The Conquest of America: The Question of the Other.* New York, 1984.

Tuveson, Ernest. *Redeemer Nation: The Idea of America's Millennial Role.* Chicago, 1968.

Twain, Mark. "To the Person Sitting in Darkness." *North American Review* 172 (February 1901): 161–76.

Vaughn, Stephen. *Holding Fast the Inner Lines: Democracy, Nationalism, and the Committee on Public Information.* Chapel Hill, N.C., 1980.

Von Eschen, Penny. *Race Against Empire: Black Americans and Anticolonialism, 1937–1957.* Ithaca, N.Y., 1997.

Walker, J. Samuel. *Henry A. Wallace and American Foreign Policy.* Westport, Conn., 1976.

Walker, R. B. J. *Inside/Outside: International Relations as Political Theory.* Cambridge, 1993.

Wallace, Henry A. "The Price of Free World Victory." In *The Century of the Common Man.* New York, 1943. Reprinted in *Prefaces to Peace: A Symposium*, 363–415. New York, 1943.

Wallerstein, Immanuel. *The Capitalist World-Economy.* New York, 1979.

———. *The Modern World-System: Capitalist Agriculture and the Origins of the European World-Economy in the Sixteenth Century.* New York, 1974.

Weathersby, Kathryn. "New Findings on the Korean War." *Cold War International History Project Bulletin* 3 (Fall 1993): 1, 14–18.

———. "New Russian Documents on the Korean War." *Cold War International History Project Bulletin* 6–7 (Winter 1995–96): 30–35.

———. "To Attack or Not to Attack? Stalin, Kim Il Sung, and the Prelude to War." *Cold War International History Project Bulletin* 5 (Spring 1995): 1, 2–9.

Weiler, Peter. "The United States, International Labor, and the Cold War: The Breakup of the World Federation of Trade Unions." *Diplomatic History* 5 (1981): 1–22.

Weinberg, Albert K. *Manifest Destiny: A Study of Nationalist Expansionism in American History.* Baltimore, 1935.

White, Donald. "History and American Internationalism: The Formulation from the Past after World War II." *Pacific Historical Review* 58 (1989): 145–72.

———. "The Nature of World Power in American History: An Evaluation at the End of World War II." *Diplomatic History* 11 (Summer 1987): 181–202.

White, Walter Francis. *A Man Called White: The Autobiography of Walter White.* New York, 1948.

Whitfield, Stephen J. *The Culture of the Cold War.* Baltimore, 1991.

Wilkins, Roy, with Tom Mathews. *Standing Fast: The Autobiography of Roy Wilkins.* New York, 1982.

Williams, William Appleman. "The Legend of Isolationism in the 1920s." *Science and Society* 18 (1954): 1–20.

Wills, Garry. *Lincoln at Gettysburg: The Words that Remade America.* New York, 1992.

Wittner, Lawrence S. *Rebels Against War: The American Peace Movement, 1933–1983.* Philadelphia, 1984.

Woodward, C. Vann. "The Irony of Southern History." In *The Burden of Southern History*, 187–211. Rev. ed. Baton Rouge, 1968.

Wyman, David S. *The Abandonment of the Jews: America and the Holocaust, 1941–1945*. New York, 1984.

Yarnell, Allen L. *Democrats and Progressives: The 1948 Election as a Test of Postwar Liberalism*. Berkeley, 1974.

Yergin, Daniel. *Shattered Peace: The Origins of the Cold War and the National Security State*. Boston, 1977.

Zelinsky, Wilbur. *Nation into State: The Shifting Symbolic Foundations of American Nationalism*. Chapel Hill, N.C., 1988.

Zieger, Robert. "George Meany: Labor's Organization Man." In *Labor Leaders in America*, edited by Melvyn Dubofsky and Warren Van Tine, 324–49. Urbana, Ill., 1987.

INDEX

Eastern Europe, 84, 156, 189. *See also specific countries*

Ebony, x, 82, 110, 179

Economic stewardship of U.S., 63–64, 67–73, 88–89

Egypt, 83

Einstein, Albert, 86

Eisenhower, Dwight, 68–69, 113

England. *See* Great Britain

Eritrea, 147

Ethyl Corporation, 96

Europe: destruction of, from World War II, 19–22, 31, 64; colonialism of, 29, 51, 81–82; pessimism of, 49; American dream for, 50–51; United States of, 50; rebuilding of, 56; War Department tour of, for top labor leaders, 57–58; food relief for, 69–71, 207 (n. 28); Marshall Plan for, 72, 86, 119, 140–44, 152, 155–56, 189, 221 (nn. 30, 32); Schuman Plan on, 173. *See also specific countries*

European Recovery Program. *See* Marshall Plan

Exemplar, United States as, 50–51, 83–88

Fair Employment Practice Committee (FEPC), 32–33, 198 (n. 48)

Fascism, 57–58, 84–85, 87, 135

Federal Council of Churches (FCC), 68, 107, 109, 113

FEPC. *See* Fair Employment Practice Committee

Ferguson, Thomas, 10

Finland, 183

Fitzgerald, Albert, 78, 149, 153, 185

Food relief and food rationing, 69–71, 206 (n. 23), 207 (n. 28)

Formosa, 176, 181

Forrestal, James, 11

Fortune, 2, 48

Four Freedoms, 42–43, 57, 77, 78, 82, 85, 119, 124

France, 39, 81–82, 173

Franco, Francisco, 156, 157, 176

Freedom: vs. slavery as metaphor of Cold War, 42, 131, 167, 176, 180, 200 (n. 8);

Roosevelt's Four Freedoms, 42–43, 57, 77, 78, 82, 85, 119; Swing on different meanings of, 43; and labor unions, 55–57, 132, 147–61; Dulles on, 119; in Truman's Baylor University speech, 128–29; capitalism equated with, 131, 161; and African Americans, 132–40, 145–47, 159–61; and pacifism, 172; and Korean War, 176. *See also* Free-world leadership

Freeland, Richard, 131

Free-world leadership: as metaphor, 130; overview of, 130–32; and "two worlds" as metaphor, 130; capitalism equated with, 131, 161; and African Americans, 132–47, 159–61; and civil rights movement, 132–40, 145–47, 157–61; and labor unions, 132, 147–61; and Marshall Plan, 140–43, 144, 221 (nn. 30, 32); and Point Four program, 143–45, 153, 156, 157; concluding comments on, 159–61

Frontier theme, 48, 50

Fukuyama, Francis, 15

Fulbright, William, 47

Fulton (Mo.) speech. *See* "Iron Curtain" speech

Gaddis, John Lewis, 1

Garrison, Ben, 61

Geertz, Clifford, 6

General Mills, 205–6 (n. 15)

Germany: destruction of, during World War II, 20, 47; Allied occupation of, after World War II, 21, 30, 51, 72, 119; and Nazism, 30, 42, 43, 51, 58, 87, 166, 183, 200 (n. 9); World War II aims against, 58; U.S. responsibility for, 72; in World War I, 110; steel industry in, 173. *See also* West Germany

Gervasi, Frank, 108, 116

Gettysburg Address, 139, 160

Globalism: American nationalist globalism, 2–3, 5, 7–8, 10, 13–15, 126, 185–91; definition of, 7; and anticommunism, 8; and white Anglo-Saxon Protestant elite, 10–11; and labor unions, 12–13, 55–62, 77–79, 148–49, 153–54, 185; Roosevelt

Markel, Lester, 164

Marshall, George, 122, 126, 128, 141–42, 145, 147, 148, 150, 152, 188

Marshall, Thurgood, 84, 87

Marshall Islands, 51–52

Marshall Plan: early ideas similar to, 72, 119; Truman on, 86; mass media on, 140–41; African Americans on, 141–43, 221 (nn. 30, 32); labor unions on, 148–53, 155–56, 160; and Communist Party, 155; congressional approval of, 189

Marx, Karl, 108

Mass media: analysis of magazines and newspapers, x; on World War II victory, 16, 25–29, 36–39, 46–52; on atomic bomb, 17–19, 26, 28–28, 114–16, 197 (n. 35); on Truman's radio address on World War II victory, 25–29; globalist imagery and iconography in, 42, 46, 53–54, 64, 73–74, 91–102; on U.S. strength and World War II victory, 46–52; on non-European peoples, 51; on military preparedness, 52–54, 111, 113–16, 174; on global responsibility and globalism, 65–76, 124–26; on economic stewardship of U.S., 67–73; on moral world leadership, 74–76; on colonialism of U.S., 80–82; on Big Three, 104, 105–6, 116–19; on Churchill's "Iron Curtain" speech, 107–9; on Baruch Plan, 115–16; on U.S.-Soviet relations, 116–23, 216 (n. 69); on Mediterranean crisis, 127–28; on Truman's NAACP Lincoln Memorial speech, 136–37; on Marshall Plan, 140–41; on Korean War, 167, 172–79, 227 (n. 30). *See also specific magazines and newspapers*

Matles, James, 153

Meany, George, 77

Media. *See* Mass media; Television

Messenger, 198 (n. 41)

Methodists, 109, 207 (n. 28)

Middle East, 40, 50, 65, 110, 173, 202 (n. 39). *See also specific countries*

Military preparedness, 52–55, 64–65, 111–16, 174

Minneapolis Star-Journal, on economic stewardship of U.S., 69–70

Mirror-imaging, 116

Monroe Doctrine, 75, 112

Montreal Star, 70

Moral leadership of U.S.: and global responsibilities, 63, 74–76, 89; and colonialism, 80–83; and African Americans, 83–86

Morgenthau Plan, 72

Morse, Wayne, 135

Murray, Philip, xi, 56–60, 78, 105, 148, 150, 152, 153, 155, 160, 161

"My Country" (Davenport), 48

Myrdal, Gunnar, 12, 85

NAACP. *See* National Association for the Advancement of Colored People

Nagasaki bombing, 16, 17–19, 22, 23, 25, 29, 32, 196 (n. 2)

National Negro Congress, 138

Nation, 206 (n. 17)

National Association for the Advancement of Colored People (NAACP): analysis of generally, x; and anticommunism, 12, 14; and racial equality, 12, 84, 134–35, 145–46, 159, 160, 182; dismissal of Du Bois from, 14, 139–40, 144, 223 (n. 47); and Fair Employment Practice Committee (FEPC), 33; and globalism generally, 77; on Truman Doctrine, 133; and Truman's Lincoln Memorial speech, 133–37; and Truman administration, 133–47, 161, 189–90, 220 (n. 27); and United Nations appeal on racial injustice in U.S., 138; criticisms of, 138, 139–40; and President's Committee on Civil Rights, 138–39; on Marshall Plan, 142–43; on Point Four program, 144–45; and State Department's foreign-policy discussion groups, 145; anticolonial and antimilitarist position of, 145, 147, 161, 223 (n. 47); Declaration of Principles of, 145–46; on NATO, 147; Spingarn Award presented to Bunche by, 147; and UAW, 157–59; on Korean War, 180–82; and U.S. Communist Party, 181

National Association of Manufacturers, 87
National-character studies, 164
National Council for a Permanent FEPC, 33
National Guard, 113, 176
Nationalism: scholarly literature on, 2–3; U.S. nationalist globalism, 2–3, 5, 7–8, 10, 13, 14–15, 126, 185–91; definition of, 3–5; and chosenness, destiny, and mission of U.S., 5–7, 11, 14–15, 125–26; and universal values, 7; and globalism, 7–8, 126; and democratic revival, 9–10; "holy nationalism," 20, 23–25, 44, 65, 68, 115–16, 170–71; of Truman, 20–22, 45–46, 47, 68, 101, 200 (n. 18), 201 (n. 20); of Roosevelt, 44, 45
National Maritime Union, 169
National security: and globalism, 10, 64–65; Truman on, 21, 22; Roosevelt on, 42; and military preparedness, 52–55, 64–65, 111–16, 174; preparedness as path to peace, 111–16; and Truman's Army Day speech, 111–13, 213 (n. 29); and atomic bomb, 115–16
National Security Council Memorandum Number 68 (NSC-68), 162–65, 176, 187
National Urban League, x, 76, 83–84
NATO. See North Atlantic Treaty Organization
Navy, 54, 81, 170, 179
Nazism, 30, 42, 43, 51, 58, 87, 166, 183, 200 (n. 9)
Niebuhr, Reinhold, 121–22, 123
Netherlands, 81, 83, 142, 221 (n. 30)
Newark Evening News, 19
New Deal, 9, 10, 61
New Hampshire Morning News, 122
New Republic, 126, 206 (n. 17)
Newspapers. See African American press; Mass media; and specific newspapers
New York Daily News: analysis of generally, x; on atomic bomb, 17, 18, 114, 116; on Roosevelt's death, 27; on World War II victory, 27–29, 197 (n. 35); on global responsibility and globalism, 52, 65, 67, 70, 76, 124, 190; on military prepared-

ness, 52, 111, 113, 114, 116; on economic stewardship of U.S., 67, 70; on Philippine independence, 80; on colonialism, 82; on "One Worldism," 105; on Churchill's "Iron Curtain" speech, 107; on Truman, 109; on Truman's Army Day speech, 111; on Baruch Plan, 116; on Korean War, 176–79
New York Times, x, 13, 99–102, 111, 123, 128
Niles, David, 134, 135, 137
Nitze, Paul, 165
Nixon, Russ, 58
Norfolk (Va.) Journal and Guide, 139
North American Aviation, 203 (n. 52)
North Atlantic Treaty Organization (NATO), 119, 131, 145, 147, 153
North Korea. See Korean War
Northwest Airlines, 73
No-strike pledge, 58–62, 204 (nn. 72, 74)
NSC-68. See National Security Council Memorandum Number 68

O'Brien, Conor Cruise, 20
O'Donnell, John, 52, 107, 177
Oil resources, 40, 110
One World, 77, 79, 103, 105, 109, 129, 150, 188
Optimism of Americans, 48–50, 201 (n. 32)
Organized labor. See Labor unions
Orwell, George, 175
Oxnam, Bishop G. Bromley, 109

Pacific Islands, 50, 81, 115, 202 (n. 39)
Padmore, George, 82
Pakistan, 181
Palestine, 83, 127
Pan American World Airways, 73
Paterson, Thomas, 1
Patterson, Robert P., 53
Peace and peace movement, 13, 16, 104–6, 111–16, 121, 124, 172
Pearl Harbor attack, 6, 9, 14, 18, 41, 53, 183, 199 (n. 3)
Pepper, Claude ("Red"), 78–79, 87, 89, 106, 120, 123, 133, 162
Peron, Eva, 146

on colonialism, 82; globe iconography in, 99; on Churchill's "Iron Curtain" speech, 107–8; on "asbestos curtain," 110; on Big Three, 116–18; on Korea, 117–18; on U.S.-Soviet relationship, 122, 123–24; on Mediterranean crisis, 127–28; on Point Four program, 144; on Korean War, 172–75, 227 (n. 30)

Schalk, Toki, 33, 34

Schatz, Ronald, 223 (n. 53)

Schlesinger, Arthur, Jr., 200 (n. 14)

Schudson, Michael, 74

Schuman Plan, 173

Schuyler, George S., 31–32, 83, 110, 132, 138, 141, 143–44, 198 (n. 41), 221 (n. 30)

Segregation. *See* Civil rights movement; Racial injustice

Senate Foreign Relations Committee, 66, 142, 144–45

Sevareid, Eric, 70, 110

Shakespeare, William, 36

Sheehan, William, 151

Shelley, Percy Bysshe, 26

Sherry, Michael, 15, 64, 196 (n. 8), 198 (n. 42)

Slavery, 37, 42, 131, 167, 176, 180, 200 (n. 8)

Smith, Anthony D., 3, 4

Snow, Edgar, 80, 82, 117, 123, 202 (n. 39), 217 (n. 76)

Somaliland, 147

South Africa, 129, 130

South Korea, 117–18, 119, 129, 181. *See also* Korean War

Soviet Union: collapse of, 3, 129, 130, 191; in World War II, 21, 26; and racial discrimination, 30, 198 (n. 39); as demonic Other, 48; America as example for, 50, 202 (n. 39); rebuilding of, 56; Churchill's "Iron Curtain" speech on, 75, 106–11; Big Three unity and peace, 104–6; U.S. public opinion on, 108–9; and "asbestos curtain," 110; air power of, 114; and atomic bomb, 114, 116, 131; and Baruch Plan, 116; and negative mirror-imaging, 116; British relations with, 116, 117; mass media on, 116–23, 174–75, 216 (n. 69);

and Roosevelt, 117; and Korea, 117–18; Dulles on, 118–20; Wallace on coexistence of U.S. and, 120–21; Niebuhr on, 121–22; Security Council veto by, 148; and Korean War, 162, 165–79, 181–86, 225 (n. 2); and NSC-68, 163–65, 176, 187; aggression against Finland before World War II, 183. *See also* Anticommunism; Cold War

Spain, 129, 156, 157, 172, 176

Spanish-American War, 11

Spellman, Archbishop Francis, 65

Spy network, 28, 105, 197 (n. 35)

Stalin, Joseph, 33, 102, 104, 105, 123, 173, 177, 201 (n. 18)

Stephanson, Anders, 5, 6

Stimson, Henry, 11, 22

Strausz-Hupé, Robert, 75

Strikes, 58–62, 67, 204 (nn. 72, 74)

Strong, Rev. Josiah, 108

Swing, Raymond Gram, 43, 109, 217 (n. 76)

Taft, Robert A., 66–67, 88, 177–79, 190, 205 (n. 11)

Taiwan. *See* Formosa

Taylor, Glen, 133, 141

Television, x, 193 (n. 6)

Thailand, 82

Thomas, R. J., 57–58, 87–88, 105

Thompson, Dorothy, 69, 74–75, 114–15, 214 (n. 47)

Thompson, E. P., 4

Time, 2

"To Secure These Rights," 139

Trans World Airline (TWA), 73–74, 93

Truman, Harry S.: citizens' letters to, ix–x, 24–25, 71, 76, 81, 87, 111–13, 169–72, 207 (n. 28); foreign policy of, 1–2, 11, 13–15, 45, 75, 76, 79, 82, 86, 89, 101, 128, 141, 153, 186; campaign and election of, in 1948, 1, 2, 201 (n. 20); Truman Doctrine speech of, 8, 79, 86, 103, 119, 124, 126–27, 129, 132–37, 141, 166, 189, 200 (n. 8); criticisms of, 13, 14, 65, 120–21, 139, 150, 152; and labor unions, 14, 79, 148, 149, 152,

161; on World War II victory, 16, 19–29, 34–36; and atomic bomb, 16–18, 22–23, 31, 196 (n. 8), 197 (n. 26); at Potsdam Conference, 19, 21, 33; nationalism of, 20–22, 45–46, 47, 101, 200 (n. 18), 201 (n. 20); victory celebrations at end of World War II, 33–36; and Roosevelt legacy, 45–46; and World War II aims, 46; and war in Pacific, 46–47; and military preparedness, 52, 54–55; Navy Day speech of, 54–55; on global responsibility, 65, 66, 68–71, 87, 129; on railroad strike, 67; domestic economic policy of, 67, 86–87; and Golden Rule, 68, 113, 206 (n. 16); on food relief for world, 69, 70–71, 207 (n. 28); on Philippine independence, 80; and civil rights movement, 86, 133–39, 141, 158; and Marshall Plan, 86, 140–43; walnut analogy of, 86, 141; and Churchill's "Iron Curtain" speech, 106–7, 109; Army Day speech of, 111–13, 213 (n. 29); State of the Union address in 1947, 124; United Nations speech by, 124; Baylor University speech of, 128–29, 218 (n. 93); NAACP Lincoln Memorial speech by, 133–37, 159; and NAACP, 133–47, 161, 189–90, 220 (n. 27); Point Four program of, 143–45; and Korean War, 162, 165–72, 177; and NSC-68, 163–65, 176, 187; public approval rating of, 197 (n. 17); V-E Day remarks of, 200 (n. 18)

Truman Doctrine: and anticommunism, 8, 103, 119, 124, 126–27, 129, 132, 166, 189, 200 (n. 8); critics of, 79, 132–33, 141; Truman on, 86; African Americans on, 132–37; and civil rights movement, 132–37; Taft on, 178. *See also* Truman, Harry S.: Truman Doctrine speech of

Turkey, 127, 129, 133

Turner, Frederick Jackson, 48, 50

Tuveson, Ernest, 6

Twain, Mark, 79

Two Worlds, 130, 147, 188–89, 191

Tydings, Millard, 112

UAW. *See* United Automobile Workers

UE. *See* United Electrical Workers

UMT. *See* Universal Military Training

Unions. *See* Labor unions; United Automobile Workers; United Electrical Workers

United Aircraft Corporation, 113–14

United Automobile Workers (UAW): analysis of generally, xi; and anticommunism, 12, 154–55; nationalism and internationalism of, 55–62, 203 (n. 60); and no-strike pledge, 59–61, 204 (n. 74); Communist influence in, 61, 88, 154, 157; Reuther as president of, 62, 88, 149, 153–58, 160–61, 223 (n. 51); and global responsibility, 78; and connection between domestic and foreign policy, 87–88; and foreign policy, 87–88, 153–59, 160, 189–90; and Big Three unity and peace, 105; freedom's meaning for Reuther, 132; compared with United Electrical Workers, 148–50; and Marshall Plan, 155–56; and Point Four, 156–57; and NAACP, 157–59; success of, 161; on Korean War, 183–84

United Electrical Workers (UE): analysis of generally, xi; nationalism and internationalism of, 55–58, 203 (n. 59); and no-strike policy, 60, 61; on global responsibilities, 77–79; expulsion from CIO, 78, 148, 153, 190; and connection between domestic and foreign policy, 87; and Big Three unity and peace, 104–5; anticapitalist critics in, 132; and foreign policy, 148, 149, 150–53, 154; compared with United Automobile Workers, 148–50; and Marshall Plan, 149, 150–53, 190; Communist influence in, 151, 153; on Korean War, 162, 184–85

United Jewish Appeal, 68–69

United Nations: purpose of, 6, 21, 36, 57, 104; and atomic bomb, 19, 114, 115; and Truman, 21, 36, 111; public opinion on U.S. membership in, 41; Charter of, 50, 54, 114; and military preparedness of U.S., 52, 54, 111, 113; and U.S. world lead-

ership, 75, 76, 108, 118; and Baruch Plan,
115; Truman's speech at, 124; and Mediterranean crisis, 133; NAACP's petition
to, on racial inequities in U.S., 138;
White as consultant to U.S. delegation
to, 140; and Point Four program, 144;
and Bunche, 146, 147, 180; and Africa,
147; and labor unions, 148, 156; Soviet
Union abuse of Security Council veto,
148; and Marshall Plan, 152; and Korean
War, 166, 179–81, 184
United Nations Human Rights Commis-
sion, 138
United Nations Relief and Reconstruction
Administration (UNRRA), 70, 133
U.S. News and World Report, 127
U.S. State Department, 133, 135, 145, 146,
162, 165, 174, 175, 180
Universal Military Training (UMT), 52, 111,
112–13, 168
UNRRA. *See* United Nations Relief and
Reconstruction Administration
Urban League. *See* National Urban
League

Vandenberg, Arthur, 66
Vaughn, Stephen, 2–3
V-E Day, 46, 47, 200 (n. 18)
Vietnam, 82, 83
Vietnam War, 13
V-J Day, 34, 35, 46
Voting rights, 58, 133, 134

Wallace, Henry: globalism of, 11, 56, 126,
190; as critic of Truman, 14, 65, 120–21,
139, 150, 152; on World War II, 42; as
vice president, 42, 45; as Roosevelt's heir,
45, 121; on Century of the Common
Man, 56, 77, 78, 89; presidential campaign of 1948, 57, 140, 141, 149, 150, 152,
161, 189; and civil rights movements, 86;
on sharing atomic bomb with Soviet
Union, 114; political cartoon on, 114; resignation of, from Truman's cabinet, 120;
on coexistence of U.S. and Soviet Union,
120–21; marginalization of views of,

120–21, 132, 190, 216 (n. 65); public opin-
ion on, 121; as *New Republic* editor, 126;
and labor unions, 149, 150, 152; on freedom, 157, 200 (n. 8); and Korean War,
162
Weaver, George L. P., 84
Weinberg, Albert K., 5–6
Welles, Sumner, 84
West Germany, 168. *See also* Germany
West Indies, 201 (n. 33)
WFTU. *See* World Federation of Trade
Unions
White, Walter: on racial injustice, 84–85,
159; and Truman administration, 86, 110,
132, 133–35, 137, 161; on Reuther's presi-
dency of UAW, 88; on Churchill's "Iron
Curtain" speech, 110; on Truman Doc-
trine, 133; and Truman's Lincoln Memo-
rial speech, 133–35, 137; and dismissal of
Du Bois, 139–40, 223 (n. 47); and Wal-
lace's presidential campaign of 1948, 140;
on Marshall Plan, 142; on Point Four
program, 145; on Atlantic Pact, 147; and
Americans for Democratic Action, 153;
on Korean War, 180–81
Widick, B. J., 223 (n. 51)
Wildcat strikes, 58–59
Wilkins, Roy, 137, 158
Willkie, Wendell, 48, 77, 85
Wilson, Woodrow, 6, 8, 20, 43, 58, 178
Wofford, Harris, Jr., 25
World Federation of Trade Unions
(WFTU), 78
World War I, 8, 43, 63, 76, 110, 178
World War II: Japanese surrender at end
of, 1, 16, 17–19, 25, 28, 33, 34; propaganda
during, 6; and bombing of Hiroshima
and Nagasaki, 6, 9, 14, 16–19, 22–24, 29,
31, 32, 196 (nn. 1–2, 8), 197 (n. 26); and
Pearl Harbor, 6, 9, 14, 18, 41, 53, 183,
199 (n. 3); and Roosevelt, 9, 41–45, 178;
African Americans during, 12; Truman
on U.S. victory in, 16, 19–29, 34–36;
destruction of Europe by, 19–22; mass
media on U.S. victory in, 25–29, 36–39;
African American press and victory in,

29–33, 39–40; and "Double V" campaign of African Americans, 32–33, 59, 183; victory celebrations after, 33–34; V-J Day, 34, 35; Italian invasion of Ethiopia, 39, 198 (n. 40); meaning of victory, 41–62; U.S. war aims, 41–44, 46, 57–58; V-E Day and, 46, 47, 200 (n. 18); portrayal of Japanese during, 51; no-strike pledge during, 58–62

Yankee skepticism, 70
Yergin, Daniel, 65
Young, P. B., Sr., 139
Yugoslavia, 122, 173, 174